D0218580

The Hub

A PLACE FOR READING AND WRITING

for North Central Texas College

Dear Instructor,

During the last six years, developmental writing and reading courses at colleges across the country have undergone immense changes: corequisite models such as the Accelerated Learning Program (ALP) are spreading quickly, reading and writing are being integrated, faculty are implementing active learning approaches, and instructors are more frequently choosing to address

Photo courtesy of Donna Crivello

the challenges students face in balancing school, work, and life issues. These seismic changes in the way we teach developmental writing and reading are the primary reasons for the creation of *The Hub: A Place for Reading and Writing*.

As faculty members at the Community College of Baltimore County, we pioneered ALP to meet the needs of our students. Our model took shape through many brainstorming sessions, conferences by active learning specialists, and continuous research around our students' outcomes and our courses. It emerged as the best model we could create to support our students, and better still, as further research by our faculty and others confirmed, it works.

Based on my experience developing ALP, and on my thirty-six years of experience teaching writing, I developed *The Hub: A Place for Reading and Writing* to bring students and instructors all of the materials and support they need to succeed in the composition classroom. I have designed *The Hub* around a series of carefully scaffolded multipart reading and writing projects that offer abundant opportunities for students to develop rhetorical knowledge, genre awareness, and critical reading and writing skills. At the same time, *The Hub* provides ideas, topics, activities, and other resources to support underprepared students and help accelerate their development into confident and successful college readers and writers.

The Hub is the result of all of the research and classroom work I've spent my career doing. The inquiry-based, active learning pedagogy you'll find in *The Hub* is thoroughly classroom-tested. The advice for instructors is based on the best practices for corequisite composition courses, as validated by outcomes research. I firmly believe it will help your students learn and succeed, just as it helped mine. So, welcome to *The Hub*! I hope you'll find it the place—your place—for reading and writing.

—*Peter*

The Hub

A PLACE FOR READING AND WRITING

Balancing School, Work, and Life

Reading/Writing Projects

Research and Documentation

Writing

Reading

for North Central Texas College

Peter Adams

Community College of Baltimore County, Emeritus

bedford/st.martin's
Macmillan Learning

Boston | New York

For Bedford/St. Martin's

Vice President, Editorial, Macmillan Learning Humanities: Leasa Burton
Program Director for English: Stacey Purviance
Senior Program Manager: Karita F. dos Santos
Marketing Manager: Lauren Arrant
Market Development Manager: Azelie Fortier
Director of Content Development, Humanities: Jane Knetzger
Senior Development Editor: Gillian Cook
Assistant Editor: Paola Garcia-Muniz
Senior Digital Content Project Manager: Ryan Sullivan
Lead Digital Asset Archivist and Workflow Manager: Jennifer Wetzel
Production Supervisor: Brianna Lester
Advanced Media Project Manager: Rand Thomas
Media Editor: Angela Beckett
Senior Manager of Publishing Services: Andrea Cava
Editorial Services: Lumina Datamatics, Inc.
Composition: Lumina Datamatics, Inc.
Text Permissions Manager: Kalina Ingham
Text Permissions Researcher: Mark Schaefer, Lumina Datamatics, Inc.
Photo Permissions Editor: Angela Boehler
Photo Researcher: Krystyna Borgen, Lumina Datamatics, Inc.
Director of Design, Content Management: Diana Blume
Text Design: Claire Seng-Niemoeller
Printing and Binding: BR Printers

Copyright © 2020 by Bedford/St. Martin's.

All rights reserved. No part of this book may be reproduced, stored in a retrieval system, or transmitted in any form or by any means, electronic, mechanical, photocopying, recording, or otherwise, except as may be permitted by law or expressly permitted in writing by the Publisher.

Manufactured in the United States of America.

3   4   5   6   25   24   23   22   21   20

For information, write: Macmillan Learning Curriculum Solutions, 14903 Pilot Drive, Plymouth, MI 48170 (macmillanlearning.com)

ISBN 978-1-319-38254-4 (North Central Texas College Edition)

Acknowledgments

Text acknowledgments and copyrights appear at the back of the book on pages 757–59, which constitute an extension of the copyright page. Art acknowledgments and copyrights appear on the same page as the art selections they cover.

At the time of publication all internet URLs published in this text were found to accurately link to their intended website. If you do find a broken link, please forward the information to TheHub@macmillan.com so that it can be corrected for the next printing.

Preface for North Central Texas College

NCTC's First-Year Composition Curriculum: An Overview

Welcome to English Composition at North Central Texas College! You've signed up for Integrated Reading and Writing (INRW 0305), Composition I (ENGL 1301), or Composition II (ENGL 1302). We are excited that you've enrolled in the course and that you're here at NCTC.

We've designed this course in keeping with the college's mission and values statement:

> **NCTC Mission:** North Central Texas College is dedicated to student success and institutional excellence.

> **NCTC Values Statement:** North Central Texas College is accountable to its students, colleagues, and the community and holds the following values to be fundamental: an affordable, quality education; stimulating learning environments; integrity; innovation; cohesive relationships; and encouragement.

This course is part of a year-long study of a common theme that centers around students' writing and reading interests. This custom rhetoric textbook is bundled with our year-long common reads and with an access code for additional resources and support. At the end of this semester, we encourage you to sign up for the next course in your communication core, so you can continue to use these texts in the spring and summer semesters. Completing your First-Year Composition (FYC) courses within an academic year will save you money on books, and research shows that students are more successful if they take FYC courses in succession and early in their academic careers. (So, be sure to keep your access code.)

This bundle consists of a custom writing textbook, the common reads, and access to the online course materials. With this bundle, we also created specific courses in Canvas designed to meet your needs. Our goal is to align our multiple campuses, dual credit sites, online courses, and developmental courses to provide you with an academically rigorous and meaningful experience. As an added benefit, proceeds from sales of the textbook will be used to bring the authors to campus.

This custom textbook is specific to NCTC and is composed of two parts:

The first part, the preface, includes a description of the course outcomes, required writing assignments, and assessment rubrics. The assignments facilitate alignment between the composition courses and provide consistent experiences that scaffold from one semester to the next. Your instructors have collaborated on course design, assessment, and best practices for our diverse students, and we have designed this custom preface so that the assignments are open-ended and that the rubrics are holistic that will complement your class's interests, your instructor's expertise, and the department's goals for consistency, transparency, and rigor.

The second part is a writing and rhetoric textbook, *The Hub*. For this custom textbook, we've carefully selected the chapters that we believe are relevant to our students. Because INRW 0305 students use the same text as students in ENGL 1301 and ENGL 1302, we hope that all students moving through the communications core feel more confident with the course readings and course design.

The common reads are books related to the year's selected theme. Each spring semester, the college will invite your texts' authors to visit with students and answer questions written by students in first-year composition.

We hope that our year-long theme and common reads encourage you to develop a "community of scholars" with each other—adding energy, excitement, and urgency to your writing courses. The English, Speech, and Foreign Language (ESFL) faculty members at NCTC are committed to your success. We all want the best *from* you and the best *for* you. We're excited to explore this topic together in a series of invitational, rigorous courses that inspire your curiosity.

> We are not here to drill pupils in spelling, punctuation, and grammar, but to bestow upon them the potentiality of service of thousands and perhaps millions of their [people]—to develop in them the power to move humanity to noble deeds by the communication of the truth. If there is in the teaching profession a higher or a more stimulating function than that, I do not know what it is.—Fred Newton Scott

First-Year Composition Focus 2020–202: Inquiry-Based Writing (What is an Essay and What Does it Mean to Study the Art of the Essay?)

> If something inside of you is real, we will probably find it interesting, and it will probably be universal. So you must risk placing real emotion at the center of your work. Write straight into the emotional center of things. Write toward vulnerability. Risk being unliked. Tell the truth as you understand it. If you're a writer you have a moral obligation to do this. And it is a revolutionary act—truth is always subversive.—Anne Lamott

Art is a human activity. It is the creation of something new, something that might not work, something that causes a viewer to be influenced. Art uses context and culture to send a message. Instead of only a contribution of beauty or craft, art adds intent. The artist works to create something generous, something that will change us. —Seth Godin

In the introduction for the *Touchstone Anthology of Contemporary Creative Nonfiction*, Scott Russell Sanders says that the term essay "suggests an experiment, a testing, a weighing out." He follows: "Experiments in language are messier than experiments in laboratories, because words do not parse the universe as neatly as numbers do, but the spirit behind both kinds of experiment is the same: to discover a tentative truth" (xvii).

Throughout INRW 0305, ENGL 1301, and ENGL 1302, we will reintroduce ourselves to the art of the essay. Our definition will become: an essay is an artful way to discover, to seek, to explore. It is a chance to question what we think we know. We will take risks and be vulnerable in order to connect with others and add something new to our world.

By focusing on *The Art of the Essay* as our theme in First-Year Composition, we will begin to wonder about everything again. To do so, we must establish a foundation on which to build our understanding of essays themselves. Think about the following questions:

- Why do we write?
- What is an essay?
- How can essays serve my community?
- What can I learn from writing essays?
- Can essays be art?

The answers to these questions are going to inevitably lead to more questions. Good. That is exactly where we want to begin. Thinking begets thinking. Once we've thought through the questions we need to ask, we will begin to write about what we find. That cycle is a perfect circle. There will never be a point where we are done learning. Nor will we ever have written enough essays to call it quits. We will practice writing something new, something that might not work, something that causes a viewer to be influenced. In doing so, we will learn how to wade through the wild nature of bias, the crisis of 24-hour information overload, the digitally connected world, and our own minds.

You might be wondering why we are going to study essays so closely. Where and how could they possibly serve us in the future after our final term paper has been submitted? The type of nonfiction writing we are going to explore belongs in all of our lives at all times. We can serve whatever occupation, role, industry, lifestyle, or job by writing through the beautiful issues and challenges we face. By studying the art of the essay, all of us have the chance to practice serving our communities and deepening our understanding. Find a field of study that is perfect and in no need of innovation. Can you think of any community that is not in need of development and progress? Search for a person who knows everything. We need essays now more than ever so we can continue to grow and change as individuals and as a society.

More specifically, this theme gives us the chance to create something in school that is meaningful. Too often, we learn that essays look, feel, and sound the same. We've grown comfortable because they follow a formula. See if this sounds familiar: Introduction with a thesis and two or three sentences, then three body paragraphs with topic sentences and evidence, and finally a conclusion with two to three sentences that restates the thesis. We know how to write that essay in our sleep. There is no challenge or room for individuality there, no need for intention or art. But true essays are wild and diverse. They are built intentionally sentence by sentence and serve the unique purpose of the task at hand. Essays are built by people who are fearless enough to question and seek answers from all different perspectives. The end result is an experiment with words that details the adventure the writer went on to find all of the tentative answers to the questions they asked.

At the core of our theme is the essence of writing nonfiction itself. We have the chance to examine all aspects of our reality and to respectfully question everything. To write a real essay is a risk, but it is one that is always worth taking. The good news is that we don't have to do this alone. Essays provide us with an opportunity to engage in the art of listening to others. They encourage us to think about complex issues that others have experienced and add to the conversation. They are an invitation to gather new perspectives and challenge all of our collective thoughts.

We are so excited to write alongside you and to explore the art of the essay. Don't let this opportunity to write on topics that you're passionate about pass you by. In school and in life, they don't present themselves very often. Every essay we write from now on is a chance to discover something new, a tentative truth. There is no longer an excuse to not write and revise until something incredible shines through. Our first-year composition classes are now a testing ground. Let us capitalize on this occasion and learn to wonder by writing again.

Strategies for Success: Writing in First-Year Composition

First-Year Composition courses have several goals: to prepare you for the demands of writing in your classes throughout your academic career, to help you understand and deconstruct writing situations so you can write effectively in the workplace, and to help you develop an appreciation and love of language that sparks your curiosity and brings you joy.

These are grand ambitions. Your instructors are committed to helping you achieve these goals. Still, you also have to do your part to succeed in this course. Here are some tips to help you be a successful student:

Consider your audience. As you write your papers, think about your audience's expectations. Specifically, academic readers favor logic over emotion, demand evidence for claims that are made (often even for what might appear to be minor claims), define "interesting" as originality of thought and potential for intellectual stimulation, favor directness and clarity over inference when they read academic papers, define "creative" more in terms of originality of ideas than in stylistic flourish, and read carefully, actively, and methodically.

Take responsibility for your learning. You can't be a passive observer in your classes and expect to learn. Active learning requires engagement, participation, focus, and time. Your instructor will work to create optimal conditions for your success; however, you still have to put in the work.

Come to class and participate. Research shows that students who regularly come to class are more successful in their courses. So come to class consistently, on time, and prepared with your book, notebook, assignments, and readings. Take notes, highlight and annotate your texts, ask questions, and avoid distractions. When in class, you'll have opportunities to get additional feedback from your instructor and peers, to ask questions, and to seek clarification. Take advantage of those opportunities so you are an active participant and not merely a passive observer. Avoid the temptation to "check out" if the conversation steers into territory that is unfamiliar or uninteresting to you. Be fully present and engaged in the class discussion to get as much out of the experience as you can. Find ways to communicate in the classroom. If you're not comfortable with sharing in front of everyone, find a different way to engage with the conversation.

Get to know your classmates. Coming to class helps you to learn from your classmates and to support each other. It's essential to "collaborate to graduate." After all, the first word in "community college" is "community." There are 4,000 other students enrolled in INRW 0305, ENGL 1301, and ENGL 1302 at NCTC, so don't be afraid to talk to your peers in your class or your other courses.

Be curious. Throughout your college career, you will take courses that do not appear to dovetail perfectly with your interests. Nonetheless, in every college course, you have the chance to explore the materials deeply, and in a manner that not only sustains your attention but that enriches your understanding. In each course, you will be encouraged to narrow the focus of consideration and discussion. Seize this opportunity to find ways to make the reading and the writing compelling and relevant to you. To achieve this, though, you must be willing to look beyond obvious answers, interpretations, and viewpoints. If you're stuck and don't know how to proceed with a topic, follow up with your instructor and your classmates. Above all, don't be afraid to ask questions.

Take risks.   Move beyond apparent observations and tired arguments. Look for opportunities to challenge the status quo, explore new ideas, and be inspired. You can even challenge an idea or belief that you have and come out on the other side okay. Be open to new ideas and respectfully question everything in the spirit of exploration.

Plan ahead.   Effective academic writing takes time, reflection, and revision. Waiting until the last minute does not provide the time and space to produce your best work. Students often think that they write their best work under pressure; but really, students do their best writing when they have time to revisit their ideas, seek feedback, and work toward greater clarity.

Visit with your instructors.   All NCTC instructors keep office hours at designated times—at least two hours each week for each course—to meet with students and provide additional feedback and support. Check your syllabus for your instructor's hours, and make a point to stop by to ask questions and get clarification on assignments or ideas. If you can't meet with your instructor during posted office hours, don't give up. Ask to schedule some time to chat before or after class, on the phone, or in Canvas Chat or Conferences. If your instructor has time online set aside to meet with students, email your instructor to schedule an appointment.

Don't cheat. Remember that your first-year composition courses are designed to prepare you for the demands of writing in your future classes and your profession. If you cheat or plagiarize, you are only hurting yourself in the long run. Ultimately, you are responsible for your education and your experience, and you will suffer consequences both immediately and in the future.

Pay attention to the details.   Read the assignment directions in this book and your instructor's specific directions, follow the minimum requirements, and review the evaluation criteria. Part of paying attention to the details is planning, so you have enough time to make minor changes and revise your drafts to meet the requirements for the assignment.

Use your resources.   You have access to the NCTC library and campus writing centers. Further, you also have access to books, academic journals, films, newspapers, and study rooms. If the NCTC libraries don't have a source that you need, the librarians will locate the source at another library and have it shipped to NCTC for you to pick up. In the writing centers, tutors can help you with all stages of the writing process: brainstorming, locating research, drafting, and revising. Successful students find and take advantage of support and resources to help them to be successful.

Strategies for Success: Reading in Academic Contexts

John Locke writes, "Reading furnishes our mind only with materials of knowledge; it is thinking [that] makes what we read ours." Reading to think and reading to write can be challenging, but they are important skills to practice. Being a stronger writer means you are also working on being a stronger reader. In college and your career, you will be expected to read, understand, and use information from textbooks, articles, reports, manuals, charts, case studies, poetry, nonfiction, editorials, fiction, brochures, and proposals. Furthermore, you will be expected to figure out what each text means to you personally and not simply what it is generally accepted to mean.

Active reading skills are vital as you progress through your courses and beyond. Active reading differs from passive reading because active reading means you do something (e.g., take notes, highlight, or annotate) while you read. Instructors will not assign reading as busy work. Your instructors choose readings for a reason, a purpose, and it's important for you to know what the reason is. Before you read, ask yourself (and, if needed, your instructor) the following questions:

- Are you preparing to write a summary, response, analysis, research paper?

- Are you preparing for class discussion?

- Are you reading to prepare for a lecture or a test?

Knowing your purpose determines your approach and engagement with the text. Your instructor will discuss many suggestions and strategies for success when reading academic texts. Here are a few to help get you started:

Read strategically.   Not everything you read in college will be enjoyable. In fact, the texts you are assigned may be dense, have unknown vocabulary, and be boring. Give yourself time to read, re-read, and comprehend the materials.

Preview the text and adjust your reading speed.   Challenging assignments will take longer to read so allow for that time. Consider what you already know about the topic and skim the text to get an idea of the organization and structure.

Annotate.   Taking notes forces you to read carefully, and understanding your purpose will help determine what you should annotate. Use a pen or a highlighter. If reading online, have a notepad in front of you to write down significant points or comments. But, don't overuse it. Easy annotations to start with are questions about the text.

Consider the rhetorical situation.   Note any words that indicate the author's stance or tone. Think about the audience and mark anything that illustrates how the author is addressing the audience's needs.

Read your textbooks.   Divide your reading into manageable pieces. If the passage is not making sense, take a break. Your brain may be tired and need a rest. Another strategy is to read the assigned material aloud. Doing so may help you process the material in a new way.

Talk back to the text.   Write comments, questions, or interesting observations in your book or a notebook, especially if you know there will be a class discussion or lecture over the material. If you cannot write in the book, use a notebook or post-it notes to keep track of main ideas, questions, and comments.

Strategies for Success: Documenting Sources (Paraphrasing, Quoting, and Citing)

A key feature of academic writing is locating research, reflecting on it (you might think about this, again, as rhetorical listening), and integrating it into your own writing to expand, develop, support, elaborate, or refute your points.

As stated earlier in this preface, academic readers favor logic over emotion, demand evidence for claims that are made (often even for what might appear to be minor claims), and define "interesting" as originality of thought and potential for intellectual stimulation.

There are three ways that we integrate sources into our work:

Direct Quote: Complete sentences are taken word-for-word from the source

Example:

In "Letter from Birmingham Jail," Martin Luther King states, "Nourished by the Negro's frustration over the continued existence of racial discrimination, this movement is made up of people who have lost faith in America, who have absolutely repudiated Christianity, and who have concluded that the white man is an incorrigible devil" (605).

Notice that King's name does not appear in the parenthetical citation because it appears in the speaker tag or signal phrase.

Example:

In her poem "The Chuppah," Marge Piercy uses a chuppah, an object similar to an altar used in traditional Jewish weddings, to symbolize her most recent marriage. According to Schneider, "Piercy will use these symbols as a springboard for lyrics that represent her distinctive relationship to Judaism ... and makes such ritual objects her own by integrating them into her life and poetry" (234).

A couple of points —

Notice the speaker tags or signal phrases: *According to Schneider* and *King states.* You need to attribute your direct quote to the source. Don't add a quote into the text without a speaker tag or signal phrase.

Regarding direct quotations: Use them sparingly. If you can paraphrase or partially quote and still convey the author's original meaning, do so. Direct quotations are often longer than necessary and contain material irrelevant to your discussion and thereby only distract your reader.

Notice the quotation marks: They must be there.

Partial Quote: Clauses, phrases, or keywords are taken directly from the outside source

Examples:

In Amy Tan's essay "Mother Tongue," Tan states that "people in department stores, at banks, and at restaurants did not take her seriously, did not give her good service, pretended not to understand her, or even acted as if they did not hear her" (489).

In addition to Piercy, other poets' works were influenced by Judaism as well. Jacqueline Osherow, a fellow Jewish poet, was greatly influenced by her religion in her collection *Dead Men's Praise*, in which Osherow describes "the tensions between being a Jew, a woman, and a poet" (Schneider 654).

Paraphrase: The text is written in your own words; however, the ideas or points come from the readings

Examples:

In Stanton's *Declaration of Sentiments and Resolutions*, she states that men have a history of wrongdoings and act as if they own the women or as if men are better than women. Even though women deserved and demanded equal rights, many men in American society still questioned their reasoning and capability of such rights (591).

As a child, Piercy had a severe case of the German measles, putting her close to death, and during this time her grandmother gave her the Hebrew name Mara, meaning bitter, because of a superstition in her culture that a bad name would keep death away. While her family tried to change her Hebrew name, she decided to keep the original name her grandmother had given her (Rodden 76).

This is very important: Notice the parenthetical citations that appear following each reference to the research. Every time you use information that you read in another source—whether you directly quote, partially quote, or paraphrase from that source, you must include a parenthetical citation.

If you are in doubt about whether you need to cite a source, ask your instructor. Failing to cite a source with a parenthetical citation appropriately is plagiarism, regardless of whether you directly quoted, partially quoted, or paraphrased.

The penalty for plagiarism can range from a verbal/written reprimand, a lower grade on the assignment, automatically failing the assignment, automatically failing the course, or being expelled from school. Again, when in doubt, ask your instructor.

Strategies for Success: Revision

Revision is one of the most exciting parts of your writing process; however, too often, we only think of revision as adding a few commas and correcting a couple of spelling errors. Correcting typographical errors is proofreading; it is not revision. In his book, *Several Short Sentences About Writing*, Verlyn Klinkenborg says, "Revision is thinking applied to language, an opening and reopening of discovery, a search for the sentence that says the thing you had no idea you could say hidden inside the sentence you're making." It is also as personal as your writing process. So, practice revising in different places and postures, finding out what works best for you.

In college, revision is a collaborative effort that works best through open-ended questions and reflective responses to feedback. Effective revision requires us to think critically and read carefully our own work, exploring new ways to speak clearly and write with power and passion. It requires that we make substantial and meaningful changes to our text, and revision takes time, practice, and planning. All of those changes cannot happen simultaneously. Like your writing process, your style of revision will grow and change as you practice it.

Do not overwhelm yourself trying to fix every issue that arises in your essay. To revise like a writer, you will have to make multiple passes through, writing and rewriting with a specific goal in mind each time. Revision is not a single action done in the writing process. It is an attitude that you develop when you engage with your text. When practiced as an art, revising helps your best work become realized.

Here are some tips and suggestions for successful revision:

- Before you begin revising:
  - Read back through your essay and think about why you created each sentence. What does each sentence say, not say, or imply?
  - Take time to reflect on your instructor's feedback. Do you agree with the observations? In what ways? Do you disagree? How so?
  - Paraphrase your instructor's feedback. What is the main point that he/she made regarding your text? What feedback back did your instructor give you in class? On the final submission?
  - Practice humility and remember that no draft is perfect from its inception. We can all grow as writers.
- During the revision process:
  - Don't be self-deprecating. The more time you spend thinking and talking about how bad your writing is, the less time you will spend making it better. All writing can be revised.
  - Start off with a single goal in mind. For example, the first time you read through your work, make sure each sentence conveys a clear and concise idea. Clarity is a great starting point for your revision process. Once you're

done with that round, choose another aspect of your essay, maybe one that your instructor pointed out, to work on.

- Ask questions. If you are confused by your instructor's comments or need further clarification, visit with your instructor and clarify anything that you did not comprehend. When you ask questions, be specific. Don't merely ask: "How do I make this paper better?" Or, "What can I do to make a better grade?" Instead, consider what you understand the comment to mean and then identify the point at which it breaks down for you.
- Solicit feedback. Make an appointment with your instructor during office hours and bring in revised versions of your assignments to get additional feedback. Visit your on-campus writing center and work with a writing tutor to improve your writing. And, make friends with your classmates and start your own writing community. Share your drafts with each other and ask for suggestions and recommendations. Collaborate to graduate!

Strategies for Success: Marketable Skills

It is important as a future college graduate that you're able to convey the knowledge and skills that you've acquired in your writing courses in your new profession. We want you to leave this course able to articulate your own marketable skills.

Marketable skills are the abilities, knowledge, attitudes, and beliefs that equip you for a fruitful career and productive life. These marketable skills—also called transferable skills, portable skills, or employability skills—are acquired through formal education, like your writing courses, and through informal experiences, such as extracurricular activities, student organizations, hobbies, and volunteer/community service work.

There are two large bodies of skills that employers are seeking: hard skills and soft skills.

Hard skills include the specific knowledge that is required for a job, such as coding or carpentry. Hard skills are teachable abilities that your instructor might grade or assess. Generally, students learn hard skills through education, apprenticeships, certification programs, and on-the-job training. These skills are usually listed on job postings. Hard skills are usually included in resumés and applications, and applicants that possess the minimum skills required will be hired. Students are usually good at highlighting these skill sets.

Soft skills are generally not job-specific and include skills such as critical thinking and communication. Soft skills are also the traits that make a good employee, such as showing up on time, being able to "read" others' emotional cues, and getting along with other people. Soft skills differ from hard skills in that they are more closely aligned with personality traits, behaviors, and attitudes rather than technical knowledge. Soft skills also are learned and developed with practice and experience. Specific soft skills may or may not be listed in job descriptions, but they are increasingly becoming an important factor in getting an interview and advancing a career. Students generally have a more difficult time highlighting these skills because they may not be required for a particular job, even though they may be as important as the hard skills.

Employers value job candidates with both sets of these marketable skills, hard and soft. Therefore, we'll continue to work on both in your writing courses. While it would be impossible to list all the skills, certain skills are often most important to employers:

- Communication
- Critical Thinking
- Problem Solving

- Creative Thinking
- Teamwork
- Leadership

- Positive Attitude
- Strong Work Ethic
- Adaptability

INRW 0305 and ENGL 1301

Introduction to INRW 0305

According to the college's catalog, INRW 0305: Integrated Reading and Writing, is a "performance-based course designed to develop students' critical reading and academic writing skills. The focus of the course will be on applying critical reading skills for organizing, analyzing, and retaining the material and developing written work appropriate to the audience, purpose, situation, and length of the assignment." The work you do in this course prepares you for the demands of writing in other academic contexts.

Perhaps you struggled with reading dense texts in the past. Maybe you struggled with coming up with ideas or writing grammatically correct sentences. If you have anxiety coming into this course based on those experiences, that's entirely reasonable. You should understand that this course creates a space—physical/or virtual—for you to develop as a reader and writer. As writing scholar Susan Naomi Bernstein states, this course "provides opportunities for students to discover the kinds of writing that they will encounter throughout college and in the workplace." Moreover, this course offers time to practice writing "intensively and extensively." Therefore, the readings and writing assignments that you do in this course will have a direct correlation to the kinds of reading and writing assignments you'll do in English 1301 and 1302.

Remember that your talents and skills inform your appropriation of academic writing conventions. For instance, in "A Framework for Understanding Latino/a Cultural Wealth," researchers Vijay Kanagala, Laura Rendon, and Amury Nora researched minority Latino students at the University of Texas at San Antonio. Kanagla, Rendon, and Nora argue that minority students, for instance, must often navigate complex discursive spaces (i.e., home community, cultural communities, academia) as well as external conflicts (i.e., financial, childrearing) when attending college (18). Many times, those who are successful relied on a network of resources. Perhaps your experience is different from those Kanagala, Rendon, and Nora studied; however, you also bring your own network of resources to this course that we invite you to draw from and lean on.

To meet those objectives, we have developed this course to align closely with the readings and writing assignments in Composition I, so that, according to the ACGM, when you complete this course, you can:

1. Locate explicit textual information, draw complex inferences, and describe, analyze, and evaluate the information within and across multiple texts of varying lengths.
2. Comprehend and use vocabulary effectively in oral communication, reading, and writing.
3. Identify and analyze the audience, purpose, and message across a variety of texts.
4. Describe and apply insights gained from reading and writing a variety of texts.
5. Compose a variety of texts that demonstrate reading comprehension, clear focus, logical development of ideas, and use of appropriate language that advance the writer's purpose.
6. Determine and use effective approaches and rhetorical strategies for given reading and writing situations.
7. Generate ideas and gather information relevant to the topic and purpose, incorporating the thoughts and words of other writers in student writing using established strategies.
8. Evaluate the relevance and quality of ideas and information in recognizing, formulating, and developing a claim.

We encourage you to participate in academic conversations and tackle relevant topics by engaging with our year-long theme. You should participate as emerging writers in the broader academic community because we need your voice and perspectives. We believe that you'll meet the course outcomes through meaningful participation and by reading a variety of texts and writing the genres that prepare you to produce the kinds of essays that you'll be writing next semester in ENGL 1301: Composition I and throughout your academic career.

Introduction to ENGL 1301

According to the college's catalog, ENGL 1301: Composition I is a course designed for "intensive study of and practice in writing processes, from invention and researching to drafting, revising, and editing, both individually and collaboratively." In Composition I, we emphasize "effective rhetorical choices, including audience, purpose, arrangement, and style." We focus the assignments in the course on writing academic essays because that genre serves "as a vehicle for learning, communicating, and critical analysis."

According to the Texas Higher Education Coordinating Board ACGM, you should, when you conclude this course, be able to

- Demonstrate knowledge of individual and collaborative writing processes.
- Develop ideas with appropriate support and attribution.
- Write in a style appropriate to the audience and purpose.
- Read, reflect, and respond critically to a variety of texts.
- Use Edited American English in academic essays.

But, what does this mean? Specifically, English 1301 is a service course designed to prepare you to write in your other classes and when you enter the workforce. It is our goal that when you conclude this course, you have the resources to write effectively and understand the importance of audience and purpose as it shapes your writing in your history, political science, humanities, literature, lab science, and art appreciation courses. We also aim to prepare you for the demands of writing on the job when you're asked to produce a cover letter and resume, reflect on a process, or problem-solve with your colleagues via email. Beyond academics and the workplace, we hope that you enjoy the challenge of reading and writing and remember the joy that each one can bring.

We also hope that this course gives you an opportunity to consider, discuss, and reflect on yourself and others. How do we present ourselves in our texts? How do we read others in theirs? How does our engagement with the writing process help us develop and hone our ideas? And, how does language shape our experiences?

To help you achieve these goals, we will spend this semester engaging with and reflecting on the arguments of others. We will spend time constructing our own thoughts and ideas through meaningful engagement with each other and with our texts, and we will continue to refine those thoughts through sustained and considerate revision that emphasizes inquiry and reflection.

INRW 0350 and ENGL 1301: This I Believe Essay

We will begin this semester by writing our own This I Believe personal essay, modeled after those in our common text.

About the personal essay. The personal essay allows you to learn how to both analyze and communicate complex ideas and meaningful experiences for a sympathetic audience. Also, as Dr. Kyle Dickson and Dr. Cole Bennett at Abilene Christian University write, the personal essay allows us to understand our commonalities and our differences:

> As readers and writers, if we believe in certain shared strands of meaning that hold all of humanity together, these commonalities are often articulated through the stories of our lives. After all, though our individual narratives vary widely, the themes are often the same: romance, family, growing up, nature, spirituality, neighbors, home, war, and death, for example. These common experiences often create a sense of community, and the personal essay can yield moments of profound clarity as the writer and the reader share complex understanding through local turns of phrase. (*This I Believe: College Writing Curriculum* 5)

The value of the personal essay is that it invites you to identify what you believe and understand the choices that led you to that belief and the decisions that you'll make in response to that belief: "Beliefs are choices. No one has authority over your personal beliefs. Your beliefs are in jeopardy only when you don't know what they are. Understanding your own beliefs, and those of others, comes through focused thought and discussion" (Allison and Gediman 6).

About *This I Believe*. For this assignment, then, you will write a This I Believe personal essay. This essay's prompt is based on a radio program, produced in 1950 and hosted by journalist Edward R. Murrow: "Each day, Americans gathered by their radios to hear compelling essays from the likes of Eleanor Roosevelt, Jackie Robinson, Helen Keller, and Harry Truman as well as corporate leaders, cab drivers, scientists, and secretaries—anyone able to distill into a few minutes the guiding principles by which they lived. These essayists' words brought comfort and inspiration to a country worried about the Cold War, McCarthyism, and racial division" ("About This I Believe").

The purpose of these essays is not to convince or persuade readers to adopt similar values or to change their core beliefs; rather, "the hope is to encourage people to begin the much more difficult task of developing respect for beliefs different from their own" (qtd in "About This I Believe").

About this assignment. Your This I Believe essay will need to adhere to these requirements.

- INRW 0305: 250 words
- ENGL 1301: 500 words
- Include a title

Strategies for Success: Writing the This I Believe Essay

This assignment invites you to identify a personal philosophy and reflect on a set of core values that guides your life. This essay also encourages you to share those experiences with others and have a lasting influence on your classmates. The work that you're doing today is just as important as it was in 1954 when the project first launched. The description of the project, as outlined in the original invitation, still resonates:

> We are sure the statement we ask from you can have a wide and lasting influence. Never has the need for personal philosophies of this kind been so urgent. Your belief, simply and sincerely spoken, is sure to stimulate and help those who hear it. We are confident it will enrich them.

Therefore, as you write your essay, consider the following strategies for success:

Identify possible topics. Think about a specific experience—maybe one that many people can see themselves experience—in which one belief was formed, put to the test, or changed. Focus on one core belief rather than listing several and offer specific details ("This I Believe Writing Suggestions"). Brandon Coon suggests that, when brainstorming your topic, complete one of these sentences:

- The biggest challenge I've ever faced is...
- Someone (person) I have unwavering faith in is...
- Something (object) I have unwavering faith in is...
- What no one knows about me is...
- What makes me angry is...
- I believe the future holds...
- The world needs more...

Identify a narrative coherence. When drafting your belief essay, you might organize it as a narrative: *introduce* yourself, your topic, and tone to the reader. Lead the reader through the *rising action* toward the *turning point* of the essay. Bring down the intensity and draw the essay to a *close*.

Develop your essay. When you have chosen a belief, reflect on what you want to say about it: Who is featured in the essay? How did these individuals contribute to your beliefs? How old were you in the essay? Where were you? What were you doing at the time? Why is this belief important? How does your experience connect to others' experiences? What cultural/social/economic/political belief does this essay illustrate? Why is your essay important? What should the reader take away from your essay?

Consider your voice and tone. Your belief essay does not need to be necessarily sad or heart-warming, but it needs to be authentic and honest. Focus, then, on "I" rather than "we" or "you." This will keep you from proselytizing, editorializing, or finger-pointing:

> Frame your beliefs in positive terms. Refrain from dwelling on what you do not believe. Avoid restatement of doctrine. ... While you may hold many beliefs, write mainly of one. Aim for truth without accusation, patriotism without political cant, and faith beyond religious dogma. (Allison and Gediman 3)

Instead, frame your essay to emphasize what you do believe, rather than what you do not. As described in the original description of this project in 1954, "Your beliefs may well have grown in clarity to you by a process of elimination and rejection, but for our part, we must avoid negative statements lest we become a medium for the criticism of beliefs, which is the very opposite of our purpose" ("Invitation").

This I Believe Essay Evaluation Criteria

	Accomplished	Emerging	Average	Below Average	Failing
Purpose (Development)	The essay clearly identifies a core belief and **consistently** develops upon it by offering **exceptionally** convincing and specific supporting details.	The essay clearly identifies a core belief and **frequently** develops upon it by offering convincing and specific supporting details.	The essay introduces a core belief and **occasionally** develops upon it by offering supporting details.	The essay **hints** at a core belief but **rarely** develops upon it by offering supporting details.	The essay **does not identify** a core belief and **does not** develop upon it by offering supporting details.
Coherence (Organization)	The essay's organization and coherence are **consistently** logical.	The essay's organization and coherence are **often** logical.	The essay's organization and coherence are **occasionally** logical.	The essay's organization and coherence are **rarely** logical.	The essay's organization and coherence are **not** logical.

Continues

	Accomplished	Emerging	Average	Below Average	Failing
Insight (Development)	The essay **consistently** draws insightful observations that are specific and relevant.	The essay **often** draws insightful observations that are specific and relevant.	The essay **occasionally** draws insightful observations that are specific and relevant.	The essay **rarely** draws insightful observations that are specific and relevant.	The essay **does not** draw insightful observations that are specific and relevant.
Convention (Style and Mechanics)	The essay **consistently** demonstrates an ability to utilize the conventions appropriate to audience and genre, including spelling, formatting, and mechanical correctness.	The essay **often** demonstrates an ability to utilize the conventions appropriate to audience and genre, including spelling, formatting, and mechanical correctness.	The essay **occasionally** demonstrates an ability to utilize the conventions appropriate to audience and genre, including spelling, formatting, and mechanical correctness.	The essay **rarely** demonstrates an ability to utilize the conventions appropriate to audience and genre, including spelling, formatting, and mechanical correctness.	The essay **does not** demonstrate an ability to utilize the conventions appropriate to audience and genre, including spelling, formatting, and mechanical correctness.

INRW 0305 and ENGL 1301: Rhetorical Listening Essay

For this assignment, you will reflect on an essay from the common read and engage in rhetorical listening to learn more about others' experiences and the sociological, political, economic, and historical circumstances that shape those experiences.

About Rhetorical Listening. It's helpful to start with the challenges that we face when we seek to understand. Scholar I. A. Richards argues that rhetoric is "a study of misunderstanding and its remedies." This view suggests that communication is difficult, and because we're limited to our words to convey complex thoughts, emotions, and desires, we're all prone to stumble and grope a bit in the dark.

To overcome these misunderstandings, one remedy suggested by Wayne Booth, another famous rhetorical scholar, is that we engage in "rhetorical listening." Rhetorical listening means that we aim to do more just to *win an argument*; instead, rhetorical listening is about *listening to understand,* comprehend, or, in the Platonic sense, strive toward "Truth" with a capital T. We can't grow as students and scholars if we only listen to voices that we agree with or to people who have similar backgrounds.

Rhetorical listening means that we aim to do more just to *win an argument*; instead, rhetorical listening is about *listening to understand*, comprehend, or, in the Platonic sense, strive toward "Truth" with a capital T. We can't grow as students and scholars if we only listen to voices that we agree with or to people who have similar backgrounds.

Krista Radcliffe explains that rhetorical listening is a "stance of *openness*" that a person may choose to assume (1). To engage in rhetorical listening, you might consider "probing for common ground" (Booth 11). You must also consider your own motives, and those of others: "Understanding means more than simply listening for a speaker/writer's intent ... or for our own self-interested intent. Instead, understanding means listening to the discourse not *for* intent but *with* intent" (Ratcliff 15). It is important as curious scholars that we engage in "rhetorical listening" and "rhetorical reading" to move toward a better understanding of others' viewpoints.

Dr. Radcliffe explains that when engaging in rhetorical listening, agreement is not necessarily the goal. We often disagree with each other; however, rhetorical listening means that we recognize others' points of view as different and work toward understanding, not agreement (Ratcliff 33).

About this assignment. For this assignment, you will use the readings from *This I Believe* to engage in rhetorical listening. Specifically, this assignment invites you to assume a *stance of openness* to others' experiences and to understand the larger context that shapes those experiences. In order to complete this assignment, you will:

- Select an essay from *This I Believe* (volume 1 or 2).

- Research, reflect, and explore the sociological, political, economic, and historical circumstances that shape those experiences.

- Write a rhetorical listening essay that seeks to understand the writer's beliefs considering those circumstances. In your assignment, be sure to reference essays from *This I Believe*.

Assignment Requirements

- INRW 0305: 500 words
- ENGL 1301: 1000 words
- Include a title

Strategies for Success: Writing a Rhetorical Listening Essay

Dr. Radcliffe offers these guiding principles when engaging in rhetorical listening:

Rhetorical listening means that we promote an understanding of self and others. In other words, when thinking about how we promote understanding, think about the essays that led you to new insights.

- What essays were surprising to you?
- Which made you feel uncomfortable, anxious, or frustrated?
- What belief or "truth" in those essays made you feel that way?

Rhetorical listening means that we proceed within an accountability logic. In other words, when thinking about an accountability logic, think about the circumstances or events that shaped the writer's life.

- What sociological, political, economic, and historical circumstances shaped the writers' lives? Your life?
- How does privilege shape the writers' experiences? Your experiences?

Rhetorical listening means that we locate identifications across commonalities and differences. In other words, how do writers' experiences and perspectives differ from each other and your own.

- What similarities do these authors share? What commonalities do you see?
- How do their experiences differ? What "points of tension" do you observe?
- Do any strategies, remedies, or opportunities exist that promote understanding of these commonalities and differences?

Rhetorical listening means that we analyze claims as well as the "cultural logics" of these claims. Cultural logics are ways of thinking or the guiding principles, values, beliefs, or ideas that people share. Some important points to consider regarding our cultural logics:

- Cultural logics are reinforced within communities. For example, they may be reinforced in the books we read and the stories we tell.
- Cultural logics or values are not fixed: they change over time and from place to place.
- We also experience different cultural logics at the same time. This can create conflict or tension within our communities or within ourselves.

Here are a few examples of different cultural logics:

- Politics: Republicans / Democrats / Libertarians / Greens
  - Republicans: Evangelical / Tea Party / Moderate
  - Democrats: Democratic Socialist / Progressive / Moderate

- Economics: Capitalists / Socialists / Fascists
- Religion: Christianity / Islam / Judaism / Buddhism
- Race: White Supremacy / Colorblindness / Multiculturalism / Critical Race Studies

Rhetorical Listening Essay Evaluation Criteria

	Accomplished	Emerging	Average	Below Average	Failing
Purpose (Development)	The essay **thoroughly** identifies and **summarily** overviews the different points-of-view.	The essay **consistently** identifies and overviews the different points-of-view.	The essay **often** identifies and overviews the different points-of-view.	The essay **hints at** identifying and overviewing the different points-of-view.	The essay **does not** identify and overview the different points-of-view.
	The writer **thoroughly** develops all of the points with examples from research.	The writer develops **most of the points** with examples from research.	The writer develops **some** of the points with examples from research.	The writer develops a **few** of the points with examples from research.	The writer develops **none** of the points with examples from research.
	The writer **thoroughly** engages in rhetorical listening throughout the essay.	The writer **consistently** engages in rhetorical listening throughout the essay.	The writer **often** engages in rhetorical listening throughout the essay.	The writer **hints at** engaging in rhetorical listening throughout the essay.	The writer **does not** engage in rhetorical listening throughout the essay.
Insight (Development)	The essay **consistently** draws insightful observations from readings/research specific and relevant to the essay's purpose.	The essay **often** draws insightful observations from readings/research specific and relevant to the essay's purpose.	The essay **occasionally** draws insightful observations from readings/research specific and relevant to the essay's purpose.	The essay **rarely** draws insightful observations from readings/research specific and relevant to the essay's purpose.	The essay **does not** draw insightful observations from readings/research specific and relevant to the essay's purpose.

Continues

	Accomplished	**Emerging**	**Average**	**Below Average**	**Failing**
Coherence (Organization)	The essay's organization and coherence are **overwhelmingly** consistent and logical.	The essay's organization and coherence are **often** consistent and logical.	The essay's organization and coherence are **occasionally** consistent and logical.	The essay's organization and coherence are **rarely** consistent and logical.	The essay **does not** demonstrate a consistent, logical, and coherent organization.
	The essay **consistently** demonstrates conventions of academic writing (i.e., **thoroughly** developed introduction, discussion sections, conclusion).	The essay **often** demonstrates conventions of academic writing (i.e., **well-developed** introduction, discussion sections, conclusion).	The essay **occasionally** demonstrates conventions of academic writing (i.e., **occasionally** developed introduction, discussion sections, conclusion).	The essay **rarely** demonstrates conventions of academic writing (i.e., **rarely** developed introduction, discussion sections, conclusion).	The essay **does not** demonstrate conventions of academic writing (i.e., **no** introduction, discussion sections, conclusion).
	The essay **consistently** demonstrates an ability to engage in rhetorical listening.	The essay **often** demonstrates an ability to engage in rhetorical listening.	The essay **occasionally** demonstrates an ability to engage in rhetorical listening.	The essay **rarely** demonstrates an ability to engage in rhetorical listening.	The essay **does not** demonstrate an ability to engage in rhetorical listening.
Convention (Style and Mechanics)	The essay **consistently** utilizes the conventions of academic prose, which include spelling, formatting, mechanical correctness, and citation practices.	The essay **often** utilizes the conventions of academic prose, which include spelling, formatting, mechanical correctness, and citation practices.	The essay **occasionally** utilizes the conventions of academic prose, which include spelling, formatting, mechanical correctness, and citation practices.	The essay **rarely** utilizes the conventions of academic prose, which include spelling, formatting, mechanical correctness, and citation practices.	The essay **does not** utilize the conventions of academic prose, which include spelling, formatting, mechanical correctness, and citation practices.

ENGL 1301: Collaborative Project, This I Believe Photo Essay

For this assignment, you will create a photo essay with peers from your class based on our common read, *This I Believe*. First, you will work in small groups to identify a common or unifying theme. Then, each member of the group will interview someone whose experience relates to that theme and write a This I Believe essay based on that interview. Finally, the group will collect the essays (including both an introduction and conclusion) in a single document.

What is a photo essay? No single, comprehensive definition of a photo essay exists, but in broad terms, a photo essay is a series of photographs collected and organized intentionally to communicate an idea, argument, or story. The photos may accompany a traditional, written essay, or they may *be* the essay.

Why create a photo essay? If you think about the adage, "a picture is worth a thousand words," you'll probably agree that some ideas simply cannot be fully expressed through written or even spoken words, alone. A photo essay—this photo essay—allows you to communicate urgency, relevancy, and other –cy's more efficiently and effectively than with words, alone.

Assignment Details

The photo essay should begin with a written introduction (around 200 words). This should be written together and should include outside research that introduces the significance of the document or theme. Look to the introduction in your book as an example.

Thoughtfully consider how you will organize your photo essay: how you will introduce the issue, how to develop the story and relevance of your issue, and how to achieve an effect on your audience.

Each essay should include a photograph of your interview subject in the presentation. (While you don't need to have or use any fancy photography equipment and the camera on your phone will suffice, the image should be clear and in focus.)

At the end of each essay, include a brief biographical sketch about the subject. Look to the examples at the end of each essay as an example.

You can use Google Docs, Google Slides, PowerPoint, or Word for your final submission.

Consider how to create a uniform final product. Each member should work singly and together to revise for clarity and other aspects that connect the pictures and writing together to form one, comprehensive essay commenting on the unifying theme you are exploring.

Photo Essay Evaluation Criteria

	Accomplished	Emerging	Average	Below Average	Failing
Purpose (Development)	The project clearly identifies core beliefs and **consistently** develops upon them by offering **exceptionally** convincing and specific supporting details.	The project clearly identifies core beliefs and **frequently** develops upon them by offering convincing and specific supporting details.	The project introduces core beliefs and **occasionally** develops upon them by offering supporting details.	The project **hints at** core beliefs but **rarely** develops upon them by offering supporting details.	The project **does not identify** core beliefs and **does not** develop upon them by offering supporting details.
Coherence (Organization)	The project's organization and coherence are **consistently** logical.	The project's organization and coherence are **often** logical.	The project's organization and coherence are **occasionally** logical.	The project's organization and coherence are **rarely** logical.	The project's organization and coherence are **not** logical.
Convention (Style and Mechanics)	The project **consistently** demonstrates an ability to utilize the conventions appropriate to the audience, including spelling, formatting, and mechanical correctness.	The project **often** demonstrates an ability to utilize the conventions appropriate to the audience, including spelling, formatting, and mechanical correctness.	The project **occasionally** demonstrates an ability to utilize the conventions appropriate to the audience, including spelling, formatting, and mechanical correctness.	The project **rarely** demonstrates an ability to utilize the conventions appropriate to the audience, including spelling, formatting, and mechanical correctness.	The project **does not** demonstrate an ability to utilize the conventions appropriate to the audience, including spelling, formatting, and mechanical correctness.
Contribution and Collaboration	The project conveys the team member's **consistent** contributions and an overwhelming commitment to collaboration.	The project conveys the team member's **frequent** contributions and a commitment to collaboration.	The project conveys the team member's **occasional** contributions and **occasionally** demonstrates a commitment to collaboration.	The project conveys the team member's **sparse** contributions and **rarely** demonstrates a commitment to collaboration.	The project **does not** convey the team member's contributions and **does not** demonstrate a commitment to collaboration.

INRW 0305 and ENGL 1301: Final Reflection

For many First-Year Composition students, there is an assumption that good writers are blessed with an innate ability to produce provocative, powerful, and poetic text. Writing just "comes easy" for these students. Magically, they can create text or write essays with little effort.

However, we hope that this semester has demonstrated that academic writing is all about consistency. Meaningful, effective writing requires critical thinking, a close reading of texts, and engagement with the writing assignments. As you should have learned, students who turn in assignments promptly, participate in class discussions, and attend class regularly write more effective texts.

Spend some time and examine your experiences in your First-Year Composition course. Then, please write a reflection addressed to your instructor in which you reflect on your writing processes over the course of the semester. This reflection helps you describe your writing processes and identify your successes and opportunities for growth.

In this final reflection, please discuss specifically how your understanding of academic discourse has developed over the course of the semester. You might think about addressing several of the questions below. You will want to use evidence from your writing assignments to support your discussions.

- How would you have described yourself as a writer and your writing processes at the beginning of the semester? How have your writing processes changed over the course of the semester? What lessons did you learn about "writing as a process"?
- What writing experiences this semester were beneficial (or not) to you as a writer? What are the areas for growth that can be identified and measured in your writing?
- What strategies did you learn about developing your ideas with support and attribution?
- What challenges did you experience when considering your audience and purpose?
- What were your strategies for reading, reflecting, and responding to the course's texts? How have your experiences in this course helped you become a more responsible and ethical writer, researcher, and student?
- What lessons did you learn that you'll take with you from this class about using edited American English in academic essays?
- How will the assignments or experiences this semester will help you in future classes or in your future career?
- What skills have you gained or improved upon as a reader, writer, and collaborator?

A well-developed reflection would be approximately 250 words.

Final Reflection Evaluation Criteria

	Accomplished	Emerging	Average	Below Average	Failing
Purpose (Development)	The reflection **identifies** and summarily overviews semester-long experience and describes the writer's process. The focus is **consistently** maintained in the self-reflective reflection that consistently demonstrates growth as a writer.	The reflection **indicates** an overview of semester-long experience and describes the writer's process. The focus is **often** maintained in the self-reflective reflection that often demonstrates growth as a writer.	The reflection **suggests** an overview of semester-long experience and describes the writer's process. The focus is **occasionally** maintained in the self-reflective reflection that consistently demonstrates growth as a writer.	The reflection **hints** at an overview of semester-long experience and describes the writer's process. The focus is **rarely** maintained in the self-reflective reflection that consistently demonstrates growth as a writer.	The reflection **does not** overview semester-long experience and describes the writer's process. The focus is **not** maintained in the self-reflective reflection that consistently demonstrates growth as a writer.
Coherence (Organization)	The reflection's organization and coherence are **consistently** logical.	The reflection's organization and coherence are **often** logical.	The reflection's organization and coherence are **occasionally** logical.	The reflection's organization and coherence are **rarely** logical.	The reflection's organization and coherence are **not** logical.
Insight (Development)	The reflection **consistently** draws insightful observations from the course assignments that are specific and relevant.	The reflection **often** draws insightful observations from the course assignments that are specific and relevant.	The reflection **occasionally** draws insightful observations from the course assignments that are specific and relevant.	The reflection **rarely** draws insightful observations from the course assignments that are specific and relevant.	The reflection **does not** draw insightful observations from the course assignments that are specific and relevant.

	Accomplished	Emerging	Average	Below Average	Failing
Convention (Style and Mechanics)	The reflection **consistently** demonstrates an ability to utilize the conventions of academic prose, which include spelling, formatting, mechanical correctness, and citation practices.	The reflection **often** demonstrates an ability to utilize the conventions of academic prose, which include spelling, formatting, mechanical correctness, and citation practices.	The reflection **occasionally** demonstrates an ability to utilize the conventions of academic prose, which include spelling, formatting, mechanical correctness, and citation practices.	The reflection **rarely** demonstrates an ability to utilize the conventions of academic prose, which include spelling, formatting, mechanical correctness, and citation practices.	The reflection **does not** demonstrate an ability to utilize the conventions of academic prose, which include spelling, formatting, mechanical correctness, and citation practices.

ENGL 1302

According to the college catalog, ENGL 1302: Composition II is a course designed for the "intensive study of and practice in the strategies and techniques for developing research-based expository and persuasive texts. Emphasis on effective and ethical rhetorical inquiry, including primary and secondary research methods; critical reading of verbal, visual, and multimedia texts; systematic evaluation, synthesis, and documentation of information sources; and critical thinking about evidence and conclusions."

As the second half of your communication core, this course encourages you to move from the structured inquiry in Composition I toward a free inquiry of the course theme in Composition II. You'll also be invited to locate and evaluate sources beyond the course readings to help you support the claims that you'll be making.

Therefore, according to the course syllabus, on successful completion of this course, students will:

1. Demonstrate knowledge of individual and collaborative research processes.
2. Develop ideas and synthesize primary and secondary sources within focused academic arguments, including one or more research-based essays.
3. Analyze, interpret, and evaluate a variety of texts for the ethical and logical uses of evidence.
4. Write in a style that clearly communicates meaning, builds credibility, and inspires belief or action.
5. Apply the conventions of style manuals for specific academic disciplines (e.g., APA, CMS, MLA, etc.).

This course is often the last dedicated writing course that students take in their academic careers; therefore, you may not have another opportunity to participate in a class focused solely on helping you become a better writer and researcher. It is vital then that this course prepares you for the demands of writing in your academic career and in the workforce. We hope that your writing courses at NCTC have helped you appreciate your power to move, inspire, challenge, or persuade others with your words.

ENGL 1302: Annotated Bibliography

For this assignment in Composition II, you will write an annotated bibliography that includes five sources you are planning to use in your research essay.

About the annotated bibliography. Completing an annotated bibliography of existing research is a fundamental component of writing an academic research essay. The annotated bibliography assignment serves several purposes:

- Locating sources and engaging in a close reading of a text help you grow as a writer. Seeing models of how other writers have approached the topic and structured their arguments is also helpful.

- The annotation summarizes the contents of the article to inform the reader of the relevance and quality of the sources cited. When collected, these annotations can serve as a "research log."

- The annotated bibliography provides an opportunity for you to evaluate the quality, breadth, and relevance of the research you've acquired. In other words, if you have five articles, each with little more than the same biographical information, then you know that you will need to do more research to find sources that offer more in-depth and robust analysis of your issue. You'll need to revisit the databases to find more diverse scholarship.

For your annotated bibliography, you need to complete the following steps:

State your tentative thesis or research question. At this point, you should have a tentative thesis or research question for your research paper. Include a one-sentence thesis or research question at the top of the bibliography, just below the title.

Keep in mind that refining your thesis or answering your research question is a recursive process. This means that while your tentative thesis or research question will guide your search, you may discover new information or arguments that persuade you to modify your thesis or approach. You can then use the revised thesis or research question to guide your research. At this point in the process, nothing should be set in stone.

Locate sources. The goal of this annotated bibliography assignment is to locate five scholarly sources that directly relate to your tentative thesis or research question. The sources can provide arguments or evidence in support of your position, or they can provide other significant positions on the topic.

Because the essays in our course readings are academic texts, you may use one of those to get your research started. The other four sources will be found using the academic research databases (e.g., Academic Search Complete, JSTOR, and Opposing Viewpoints in Context).

Write the annotations. The annotation should be written in complete sentences and should include the following information:

- A summary of the source's thesis and supporting arguments. Use active verbs.
- If the source supports your thesis or research question, an explanation of which information or arguments you will use in your essay.
- If the source provides a different or opposing position, an explanation of how you will respond to that position.
- An analysis of what makes this source a good one, including the credentials of the author(s) and the reliability of the arguments and information.

Formatting the bibliography. When writing the annotated bibliography, consider the following guidelines:

- Use MLA or APA style to provide a complete citation for the article.
- MLA or APA formatting and heading
- MLA or APA formatted citations

Annotated Bibliography Evaluation Criteria

	Accomplished	Emerging	Average	Below Average	Failing
Development	Annotations **summarily overview** and identify the main argument. Annotations **consistently** describe the supporting points. The descriptive focus **is maintained** throughout the bibliography.	Annotations **overview** and identify the main argument. Annotations **indicate** the supporting points. The descriptive focus is **consistently** maintained throughout the bibliography.	Annotations **suggest** the main argument. Annotations **occasionally** describe the supporting points. The descriptive focus is **often** maintained throughout the bibliography.	Annotations **hint at** the main argument. Annotations **rarely** describe the supporting points. The descriptive focus is **rarely** maintained throughout the bibliography.	Annotations **do not** identify the main argument. Annotations do not describe the supporting points. The descriptive focus **is not** maintained throughout the bibliography.

Continues

	Accomplished	**Emerging**	**Average**	**Below Average**	**Failing**
Coherence	Annotations **consistently** unfold logically.	Annotations **often** unfold logically.	Annotations **occasionally** unfold logically.	Annotations **rarely** unfold logically.	Annotations **do not** unfold logically.
	Annotations **consistently** identify information or arguments that are relevant to the thesis statement.	Annotations **often** draw identify information or arguments that are relevant to the thesis statement.	Annotations **occasionally** identify information or arguments that are relevant to the thesis statement.	Annotations **rarely** draw identify information or arguments that are relevant to the thesis statement.	Annotations **do not** draw identify information or arguments that are relevant to the thesis statement.
Analysis	Annotations **consistently** demonstrate an ability to evaluate the quality of the sources.	Annotations **often** demonstrate an ability to evaluate the quality of the sources.	Annotations **occasionally** demonstrate an ability to evaluate the quality of the sources.	Annotations **rarely** demonstrate an ability to evaluate the quality of the sources.	Annotations **do not** demonstrate an ability to evaluate the quality of the sources.
Convention (Style and Mechanics)	Annotations **consistently** demonstrate an ability to utilize the conventions of academic prose, which include spelling, formatting, mechanical correctness, and citation practices.	Annotations **often** demonstrate an ability to utilize the conventions of academic prose, which include spelling, formatting, mechanical correctness, and citation practices.	Annotations **occasionally** demonstrate an ability to utilize the conventions of academic prose, which include spelling, formatting, mechanical correctness, and citation practices.	Annotations **rarely** demonstrate an ability to utilize the conventions of academic prose, which include spelling, formatting, mechanical correctness, and citation practices.	Annotations **do not** demonstrate an ability to utilize the conventions of academic prose, which include spelling, formatting, mechanical correctness, and citation practices.

ENGL 1302: Research Essay

Throughout Composition I and II, you have engaged in many academic conversations. The texts and research you've studied have offered new insights, research findings, and perspectives that you might not otherwise have known.

For this next essay, then, you'll incorporate your reading and research into an academic research-based, argumentative essay. Meaningful academic and civic discourses go beyond merely reporting research findings; instead, academic papers add to these broader conversations by going beyond reiterating what others have said (or what most already know) and add new "voices" to the conversation. This essay is your opportunity to join the academic conversation.

Keep in mind that an effective research essay does not exhort the audience as if the essay were a personal blog post or opinion piece in a newspaper. Nor does academic argument attempt to appeal to or replicate popular opinion. Instead, seize the chance to showcase your critical thinking about complex and diverse issues.

Your research essay should:

- Be appropriate for an audience of your peers at NCTC,

- Be unified around a research question rather than merely reporting on several different aspects of a topic,

- Be "original" in that it attempts to wrestle with a topic that has not already been rehashed again and again in print, and

- Incorporate research, which may mean textual study, library sources, historical sources, or media sources.

As for all writings this semester, this paper will be written for your peers and your instructor. Therefore, you should assume that your reader is favorable to your analysis but might be unfamiliar with your sources. Your paper will need to background and clarify the content of the articles that you cite in your text.

Assignment Requirements

- 12-point font, Times New Roman

- Double-spaced, approximately 1750 words

- MLA or APA guidelines for submission, citation, and documentation

- Minimum of 5 cited sources

Strategies for Success: Writing a Research Essay

To begin this assignment, you'll want to first think of a research topic. You'll want to narrow your focus to an issue addressed or explored throughout our year-long discussion. Talk to your instructor about possible topics. Your research essay might focus on ethical arguments, proposal arguments, cause/effect arguments, classification arguments, or arguments of definition.

Once you have narrowed down a research topic, you need to construct a series of questions that you will attempt to answer throughout your research. You may not know the answers to these questions, but you probably won't. That's a good thing because your research is an opportunity for you to investigate the answers.

When considering research questions, you might focus on issues specific to a particular time, place, media, or circumstance. You can transition from your research topic to your research questions by narrowing your focus and looking at what would make your research "original."

Coming up with an "original topic" might mean:

- **You frame your research topic within a particular time.** *This topic is relevant and original because I'm focusing on recent advancements and concerns.*

- **You frame your research topic by examining particular examples.** *This topic is relevant and original because I'm focusing on these specific examples.*

- **You go against the grain.** *This topic is relevant and original because I'm going to present counter-arguments that are often overlooked or dismissed.*

- **You frame your research topic by examining specific locations.** *This topic is relevant and original because I'm focusing my research on North Texas.*

Construct specific research questions that avoid questions that have simple "yes" or "no" answers. Compose questions that ask "what," "how," and "why." As an example, rather than begin a research report on the facts about genetically modified food, begin your research based on questions that are specific to time, location, utilization, or motivation. Delve into questions that move beyond merely summarizing a topic toward presenting an original argument. Such questions might look something like these:

- How are organic foods discussed in news articles throughout the past five years?

- Why is the news coverage of organic foods relevant?

- And, how do these news stories shape public opinion and, in turn, shape public policy?

When narrowing your research topic, consider alternative research methods to explore the issue from an original or unique perspective by developing question-naires; conducting interviews; engaging in close readings of film, television, or social media; or crafting and distributing surveys. While you'll need to include scholarly research from the NCTC library databases to locate your topic in a broader conversation and support your claims, you may also use other research methods to develop a more robust and original focus.

Research Essay Evaluation Criteria

	Accomplished	Emerging	Average	Below Average	Failing
Description (Development)	The essay **identifies** and **summarily overviews** arguments and describes the main points. The focus is **maintained** on making and supporting arguments throughout the essay.	The essay **indicates** a fully-developed argument and describes most of its points. The focus is **consistently maintained** on making and supporting arguments throughout the essay.	The essay **suggests** an argument and describes some of its main points. Original research focus is **often** maintained throughout the essay.	The essay **hints** at an argument and describes a few main points. Original research focus is **rarely** maintained throughout the essay.	The essay **fails** to identify an argument and does not describe the main points. Original research focus is **not** maintained throughout the essay.
Insight and Evaluation (Development)	The essay **consistently** draws insightful observations from sources that are specific and relevant to the essay's purpose. The essay **meaningfully** engages with the ethical challenges.	The essay **often** draws insightful observations from sources that are specific and relevant to the essay's purpose. The essay **often** engages with the ethical challenges.	The essay **occasionally** draws insightful observations from sources that are specific and relevant to the essay's purpose. The essay **occasionally** engages with the ethical challenges.	The essay **rarely** draws insightful observations from sources that are specific and relevant to the essay's purpose. The essay **rarely** engages with the ethical challenges.	The essay **does not** draw insightful observations from sources that are specific and relevant to the essay's purpose. The essay **does not** engage with the ethical challenges.

Continues

	Accomplished	Emerging	Average	Below Average	Failing
Coherence (Organization)	The essay's organization and coherence are **consistent and logical.** The essay **consistently** demonstrates conventions of academic writing. The essay **consistently** demonstrates an ability to support points with research.	The essay's organization and coherence are **often** consistent and logical. The essay **often** demonstrates conventions of academic writing. The essay **often** demonstrates an ability to support points with research.	The essay's organization and coherence are **occasionally** consistent and logical. The essay **occasionally** demonstrates conventions of academic writing. The essay **occasionally** demonstrates an ability to support points with research.	The essay's organization and coherence are **rarely** consistent and logical. The essay **rarely** demonstrates conventions of academic writing. The essay **rarely** demonstrates an ability to support points with research.	The essay **does not** demonstrate a consistent, logical, and coherent organization. The essay does not demonstrate conventions of academic writing. The essay **does not** demonstrate an ability to support points with research.
Convention (Style and Mechanics)	The essay **consistently** demonstrates an ability to utilize the conventions of academic prose, which include spelling, formatting, mechanical correctness, and citation practices.	The essay **often** demonstrates an ability to utilize the conventions of academic prose, which include spelling, formatting, mechanical correctness, and citation practices.	The essay **occasionally** demonstrates an ability to utilize the conventions of academic prose, which include spelling, formatting, mechanical correctness, and citation practices.	The essay **rarely** demonstrates an ability to utilize the conventions of academic prose, which include spelling, formatting, mechanical correctness, and citation practices.	The essay does not demonstrate an ability to utilize the conventions of academic prose, which include spelling, formatting, mechanical correctness, and citation practices.

ENGL 1302: Collaborative Project: Social Media Rhetorical Inquiry

Our task is to learn how to build smart rooms—that is how to build smart networks that make us smarter, especially since, when done badly, networks can make us distressingly stupider.—David Weinberger

Think about where you connect with others most often. Is it digital or person-to-person? What about how you consume media, the news, facts and figures, and new information? We spend more time than we ever have networking with others and learning in online platforms. Learning how to navigate this new world together will be easier than going at it alone. Not only will it benefit us to do so, we have an obligation to build networks that will allow everyone to grow collectively.

Our collaborative project, then, for ENGL 1302 will do just that: We are going to dive inside our text and think critically about the opportunities and/or dangers that are present in our social media networks.

For this assignment, you will work in small groups to create a visual artifact that examines and critically adds to one of the arguments presented in our text. Specifically, the final product must examine one of the ten arguments presented in the text and provide adequate proof of the position taken by the group. It will be an experimental essay in digital form. In First-Year Composition classes, you have been learning how to rhetorically listen, to argue well, to read critically, and to write intentionally. This assignment, then, will require that you listen to the text and analyze the content. It will challenge you to think about all aspects of the argument, and then push you to comment academically, adding to the argument in support or refutation.

For this assignment, you can use any platform(s) of social media or digital platforms where users can create online communities to share information, ideas, personal messages and/or other content. A few examples are Instagram, Facebook, a blog, TikTok, a podcast, forum-based website, Snapchat, etc.

Each group will be responsible for creating an artifact that is viewable online and can be uploaded to Canvas.

When producing your collaborative project, follow these directions:

1. As a group, choose a section from the text.
2. Every group member needs to read, annotate, and think about your chosen section.
3. Create and share a Google doc that explores the section(s) entirely. Share your notes and thoughts with one another. Ask questions and outline the details living inside the argument(s) you've chosen.
4. Decide as a group whether you want to add to the argument(s) and prove its validity or you want to oppose the argument(s) and attempt to provide a counter argument.
5. Either create a social media platform that will house your project or collect from social media platforms (or both) to complete the project.

   ○ Projects need to incorporate digital media supported by words.
   ○ Each post created or collected needs to be done so with intention.

- Be sure you keep all details in order: date created, content created, platform used, etc.
- Each member needs to add/collect content in a meaningful way. Everyone must participate for the project to be successful.
6. Intentionally craft your final project for submission. To do so, think through the following questions: How will you present your argument? What will act as evidence? Is your message clear? Did you accomplish the original goal? Why did you use the specific platform for your final project?
7. Every student must upload the project to Canvas.

This assignment is designed to challenge you to listen well, argue in the true sense, and create intentionally with a nontraditional medium. It will help you collaborate with others effectively and to learn how to work as a team to accomplish a common goal. Our arguments will add to a larger conversation and not be designed so we "win." Our goal is to create something as a group that will stand as evidence, furthering our understanding of how social media affects our lives.

Collaborative Project Evaluation Criteria

	Accomplished	Emerging	Average	Below Average	Failing
Purpose (Development)	The project clearly identifies core beliefs and **consistently** develops upon them by offering **exceptionally** convincing and specific supporting details.	The project clearly identifies core beliefs and **frequently** develops upon them by offering convincing and specific supporting details.	The project introduces core beliefs and **occasionally** develops upon them by offering supporting details.	The project **hints** at core beliefs but **rarely** develops upon them by offering supporting details.	The project **does not identify** core beliefs and **does not** develop upon them by offering supporting details.
Coherence (Organization)	The project's organization and coherence are **consistently** logical.	The project's organization and coherence are **often** logical.	The project's organization and coherence are **occasionally** logical.	The project's organization and coherence are **rarely** logical.	The project's organization and coherence are **not** logical.

	Accomplished	Emerging	Average	Below Average	Failing
Convention (Style and Mechanics)	The project **consistently** demonstrates an ability to utilize the conventions appropriate to the audience, including spelling, formatting, and mechanical correctness.	The project **often** demonstrates an ability to utilize the conventions appropriate to the audience, including spelling, formatting, and mechanical correctness.	The project **occasionally** demonstrates an ability to utilize the conventions appropriate to the audience, including spelling, formatting, and mechanical correctness.	The project **rarely** demonstrates an ability to utilize the conventions appropriate to the audience, including spelling, formatting, and mechanical correctness.	The project **does not** demonstrate an ability to utilize the conventions appropriate to the audience, including spelling, formatting, and mechanical correctness.
Contribution and Collaboration	The project conveys the team member's **consistent** contributions and an overwhelming commitment to collaboration.	The project conveys the team member's **frequent** contributions and a commitment to collaboration.	The project conveys the team member's **occasional** contributions and **occasionally** demonstrates a commitment to collaboration.	The project conveys the team member's **sparse** contributions and **rarely** demonstrates a commitment to collaboration.	The project **does not** convey the team member's contributions and **does not** demonstrate a commitment to collaboration.

ENGL 1302: Final Reflection

For many First-Year Composition students, there is an assumption that good writers are blessed with an innate ability to produce provocative, powerful, and poetic text. Writing just "comes easy" for these students. Magically, they can create text or write essays with little effort.

However, we hope that this semester has demonstrated that academic writing is all about consistency. Meaningful, effective writing requires critical thinking, a close reading of texts, and engagement with the writing assignments. As you should have learned, students who turn in assignments promptly, participate in class discussions, and attend class regularly write more effective texts.

Spend some time and examine your experiences in your First-Year Composition course. Then, please write a reflection addressed to your instructor in which you reflect on your writing processes over the course of the semester. This reflection helps you describe your writing processes and identify your successes and opportunities for growth.

In this final reflection, please discuss specifically how your understanding of academic discourse has developed over the course of the semester. You might think about addressing several of the questions below. You will want to use evidence from your writing assignments to support your discussions.

- How would you have described yourself as a writer and your writing processes at the beginning of the semester? How have your writing processes changed over the course of the semester? What lessons did you learn about "writing as a process"?
- What writing experiences this semester were beneficial (or not) to you as a writer? What are the areas for growth that can be identified and measured in your writing?
- What strategies did you learn about developing your ideas with support and attribution?
- What challenges did you experience when considering your audience and purpose?
- What were your strategies for reading, reflecting, and responding to the course's texts? How have your experiences in this course helped you become a more responsible and ethical writer, researcher, and student?
- What lessons did you learn that you'll take with you from this class about using edited American English in academic essays?
- How will the assignments or experiences this semester will help you in future classes or in your future career?
- What skills have you gained or improved upon as a reader, writer, and collaborator?

A well-developed reflection would be approximately 250 words.

Final Reflection Evaluation Criteria

	Accomplished	Emerging	Average	Below Average	Failing
Purpose (Development)	The reflection **identifies** and summarily overviews semester-long experience and describes the writer's process. The focus is **consistently** maintained in the self-reflective reflection that consistently demonstrates growth as a writer.	The reflection **indicates** an overview of semester-long experience and describes the writer's process. The focus is **often** maintained in the self-reflective reflection that often demonstrates growth as a writer.	The reflection **suggests** an overview of semester-long experience and describes the writer's process. The focus is **occasionally** maintained in the self-reflective reflection that consistently demonstrates growth as a writer.	The reflection **hints at** an overview of semester-long experience and describes the writer's process. The focus is **rarely** maintained in the self-reflective reflection that consistently demonstrates growth as a writer.	The reflection **does not** overview semester-long experience and describes the writer's process. The focus is **not** maintained in the self-reflective reflection that consistently demonstrates growth as a writer.

	Accomplished	Emerging	Average	Below Average	Failing
Coherence (Organization)	The reflection's organization and coherence are **consistently** logical.	The reflection's organization and coherence are **often** logical.	The reflection's organization and coherence are **occasionally** logical.	The reflection's organization and coherence are **rarely** logical.	The reflection's organization and coherence are **not** logical.
Insight (Development)	The reflection **consistently** draws insightful observations from the course assignments that are specific and relevant.	The reflection **often** draws insightful observations from the course assignments that are specific and relevant.	The reflection **occasionally** draws insightful observations from the course assignments that are specific and relevant.	The reflection **rarely** draws insightful observations from the course assignments that are specific and relevant.	The reflection **does not** draw insightful observations from the course assignments that are specific and relevant.
Convention (Style and Mechanics)	The reflection **consistently** demonstrates an ability to utilize the conventions of academic prose, which include spelling, formatting, mechanical correctness, and citation practices.	The reflection **often** demonstrates an ability to utilize the conventions of academic prose, which include spelling, formatting, mechanical correctness, and citation practices.	The reflection **occasionally** demonstrates an ability to utilize the conventions of academic prose, which include spelling, formatting, mechanical correctness, and citation practices.	The reflection **rarely** demonstrates an ability to utilize the conventions of academic prose, which include spelling, formatting, mechanical correctness, and citation practices.	The reflection **does not** demonstrate an ability to utilize the conventions of academic prose, which include spelling, formatting, mechanical correctness, and citation practices.

Special Event Attendance Documentation

Research shows that students who participate in their academic communities—like joining academic and nonacademic organizations, soliciting academic support, and attending extracurricular events—have better grades, are more likely to complete their degrees, and are more satisfied and happy throughout their academic studies.

You are invited to attend special events on the NCTC campus and can receive one absence forgiveness. To earn the credit, you must complete the following form within one week of the event and submit it to your instructor. If the reflection is incomplete, it may not be accepted for credit.

It is also important that you present yourselves as polite and serious students. Therefore, to receive full credit for this assignment, you must 1) stay for the entire event and 2) should not get up and leave while the speaker is talking or answering questions. A failure to demonstrate this sort of professionalism means that you will not receive full credit for your attendance.

To receive full credit, please provide the following information:

1. A description of the event (i.e., title, day, time, location).
2. An explanation of how this event enhanced your experience in your INRW 0305, ENGL 1301, or ENGL 1302 course.
3. Questions that you would like to ask as a result of attending this event.

NCTC's Statement on Plagiarism in First-Year Composition

Over the course of this academic year, you'll learn how to locate, synthesize, paraphrase, and quote outside sources to support your points. Learning to integrate sources to avoid "double-voicing" (when it's unclear when your voice ends and your sources begin) is a foundational component of academic research and is why both ENGL 1301 and 1302 include *attribution* and *documentation* in the learning outcomes.

- ENGL 1301: Develop ideas with appropriate support and attribution
- ENGL 1302: Apply the conventions of style manuals for specific academic disciplines (e.g., APA, CMS, MLA, etc.)

It's essential that you learn how to document your sources and have the time and space to practice those skills. You'll probably make mistakes, and it's our job to help you see those errors and learn from them.

However, there is a difference between incorrectly documenting your sources and intentionally trying to deceive your instructor by submitting someone else's work or thoughts and claiming them to be your own. A deliberate attempt to circumvent doing your own writing—whether it's a sentence, paragraph, or entire essay—is considering scholastic dishonesty or plagiarism.

For our part, we've taken several measures to create a classroom environment that discourages plagiarism: First, we've designed your courses so that the readings and writing assignments are specific to NCTC and our course discussions. We do this to engage you in the course activities so that you feel invested and motivated to participate fully in the course. Second, we customize our courses to prevent students from turning in generic, tired writing assignments about topics that have been hashed out time and time again online. The assignments in your courses are also designed so that papers cannot be easily copied from online paper mills.

For your part, we ask you to consider how you can avoid plagiarism by not engaging in the following actions:

1. Turning in someone else's ideas, opinions, theories, or work as your own;
2. Unintentionally or inadvertently turning in someone else's ideas, opinions, theories, or work as your own as the result of failing to document sources both internally and on the Works Cited page;
3. Copying words, ideas, or images from someone without giving credit and failing to put a quotation in quotations marks;
4. Giving incorrect information about the source of information, quotations, or images;
5. Changing words but copying the sentence structure of a source without giving credit; and/or
6. Copying so many words, ideas, or images from a source that it makes up the majority of the student's work, whether or not the student gives credit.

In other words, according to the student handbook, scholastic dishonesty shall include, but is not limited to, cheating on a test, plagiarism, and collusion. (See *Student Handbook* "Student Rights & Responsibilities: Student Conduct [FLB- (LOCAL)]" #18.)

Please pay careful attention to the consequences of scholastic dishonesty:

> *Disciplinary Actions* [*Student Handbook*, #5]: When cheating, collusion, or plagiarism has occurred beyond any reasonable doubt, the instructor may give the student or students involved an "F" on a particular assignment or in the course. [See Scholastic Dishonesty FLB (Local)] The instructor shall make a written report of the incident and the planned action to the Department Chair. The Department Chair shall report the incident and action to the appropriate instructional dean who shall review the case, notify the student and, if necessary, take further action. This may involve either probation or suspension of the student or students in question. If such disciplinary action is deemed necessary, the Dean of Student Services shall be notified, and the action shall be taken through that office.

Please be advised that your instructor and our department take scholastic dishonesty seriously. To avoid plagiarism, we encourage you to do your own work, embrace any struggles or challenges as part of the learning process, start early on your assignments, and seek out feedback or clarification from your instructor or the writing center if you're confused about whether you've appropriately documented your sources.

Works Cited

"A Useful Definition of Art." *Seth's Blog*, 13 Sept 2019, https://seths.blog/2019/09/a-useful-definition-art/.

"About This I Believe." *This I Believe*, 2020, https://thisibelieve.org/about/.

Allison, Jay and Dan Gediman. *This I Believe*. Vol 1. New York: Holt, 2007.

Booth, Wayne C. *Rhetoric of Rhetoric: The Quest for Effective Communication*. Hoboken, NJ: Blackwell Publishing.

Coon, Brandon. *This I Believe Personal Essay*, 3 Oct 2017, https://www.bulbapp.com/u/this-i-believe-personal-essay.

"Feature." *This I Believe*, 2020, https://thisibelieve.org/feature/.

Klinkenborg, Verlyn. *Several Short Sentences About Writing*. Vintage Books Edition, New York, NY: Random House, 2013.

Lamott, Anne. *Bird by Bird: Some Instruction on Writing and Life*. New York: Anchor, 1994. Print.

Ratcliffe, Krista. *Rhetorical Listening: Identification, Gender, Whiteness*. Carbondale: Michigan UP, 2005.

Russell, Scott. "Introduction." *Touchstone Anthology of Contemporary Creative Nonfiction*, New York: Touchstone, xvii-xviii. Print.

"Themes." *This I Believe*, 2020, https://thisibelieve.org/themes/.

"Themes." *This I Believe at TCU*. Texas Christian University. https://tcuthisibelieve.wordpress.com/category/stories/themes/. Accessed 6 Apr 2020.

This I Believe: College Writing Curriculum, PDF, 2015.

Preface for Instructors

The Hub: A Place for Reading and Writing consists of a series of carefully curated, inquiry-based reading/writing projects supported by crucial instruction and activities related to reading, writing, research, and life issues. It is available both in print and in a powerful digital format: *Achieve with Adams, The Hub.* For corequisite composition courses, it can serve as the complete "text" for both the composition course and the paired developmental section.

One Text for Two Courses

The breadth and depth of content in *The Hub* allows instructors the opportunity to select those elements that make the most sense for their students, their teaching styles, and the context in which they are teaching. Experienced instructors, for example, can select just the materials they want and assemble them into a powerful syllabus. Less experienced instructors (or those with less time to prepare) can choose from suggested schedules in the Instructor's Manual that combine selections of the materials into effective teaching plans for a variety of course types.

The Hub addresses the major topics typically covered in a composition rhetoric or reader: the rhetorical situation, thesis and unity, developing an argument, supporting assertions, diction, editing to reduce the frequency and severity of sentence-level errors, and research and documentation. (See the WPA Outcomes correlation chart on p. xiv for more details.) But it also addresses important issues that are not covered by other texts or digital products currently on the market:

- It features a strong and innovative approach to integrating reading and writing.

- It tackles the noncognitive issues that so often cause students to give up on college (e.g., life issues such as those related to finances, housing, health, child care, and so on, as well as affective issues like stress and impostor syndrome).

- It emphasizes active learning in small groups, which allows students to discover ideas about writing for themselves rather than simply read about them.

- It places more emphasis on the importance of inquiry and critical thinking.

One reason so many students drop out of college before they complete their developmental coursework is that the classes make them feel like they are back in seventh grade. *The Hub* does not do this. The materials in this collection ask students to read college-level essays, to complete college-level activities, and to write college-level essays. However, the additional materials provided for corequisite students offer the option of proceeding at a slower pace with more scaffolding, more support, and more opportunity for revisions.

Uniquely Flexible Content

Ideal for corequisite composition courses, *The Hub* was conceived of and designed as an in-depth suite of digital materials accompanied by a printed companion text. Seven multipart reading/writing projects on high-interest topics form the base of *The Hub*, with additional reading, writing, life skills, and research topics available in Parts 2–5. As your students work on readings and assignments in any of the projects, this rich library of additional content allows you to easily find and assign the exact materials and activities your students need when they need them. Whether it's detailed writing instruction on thesis development, a concise explanation of reading strategies like previewing or annotation, or advice on time management, it's all available for you to select from and combine in whatever order makes sense for your students.

To maximize the effectiveness of this unique resource, use *Achieve with Adams, The Hub* (see macmillanlearning.com for details). Achieve puts student writing at the center of your course and keeps revision at the core, with a dedicated composition space that guides students through draft, review, source check, and revision. In Achieve, students can read the complete text of *The Hub*, watch presentations on key topics narrated by the author, link to relevant websites, complete short writing assignments and reflection activities, get feedback from peers, and work on the end-of-project essay assignments.

Organization

The Hub consists of five parts:

Part 1: Reading/Writing Projects.   This is the core of *The Hub* and consists of seven thematically organized projects of different lengths on a variety of high-interest topics, such as freedom of speech, what constitutes fake news, and choosing a career. These projects can be used in any order, and each takes 3–6 weeks to complete.

Part 2: Writing.   This section of *The Hub* contains eleven Topics (8–18), each made up of several units that address essential writing issues, including the following: the rhetorical situation; the writing process; finding a focus; developing and organizing support; thesis, unity, and coherence; types of writing; argument; reducing sentence-level errors; and more. It includes several student essays, some annotated, and a series of drafts of an essay that illustrate the revision process.

Part 3: Reading.   Three Topics (19–21), also made up of subunits, discuss active and critical reading strategies. These include purposes for reading, constructing meaning, activating schema, previewing, annotating, evaluating, identifying biases and assumptions, making inferences, distinguishing between facts and opinions, decoding difficult language, reading as a believer and doubter, and more.

Part 4: Research and Documentation.   Topic 22 provides coverage of the research process: finding and evaluating sources; quoting, paraphrasing, and summarizing; conducting interviews and surveys; and avoiding plagiarism. Topics 23 and 24 provide detailed information on MLA and APA documentation, with numerous examples and a sample student paper in each.

Part 5: Balancing School, Work, and Life.   An important feature of *The Hub* is the attention devoted to noncognitive issues, which can significantly impact student success. Topics 25–28 cover a broad range of issues students can find challenging: finances, health care, time management, goal setting, responding to setbacks, college terminology, asking for help, and more.

Elements and Features

The Hub contains a variety of important structural elements and features designed to support the overall pedagogical approach:

Reading/Writing Projects.   Following best practices for teaching composition, each of the seven high-interest projects involves a variety of activities—reading articles, watching videos, engaging in class discussions, writing short papers, creating group responses to readings, analyzing data, interviewing someone who has knowledge or experience of the topic, and more. This approach inspires deep and prolonged thinking, encouraging students to articulate, analyze, and evaluate both their ideas and those of the authors they are reading, and to synthesize these ideas in their writing. In the end, the work students do for all of the shorter activities and assignments forms the basis of a longer paper or multimodal composition.

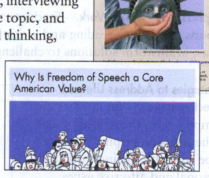

↳ **3.10** Writing
Explaining the Senate's Reservations
Write a short paper—about a page—in which you explain the reservations that the US Senate registered in the document that can be found in the US Senate Response to the International Convention on the Elimination of All Forms of Racial Discrimination (3.9, p. 93). What were the government's reservations about the International Convention on the Elimination of All Forms of Racial Discrimination and why did it have those reservations?

Integration of Reading and Writing. Throughout the projects in Part 1, reading and writing are seamlessly integrated: when students read, they are asked to preview, annotate, paraphrase, summarize, analyze, evaluate, discuss, reflect on, and write in response to reading, and finally to draw on everything they have read to write a culminating essay or create a multimodal composition.

Top photo: (*statue*) Bryan Busovicki/Shutterstock; (*hand*) DenisNata/Shutterstock. Middle photo: rob zs/Shutterstock

Emphasis on Critical Thinking.
Group activities, discussion
prompts, short writing assignments, readings from a variety
of genres, and videos on related
topics all challenge students to

> **3.11** Activity
> **Defining *Hate Speech***
> Much of current discussion about freedom of speech revolves around what is referred
> to as *hate speech*. Working in your group, write a definition of *hate speech*, explain-
> ing what your group agrees it is and what it isn't. If you need a refresher on how to

question what they read in any medium; evaluate the credentials, assumptions, and
biases of authors; fact-check to distinguish between facts and opinions, truth and lies;
and explore their own thinking.

> **19.1** Presentation
> **Reading Is Thinking**
> To watch this presentation, which discusses the importance of thinking, questioning,
> and extracting meaning from a text as you read, go to *Achieve for The Hub*, Topic 19,
> and open Unit 19.1.

Focus on Active Learning. *The
Hub* uses an array of activity types
to engage students' interest, promote critical thinking, and teach
fundamental reading and writing
skills: group and individual read-
ing assignments, videos, narrated presentations, class discussions, small-group and
whole-class exercises, short writing assignments, data analysis, interviewing, surveying, researching in class and out, essay assignments, peer review, and more.

Emphasis on Group Work. Students are frequently asked to work together in small
groups to practice reading and writing skills, discuss readings, explore and debate
ideas, brainstorm solutions to challenging life issues, and determine grammar rules.

**Strategies to Address Life and
Affective Issues.** An important
component of the ALP approach
is the focus on helping students
cope with challenging work and
personal and affective issues.
Topics 25–28, in Part 5, contain
activities that aid students in
identifying issues and brain-

> **26.7** Activity
> **Time Management: Strategies**
> Working together as a group, make a list of time-management strategies. To get you
> started, here's one strategy:
>
> **Do the hardest task first.** Sometimes a difficult task gets pushed to later in the day
> or even later in the week. Then you spend time dreading it, which makes you less
> effective at completing other tasks. There's nothing more satisfying than taking on
> that hard task first, preferably earlier in the day when you are at your most alert, and
> getting it done.

storming solutions to them in a group setting. In addition, the instructor-facing support
for these activities provides suggestions to faculty on how to address these issues in the
classroom as well as information on resources students could access and use.

Inductive Approach to Grammar. In contrast to traditional approaches, *The Hub*
teaches grammar inductively. Grammar activities encourage students to work with
peers to infer grammar rules from pairs and groups of sentences that illustrate correct

and incorrect usage, work with them to articulate and record these rules, and apply what they have learned in the context of their own writing.

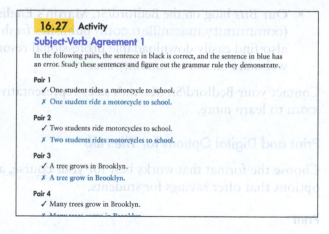

16.27 Activity

Subject-Verb Agreement 1

In the following pairs, the sentence in black is correct, and the sentence in blue has an error. Study these sentences and figure out the grammar rule they demonstrate.

Pair 1
✓ One student rides a motorcycle to school.
✗ One student ride a motorcycle to school.

Pair 2
✓ Two students ride motorcycles to school.
✗ Two students rides motorcycles to school.

Pair 3
✓ A tree grows in Brooklyn.
✗ A tree grow in Brooklyn.

Pair 4
✓ Many trees grow in Brooklyn.
✗ Many trees grows in Brooklyn.

Instructor Support for Teaching with *The Hub*

Very few faculty have received preparation to teach an ALP or corequisite course, to address noncognitive issues, or to help students develop as readers. Recognizing this problem, *The Hub* provides extensive assistance for instructors. In *Instructor's Manual for The Hub*, every activity, assignment, or reading in Projects 1–7 has a corresponding unit of suggestions, tips, and answers for instructors. In addition, there is specific guidance on teaching every unit in the Topics in Parts 2–5.

Two sections in the Instructor's Manual, Chapter 2 and Teaching Part 3: Reading (in Section 3: Teaching the Topics), address reading issues in some depth, and these pages will be extremely helpful for instructors with little preparation to encourage students to develop as readers. Also included are chapters for faculty explaining the history and development of ALP and corequisite models, how to teach integrated reading and writing, how to integrate group work and inductive learning, how to address noncognitive issues in the classroom, and how to use *The Hub* to design a syllabus for a composition or corequisite course.

Bedford/St. Martin's Puts You First

From day one, our goal has been simple: to provide inspiring resources that are grounded in best practices for teaching reading and writing. For more than 35 years, Bedford/St. Martin's has partnered with the field, listening to teachers, scholars, and students about the support writers need. We are committed to helping every writing instructor make the most of our resources.

How can we help *you*?

- Our editors can align our resources to your outcomes through correlation and transition guides for your syllabus. Just ask us.

- Our sales representatives specialize in helping you find the right materials to support your course goals.

- Our *Bits* blog on the Bedford/St. Martin's English Community site (community.macmillan.com) publishes fresh teaching ideas weekly. You'll also find easily downloadable professional resources and links to author webinars on our community site.

Contact your Bedford/St. Martin's sales representative or visit macmillanlearning .com to learn more.

Print and Digital Options for *The Hub*

Choose the format that works best for your course, and ask about our packaging options that offer savings for students.

Print

- *Paperback.* To order the paperback edition, use ISBN 978-1-319-36235-5. To order the paperback edition packaged with *Achieve with Adams, The Hub*, contact your Bedford/St. Martin's sales representative.

- *Loose-leaf edition.* This format does not have a traditional binding; its pages are loose and hole-punched to provide flexibility and a lower price to students. To order this version of *The Hub*, use ISBN 978-1-319-36236-2. To order the loose-leaf packaged with Achieve, contact your Bedford/St. Martin's sales representative.

Digital

- *Achieve with Adams, The Hub.* For details, visit macmillanlearning.com.

- *Popular e-book formats.* For details about our e-book partners, visit macmillanlearning.com/ebooks.

- *Inclusive Access.* Enable every student to receive their course materials through your LMS on the first day of class. Macmillan Learning's Inclusive Access program is the easiest, most affordable way to ensure all students have access to quality educational resources. Find out more at macmillanlearning.com/ inclusiveaccess.

Your Course, Your Way

No two writing programs or classrooms are exactly alike. Our Curriculum Solutions team works with you to design custom options that provide the resources your students need. (Options below require enrollment minimums.)

- *ForeWords for English.* Customize any print resource to fit the focus of your course or program by choosing from a range of prepared topics, such as Sentence Guides for Academic Writers.

- *Macmillan Author Program (MAP).* Add excerpts or package acclaimed works from Macmillan's trade imprints to connect students with prominent authors and public conversations. A list of popular examples or academic themes is available upon request.

- *Bedford Select.* Build your own print handbook or anthology from a database of more than 800 selections, and add your own materials to create your ideal text. Package with any Bedford/St. Martin's text for additional savings. Visit macmillanlearning.com/bedfordselect.

Instructor Resources

You have a lot to do in your course. We want to make it easy for you to find the support you need—and to get it quickly.

The Instructor's Edition for *The Hub: A Place for Reading and Writing* is available in print (ISBN 978-1-319-32942-6) and includes a sixteen-page insert that provides concise information on how to use *The Hub*, as well as sample schedules for teaching the ENG 101 and corequisite sections for three of the reading/writing projects.

Instructor's Manual for The Hub is available both in print (ISBN 978-1-319-32943-3) and as a PDF that can be downloaded from macmillanlearning .com. Section 1 provides detailed information on how to teach corequisite composition courses—discussing how to integrate reading and writing, use group work and inductive learning to create an active learning environment, and address noncognitive issues—as well as providing information on how to design a syllabus using content from *The Hub*. Section 2 includes sample schedules for using the projects in conjunction with content from Parts 2–5 of *The Hub* in composition and corequisite classes, and both Sections 2 and 3 provide unit-by-unit teaching tips, suggestions, and answers to exercises.

Acknowledgments

I am grateful to my colleagues at the Conference (now, Council) on Basic Writing for their support of my early thinking about corequisites (or, as we called it then, "mainstreaming" basic writers): Suellynn Duffey, Greg Glau, Barbara Gleason, Sugie Goen-Salter, Carolyn Kirkpatrick, Bill Lalicker, Rebecca Mlynarczyk, Deborah Mutnick, and Karen Uehling. I owe equal gratitude to my colleagues at the Community College of Baltimore County: Linda De La Ysla, Susan Gabriel, Jamey Gallagher, Sarah Gearhardt, Terry Hirsch, Patrick Kelleher, Donna McKusick, Bob Miller, Anne Roberts, Jackie Scott, and Monica Walker. The corequisite idea also received important support from Tom Bailey at the Community College

Research Center, from Bruce Vandal at Complete College America, and from David Bartholomae, whose "Tidy House" presentation at the CBW conference in 1992 provided reassurance that corequisite developmental writing was not a crazy idea.

For the development of *The Hub*, I was fortunate to have a faculty advisory board who provided insights, suggestions, corrections, and examples that have greatly improved the final manuscript under extremely tight time constraints. Warm thank-yous to Paul Beehler, *University of California–Riverside*; Mark Blaauw-Hara, *North Central Michigan College*; Brian Dickson, *Community College of Denver*; Jacqueline Gray, *St. Charles Community College*; Angelique Johnston, *Monroe Community College*; Meridith Leo, *Suffolk County Community College*; Angelina Oberdan, *Central Piedmont Community College*; Kelli Prejean, *Marshall University*; Sarah Snyder, *Western Arizona College*; and Christina Tarabicos, *Delaware Technical Community College*.

I also want to thank colleagues across the country who found time to review the manuscript and to participate in focus groups:

Susan Achziger, *Community College of Aurora*; Nancy Alexander, *Methodist University*; Eric Atchison, *Mississippi Institutions of Higher Learning*; Patricia Biebelle, *New Mexico State University*; Janice Brantley, *University of Arkansas at Pine Bluff*; Erin Breaux, *South Louisiana Community College*; Elizabeth Burton, *Hopkinsville Community College*; Katawna Caldwell, *Eastfield College*; Helen Ceraldi, *Cedar Valley College*; Mollie Chambers, *Lorain Community College*; Nancy Cheeks, *California State University–Northridge*; Emily Cosper, *Delgado Community College*; Jill Darley-Vanis, *Clark College*; Lacy Davis, *New Mexico State University–Carlsbad*; Darren DeFrain, *Wichita State University*; Elizabeth Donley, *Clark College*; Summer Doucet, *Baton Rouge Community College*; Amy Drees, *Northwest State Community College*; Karen Dulweber, *Kilgore College*; Margot Edlin, *Queensborough Community College*; Jennifer Ferguson, *Cazenovia College*; Jennifer Garner, *Howard Community College*; Tracie Grimes, *Bakersfield College*; Sharon Hayes, *Baltimore County Community College–Essex*; Cynthia Herrera, *Lone Star College*; Jennifer Hewerdine, *The University of Tennessee–Knoxville*; Josh Hite, *Hagerstown Community College*; Elizabeth Hope, *Delgado Community College*; Daniel Hutchinson, *Arkansas State University Mid-South*; Lisa Joslyn, *Community College of Denver*; Julia Laffoon-Jackson, *Hopkinsville Community College*; Rebekah Maples, *California Polytechnic State University*; Jennifer Martin, *Salem Community College*; April Brook Mayo, *Ashville-Buncombe Technical Community College*; Jeffrey Miller, *St. Charles Community College*; Elizabeth Newman, *Texas Southmost College*; Karen O'Donnell, *Finger Lakes Community College*; Pam Ortega, *Amarillo College*; Denise Parker, *Baltimore County Community College–Catonsville*; Stephanie Paterson,

California State University–Stanislaus; Jim Richey, *Tyler Junior College*; Elvis Robinson, *Jackson State University*; Laurie Rowland, *Cleveland State Community School*; Heather Sinnes, *Boise State University*; Daniel Stanford, *Pittsburgh Community College*; Lisa Tittle, *Harford Community College*; Charlie Warnberg, *Brookhaven College*; Kyle Warner, *Craven Community College*; Jonathan Warnock, *Tri-County Technical College–Pendleton*; Audrey Wick, *Blinn College*; Tina Willhoite, *San Jacinto College–South*; and Jason Ziebart, *Central Carolina Community College*.

It has been a great pleasure to work with the team at Bedford/St. Martin's. Their knowledge of the fields of composition and basic writing, their experience in text-book development, their willingness to talk through complex issues, and the breadth of their expertise have meant that working on this project for five years has been an exhilarating experience for me. I, first, want to thank my senior development editor, and friend, Gillian Cook, who guided and inspired my work with her wit, her expertise, her insight, and her encouragement. Her brilliance and hard work are present on every page. Karita dos Santos, Senior Program Manager for the project, managed it so gracefully that I seldom realized I was being managed. Ryan Sullivan, Senior Digital Content Project Manager, coordinated all the moving parts masterfully, and was very ably assisted by Andrea Cava, Senior Manager of Publishing Services. Heartfelt thanks to Paola Garcia-Muniz, Assistant Editor, for her dedication to this project. Leasa Burton, Vice President, Editorial, Macmillan Learning Humanities; Stacey Purviance, Program Director for English; and Edwin Hill, former Vice President, Editorial, Macmillan Learning Humanities, provided the kind of advice, support, and encouragement any author would hope for.

Thanks also to Lauren Arrant, Marketing Manager, and Azelie Fortier, Market Development Manager, who brilliantly organized meetings, brochures, letters, and blogs to spread the word about *The Hub*. I am also grateful to the digital experts—Adam Whitehurst, Director of Media Editorial, Humanities; Doug Silver, Product Manager; Rand Thomas, Advanced Media Product Manager; and Angela Beckett, Media Editor—for making my dream of a digital publication into a reality. My thanks also to William Boardman, Senior Design Manager, for *The Hub*'s delightful cover design.

Finally, I want to express my loving gratitude to my wife, Donna, and my mother-in-law, Rosemarie, who have provided the kind of environment that allowed me to hole up in my office for the past three years to work on this book and who were always ready with thoughtful suggestions when I needed them. I also owe thanks to my daughters, Melia and Emily, who have kept me connected to a younger generation, and to my grandchildren, Casey and Nick, who have provided the same connections to an even younger generation.

How *The Hub* Supports WPA Outcomes for First-Year Composition

This chart aligns *The Hub* with the latest WPA Outcomes Statement, ratified in July 2014.

WPA Outcomes	Most Relevant Features of *The Hub*
Rhetorical Knowledge	
Learn and use key rhetorical concepts through analyzing and composing a variety of texts.	• **Topic 9: Preparing to Write** discusses key rhetorical concepts as they apply to writing. • In **Topic 20: Reading Strategies**, Unit 20.2 discusses key rhetorical concepts as they apply to reading. • In **Projects 1–7**, as part of previewing texts, students are asked to analyze the rhetorical situation for each.
Gain experience reading and composing in several genres to understand how genre conventions shape and are shaped by readers' and writers' practices and purposes.	• The readings in **Projects 1–7** represent a range of genres including essays; editorials; newspaper, magazine, and research articles; nonfiction books; arguments; web pages; videos; and historical writings. • **Topic 18: Writing Strategies** provides strategies for composing arguments and writing using description, narration, process, comparison/contrast, cause/effect, definition, and classification as their purpose for writing requires. • Essay assignments in **Projects 1–7** ask students to write in a wide variety of genres.
Develop facility in responding to a variety of situations and contexts calling for purposeful shifts in voice, tone, level of formality, design, medium, and/or structure.	Throughout **Projects 1–7**, students encounter, analyze, discuss, and write in response to a wide variety of genres, using a variety of formats ranging from reflective, to short response, to full-length essays or multimodal compositions. Assignments also call for writing editorials, proposals, brochures, op-eds, and more.
Understand and use a variety of technologies to address a range of audiences.	The range of texts and technologies students interact with in the print and digital versions of *The Hub* helps them understand the variety of technologies they can use to address their own audiences.

WPA Outcomes	Most Relevant Features of *The Hub*
Match the capacities of different environments (e.g., print and electronic) to varying rhetorical situations.	• **Topic 18: Writing Strategies** provides information on writing using a variety of patterns, which can be modified according to the writing task or environment. • In **Projects 1–7**, students analyze web and blog sites, watch videos, and use online sites to find information, allowing them to see how environment influences text and rhetorical devices.
Critical Thinking, Reading, and Composing	
Use composing and reading for inquiry, learning, critical thinking, and communicating in various rhetorical contexts.	The **seven inquiry-based reading/writing projects in Part 1**, each consisting of several thematic readings from a variety of genres and accompanied by group and individual activities, are designed to develop critical thinking and reading skills, challenge students to learn new concepts and ideas, model rhetorical options, and provide content for writing thoughtful essays.
Read a diverse range of texts, attending especially to relationships between assertion and evidence, to patterns of organization, to the interplay between verbal and nonverbal elements, and to how these features function for different audiences and situations.	• **Topic 19: Active Reading** discusses reading as a thinking process, optimizing reading and recall, using different reading techniques based on the text and purpose for reading it, and how to construct meaning from a text. • **Topic 20: Reading Strategies** explains what to do before, during, and after reading, covering activating schema, previewing, predicting, annotating, keeping a reading journal, decoding difficult language, reading as a believer and doubter, and using graphic organizers. • **Topic 21: Critical Reading** addresses how to evaluate the author and source of a text; distinguish between facts and opinions, assertions and evidence; make inferences; and recognize assumptions and biases.
Locate and evaluate (for credibility, sufficiency, accuracy, timeliness, bias, and so on) primary and secondary research materials, including journal articles and essays, books, scholarly and professionally established and maintained databases or archives, and informal electronic networks and internet sources.	• In **Topic 22: Research**, Units **22.1–22.3** address the research process, Unit **22.4** is a presentation on finding online sources, Unit **22.5** discusses how to locate books and articles in libraries and use databases, Unit **22.6** covers evaluating sources, Unit **22.10** describes how to conduct interviews, and Unit **22.11** addresses how to conduct surveys. • **Project 4: Truth, Lies, and Fake News** contains readings that discuss issues related to truth, lies, facts, opinions, the ways statistics can be misused, and how to fact-check. It is designed to provide students with the tools to make thoughtful, informed decisions about what they read, see, and hear.

WPA Outcomes	Most Relevant Features of *The Hub*
Use strategies—such as interpretation, synthesis, response, critique, and design/redesign—to compose texts that integrate the writer's ideas with those from appropriate sources.	• **Units 18.23–18.26** discuss how to accurately summarize text. • **Unit 22.8: Quoting and Paraphrasing** explains and shows how to accurately and ethically paraphrase and quote sources. • **Unit 22.14: Synthesis** explains and shows how to interpret, synthesize, and integrate sources with the writer's own ideas.
Processes	
Develop a writing project through multiple drafts.	• **Topic 8: The Writing Process** discusses the stages of the writing process and shows the recursive nature of good writing in the **Unit 8.2** narrated presentation. • In **Projects 1–7**, students participate in low-stakes writing they can use in the final assignments, write and revise definitions based on new information (e.g., in **Project 7: What Is Art?**), and complete full-length writing assignments.
Develop flexible strategies for reading, drafting, reviewing, collaborating, revising, rewriting, rereading, and editing.	**Part 2: Writing** covers all aspects of the writing process: process (**Topic 8**); rhetorical situation, audience and purpose, planning (**Topic 9**); invention strategies, topic and thesis development (**Topic 10**); developing support (**Topic 11**); organizing ideas (**Topic 12**); language denotation/connotation, concrete and figurative (**Topic 13**); thinking while writing (**Topic 14**); revision strategies (**Topic 15**); editing for grammar and sentence structure (**Topic 16**); titles, introductions, and conclusions (**Topic 17**); and writing strategies, including argumentation, modes, summary, proposal, and reflection (**Topic 18**).
Use composing processes and tools as a means to discover and reconsider ideas.	**Topic 14: Thinking While Writing** contains units that encourage students to think deeply and broadly about their topic, finding new ideas and deepening their understanding of their original ones.
Experience the collaborative and social aspects of writing processes.	*The Hub* has an active learning, collaborative, group-work focus, and students have numerous opportunities to write together.
Learn to give and to act on productive feedback to works in progress.	• **Unit 8.4: Peer Review** is a tutorial on how to give and receive feedback on works in progress. • In **Projects 1–7**, students often work in groups to write together and provide feedback on each other's work.

WPA Outcomes	Most Relevant Features of *The Hub*
Adapt composing processes for a variety of technologies and modalities.	• Students are exposed to a wide range of print modalities in **Projects 1–7**, and they also visit and evaluate websites and blog posts and watch videos and narrated PowerPoint presentations, learning how content is adapted for different purposes and modalities. • Culminating assignments for each of **Projects 1–7** include a "real world essay" (e.g., a proposal, op-ed piece, article, etc.), "academic essay" (suitable for an English or content course), and a multimodal composition, for which students can produce a document with graphics, a PowerPoint presentation, blog, website, etc.
Reflect on the development of composing practices and how those practices influence their work.	• Low-stakes writing assignments throughout **Projects 1–7** ask students to reflect on what they've read, how it's written, rhetorical purpose, etc. • A **reflection activity** at the end of each of **Projects 1–7** asks students to report on what they've learned and how it will influence them in the future.
Knowledge of Conventions	
Develop knowledge of linguistic structures, including grammar, punctuation, and spelling, through practice in composing and revising.	• **Topic 16: Editing** contains 49 units covering issues in grammar (e.g., fragments, comma splices, subject-verb agreement, pronoun reference issues), punctuation, and sentence development. • A **unique inductive approach to grammar** prompts students working in small groups to discover important grammar rules for themselves and express them in language they understand and remember. • **Units 13.7–13.9** discuss dictionary usage, diction, and the spelling of confusing words.
Understand why genre conventions for structure, paragraphing, tone, and mechanics vary.	Throughout **Projects 1–7** students are exploring readings from a variety of sources and genres on many levels, including author, purpose, audience, topic, and context, leading to discussion of differences in structure, tone, paragraphing, and mechanics.
Gain experience negotiating variations in genre conventions.	Students read a wide variety of texts in **Projects 1–7**, ranging from straightforward news articles to excerpts from research papers and Aristotle's "Nicomachean Ethics." Annotations and scaffolded instruction explain and illustrate variations in genre conventions.

WPA Outcomes	Most Relevant Features of *The Hub*
Learn common formats and/or design features for different kinds of texts.	Throughout **Projects 1–7**, students are reading, analyzing, and discussing text presented in a variety of formats, including PowerPoints, videos, and web and blog sites.
Explore the concepts of intellectual property (such as fair use and copyright) that motivate documentation conventions.	• **Unit 22.13: Avoiding Plagiarism** explains what plagiarism is and why and how to avoid it. • **Unit 22.8: Quoting and Paraphrasing** provides information on how to accurately and ethically quote and paraphrase sources. • **Topics 23 and 24** explain MLA and APA documentation conventions.
Practice applying citation conventions systematically in their own work.	• **Topic 23: MLA Documentation** explains how to provide in-text citations and create a works cited list and includes an annotated essay. • **Topic 24: APA Documentation** explains how to provide in-text citations and create a references list and includes annotated examples.

Knowledge of Conventions

Develop knowledge of linguistic structure, including grammar, punctuation, and spelling through practice in composing and revising.	• **Topic 16: Editing** contains 49 units covering issues in grammar (e.g., fragments, comma splices, subject-verb agreement, pronoun reference issues), punctuation, and sentence development. • A unique inductive approach to grammar prompts students working in small groups to discover important grammar rules for themselves and practice them in language they understand and remember. • **Units 13.7–13.9** discuss dictionary usage, diction, and the spelling of confusing words.
Understand why genre conventions for structure, paragraphing, tone, and mechanics vary.	Throughout **Projects 1–7** students are offering readings from a variety of sources and genres on many levels, including author, purpose, audience, topic and context, leading to discussion of differences in structure, tone, paragraphing, and mechanics.
Gain experience in negotiating variations in genre conventions.	Students read a wide variety of texts in **Projects 1–7** ranging from "straightforward" news article to excerpts from research papers and Aristotle's "Nicomachean Ethics." Annotations and scaffolded instruction explain and illustrate variations in genre conventions.

Contents

Note: This custom edition of *The Hub* for North Central Texas College omits Part 1 (chapters 1 through 7), which is not covered by your instructor.

Brief Contents   inside front cover
Preface for North Central Texas College   v
Preface for Instructors   xlvii
How *The Hub* Supports WPA Outcomes for First-Year Composition   lvi

Writing 1

Topic 8: The Writing Process 3

Introduction to the Writing Process 3

8.1 Activity How Do *You* Write an Essay? 4

8.2 Presentation The Writing Process 4

8.3 Tutorial How Effective Writers Go about Writing 4 | How Juanita Wrote Her Essay 6 | How Juanita's Process Relates to You 7

8.4 Tutorial Peer Review 8 | Guidelines for Peer Review 8 | Guidelines for Responding to Peer Review 10

8.5 Activity Practicing Peer Review 10

Topic 9: Preparing to Write 11

Introduction to Preparing to Write 11

9.1 Tutorial Reading an Assignment 12

9.2 Activity Analyzing an Assignment 12 | Assignment: The Significance of Grit 12

9.3 Tutorial The Rhetorical Situation 13 | Traditional Components of Rhetorical Analysis 13 | Additional Components of Rhetorical Analysis 14

9.4 Tutorial Thinking about Audience 14 | Identify Your Audience 15 | Analyze Your Audience 15

KEY | Units that work together are placed in groups.   ▢ Boxed units provide reinforcement for other items in each group.

See page lxxv for more information on the unit types in this book.

9.5 Activity Practice Thinking about Audience 16

9.6 Tutorial Thinking about Purpose 17

9.7 Activity Practice Thinking about Purpose 18

9.8 Tutorial Making a Plan 19

Topic 10: Finding a Focus 21

Introduction to Finding a Focus 21

10.1 Tutorial Invention Strategies 22 | Brainstorming 22 | Freewriting 24 | Browsing and Reading 25 | Mapping 26 | Outlining 28

10.2 Presentation Brainstorming 30

10.3 Tutorial How to Use Invention Strategies to Select a Topic 30

10.4 Activity Using Brainstorming to Narrow a Topic 31

10.5 Tutorial Thesis Statements 32 | Avoid These Common Mistakes 34 | A Thesis with More Than One Point 35

10.6 Tutorial Using Invention Strategies to Arrive at a Thesis 35

10.7 Activity Where Should the Thesis Be Located? 36 | Know Your Instructor's Preferences 40

Topic 11: Developing Ideas 41

Introduction to Developing Ideas 41

11.1 Tutorial Options for What to Include in an Essay 42 | Ways to Make Essays More Interesting 42

11.2 Activity Evidence and Assertions 43

11.3 Tutorial Development, Support, or Evidence 48 | Connecting Evidence to Your Topic Sentences and Thesis 48 | Types of Support 49

11.4 Activity Developing Strong Support for an Argument 52

11.5 Activity Recognizing Development Strategies in "Violence Vanquished," Steven Pinker 53

11.6 Tutorial Three Types of Appeal: Logos, Ethos, and Pathos 58

11.7 Tutorial Avoiding Logical Fallacies 59 | Common Rhetorical Fallacies 59

Topic 12: Organizing Ideas 62

Introduction to Organizing Ideas 63

12.1 Tutorial Unity 63 | Unity Problems Caused by Unrelated Material 63 | Unity Problems Caused by a Change of Focus 65

12.2 Activity Evaluating Thesis and Unity 67

12.3 Writing One Unusual Thing 68

12.4 Activity Thesis and Unity in One Unusual Thing 69

12.5 Presentation Chunking and Ordering 69

12.6 Activity Practice Chunking 69

12.7 Activity Practice Ordering Ideas 70

12.8 Tutorial Coherence 70 | Logical Organization 71 | Repetition of Key Words and Pronouns 72 | Use of Transitional Expressions 73

12.9 Activity Editing for Coherence 74

Topic 13: Using Language Powerfully 77

Introduction to Using Language Powerfully 78

13.1 Tutorial Connotation and Denotation 78 | Activity: Explaining Differences in Meaning 79

13.2 Activity Seeing How Concrete Language Works 79

13.3 Tutorial Using Concrete Language to Bring Writing to Life 80

13.4 Activity Adding Concrete Language 81

13.5 Activity Words, Fancy and Plain 82

13.6 Tutorial Figurative Language 84 | Similes 85 | Metaphors 85 | Personification 86 | When to Use Figurative Language 86

13.7 Tutorial Using a Dictionary to Understand Words 87

13.8 Activity Using a Dictionary to Select the Right Word 88

13.9 Activity Determining the Meanings of Confusing Words 89

Topic 14: Thinking While Writing 92

Introduction to Thinking While Writing 93

14.1 Writing One Interesting Thing about You 93

14.2 Activity Class Discussion on Interesting Writing 93

14.3 Tutorial Avoid Proving the Obvious 94

14.4 Tutorial Use Thinking to Find an Interesting Thesis 94 | Example 1: Thinking about Helping Children "Get Ahead" 94 | Example 2: Thinking about Drunk Driving 95

14.5 Writing Who Should Get Reserved Parking? 96

14.6 Activity Thinking about Reserved Parking 96

14.7 Presentation Thinking about Alex's Paper 97

14.8 Presentation Thinking Deeply 98

14.9 Presentation Thinking Broadly 98

14.10 Writing Revising Your Reserved Parking Paper 98

Topic 15: Revising 99

Introduction to Revising 100

15.1 Tutorial Revision Basics 100

15.2 Tutorial Revising for Assignment, Audience, and Purpose 101

15.3 Tutorial Backward Outlining 101

15.4 Tutorial Revising for Thesis and Unity 105 | Using a Backward Outline to Check on Thesis and Unity 106

15.5 Tutorial Revising for Organization 107

15.6 Tutorial Revising for Support 109

15.7 Tutorial Revising for Coherence 114

15.8 Activity Backward Outlining Applied 118

15.9 Tutorial Reviewing Options for What to Include in an Essay 118 | Ways to Make Essays More Interesting 119

15.10 Tutorial A Revision Checklist 120

Topic 16: Editing 121

Thinking about Grammar 124

16.1 Activity Good and Bad English 124

16.2 Presentation The Grammar in Your Head 124

Punctuating to Avoid Fragments, Run-Ons, and Comma Splices 124

16.3 Tutorial What Is a Sentence? 125 | Using a Test Frame 125 | Activity: Is This a Sentence? 126

16.4 Activity Fragments 126

16.5 Activity Correcting Fragments 127

16.6 Activity What Is an Independent Clause? 128

16.7 Activity Run-Ons and Comma Splices 128

16.8 Activity Correcting Run-Ons and Comma Splices 130

16.9 Activity Correcting Fragments, Run-Ons, and Comma Splices 132

16.10 Activity Punctuating Independent Clauses 1 133

16.11 Activity Punctuating Independent Clauses 2 133

16.12 Activity Punctuating Independent Clauses 3 134

16.13 Activity Punctuating Independent Clauses 4 135

16.14 Activity Punctuating Introductory Elements 1 137

16.15 Activity Punctuating Introductory Elements 2 138

16.16 Activity Editing an Essay for Punctuation 1 139

16.17 Activity Editing an Essay for Punctuation 2 141

Using Apostrophes to Show Possession and to Indicate Contractions 144

16.18 Tutorial Apostrophes 1 (Possessives) 144

16.19 Activity Apostrophes 2 (Possessives) 145

16.20 Activity Apostrophes 3 (Possessives) 146

16.21 Activity Apostrophes 4 (Possessives) 147

16.22 Activity Apostrophes 5 (Possessives) 148

16.23 Tutorial Apostrophes 6 (Contractions) 149 | Activity: Practice with Contractions 149

16.24 Activity Contractions versus Possessive Pronouns 149

Contents **lxv**

16.25 Activity Editing an Essay for Apostrophes 1 151

16.26 Activity Editing an Essay for Apostrophes 2 153

Ensuring Subject-Verb Agreement 155

16.27 Activity Subject-Verb Agreement 1 155

16.28 Activity Subject-Verb Agreement 2 156

16.29 Activity Subject-Verb Agreement 3 157

16.30 Activity Subject-Verb Agreement 4 (Indefinite Pronouns 1) 158 | Indefinite Pronouns 1 159

16.31 Activity Subject-Verb Agreement 5 (Indefinite Pronouns 2 and 3) 159 | Indefinite Pronouns 2 159 | Indefinite Pronouns 3 160

16.32 Activity Editing an Essay for Subject-Verb Agreement 1 161

16.33 Activity Editing an Essay for Subject-Verb Agreement 2 163

Avoiding Pronoun Reference and Agreement Errors 165

16.34 Activity Pronouns and Antecedents 165 | Identifying Antecedents 166

16.35 Activity Vague Pronoun Reference 1 166

16.36 Activity Vague Pronoun Reference 2 167

16.37 Activity Vague Pronoun Reference 3 167

16.38 Tutorial Pronoun Agreement 168 | A Note about "Singular" *They* 169 | Gender-Neutral Pronouns 170 | Agreement and Indefinite Pronouns 171

16.39 Activity Correcting Pronoun Errors 172

16.40 Activity Editing an Essay for Pronoun Errors 1 172

16.41 Activity Editing an Essay for Pronoun Errors 2 174

Combining Sentences in Interesting Ways 176

16.42 Tutorial Sentence Combining 176

16.43 Activity Sentence Combining 1 177

16.44 Activity Sentence Combining 2 178

16.45 Activity Sentence Combining 3 179

16.46 Activity Sentence Combining 4 180

16.47 Activity Sentence Combining 5 182

Language and Computers 183

16.48 Activity Computers and Editing 1 183 | Activity: Testing Grammar Checkers 184

16.49 Tutorial Computers and Editing 2 184

Topic 17: Titles, Introductions, and Conclusions 186

Introduction to Titles, Introductions, and Conclusions 187

17.1 Tutorial Titles 187 | Options for Titles 187

17.2 Activity Writing Titles 189

17.3 Tutorial Introductory Paragraphs 189 | Elements of a Good Introduction 190 | Types of Introductory Paragraphs 190

17.4 Activity Writing Introductory Paragraphs 192

17.5 Tutorial Closing Paragraphs 193 | Strategies for Effective Conclusions 193 | Examples of Effective Conclusions 193 | Concluding Strategies to Avoid 195

17.6 Activity Writing Conclusions 195

Topic 18: Writing Strategies 196

Introduction to Writing Strategies 198

Argumentation 198

18.1 Tutorial What Is an Argument? 199

18.2 Activity What Are the Features of Effective Arguments? 199

18.3 Tutorial The Features of Effective Arguments 199

18.4 Tutorial Thinking about Audience and Purpose 200

18.5 Tutorial How to Answer Counterarguments 200 | Identifying and Refuting Counterarguments 201

18.6 Writing Answering Counterarguments 202

18.7 Tutorial Three Types of Appeal: *Logos, Ethos,* and *Pathos* 202 | "Gifted and Talented Programs: More Harm Than Good?" *Kevin Turner* 203 | Rogerian Argument: A Different Way of Arguing 207

Description and Observation 208

18.8 Tutorial Strategies for Writing Descriptions and Observations 208 | Writing Descriptions 208 | Writing Observations 209

18.9 Writing Describing/Observing a Person, Place, Thing, or Event 211

Narration 212

18.10 Tutorial Strategies for Writing Narratives 212 | Features of Effective Narrative Writing 213

18.11 Writing Narrating an Event 215

Process 216

18.12 Tutorial Strategies for Process Writing 216 | How to Do Something 216 | How Something Works 217

18.13 Writing Explaining a Process or How Something Works 218

Comparison and Contrast 219

18.14 Tutorial Strategies for Writing Comparison and/or Contrast 219 | Point-by-Point Method 219 | Subject-by-Subject Method 221

18.15 Writing Comparing and/or Contrasting Two Items 223

Cause and Effect 223

18.16 Tutorial Strategies for Writing Cause and Effect 223

18.17 Writing Explaining the Causes or Effects of an Event or Action 226

Definition 226

18.18 Tutorial Strategies for Writing Definitions 226 | Simple Definitions 226 | Extended Definitions 228 | Guidelines for Writing a Definition 228

18.19 Activity Revising Definitions 229

18.20 Writing Providing Simple or Extended Definitions 230

Classification 230

18.21 Tutorial Strategies for Writing Classification 230 | Guidelines for Effective Classification 231

18.22 Writing Breaking a Topic into Categories 232

Summary 232

18.23 Writing What Makes a Good Summary? 233

18.24 Activity Analyzing Summaries 233

18.25 Tutorial Strategies for Writing a Summary 233 | Writing a Good Summary 234

18.26 Writing Summarizing Baldwin 235 | "On Being 'White' . . . and Other Lies," *James Baldwin* 235

Proposal 238

18.27 Tutorial Strategies for Writing a Proposal 238 | How to Write a Successful Proposal 238

18.28 Writing Making a Proposal to Solve a Problem 241

Reflection 241

18.29 Tutorial Strategies for Writing a Reflection 241

18.30 Writing Reflecting on an Important Experience 242

Weaving Strategies into a Strong Essay 243

18.31 Tutorial Using Multiple Writing Strategies in an Essay 243

18.32 Activity Identifying Multiple Writing Strategies in an Essay 243 | "Words and Worlds," *Steven Pinker* 244

PART 3 Reading 247

Topic 19: Active Reading 248

Introduction to Active Reading 248

19.1 Presentation Reading Is Thinking 249

19.2 Presentation The Reading Process 249

19.3 Tutorial Optimizing Your Reading 249

19.4 Tutorial Remembering What You've Read 250

19.5 Activity Purposes for *Your* Reading 251

19.6 Tutorial Purposes for Reading 251

19.7 Tutorial Constructing Meaning 252

19.8 Activity Constructing Mike Rose's Meaning in "'Grit' Revisited" 253 | "'Grit' Revisited: Reflections on Our Public Talk about Education," *Mike Rose* 254

Topic 20: Reading Strategies 259

Introduction to Reading Strategies 260

20.1 Tutorial Activating Schema 260 | Activity: Activating Your Schema for Dishonest Numbers 261

20.2 Tutorial Previewing a Text 261 | Step 1: Preview the Text 261 | Step 2: Analyze the Rhetorical Situation 262 | Step 3: Predict What the Text Is About 263 | Step 4: Think about Yourself in Relation to the Text 263

20.3 Activity Previewing *The Stuff of Thought, Steven Pinker* 264

20.4 Activity Previewing a Website 268

20.5 Activity Previewing Other Students' Essays 269

20.6 Tutorial Annotation Explained 269 | Some Reasons to Annotate 270 | Activity: Explaining Annotations 270

20.7 Activity Annotating a Text 273

20.8 Tutorial Keeping a Reading Journal 274 | "Words and Worlds," *Steven Pinker* 274

20.9 Tutorial Dealing with Difficult Language 280 | Use Context Clues 280 | Use Word Parts 281 | Reread the Passage 282 | Keep Reading 282 | Decide the Word Is Not Important 282 | Use a Dictionary 282

20.10 Activity Decoding Difficult Language 283

20.11 Tutorial Believing and Doubting 283

20.12 Activity Reading as a Believer and Doubter 284

20.13 Tutorial Creating Timelines and Family Trees 284 | Timelines 285 | Family Trees 285

Topic 21: Critical Reading 287

Introduction to Critical Reading 288

21.1 Tutorial How to Evaluate the Author and Source of a Text 288 | Evaluating the Author 288 | Evaluating the Source 288

21.2 Activity Evaluating the Author and Source of a Text 289

21.3 Tutorial Distinguishing among Facts, Statements Most Experts Agree On, and Opinions 290 | What Are Facts? 290 | How Do We Decide Whether the Experts Agree? 291 | How Should Readers Respond to Conclusions, Claims, and Opinions? 291

21.4 Activity Recognizing Facts, Statements Most Experts Agree On, and Opinions 292

21.5 Activity Evaluating Evidence 293 | Report 1 293 | Report 2 293 | Report 3 294

21.6 Tutorial How to Make Inferences 295 | Guidelines for Making Inferences 296 | Making an Inference 296

21.7 Activity Making Inferences 297 | Passage 1: Excerpt from *Better: A Surgeon's Notes on Performance* 297 | Passage 2: Excerpt from *Outliers: The Story of Success* 297

21.8 Tutorial Recognizing Assumptions and Biases 298 | Assumptions 299 | Biases 300

21.9 Activity Recognizing Assumptions and Biases in Three Passages 300

PART 4

Research and Documentation 303

Topic 22: Research 305

Introduction to Research 306

22.1 Writing Thinking about the Research Process 306

22.2 Tutorial The Research Process 306 | Checklist for Steps in the Research Process 306

22.3 Activity Choosing Relevant Steps in the Research Process 308 | Checklist for Steps in the Research Process 308 | Assignment 1: Evolution of Thinking on Delayed Gratification 310 | Assignment 2: Freedom of Speech 310 | Assignment 3: Taking a Position on the Minimum Wage 311

22.4 Presentation Finding Sources Online 312

22.5 Tutorial Finding Sources in the Library 312 | Locating Books 313 | Locating Articles in Journals and Magazines 314 | Using Library Databases 316

22.6 Activity Evaluating Sources 317 | Assignment 1: Exploring Mistakes Made during the Vietnam War 317 | Assignment 2: Evaluating the Affordable Care Act 319

22.7 Tutorial Notetaking 319 | Strategies for Effective Notetaking 320

22.8 Tutorial Quoting and Paraphrasing 321 | Quotations 322 | Paraphrases 326

22.9 Activity Quoting and Paraphrasing Shaughnessy 327 | Practice Quoting 328 | Practice Paraphrasing 328

22.10 Tutorial Conducting Interviews 328 | Checklist for Steps for Conducting Interviews 329

22.11 Tutorial Conducting Surveys 330 | Developing Survey Questions 330 | Conducting a Survey 332

22.12 Writing Questions about Plagiarism 332

22.13 Tutorial Avoiding Plagiarism 332 | Use Quotation Marks and Document Your Sources 333

22.14 Tutorial Synthesis 334 | How to Synthesize Sources 334 | Examples of Synthesis 335

Topic 23: MLA Documentation 336

Introduction to MLA Style 336

23.1 Tutorial Documenting Sources in MLA Style 337 | Author and Title 337 | Containers 337

23.2 Tutorial MLA In-Text Citations 338 | Guidelines for In-Text Citations 339

23.3 Tutorial MLA Works Cited List 344 | General Guidelines for the Works Cited List 345 | General Guidelines for Listing Authors 347 | Articles and Other Short Works 349 | Books and Other Long Works 350 | Online Sources 353 | Visual, Audio, Multimedia, and Live Sources 354 | Other Sources 357

23.4 Tutorial MLA-Style Formatting 359 | Formatting an MLA Project 359 | Formatting an MLA Works Cited List 360 | Sample Pages from Student Writing in MLA Style 360

Topic 24: APA Documentation 373

Introduction to APA Style 373

24.1 Tutorial Documenting Sources in APA Style 374

24.2 Tutorial APA In-Text Citations 374 | Basic Format for a Quotation 375 | Basic Format for a Summary or a Paraphrase 375 | Guidelines for In-Text Citations 376

24.3 Tutorial APA Reference List 379 | General Guidelines for Listing Authors (Print and Online) 380 | Articles in Periodicals (Print) 383 | Books (Print) 386 | Online Sources 390 | Other Sources (including Online Versions) 398

24.4 Tutorial APA-Style Formatting 401 | APA Guidelines for Student Papers 402 | Preparing the List of References 403 | Sample Pages from Student Writing in APA Style 404

PART 5 Balancing School, Work, and Life 417

Topic 25: Getting Acquainted 418

Introduction to Getting Acquainted 418

25.1 Activity Interesting Interviews 419

25.2 Activity Meet and Greet Bingo 419

25.3 **Activity** Getting to Know You 420

25.4 **Activity** Two Truths and a Lie 420

Topic 26: Life Issues 421

Introduction to Life Issues 421

26.1 **Writing** Money Matters 422 | Researching a Financial Topic 422 | Quoting Sources 422 | Activity: Writing about Money 423

26.2 **Activity** Renting 424

26.3 **Activity** Health Care 424

26.4 **Activity** Child Care 424

26.5 **Activity** Time Management: Activity Log 424 | Advice for the Specific Columns 425 | Sample Activity Log 425

26.6 **Activity** Time Management: Analyzing Activity Logs 427

26.7 **Activity** Time Management: Strategies 427

26.8 **Activity** Time Management: Calendars 427 | Creating a Calendar 428

26.9 **Activity** Plan B 430 | Activity: Listing Strategies for Coping with Stress 430

Topic 27: Staying the Course 431

Introduction to Staying the Course 431

27.1 **Writing** Why Are You in This Class? 432

27.2 **Activity** Thinking about Why Are You in This Class? 432

27.3 **Activity** What Worries You? 433

27.4 **Writing** Who Is "College Material"? 433

27.5 **Writing** Responding to Setbacks 434

27.6 **Writing** Goal Setting and Planning 434 | Activity: Twelve-Month Goals 434

Topic 28: College Knowledge 435

Introduction to College Knowledge 435

28.1 Writing College Terminology 436

28.2 Writing Terms for Writing Assignments 436 | Activity: Defining Terms 436

28.3 Activity Asking for Help 437

28.4 Activity Locating Resources 437

28.5 Tutorial What Is Group Work, and Why Are We Doing It? 439 | Tips for Successful Group Participation 439 | Tips for Group Success 440

Definitions of Terms Used in *The Hub*	
Academic Essay	At the end of each reading/writing project, there are three writing assignments. One of the three is a traditional academic essay.
Activity	A unit designed for students to do some thinking, usually in a group, but most of these can be assigned as individual work if preferred.
Multimodal Composition	At the end of each reading/writing project, there are three writing assignments, one of which asks students to produce a multimodal composition.
Part	One of the five major divisions of *The Hub*—Part 1: Reading/Writing Projects, Part 2: Writing, Part 3: Reading, Part 4: Research and Documentation, and Part 5: Balancing School, Work, and Life. Each part contains a series of Topics on major subjects relevant to the part.
Presentation	A five-minute video narrated by the author.
Project	One of the seven reading/writing projects that constitute Part 1.
Reading	A reading can be an essay, newspaper article, journal article, blog post, excerpt from a nonfiction or fiction text, chapter from a book, legal statute, set of college policies, and more. These readings are the primary material in the reading/writing projects in Part 1. Students are expected to read them in preparation for class.
Real World Essay	At the end of each reading/writing project, there are three writing assignments. The "Real World Essay" asks students to write an essay that addresses an audience outside their classroom (e.g., next year's students, the community, visitors to an art museum, a career counselor, a college committee, or readers of a newspaper).
Topic	One of the major sections of each of Parts 2–5 (equivalent to a chapter). Each Topic contains a series of units that address relevant subjects.
Tutorial	Instructional text that discusses issues and strategies for writing, reading, and research, designed to be read in preparation for class.
Unit	Each topic consists of a series of units that provide instruction (tutorials and presentations), practice (activities), and reading and writing opportunities (readings, writing prompts, and essay assignments).
Video	A short video, almost always less than five minutes, and usually available on YouTube.
Writing	The word *Writing* is used in the titles of units in the Contents to indicate the many short writing assignments. These usually call for a page or so of writing, but sometimes even less. The idea, especially in Part 1, is that some of this writing may later be incorporated into the major writing projects, such as those at the end of each reading/writing project.

Definitions of Terms Used in The Hub

Academic Essay	At the end of each reading/writing project, there are three writing assignments. One of the three is a traditional academic essay.
Activity	A unit designed for students to do some thinking, usually in a group, but most of these can be assigned as individual work if preferred.
Multimodal Composition	At the end of each reading/writing project, there are three writing assignments, one of which asks students to produce a multimodal composition.
Part	One of the five major divisions of The Hub—Part 1: Reading/Writing Projects, Part 2: Writing, Part 3: Reading, Part 4: Research and Documentation, and Part 5: Balancing School, Work, and Life. Each part contains a series of Topics on major subjects relevant to the part.
Presentation	A five-minute video narrated by the author.
Project	One of the seven reading/writing projects that constitute Part 1.
Reading	A reading can be an essay, newspaper article, journal article, blog post, excerpt from a nonfiction or fiction text, chapter from a book, legal statute, set of college policies, and more. These readings are the primary material in the reading/writing projects in Part 1. Students are expected to read them in preparation for class.
Real World Essay	At the end of each reading/writing project, there are three writing assignments. The "Real World Essay" asks students to write an essay that addresses an audience outside their classroom (e.g., next year's students, the community, visitors to an art museum, a career counselor, a college committee, or readers of a newspaper).
Topic	One of the major sections of each of Parts 2–5 (equivalent to a chapter). Each Topic contains a series of units that address relevant subjects.
Tutorial	Instructional text that discusses issues and strategies for writing, reading, and research, designed to be read in preparation for class.
Unit	Each topic consists of a series of units that provide instruction (tutorials and presentations), practice (activities), and reading and writing opportunities (readings, writing prompts, and essay assignments).
Video	A short video, almost always less than five minutes, and usually available on YouTube.
Writing	The word Writing is used in the title of units in the Contents to indicate the many short writing assignments. These usually call for a page or so of writing, but sometimes even less. The idea, especially in Part 1, is that some of this writing may later be incorporated into the major writing projects, such as those at the end of each reading/writing project.

The Hub

A PLACE FOR READING AND WRITING

for North Central Texas College

The Hub

A PLACE FOR READING
AND WRITING

for North Central Texas College

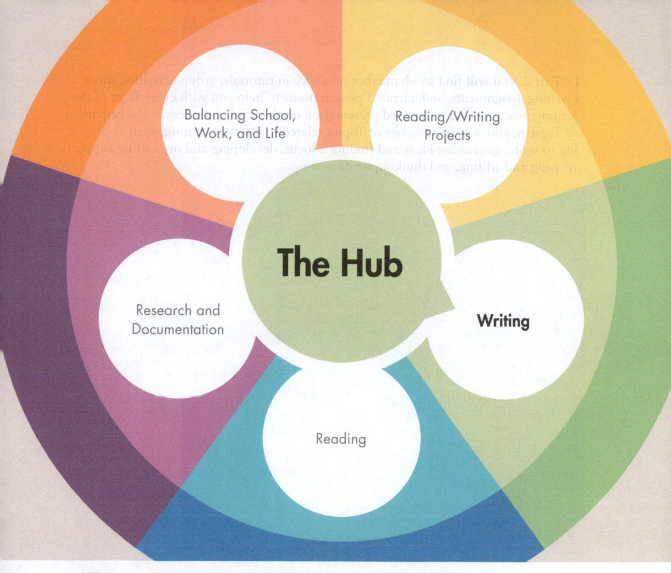

2 Writing

Topic 8 The Writing Process 3
Topic 9 Preparing to Write 11
Topic 10 Finding a Focus 21
Topic 11 Developing Ideas 41
Topic 12 Organizing Ideas 62
Topic 13 Using Language Powerfully 77
Topic 14 Thinking While Writing 92
Topic 15 Revising 99
Topic 16 Editing 121
Topic 17 Titles, Introductions, and Conclusions 186
Topic 18 Writing Strategies 196

I n Part 2, you will find an abundance of advice in tutorials, group activities, short writing assignments, and narrated presentations to help you with every facet of the writing process. After a narrated presentation on the writing process at the beginning of Topic 8, you will find a series of Topics related to effective writing, such as preparing to write, generating ideas and finding a focus, developing and organizing support, revising and editing, and thinking while writing.

TOPIC 8
The Writing Process

This Topic does not discuss what effective writing is; instead, it explores what you need to do to produce effective writing by examining the process that effective writers follow.

Navigating Topic 8

The tutorials and presentation listed below provide information about the writing process. You can work through the entire Topic on your own, learning about all the strategies and practicing them; work on items you've been assigned by your instructor; or choose just the ones you find helpful.

Introduction to the Writing Process   3

8.1	Activity	How Do *You* Write an Essay? 4
8.2	Presentation	The Writing Process 4
8.3	Tutorial	How Effective Writers Go about Writing 4
8.4	Tutorial	Peer Review 8
8.5	Activity	Practicing Peer Review 10

Introduction to the Writing Process

This Topic focuses on the writing process and begins with an activity asking about your current writing strategies. It's followed by a presentation that discusses the different elements of an effective writing process—prewriting strategies, finding a focus, developing and organizing ideas, drafting, revising and editing—and, very importantly, emphasizes how good writers move back and forth among these different steps in the process. Next, you will follow a student writer as she thinks through how to focus a topic and write for a specific assignment. Finally, you will learn about and practice peer review.

8.1 Activity

How Do *You* Write an Essay?

For this activity, you're going to do a short piece of informal writing. Your instructor will let you know whether you will write this in class or at home and when it should be turned in.

For this assignment, you will need to think back to a time when you had to write an essay, perhaps in high school, in another course, or even earlier in this course. Write a numbered list of the steps that you took to write the paper.

If it's been a while since you wrote an essay in a class and you cannot remember a specific essay you had to write, you can use the following assignment and make a list of the steps you would take today to write this essay.

> **Essay Assignment**
>
> Write a letter to the editor of the *New York Times* in which you discuss an event or an issue reported in the paper this week. A selection of letters written to the editor are published each day. They are seldom more than 250 words long. Your goal is to get your letter published in the *New York Times*.

8.2 Presentation

The Writing Process

To watch this presentation on the writing process and the steps involved in reading an assignment, narrowing a topic, deciding on a thesis, generating ideas, drafting, revising, and editing an essay, go to *Achieve for The Hub*, Topic 8, and open Unit 8.2.

8.3 Tutorial

How Effective Writers Go about Writing

Good writing takes time and effort. Developing a process that you can follow and change as needed based on a specific assignment will improve your writing. The chart below lists six major activities involved in the writing process.

Preparing to Write	Finding a Focus	Developing Ideas	Organizing Ideas	Writing	Editing

Thoughtful writers do not simply move through the steps listed in the chart, performing each activity once and then moving on to the next in the linear fashion shown in the following diagram.

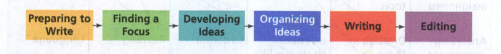

Instead, as illustrated in the diagram below, they weave back and forth among these activities as they find new information, generate new ideas, revise their thesis, reorganize their ideas, add support, revise their writing, and edit their final draft. Their process is messy and involves lots of circling back to improve parts of the paper they worked on earlier—messy, yes, but very productive.

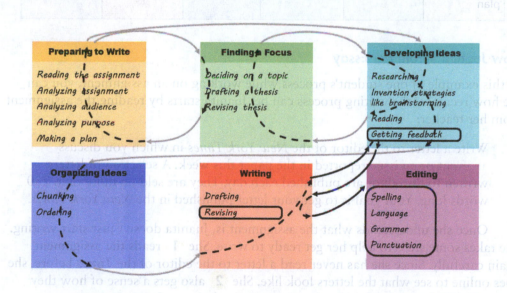

The diagram that follows represents the way one writer, named Juanita, carried out the recursive process of writing discussed above and in more detail on page 6.

Preparing to Write	Finding a Focus	Developing Ideas	Organizing Ideas	Writing	Editing
1 Reading the assignment	**6** Deciding on a topic	**2** **8** Researching	Chunking	**9** **12** Drafting	**14** Style
Analyzing assignment	Drafting a thesis **7**	**5** **11** Invention strategies like brainstorming	Ordering	**13** Revising	Language
4 Analyzing audience	Revising **10** thesis	Reading			Grammar
3 Analyzing purpose		Getting feedback			Punctuation
Making a plan					

How Juanita Wrote Her Essay

In this example of one student's process while working on an assignment, you can see how recursive the writing process can be. Juanita starts by reading the assignment from her teacher:

> Write a letter to the editor of the *New York Times* in which you discuss an event or an issue reported in the paper this week. A selection of letters written to the editor are published each day. They are seldom more than 250 words long. Your goal is to get your letter published in the *New York Times*.

Once she understands what the assignment is, Juanita doesn't just start writing. She takes some steps to help her get ready to write. She **1** **reads the assignment** again carefully. Since she has never read a letter to the editor of the *Times* before, she goes online to see what the letters look like. She **2** also gets a sense of how they "sound" and the kinds of topics they are written about.

She returns to the assignment and sees that her essay should be fewer than 250 words and that her **3** purpose is to get it published in the *Times*. She thinks, at first, that her **4** audience is people who read the *Times*, and it is; but there is also another audience: the editors at the paper who decide which letters to publish. From the letters she reads in the library, she decides the editors at the *Times* seem to prefer letters that take a strong stand and back up their positions with thoughtful arguments.

Looking in the *New York Times* online, Juanita notices that just one day earlier there had been a shooting at a Burger King. An angry employee had returned to work with a pistol and shot the manager, two workers, and a customer. The manager died, and the other victims were in serious condition in the hospital. The shooter, who had been diagnosed as schizophrenic, was shot and killed by police as he fled the scene.

Juanita thinks maybe she could write a letter about the need for greater gun control laws, and she starts **5** **brainstorming**, making a list of ideas for her letter. After a few minutes, she discovers that her ideas about gun control are not very original; she is just repeating what she has heard lots of other people say. Then she remembers the struggles of her older half-brother Jake, who suffers from a bipolar disorder that often leads him to violent behavior. Jake has struggled for years to get help with his condition, but he has been continually sent back out onto the streets because he has no health insurance. Juanita **decides to** **6** **write** about the lack of treatment for people with mental illnesses in our society. Thinking about the shooting at Burger King, Juanita decides that, at least for now, her thesis—**the** **7** **point** of her letter—will be that neglecting to treat people with mental health issues in this country endangers us all.

Juanita **next** **8** **goes online** and finds a website that provides statistics on how many people arrested for violent crimes are suffering from mental illness. She **returns to her** **9** **draft** and starts writing, combining her brother's story with the statistics she has found.

At this point, Juanita pauses to read over what she has written and comes to a disappointing conclusion. There is no way she can say all she has to say in 250 words or less, so she decides **to** **10** **narrow** down her thesis to focus only on the treatment her brother received when he was in high school, where all his troubles began.

At this point, Juanita remembers a conversation with her school's guidance counselor, who had tried to help her brother but was overwhelmed by the number of troubled students she needed to help as she worked only two days per week. Juanita **decides to** **11** **add this information** to her argument.

She **returns** **12** **to her draft** and adds a few sentences about the overworked guidance counselor. Next, **she** **13** **reads the paper** over looking for places that might need revising—changing the order of ideas, providing more support for her assertions and adding coherence to her essay. Finally, she pours herself a fresh cup of coffee and **14** **reads the entire paper** several times looking for problems with spelling, grammar, punctuation, wording, and style.

How Juanita's Process Relates to You

Although every writer's process is different, and even the same writer's process is different for different writing tasks, the most effective writers carry out all the stages listed above and keep circling back to do them over and over. This kind of recursive process may take more time than you're used to devoting to an essay, but it produces consistently better results. In addition, following this kind of process will significantly improve the quality of the writing you submit for assignments.

8.4 Tutorial

Peer Review

After finishing a draft of a piece of writing, many writers like to ask a friend, a classmate, a coworker, or someone else to look their writing over and give them some feedback. Because this practice—asking someone else to review writing—is so common in the world outside college, many instructors in college writing courses ask their students to review each other's drafts, a process known as *peer review*. A *peer* is someone who has the same standing as you, someone like one of your classmates.

There are two ways you might participate in peer review this semester. Your instructor may organize a peer review session either in class or online. Or you may decide, on your own, to ask a classmate or a friend to look over a draft of your writing. In this tutorial, you will learn how to ask for and receive such feedback and get some ideas about how to give others feedback on their drafts. These ideas should be useful whether you are informally asking a friend for feedback or you are more formally asking for feedback in class or online.

Guidelines for Peer Review

Here are some suggestions for how to respond when you are asked to review someone else's writing.

1. **Make sure you understand the assignment for the piece of writing.** Be sure to check whether the writer is actually doing the kind of writing the assignment asks for.

2. **Determine where the writer is in the process of writing this paper.** If you are reviewing a very early rough draft, you will want to concentrate on the big issues. Is it clear what the point, the thesis, of the paper is? Does the paper include convincing evidence to support that thesis? On the other hand, if the writer is almost finished with a paper that has been revised several times, it probably makes more sense to focus on the little stuff: places where the writing is unclear, errors with grammar and punctuation, and spelling errors.

3. **Keep in mind that receiving criticism is not exactly fun.** The writer of the paper wants to hear what can be improved but is probably also dreading hearing your feedback. One way to make your comments easier for the writer to hear is to make sure you praise what you really like about the paper. Find a place where the writer has made a good point or expressed an idea in particularly powerful language. Be sure you are sincere in this praise; most writers can see right through empty compliments.

4. **Use a guide (rubric) if one has been assigned.** If you are reviewing a piece of writing because your instructor has required the class to do so, you may have received a list of topics or questions to guide your review. Be sure you follow this guide.

5. **If you are not given a guide (rubric) for your review, you might want to use the following suggestions.**

   a. *Comment on the focus of the writing.* Is the main argument—the thesis of the writing—clear? Does that thesis remain the focus of the whole paper or does the writer lose track and wander into other topics in some places? Is the main idea of the paper the same at the end of the paper as it was at the beginning? If there are problems with the thesis and unity, point out exactly where the problems occur and, if possible, suggest how they might be eliminated.

   b. *Comment on how well the writer provided convincing evidence to support the thesis.* Compliment the writer on evidence that really "works," but also point out where the writer has made assertions without convincing support or where evidence seems to be presented that doesn't really belong because it does not support the argument.

   c. *Comment on how well the writer has responded to possible opposing arguments.* Does the essay simply ignore obvious arguments that those who disagree with its thesis would raise? When the writer acknowledges arguments that opponents would make, does he or she provide effective counterarguments? Or, when it seems necessary, does the writer concede the point and then explain why the point is of minimal importance?

   d. *Comment on how easy it was to follow the paper's argument.* Are there places that confused you? Are there places where the paper seemed to jump from one point to the next and it was difficult to see the connection between the points? If possible, suggest changes to the organization that would make the argument easier to follow.

6. **Try to make your comments as specific as possible.** Don't just write, "You need more evidence to support your assertions." Instead, point out a specific assertion that needs more evidence and, if possible, give some suggestions about what kind of evidence might help.

7. **If you are reviewing an essay that you receive as a Word document, you may want to use the "Review" function in Word to make your comments.** The illustration below demonstrates how to do this.

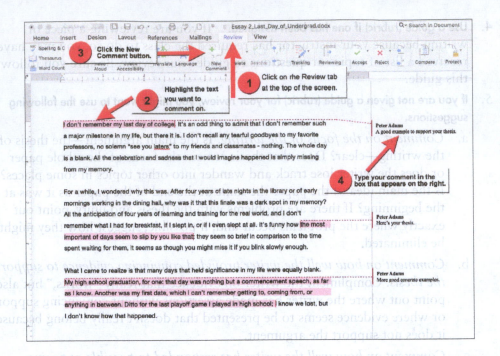

Guidelines for Responding to Peer Review

Here are some suggestions for how to respond when someone reviews your writing.

1. Ask your reviewer to address some specific things you'd like to know about your draft.

2. If your reviewer is giving feedback orally, be sure to take notes.

3. If your reviewer's comments are not clear, ask questions.

4. Don't get in an argument with your reviewer. If the reviewer is making criticisms or suggestions you don't agree with, listen carefully to what is said, but feel free to ignore comments you simply don't agree with. It's your paper.

8.5 **Activity**

Practicing Peer Review

Your instructor will give you instructions about working in pairs to review each other's drafts of an essay. If you need to refresh your understanding of peer review, see Peer Review (8.4, p. 8).

TOPIC 9
Preparing to Write

In this Topic, you'll learn about some important steps you can take before starting to write an essay, steps that will take only a few minutes but will greatly improve the effectiveness of what you write.

Navigating Topic 9

The tutorials listed below provide information on preparing to write. Each is followed by an opportunity to apply the skills you have just learned. You can work through the entire Topic on your own, learning about all the strategies and practicing them; work on items you've been assigned by your instructor; or choose just the ones you find helpful.

Introduction to Preparing to Write 12

9.1	Tutorial	Reading an Assignment 12
9.2	Activity	Analyzing an Assignment 12
9.3	Tutorial	The Rhetorical Situation 13
9.4	Tutorial	Thinking about Audience 14
9.5	Activity	Practice Thinking about Audience 16
9.6	Tutorial	Thinking about Purpose 17
9.7	Activity	Practice Thinking about Purpose 18
9.8	Tutorial	Making a Plan 19

Introduction to Preparing to Write

Topic 9 starts by giving advice on how to read writing assignments and ensure you understand what they are asking you to do. Then it discusses the elements of the rhetorical situation (author, audience, topic, purpose, context, genre, and medium), providing more detailed information on audience and purpose, and ends by explaining how to create a plan for completing a writing assignment.

9.1 Tutorial
Reading an Assignment

To write effectively in a college class, it is essential that you carefully read each assignment and make sure you understand exactly what the instructor expects you to do. If possible, read the assignment when it's handed out in class and ask any questions you have about it then. When you are ready to start working on the assignment later, read it again slowly, perhaps marking it up with comments, reminders, and questions. If you do have questions, check whether your instructor is open to receiving them via email.

When reading an assignment, be particularly attentive to the verbs your instructor has used. Were you asked to *explain* something? To *define* something? To *propose* something? If you have already completed Terms for Writing Assignments (28.2, p. 436), you'll have a list of these terms and their definitions (if not, you might consider working on Unit 28.2 now). These kinds of words are important clues to the kind of writing your instructor expects. Also, you need to note the specific requirements of the assignment—length, format, type of citations required, due dates for drafts, and the due date for the final paper.

9.2 Activity
Analyzing an Assignment

Below is a writing assignment on the topic of grit (defined by Angela Duckworth as "perseverance and passion for long-term goals"). Working in your group, make a numbered list of everything this assignment asks you to do.

Assignment: The Significance of Grit

For this assignment, you will write a three- to four-page essay that grows out of your reading, discussion, and thinking about grit.

> You will write an academic essay suitable for a class in psychology, sociology, education, or even freshman composition. In this essay, you will explain the concept of grit, present the arguments on both sides of the controversy about grit, and take a position on the significance of grit, a position you support with evidence.

As you write this essay, you will want to include information from the three articles you have read in this project and at least one article you find on your own by quoting, paraphrasing, or summarizing relevant passages. When you do this, be sure to provide appropriate citations for any words you quote, paraphrase, or summarize and include a works cited list or list of references at the end of your essay. . . .

If you want to use your sources most effectively to support your argument, it's not enough to simply include them as a series of unrelated sources; you need to tie them together, explain their relationships with each other, and express your conclusions about them.

9.3 Tutorial

The Rhetorical Situation

As long ago as classical Greece—300 BC or so—thinkers have been aware that four important components exist for every text: the *author* of the text, the *audience* for the text, the *topic* of the text, and the *purpose* of the text. These four important elements are discussed from the point of view of the reader in Previewing a Text (20.2, p. 261). There readers are urged, before diving into reading a text, to take a few minutes to analyze the rhetorical situation, as it will help them to better understand and analyze what they are reading. These same four components are also important for a *writer* to think about before and during any writing project. You will need to analyze them as you prepare to write.

Traditional Components of Rhetorical Analysis

The following are the four traditional components of rhetorical analysis.

1. **Author.** Of course, you know who the author is; it's you. But what version of *you* do you want your readers to encounter? Having done considerable research and thinking about your topic, do you want to take on the role of an expert? Or would it be a better strategy to be up front about the fact that you are "just a college student" and argue that being a college student gives you a valuable perspective on the topic? If you have been personally affected in some way by the topic, do you want your readers to see you as someone with personal experience of the issue?

2. **Audience.** What do you know about your audience, the people who will read what you have written? Audience analysis is discussed more fully in Thinking about Audience (9.4, p. 14).

3. **Topic.** What will you be writing about? Early in the process your topic may be very broad, but before you start to write, you will need to narrow it down to something manageable. (See How to Use Invention Strategies to Select a Topic [10.3, p. 30].)

4. **Purpose.** What is your purpose for writing? What do you want to have happen as a result of people reading your essay? Read more about this in Thinking about Purpose (9.6, p. 17).

Additional Components of Rhetorical Analysis

In addition to the four traditional components of rhetorical analysis, before starting to write, you should also think about three additional elements that have come to be considered part of a rhetorical analysis in the modern world:

1. **Context.** *Where* does the writing you're doing fit into the world in which it will be read? Is your topic the center of a firestorm of public argument? Are you writing about a topic that most of the world views as already settled and not in need of more discussion? Are you writing about a topic that has been neglected, that most people have not been thinking about? Are you breaking new ground? Are you writing about a topic that has been much discussed already, but which you are addressing from a new perspective or as a result of new evidence? Thinking about where your writing fits into the broader conversation will help you to adopt the most effective tone and style.

2. **Genre.** What *kind* of writing are you doing? Is this going to be a memo, a formal report, an essay for publication, an application for a job, a letter to potential supporters of a project? What style and tone of writing is expected in this genre of writing? What length is expected? What kind of evidence? What kind of documentation of sources? Does the type of writing you're doing call for the use of a series of paragraphs, or would the use of bulleted or numbered lists be more effective?

3. **Medium.** Give some thought to what medium would be most effective for presenting your argument. Don't assume that a ten-page formal written report is your best option. Depending on the situation, your writing may be more effective if it's enriched with images, charts, and diagrams. Is a PowerPoint or web page an option? Considering your topic, purpose, and audience, what medium would be most effective?

9.4 Tutorial

Thinking about Audience

Before starting any writing task, most writers find it helpful to think about who their audience will be. Who will be reading what they are about to write? This knowledge will shape the tone of their writing, the content, the examples, and the amount of detail they provide.

Identify Your Audience

This task can actually be a little more complicated than it seems. Suppose the writing assignment you are responding to asks you to write to your college or university's Committee on the Student Code of Conduct to propose a change in its policy on bringing children on campus. As with most assignments in college English classes, your essay will have two different audiences. The first is the committee, but the second is your instructor. And if that's not complicated enough, your instructor will be reading and evaluating your essay based on how well he or she thinks it addresses the committee as audience.

Writing tasks in the workplace can just as easily have multiple audiences. Imagine that a company you work for has discovered a flaw in a product it sells. Your boss has asked you to write a letter to customers explaining what the flaw is and what steps the company will take to correct it. Your audience is, obviously, the people who bought the product, but remember that first your letter will be read by your boss. In addition, it may be sent to other offices, like the legal affairs office, for their approval.

Analyze Your Audience

Once you know who your audience is, you will need to think about them and answer questions such as the following.

- **How much does your audience already know about the subject you are writing about?** Do you need to provide some background information as context, such as a brief overview of events preceding a political crisis you are analyzing or the different ways people in the past have addressed a problem to which you are proposing a solution?

- **How technical should you be with this audience?** If you are writing for a general audience, you may need to define important terms and be careful not to assume your readers know more than they do. On the other hand, if you are writing for people knowledgeable about your topic, you may be able to use more technical language and assume that they are familiar with certain basic information.

- **Are they likely to agree or disagree with what you have to say?** How you think an audience might react to your writing can help you determine how to present your position. For those who agree, you might only need to present a well-researched and supported argument. For those who hold different opinions, you might also need to acknowledge their positions and provide well-supported counterarguments.

- **Are there characteristics about them you should take into account as you write?** Do most of them have children? Are most of them in school? Do most of them read a newspaper? Are there demographic characteristics (e.g., race, gender, sexual orientation, religion, economic status) you should be aware of? What style of writing is most likely to be successful with this group of readers?

9.5 Activity

Practice Thinking about Audience

Below is an assignment you might be asked to write about later in the course. For this activity, you're not going to write the paper; you're just going to do some thinking about audience.

Your instructor will form the class into groups of four or so. In your group, discuss who the audience will be for this writing assignment. Who will be the readers of this essay? What do you know about them? Is there only one audience for this assignment? If you think there is more than one, what do you know about the second audience? Who might they be?

How much does each audience know about the topic of delayed gratification? How much are they likely to agree or disagree with your point? What will be the most effective stance for you to take? Can you pull off being an expert? Or should you emphasize that you are "just a student"? Remember, you are not being asked to actually write a paper at this time.

NOTE: *Delayed gratification* is when you put off something that you'd like to do until later in order to achieve a more important goal. For example, you want to watch a football game on TV on Sunday afternoon, but instead, you tape it for later so you can finish your English essay.

For this assignment, you will write a three- to four-page essay that grows out of your reading, discussion, and thinking about delayed gratification. Your audience for this paper is students who will be arriving at your institution next year. Your essay, if accepted by the college's New Student Orientation Committee, will be included in a packet of information new students will receive to help them understand how to be more successful in college.

Think deeply about *delayed gratification*—what it is, when it is a good strategy, how one might be successful at doing it. Support your argument with information from the articles you have read or others you locate yourself and/or with examples from your own life or from the lives of people you know.

9.6 Tutorial

Thinking about Purpose

Before starting any writing task, most writers find it helpful to think about the purpose of the writing they are about to do. Knowing what they want to accomplish will shape the tone of their writing, the examples they use, the amount of detail they include, and the way they present their ideas.

Traditionally, a small number of possible purposes for writing have been identified:

1. To persuade
2. To explain
3. To express (feelings or thoughts)
4. To entertain

However, you could add to the list some additional purposes for writing:

5. To request
6. To recommend
7. To reassure
8. To summarize

Lots of writing certainly does have one of these as its purpose, although more often a piece of writing will combine several of them.

Nonetheless, instead of thinking about purpose in terms of these very broad and general descriptions, you can think about purpose in another way: you can think more specifically and concretely about *your* purpose. To identify a specific focused purpose, think about this question: *What do you want to happen as a result of this writing?*

Realistically, most times when you write, you will have several different purposes. Consider the following example.

One Saturday afternoon, Tanya Jennings was backing her car out of a parking space at a local mall when she heard a sickening crashing sound. She had backed into a car parked beside her. When she got out and saw the damage she had done, she was horrified. The other car's fender, taillight, and bumper were all damaged, although her own car was not even dented. She also noticed a small crowd had gathered and was watching her.

Tanya was late for a doctor's appointment, so she decided to write a note to the owner of the other car and leave it under the windshield wiper.

The note she wrote had several different purposes, illustrating how complicated the purpose of a piece of writing can be:

1. To apologize to the owner of the car
2. To provide contact information so the owner of the car could reach her
3. To convince the people gathered around, who might read the note after she left, that she had really left contact information
4. To make the point that the other car was parked over the line into her parking space in case the accident ended up in court

This next example demonstrates how thinking carefully about purpose can help someone be a more effective writer.

> Imagine that you've heard about a job you would really like: an evening receptionist position in a hospital that's within walking distance of your college. Perfect. You make sure your résumé is up to date, and then you go to work on a cover letter to go with the résumé.

If you don't give it a lot of thought, the purpose of the cover letter may seem almost obvious: you want to be hired for the job. However, the actual purpose for a cover letter is slightly different. Seldom do employers hire someone based simply on a résumé and cover letter. They will invite some of the applicants in for an interview and then hire one person based on the interviews, the résumé and letter, and perhaps other factors like recommendations or college transcripts.

The purpose of the cover letter is to be invited for an interview, which you hope will lead to the job. If you keep this purpose in mind, you will probably close the letter by saying something like "I would be available for an interview any day next week." But if you do not realize what the true purpose of the letter is, you might close with something like "If you hire me, I can be available to start in one week." The latter closing is inappropriate in this scenario and could lead the employer to think you are not "savvy" enough about the working world to be considered for the job.

9.7 Activity
Practice Thinking about Purpose

For this activity, your instructor will divide the class into groups of three or four. Each group will read the following text. Working in your group, come up with a list of as many different possible purposes for the letter you would write about the experience described below as you can.

> A few weeks ago, you purchased a laptop computer at a local electronics store. When you got home and set up your computer, all that appeared on the screen was "Error Message 134," which informed you that your computer was damaged, and you would have to take it to an authorized repair shop.
>
> When you returned the computer to the store where you had purchased it, the salesperson said you must have damaged the computer while taking it home and refused to repair it for free. When you explained that you had taken it home in its factory packaging and had opened it up very carefully when you got there, he insisted that you must have done something to damage it. He argued that "Error Message 134" could only be the result of extreme carelessness. When you asked to see the manager, he informed you that he was the manager and suggested you were being unreasonably difficult.
>
> Before you completely lost your cool, you decided to leave the store. The salesperson yelled something at you as you left, but you couldn't hear what it was.
>
> When you arrived home, you decided to write a letter about your experience to the general manager of the store.

9.8 Tutorial
Making a Plan

Taking some time before you start to write to make a plan for a writing project is well worth it. If you have four weeks to complete an elaborate research project that culminates in a twelve-page research paper, you will clearly need to develop a work plan. Many students like to do this planning on a calendar like the one on page 20.

Sunday	Monday	Tuesday	Wednesday	Thursday	Friday	Saturday
3	4 Read assignment. Analyze audience and purpose.	5	6 Brainstorm for a topic.	7 Browse library and online resources.	8 Select a narrowed topic. Draft thesis.	9 Conduct research focused on topic. Start bibliog.
10 Brainstorm ideas for paper.	11	12 Chunk ideas and order them.	13 Revise thesis.	14	15 Identify ideas that need more sources.	16 Conduct research for missing sources.
17 Start first draft.	18	19 Continue work on draft.	20 Draft for peer review.	21 Revise.	22	23 Create works cited list.
24 Revise.	25 Edit MLA citations and works cited list.	26	27 Do a careful edit for the little stuff.	28 Research paper due!	29	30

Of course, you don't need an elaborate plan like this if you're writing something much shorter, but believe it or not, even if you are writing an in-class essay and have only an hour, it is still a good idea to take a minute to plan your time. A brief outline like the one that follows will remind you when it's time to move on to the next step in the process. In fact, some students even use the alarm on their phones to alert them to when they need to move on.

> 5 mins: Reading assignment and analyzing audience and purpose
> 5 mins: Brainstorming & ordering
> 30 mins: Drafting
> 10 mins: Revising
> 10 mins: Editing

TOPIC 10
Finding a Focus

In this Topic you'll learn to use various invention strategies to develop a focus for your writing and create a draft thesis.

Navigating Topic 10

The tutorials and presentation listed below discuss how to focus a broad subject, and the activities provide opportunities for practice. You can work through the entire Topic on your own, learning about all the strategies and practicing them; work on items you've been assigned by your instructor; or choose just the ones you find helpful.

Introduction to Finding a Focus   21

10.1	Tutorial	Invention Strategies 22
10.2	Presentation	Brainstorming 30
10.3	Tutorial	How to Use Invention Strategies to Select a Topic 30
10.4	Activity	Using Brainstorming to Narrow a Topic 31
10.5	Tutorial	Thesis Statements 32
10.6	Tutorial	Using Invention Strategies to Arrive at a Thesis 35
10.7	Activity	Where Should the Thesis Be Located? 36

Introduction to Finding a Focus

Topic 10 starts with an explanation of five different *invention strategies* (brainstorming, freewriting, browsing and reading, mapping, and outlining), sometimes known as *prewriting*, which is followed by a more detailed presentation on brainstorming. It then discusses how to use invention strategies to select and narrow a topic and develop a draft thesis. It ends with an activity to get you thinking about where you might place your thesis in an essay, based on your topic, purpose, and audience.

Invention Strategies

For many writers, getting started is the hardest part. In this tutorial, you will find many ideas and strategies to help you generate ideas and identify and narrow a topic.

Sometimes when you are asked to write in college, you are given complete freedom to write about a topic of your choosing or, at least, a very wide topic area in which to carve out a specific topic. Broad assignments might sound like this:

- Write a three-page essay in which you argue for a cause you believe in.
- Write a three- to four-page essay discussing an issue involving the labor movement in America.
- Write a fifteen-page research paper on American immigration policy over the past fifty years.
- Write a three-page essay discussing one issue raised by the book you read last week for this course.

Sometimes your professors will give you more specifics about what they want you to write about:

- Write a three-page essay in which you explain why the global-warming resisters are wrong.
- Write a four-page essay in which you agree or disagree with this statement: Public schools in America do not provide an equal education to all citizens.

At work, your boss might ask for writing that addresses certain situations:

- The copiers in the office are old and break down frequently. Investigate options for replacing them and have a proposal for new copiers on my desk by noon on Friday.
- Write a letter to customer X explaining why the television he ordered took three weeks to arrive and explaining what we will do to compensate him for the inconvenience.

Whether you have significant leeway in finding a topic or fairly narrow guidelines to work with, the following material offers some techniques, with examples, for generating ideas and then focusing in on a specific topic, including brainstorming, freewriting, browsing and reading, mapping, and outlining.

Brainstorming

To brainstorm, you have to turn your internal censor off. Just write down every idea that comes to you. Don't worry about writing complete sentences; phrases are fine.

Don't even worry about spelling. Just get every idea you can think of written down. When you run out of ideas, read over what you've written. That will often generate additional ideas. When you run out again, go get a cup of coffee or take a break. When you come back, more ideas may come to you.

Many people like to brainstorm on a blank sheet of paper; others prefer to do it in a blank document on a computer. Try both to see what works best for you, but keep in mind that the next step, organizing your list, is much easier to do on a computer, so you may want to choose that approach.

For an example of how brainstorming works, see the presentation in Brainstorming (10.2, p. 30).

Brainstorming Example

Tania was preparing to write an essay on disciplining her five- and seven-year-old daughters. Working on her computer, she began by typing short phrases as they popped into her head.

spanking

"time out"

no TV

chores

yelling

a formal sit-down talk

setting clear rules and limits that everyone understands

talking about the rules from time to time, not just when they are broken

explaining the reasons behind the rules

what kinds of rules?

rules about cleaning up after making a mess

rules about teasing your sister

rules about not eating snacks between meals

rules about going to be on time

rules about lying

rules about throwing balls in the house

do I need all these rules???

Something really interesting (and not that unusual) happened as Tania did this brainstorming. She started out thinking about how to discipline children, but at the point where she drew the first line, her focus seems to shift. Instead of thinking about what she might do when her daughters misbehave, she starts thinking about what she might do to reduce the times when a need for discipline comes up. Below the second line, Tania's focus shifts again. She starts listing all the rules she might need to discuss, and then pauses and wonders whether she really needs all these rules.

Brainstorming, as it did for Tania, often goes in directions the writer wasn't even thinking about when he or she started. Tania has ended up with some good ideas for three different topics:

1. What kind of discipline to use with her daughters
2. Steps she could take to reduce the need for discipline
3. Why does she need so many rules?

But now Tania will have to make a decision. She cannot write about three different topics, even though they are somewhat related. She'll have to settle on one of these and then do some more brainstorming on that topic.

Freewriting

Other writers use a system called freewriting when they are trying to find ideas. They just start writing about whatever comes to mind, and they keep writing for an extended time without worrying about whether what they are writing is coherent, whether it has unity, or whether it even makes sense. Some writers like to set themselves a goal: they will write for twenty minutes or until they have filled two pages. The idea is to write freely, hoping to generate a few good ideas surrounded, usually, by a lot of not-so-good stuff.

When they're finished, they read over what they've written, searching for a few good ideas. They may end up discarding a large percentage of what they wrote, but the effort will have been worthwhile if it produced a few good ideas.

Freewriting Example

When Alethea started working on a paper about racism for her political science class, she chose freewriting as her invention strategy.

> Racism . . . well, I know its bad. I know it involves treating people of some races badly and giving privileges to other people, usually white like me. And when it gets really ugly with terrible words like the n-word. That's clearly racism. But is racism always that obvious? How bout when I'm walking home at night and see a black man walking in my direction. Do I have a

> different reaction cos he's black? What neighborhoods do I make sure I lock my car door in? Do I feel different when a couple of black dudes are talking, joking real loudly in the mall than if its a coupla white guys making a racket?

Alethea took a break at this point, but she had at least started on her paper. She'd raised some interesting questions. When she returned, she reread what she'd written and got some new ideas and even a new direction to take her paper in.

> Those sentences are all about me . . . my feelings, actions. But does racism have to be about one person??? Can organizations be racist? Can structures be racist? What about the way schools are funded in America—property taxes. Doesn't that mean schools in places where people have big houses and lots of money get more $s than schools in neighborhoods where poorer people live? People of color? What about who goes to prison for long sentences? Don't black people get longer sentences? Why is that?

After her break, Alethea had moved in a new direction—structural racism instead of individual racism. She may end up needing to choose one or the other to write about, or she might end up writing about both in a paper that compares these two types of racism. In any case, she has a great start on her paper. Notice she didn't spend time correcting typos and grammar errors—this is freewriting, getting ideas down as fast as you can.

Browsing and Reading

Another great way to generate ideas to write about is through browsing and reading, either in the library or online. Using the card catalog or the computer database in the library, browse titles or subjects until something catches your eye. Using Google, start a search for a broad topic and then follow links to wherever they lead. Skim articles or browse books making lots of notes of ideas that hold promise. When you finish, you'll have a long list of ideas that need to be organized and focused.

Browsing and Reading Example

Lani knew she wanted to write about health care and the elderly. Her mother was in her late seventies, and it was clear she was not going to be able to live alone too much longer without some in-home support, so this topic was important to Lani. She first visited her college library, where she went to the computerized database for books and found listings for a couple that looked promising. She made a note of the titles, authors, and call numbers, in case she would decide to use these in her works cited list, and headed to the stacks to locate the actual books.

The Psychology of Aging: Theory, Research, and Practice by Janet Belsky
(BF724.55.A35 B44 1984)

Learning to Be Old: Gender, Culture, and Aging by Margaret Cruikshank
(BF724.55.A35 C78 2013)

When Lani found these two books on a shelf on the second floor of the library, she took them to a table and started browsing. In the Belsky book, Chapter 6 discusses cognition and aging. Lani had worried that her mother was getting a little forgetful and sometimes seemed confused, so that chapter caught her attention. The Cruikshank book didn't have a chapter on cognition, so Lani headed back to the shelf where she'd found the first two books. Lani returned the second book to the shelf, and when she looked a little farther down the shelf, she was really excited. There were three more books focused specifically on cognition and aging.

Aging and Cognition: Research Methodologies and Empirical Advances,
edited by Hayden B. Bosworth (BF724.55.C63 A47 2009)

Everyday Cognition in Adulthood and Late Life, edited by Leonard W. Poon,
David C. Rubin, Barbara A. Wilson (BF724.55.C63 P66 1989)

*Adult Cognition and Aging: Developmental Changes in Processing,
Knowing and Thinking* by John M. Rybas (BF724.55.C63 R93 1986)

Armed with these four books, Lani headed for the library's computer where databases for periodicals were available. She decided to use the ProQuest Nursing and Allied Health database. She typed in the words "aging and cognition" and was startled to learn 21,268 articles were available. She was greatly relieved to learn that she could search the titles from her computer at home and narrow her search criteria so she would get a smaller, more focused list of articles, which she could print out.

Lani's trip to the library was very productive. She not only focused her topic on a narrower topic—aging and cognition—but she was headed home with four books on the subject and access to lots of articles.

Mapping

Mapping is much like brainstorming, only more visual. Start by writing down a single idea in the center of a blank page and drawing an oval around it. Then add additional ideas and position them around the first idea. Draw lines to show connections among the ideas. Keep going until you run out of ideas or the page is full.

At this point, you might want to select one of the more promising ideas, write it in the middle of a fresh sheet of paper, and start an entirely new map with it.

Some writers like to do their mapping using sticky notes that can be rearranged as the map grows larger. Mapping can even be done in a word processing program. Most of them have a function under the "insert" menu called "text box." Click on it and then click in the center of your page to insert a text box, in which you can write your first idea. Then add additional ideas each in its own text box. These can be rearranged easily by dragging them around the screen. Lines showing connections among the boxes can be added by clicking on the "insert" menu, clicking on "shape," and selecting "line."

Mapping Example

John was interested in writing about the dangers of driving, so he created a map using text boxes in a Microsoft Word document. He placed "dangers of driving" at the center, and then added four boxes for what he considered the major categories of danger: other drivers, bad weather, road hazards, and driver error. For each of these categories, he added related ideas. Using this process, he came up with enough ideas that he could use any one of the four major topics as the basis for a paper.

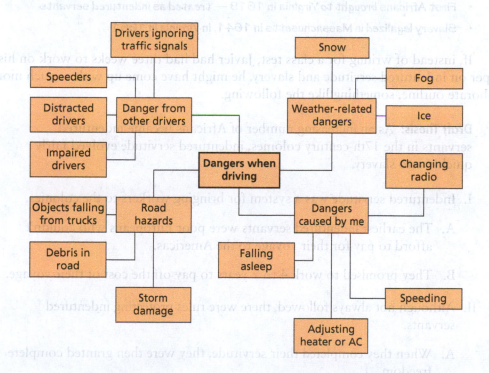

Outlining

Outlines range from quick lists of three or four ideas to highly structured documents complete with indentations, capital and lowercase letters, and Roman and Arabic numbers. For short writing assignments, or assignments when you don't have much time, such as an exam, a scratch outline can still be very helpful.

However, when you are working on an essay assignment, creating a more detailed outline can be really useful once you have narrowed your topic, drafted a working thesis statement, and generated some supporting evidence. An outline helps you to organize your ideas, decide on what order to present them, and identify where you need more support; it provides a road map for your essay that will guide your writing.

Outlining Example

When asked in a history class to write an in-class essay on the beginnings of slavery in America, Javier jotted down a few quick ideas before beginning to write.

- Indentured servitude brought many poor Europeans to the colonies in the 17th century
- How it worked
- First Africans brought to Virginia in 1619 — treated as indentured servants
- Slavery legalized in Massachusetts in 1641, in Virginia in 1661

If, instead of writing for a class test, Javier had had three weeks to work on his paper on indentured servitude and slavery, he might have come up with a much more elaborate outline, something like the following.

Draft Thesis: As an increasing number of Africans became indentured servants in the 17th-century colonies, indentured servitude evolved fairly quickly into slavery.

I. Indentured servitude was a system for bringing workers to the colonies.

   A. The earliest indentured servants were poor Europeans who couldn't afford to pay for their voyage to the Americas.

   B. They promised to work 4 to 7 years to pay off the cost of their voyage.

II. Although not always followed, there were rules protecting indentured servants.

   A. When they completed their servitude, they were then granted complete freedom.

B. Most were also given their "freedom dues" of something like 25 acres of land, seed for a year, fresh clothes, and a firearm.

III. Although initially classified as indentured servants, Africans were never treated the same way as Europeans.

A. Most were captured in Africa and *forcibly* transported to the colonies.

B. Beginning in 1619, Africans were brought to Virginia and categorized as indentured servants, but even then, their treatment was not the same as the treatment of the Europeans.

1. Some Africans actually achieved freedom after serving out their period of indenture, but most of these were not given "freedom dues."

2. By 1650, the total number of Africans in Virginia had risen to only 400; the total number of Europeans was nearly 19,000.

IV. Indentured servitude evolves into slavery.

A. Slavery in England had been reserved for "non-Christians," and was not usually related to race.

B. The number of freed Europeans in the colonies was growing and creating pressure on land ownership.

C. The colonists began to see slavery as a more economically feasible option than indenture.

1. Slaves could be enslaved for life.

2. The children of slaves would become slaves as well.

3. Slavery, originally based on religion—only non-Christians could be enslaved—had a problem: slaves could convert to Christianity and demand freedom.

4. Gradually, the basis for slavery changed from religion to race, an unchangeable and easily identified category.

A formal outline like this is different in several ways from the scratch outline Javier used when he had to write a paper quickly.

1. It is much more detailed. Although he started with a brief outline, as Javier did more research and thinking, he added more and more detail.

2. An elaborate system of letters, numbers, and indentation is used to indicate where the ideas fit in the hierarchy of the argument.

3. Each entry is a complete sentence. This is only necessary in the most formal kind of outline—a sentence outline. In a less formal outline, each entry could just be a phrase.

4. At every level, where there is one entry, there is at least one more. For example, there are no 1's without 2's; no A's without B's.

Some instructors require that an outline like this one be turned in along with a research paper.

Most writers who use an outline to guide their writing consider it a very fluid document that is constantly revised, pruned, and added to. In many cases, as the writer fleshes out the outline, the draft thesis is revised significantly, paragraphs are reordered, new evidence is added, and support that is not relevant is deleted.

10.2 Presentation

Brainstorming

To watch this presentation on brainstorming, a particularly useful prewriting strategy that can help you to find and narrow a topic, develop a working thesis, and generate ideas to support it, go to *Achieve for The Hub*, Topic 10, and open Unit 10.2.

10.3 Tutorial

How to Use Invention Strategies to Select a Topic

Using invention strategies to come up with a topic to write about is often a two-stage process. In the first stage, you use one or more of the strategies described in Invention Strategies (10.1, p. 22) to develop a collection of potential ideas to write about. Then you read through your list, crossing out or deleting any ideas that no longer appeal to you, that don't match the assignment, or that you don't think you have much to say about. Now you should have a handful of ideas that might work as a topic for a paper. You might try them out on other people. Get their reactions and suggestions. Or you might select one of the ideas and try writing about it. If it seems to work, you may have your topic. If it doesn't, try another one.

Finally, with luck and perseverance, you will arrive at one topic that seems like it will work for your essay. Topics at this stage often look something like these:

- Solar energy
- Prison reform
- Transsexuals in the army

- Freedom of speech at college
- Religious freedom
- Right to die

The most common problem that students have with these early topics is that they are too broad. Most of those listed above would require many pages to discuss adequately. So, in the second stage, you take the broad topic you've selected and use an invention strategy to find more ideas that relate to it. If you had chosen, for example, "religious freedom," you might have brainstormed a list that looks something like this:

Freedom to worship the way your faith tells you to

Freedom to refuse to do anything your religious beliefs say you shouldn't do

Freedom to raise your children in accordance with your beliefs

Freedom to marry in accordance with your religious beliefs

Freedom to engage in rituals and ceremonies dictated by your religion

Freedom to refuse medical treatment for yourself and your children when your religion forbids such treatment

Once again, it's time to make a decision. Following the same technique that you did in the first stage, read through your list, deleting any ideas that no longer appeal to you, that don't match the assignment, or that you don't think you have much to say about. At this point, you should have a narrowed topic that you can address within the page limits of your assignment.

10.4 Activity

Using Brainstorming to Narrow a Topic

Use the following steps to narrow a broad topic to one you could write about in a paper of three to four pages in length.

1. Choose one of the broad topics listed below or one from the next essay assignment for this course and brainstorm a list of more focused topics you might write about.

- Patriotism
- Lying
- Success
- Religion
- The environment

- Race in America
- Drugs
- Education
- Transportation
- Criminal justice

2. After you've had enough time to do this brainstorming, your instructor will organize you into groups of three or four to compare the lists you have come up with. If you like some of the topics on a classmate's list, feel free to add them to your list.

3. Working individually, go over your list to eliminate any topics that don't seem very promising, that you don't know enough about, or that you simply aren't interested in writing about. Then review the remaining topics to see if any can be combined into one topic. Finally, select the one topic you could write an essay about.

4. Complete a second round of brainstorming. Make a list of all the ideas you might include in a paper about the topic you have chosen. If you run out of ideas, you might want to take a short break and relax for a few minutes. Then return to the brainstorming to see if you can come up with some more ideas, or try one of the other invention strategies listed in Unit 10.1 (p. 22).

5. As you did in step 4, review your list of ideas eliminating any that don't seem to fit under your topic, that you don't know enough to write about, or that you are not interested in writing about.

For information on how to further organize the ideas you have now listed for your topic, see Chunking and Ordering (12.5, p. 69).

10.5 Tutorial

Thesis Statements

Most successful college essays focus on a single idea or main point, which is referred to as a *thesis* or *thesis statement*. The thesis of an essay includes two major parts: (1) a statement of the subject or topic for the essay and (2) an assertion about that subject or topic.

Subject — Assertion about the Subject

Here are some examples:

- Global warming is a threat to the US economy.
- A police officer's life is frequently at risk.
- Today's automobiles are much safer than those of ten years ago.

Notice that each of these theses (*theses* is the plural form of thesis) has two parts:

A thesis statement must do these two things—identify the topic and make an assertion about that topic—but it can also do other things.

1. It can provide some background information about the topic of the paper.

- *Because it threatens our ability to produce enough food to feed our nation,* global warming is a threat to the US economy.
- A police officer's life is frequently at risk *as a result of the widespread ownership of handguns in America.*
- *Since computers have become widespread in our cars,* today's automobiles are much safer than those of ten years ago.

2. It can also give a preview of the organization of the argument to follow.

- Global warming is a threat to the US economy *because of its effect on agriculture, coastal cities, flooding, and wildfires.*
- A police officer's life is frequently at risk *from attacks by violent criminals, accidental shootings, and deranged individuals.*
- Today's automobiles are much safer than those of ten years ago *because they are fitted with a significant number of safety devices and include software that can alert drivers to potential dangers.*

Avoid These Common Mistakes

Avoid these common mistakes when creating a thesis.

- **Stating a fact.** A thesis that simply states a fact will not work well because there is not enough to write about; an essay is not necessary to prove something that is factually true. The theses here state a fact:

  - Newspapers provide news to many people.
  - Some foods are healthier than others.
  - Many children are born each year.

- **Taking an uncontested position.** A thesis that simply argues something that most people already agree with will not produce an interesting essay:

  - Drunk driving is a terrible thing.
  - Child abuse should not be tolerated.
  - Not showing up regularly for work will lead to losing your job.

- **Reusing language that is in the actual assignment.** If the assignment reads, "Write a three-page essay in which you discuss at least three causes of global warming," your thesis should not recycle the same language:

  - In this essay I will discuss three causes of global warming.

- **Making sweeping statements about what you are going to write about.**

  - In this essay, I will explain why America's groundwater is in danger.
  - This essay will prove that we need lower speed limits on interstate highways.

- **Stating your thesis as your opinion.**

  - In my opinion, we need a major revision of immigration laws in this country.

  - My belief is that racial justice should be the top priority.

A Thesis with More Than One Point

Some teachers insist that a thesis argue only a single point, but others recognize that it is possible, although more difficult, to write a fine essay that argues more than one point. Here are some examples:

- *America is in danger of spending too much on the military* and of not spending enough on education.

- *Children's television can have a positive effect on children's development,* but it can also have a very negative effect.

- *Americans who break some laws receive excessively harsh sentences,* while those who break other laws receive sentences that are far too light.

Check with your professor whether he or she will accept a more complex thesis statement like one of these.

10.6 Tutorial

Using Invention Strategies to Arrive at a Thesis

Once you have a topic, how do you turn it into a *thesis*? Using an invention strategy, or more than one, that works for you, you can come up with a variety of ideas about your topic. Freewriting, brainstorming, mapping, and reading about the topic can all help you to develop a thesis about that topic.

Here is the list of possible topics brainstormed for "religion" in Using Brainstorming to Narrow a Topic (10.4, p. 31):

Freedom to worship the way your faith tells you to

Freedom to refuse to do anything your religious beliefs say you shouldn't do

Freedom to raise your children in accordance with your beliefs

Freedom to marry in accordance with your religious beliefs

Freedom to engage in rituals and ceremonies dictated by your religion

Freedom to refuse medical treatment for yourself and your children when your religion forbids such treatment

At this point, the writer needs to make a choice. In most cases, a well-organized essay has only one thesis, so one topic will need to be selected. For this example, the writer decides on "freedom to marry in accordance with your religious beliefs" as his topic. He then chooses to brainstorm a list of possible theses:

> The government should not pass laws controlling who can marry whom.
>
> The government should not impose the beliefs of one religion about marriage on people who practice another religion.
>
> Marriage is a religious practice; the government should have no role and should not issue marriage licenses.
>
> The age at which people can marry should be set by their religion, not by the government.
>
> Two major world religions, Islam and Hinduism, as well as many smaller religions allow polygamy; the government should not outlaw polygamy.

Again, it's time to make a choice. The writer thinks about his list of potential theses and rereads the assignment to make sure they fulfill the requirements. Then he thinks about the audience for and purpose of the writing as detailed in the assignment and eliminates theses that would not address both sufficiently. He asks for opinions from friends or classmates to help him make a choice. As he focuses in on one of the theses, he decides to try freewriting about it to see whether that produces enough ideas for an essay. If it does, he's ready to start drafting. If not, he will try finding ideas for another thesis in his list.

The choice of a thesis is important, but it is not irrevocable. Later in the writing process, your thesis can be modified or even replaced, based on where your reading, research, or writing takes you.

10.7 Activity

Where Should the Thesis Be Located?

Read over the following short essays that were written to argue that the city of Baltimore should install a traffic light at the intersection of Northern Parkway and Chinquapin Parkway. These essays were intended to be sent as letters to the director of transportation for the city.

The three essays are quite similar, but they are organized in different ways. Working in groups, study them carefully, looking particularly at the location of the thesis in each. Discuss which way of organizing the essay your group thinks is most effective.

Essay 1

For the past six years, I've been living a few houses away from the intersection of Northern Parkway and Chinquapin Parkway, a busy intersection in a neighborhood where many families have children. I urge the city to install a traffic light at this intersection.

In the years I've lived here I've seen and heard far too many accidents at this intersection. In the last month, I have observed two, one of which involved serious personal injury. In the past year, I have personally witnessed twenty-one accidents. While I was out of town last summer, a terrible four-car accident occurred after which five people were admitted to the hospital. I know that two accidents at this busy intersection have resulted in loss of life. Something needs to be done.

This morning as I was leaving my house for work, I heard the squealing sound of the brakes of a large city bus trying to stop suddenly, followed by the sickening sound of that bus crashing into the side of a station wagon carrying three small children. As I ran to the station wagon, I saw that two children were scared but had been restrained by their seatbelts. The third child, unfortunately, had not been wearing her seatbelt. She flew through the windshield and landed in a forsythia bush on the opposite side of the intersection. Fortunately, the bush cushioned her impact. She was bleeding from many scratches and cuts, but did not suffer any serious injuries. We were lucky this time.

I checked with the Department of Transportation and learned that the minimum traffic requirement to trigger a new traffic light is at least 1,200 vehicles per hour on the more congested road at peak traffic periods and at least 50% of that volume on the less congested road. My neighbor and I sat near the intersection on three different work days last week. On Northern Parkway, I counted more than 1,500 vehicles per hour each day. My neighbor counted 855 vehicles per hour on Chinquapin Parkway. In addition to exceeding the minimum traffic requirements for a new traffic light, I'd like to point out that there is a large public school just a block away from this intersection, meaning that large numbers of children cross at this intersection every school day.

In light of the alarming number of accidents at this intersection and the fact that the traffic density exceeds the minimum requirements, I urge the Department of Transportation to install a traffic light at the intersection of Northern and Chinquapin Parkways.

Essay 2

This morning as I was leaving my house for work, I heard the squealing sound of the brakes of a large city bus trying to stop suddenly, followed by the sickening sound of that bus crashing into the side of a station wagon carrying three small children. As I ran to the station wagon, I saw that two children were scared but had been restrained by their seatbelts. The third child, unfortunately, had not been wearing her seatbelt. She flew through the windshield and landed in a forsythia bush on the opposite side of the intersection. Fortunately, the bush cushioned her impact. She was bleeding from many scratches and cuts, but did not suffer any serious injuries. We were lucky this time.

In the years I've lived here I've seen and heard far too many accidents at this intersection. In the last month, I have observed two, one of which involved serious personal injury. In the past year, I have personally witnessed twenty-one accidents. While I was out of town last summer, a terrible four-car accident occurred after which five people were admitted to the hospital. I know that two accidents at this busy intersection have resulted in loss of life. Something needs to be done.

For the past six years, I've been living a few houses away from the intersection of Northern Parkway and Chinquapin Parkway, a busy intersection in a neighborhood where many families have children. I urge the city to install a traffic light at this intersection.

I checked with the Department of Transportation and learned that the minimum traffic requirement to trigger a new traffic light is at least 1,200 vehicles per hour on the more congested road at peak traffic periods and at least 50% of that volume on the less congested road. My neighbor and I sat near the intersection on three different work days last week. On Northern Parkway, I counted more than 1,500 vehicles per hour each day. My neighbor counted 855 vehicles per hour on Chinquapin Parkway. In addition to exceeding the minimum traffic requirements for a new traffic light, I'd like to point out that there is a large public school just a block away from this intersection, meaning that large numbers of children cross at this intersection every school day.

In light of the alarming number of accidents at this intersection and the fact that the traffic density exceeds the minimum requirements, I urge the Department of Transportation to install a traffic light at the intersection of Northern and Chinquapin Parkways.

Essay 3

This morning as I was leaving my house for work, I heard the squealing sound of the brakes of a large city bus trying to stop suddenly, followed by the sickening sound of that bus crashing into the side of a station wagon carrying three small children. As I ran to the station wagon, I saw that two children were scared but had been restrained by their seatbelts. The third child, unfortunately, had not been wearing her seatbelt. She flew through the windshield and landed in a forsythia bush on the opposite side of the intersection. Fortunately, the bush cushioned her impact. She was bleeding from many scratches and cuts, but did not suffer any serious injuries. We were lucky this time.

In the years I've lived here I've seen and heard far too many accidents at this intersection. In the last month, I have observed two, one of which involved serious personal injury. In the past year, I have personally witnessed twenty-one accidents. While I was out of town last summer, a terrible four-car accident occurred after which five people were admitted to the hospital. I know that two accidents at this busy intersection have resulted in loss of life. Something needs to be done.

I checked with the Department of Transportation and learned that the minimum traffic requirement to trigger a new traffic light is at least 1,200 vehicles per hour on the more congested road at peak traffic periods and at least 50% of that volume on the less congested road. My neighbor and I sat near the intersection on three different work days last week. On Northern Parkway, I counted more than 1,500 vehicles per hour each day. My neighbor counted 855 vehicles per hour on Chinquapin Parkway. In addition to exceeding the minimum traffic requirements for a new traffic light, I'd like to point out that there is a large public school just a block away from this intersection, meaning that large numbers of children cross at this intersection every school day.

In light of the alarming number of accidents at this intersection and the fact that the traffic density exceeds the minimum requirements, I urge the Department of Transportation to install a traffic light at the intersection of Northern and Chinquapin Parkways.

Know Your Instructor's Preferences

There is some disagreement among English teachers about *where* a thesis statement should be located in an essay. Some insist that it appear in the first paragraph; some even specify a particular location in that paragraph, like the last sentence. Others recognize that the thesis can effectively be withheld until later in the paper, even until the final paragraph. Making sure you understand your instructor's preferences about thesis placement before you start writing is always a good idea. (For more on thesis placement, see Introductory Paragraphs [17.3, p. 189].)

TOPIC 11
Developing Ideas

One of the most effective ways to make an essay stronger is to provide more "development," more reasons for readers to agree with your thesis. In this Topic, you will learn a variety of strategies for providing support for your thesis and topic sentences.

Navigating Topic 11

The tutorials listed below provide information on how to generate support for an argument. You can work through the entire Topic on your own, learning about all the strategies and practicing them; work on items you've been assigned by your instructor; or choose just the ones you find helpful.

Introduction to Developing Ideas 41

11.1	Tutorial	Options for What to Include in an Essay	42
11.2	Activity	Evidence and Assertions	43
11.3	Tutorial	Development, Support, or Evidence	48
11.4	Activity	Developing Strong Support for an Argument	52
11.5	Activity	Recognizing Development Strategies in "Violence Vanquished," Steven Pinker 53
11.6	Tutorial	Three Types of Appeal: Logos, Ethos, and Pathos	58
11.7	Tutorial	Avoiding Logical Fallacies	59

Introduction to Developing Ideas

Topic 11 is all about making your argument stronger and more convincing. It opens with an explanation of ways to make your essays more interesting, followed by an activity that gets you thinking about evidence and assertions, which leads to an overview of the kinds of support you could use in an essay, such as examples, statistics, interviews, expert testimony, and more. Group activities are designed to give you practice at providing support for a thesis and recognizing support in someone else's essay. The Topic also offers advice on three types of appeals and how to avoid logical fallacies.

11.1 Tutorial

Options for What to Include in an Essay

At its most basic, an essay consists of these three components:

- An introduction
- Body paragraphs that provide support for the thesis; for example, a series of paragraphs that provide, explain, and support reasons for an argument or position
- A conclusion

These three components can make a perfectly satisfactory essay, but many other components can make your essay more interesting, more convincing, and more appealing to the reader, as outlined below. Think about including some of these in your next essay. Also think about your audience. What will it take to win them over to your position? What is likely to be their primary reservation?

Ways to Make Essays More Interesting

1. **Add more arguments.**   Just because you've come up with three reasons that support the position you have taken in your thesis, there is no reason to stop thinking. Most essays can be made more convincing if they include more reasons, more arguments, to support the thesis.

2. **Provide definitions of key terms.**   If there are several words or phrases that are central to your argument, you may want to use a paragraph near the beginning of your essay to explain how you will be using them. For example, if you're writing about juvenile delinquency, you may want to explain what that term will mean in your discussion. It's not that you think your reader has never heard of the term; it's just that it has a wide range of meanings, and you want to make clear what you mean when you use the term. Does it, for example, include juveniles who commit murder? How about juveniles who spray paint graffiti?

3. **Recognize negative effects.**   Your thesis may be a good idea, and you may have presented a number of positive outcomes that will result from it, but it is often

a good strategy also to admit that there are some negative outcomes that may result. Recognizing these can add to your credibility. They demonstrate that you are knowledgeable enough to be aware of these negatives and honest enough to admit they exist. Of course, it is a good idea if you can also explain why these negatives are less serious than they appear or how they can be mitigated.

4. **Recognize what opponents may say.** Closely related to recognition of negative effects is the recognition of opponents' arguments, especially if those arguments are well known. Summarize them as objectively as you can and then answer, rebut, or counter them.

5. **Include some history of the topic you're writing about.** How long has it been an issue? What positions have others taken about it?

6. **Make suggestions for implementation.** If you are trying to convince your reader to agree with you about some issue, it can be a great idea to include some advice, toward the end of the essay, about what steps will be needed to implement the change you are proposing.

7. **Make a call to action.** Even stronger than advice about implementation is a call to action, urging the reader not just to begin implementing some change, but to actually commit to some cause.

8. **Include background about who you are and/or why you decided to write about the topic.** Especially if it makes you a more credible author or demonstrates you are an author with a particular viewpoint, it can be very helpful to take a paragraph or two to give the reader some information about who you are and why you are writing about the topic.

11.2 Activity

Evidence and Assertions

On October 15, 2018, police found a man unconscious on the sidewalk at the intersection of Charles and Lombard Streets in Baltimore, Maryland. They called an ambulance to take the man to the emergency room, but they also emptied his pockets into an evidence container to help them figure out who he was. The following items were found in his pockets and in his wallet.

Working in groups, make a list of observations about the man based on the contents of his pockets. You will have about fifteen minutes to complete your list.

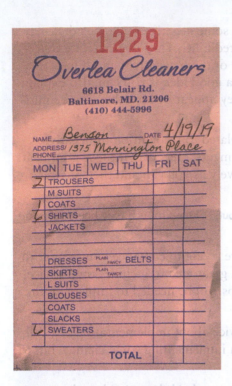

(Photos) Peter Adams

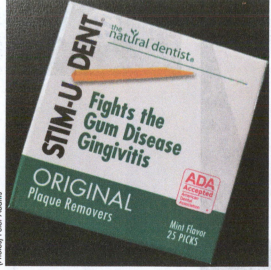

(Photos) Peter Adams

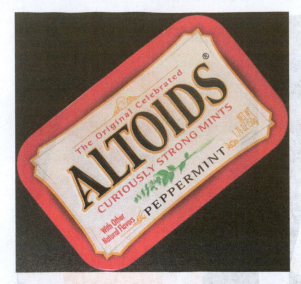

(Photos) Peter Adams

(Photos) Peter Adams

Development, Support, or Evidence

At one time or another, you've probably been told that something you've written needs more development, more support, or more evidence. These kinds of suggestions usually indicate that the reader feels that you've expressed an opinion or made an assertion that he or she finds unconvincing. Providing more development, support, or evidence will make it more likely that your readers will be persuaded to agree with your assertion. In this discussion, these words—development, support, and evidence—will be used interchangeably, although sometimes people do make fine distinctions among them.

One way to improve the evidence you provide to support your assertions is to think about your audience. What will it take to win them over to your position? What do they need to know in order to understand your point of view? What kinds of assumptions or biases might they have? Another way is to consider your purpose. What do you want to achieve through your writing? How can you choose evidence to support your goal?

When in doubt about whether you have been convincing, think harder to come up with more evidence to support your position. Below you will find a variety of types of evidence you might use.

Connecting Evidence to Your Topic Sentences and Thesis

It is usually quite clear to the *writer* of an essay why a particular piece of evidence is there and how it relates to the topic sentence of a paragraph or thesis of an essay, but sometimes this connection is not so clear to the *reader*. For example, in a paper arguing that schools in America attended by children from affluent families receive much greater financial support than schools that children from poorer families attend, a student might provide this evidence in a paragraph to support a topic sentence that addresses the fact that where students live impacts their education:

> The value of homes in affluent neighborhoods can be ten times as high as the value of those in poorer neighborhoods.

The writer knows why this is important support but hasn't made the connection clear to the reader. The writer knows that schools in America are funded by local property taxes, so wealthy neighborhoods will produce more revenue to support their schools than poorer ones. In order to make the connection explicit, she could have written this:

Because property taxes are used to fund schools, neighborhoods with a greater proportion of wealthy families who pay higher taxes will have schools with more and better resources than neighborhoods with predominantly poorer residents who pay less.

In the same way, you want to make clear the connection between the evidence you discuss in each paragraph and your thesis. One way to do this is to ensure that each topic sentence clearly supports your main point: outlining before, during, and after drafting can help you to see the connections between the different parts of your essay. Delete or revise topic sentences that do not support your main argument. Once you are sure of your major support and how you want to present it, be sure to connect your evidence to your topic sentences, explaining how each piece supports your argument.

Types of Support

Suppose you wanted to argue that the country is not doing enough to address poverty. To support your opinion, you would need to provide evidence. As you can supply evidence to support an assertion in several different ways, similar kinds have been grouped together here. They include facts, examples, statistics or numerical evidence, expert testimony, and appeals.

Facts

It was John Adams who said that "facts are stubborn things," and indeed they are. Facts are based on reality; they are known to exist or to have happened because they have been experienced or observed. They don't leave room for argument. They establish the credibility of a writer who "knows the facts," and they can be assembled into a well-structured argument. An essay on poverty would be strengthened by the inclusion of facts like these:

- According to the US Census Bureau, a family of four earning less than $25,465 a year is living in poverty.

- According to the Center for Poverty Research at the University of California, Davis, 39.7 million Americans lived in poverty in 2017.

- According to the US Census Bureau, 13.9% of Americans were living in poverty in 2017.

For more discussion of facts, see Distinguishing among Facts, Statements Most Experts Agree On, and Opinions (21.3, p. 290).

Examples

One of the most common and most effective ways to provide support is to present examples, descriptions of situations that illustrate the point a writer is making. Examples can take several different forms such as a single brief example, an extended example with more detail, a story, or a report of the results of an interview:

- **Brief examples.** You might tell about a person you know who is living in extreme poverty. To make your argument more convincing, you might add three more examples of people living in poverty, or even add ten more. At some point, however, examples alone begin to lose their power to convince, and you need to use other types of evidence as well.

- **Extended examples.** Another way to add support to your argument might be to dig down into an example of living in poverty in greater detail: to describe what it's like to run out of food before your next payday, to be afraid to answer the phone because it might be a collection agency trying to pressure you into paying off a debt, to worry when there's a knock at the door that might mean you're being evicted, or to have to watch your daughter crying because you cannot afford the medicine to treat her earache.

- **Stories.** One of the oldest methods that human beings have used to convince an audience of a point is to tell a story. Sometimes a narrative will move a reader far more than cold statistics or expert testimony.

- **Interviews.** Another way to "dig down" into a subject is to interview one or more people who are living in poverty. Be sure to plan your interview(s) in advance, to choose relevant quotes that accurately represent your interviewee(s), and to report and document his or her words accurately. For more details on interviewing, see Conducting Interviews (22.10, p. 328).

Statistics or Numerical Evidence

Statistics are a powerful form of evidence because they represent many examples, not just one or two. Statistics as a subject is a branch of mathematics related to collecting, organizing, analyzing, and interpreting large quantities of numerical data. Statistical analysis is particularly useful for inferring general conclusions based on representative samples of people who have been asked to answer questions on specific topics. Statistical data are often presented in a visual format—a graph, chart, or infographic—that can make it easy to see trends or to compare sets of information:

- **Statistics.** Instead of adding examples to your essay on poverty one at a time, you might decide to make your argument more convincing by adding statistics that show the scale of the problem. You might do some research and report how many people in this country are living in poverty, or how many

African-American men under twenty-five live in poverty, or how many children live in poverty. You could also create graphics to illustrate and/or compare statistical information or incorporate graphs and charts from material you have researched, providing you clearly document your sources.

- **Survey results.**   Sometimes it is possible to conduct a survey to support your position. If you are arguing that a large percentage of community college students are living in poverty, for example, you could conduct a survey at your college and present the information you gather. For more details on surveying, see Conducting Surveys (22.11, p. 330).

- **Analysis of trends.**   When you analyze trends, you are not just looking at statistics at one point in time. You are showing how those statistics are changing over time. In the essay on poverty, for instance, you could bolster your argument by analyzing trends over time and demonstrating that the percentage of people living in poverty has increased dramatically in recent years. You could even project into the future: if nothing is changed, what percentage of Americans will be living in poverty in ten years?

Expert Testimony

On almost any topic, a little research will lead you to people who are recognized experts in their field. Supporting your argument with expert testimony, such as a quotation from economist Paul Krugman or conservative commentator David Brooks that points out that increasing levels of poverty are harmful to the nation, can make your argument more convincing. To determine whether individuals are experts in their fields, take note of their titles, publications, credentials, and how often other experts mention them. For more discussion on identifying experts, see Distinguishing among Facts, Statements Most Experts Agree On, and Opinions (21.3, p. 290).

At some point in your argument about poverty, you might want to explain why your opinion is worthy of consideration, in what way you are an "expert" who should be listened to. For example, if you grew up in poverty, you may have insights that others don't have. If you worked for three years in a shelter for the homeless, you may have unique experiences. Explaining the source of your "expertise" is often a good way of supporting your argument.

Appeals

Writers often appeal to their readers to take a stand, to provide support, to express sympathy, or to change their behavior. Appeals can take many forms, including traditional appeals to ethos, logos, and pathos (see Three Types of Appeal [11.6, p. 58]), as well as appeals to people's values.

When you appeal to a reader's values, it is important that you know your audience or at least know them well enough to have some idea of their values. For example, if you are writing to a conservative and fairly wealthy audience, perhaps readers of the *Wall Street Journal*, you might want to discuss the longstanding belief in the American Dream, something many wealthy Americans support. Then you could point out that the American Dream is in danger of disappearing as more people become trapped in generational poverty.

11.4 Activity

Developing Strong Support for an Argument

Below is a thesis statement followed by a brainstormed list of the kinds of strong, convincing evidence that could be used to support it. Read the thesis and supporting evidence carefully. Then, using this example as a model, work with your group to select one of the following six theses and make a list of all the kinds of evidence that would help provide strong evidence to support it.

> **Thesis:** The United States should not attempt to overthrow rulers of Near Eastern countries, even if they are tyrannical dictators.
>
> - Examples of countries in which we have intervened with results that are disastrous (Iran, Somalia, Afghanistan, Iraq, Libya)
>
> - Statistics on the numbers of Americans who have died in several of our wars
>
> - Statistics on the number of civilians who died in the same wars
>
> - Ethical reason: It is morally wrong for one country to attempt to dictate who rules in another country.
>
> - Statements by respected officials like former Secretary of State Colin Powell, who has argued that we should not attempt such interventions

1. We need laws in this country that will make it less likely that guns will end up in the hands of violent or mentally unstable people.

2. Laws to limit people from buying guns will not keep guns out of the hands of violent or mentally unstable people.

3. The American people are losing their morality.

4. The American people are becoming more moral.

5. America is becoming more unfair than it used to be.

6. America is not perfect, but it is fairer than it used to be.

11.5 Activity

Recognizing Development Strategies in "Violence Vanquished," Steven Pinker

Read the following essay by Steven Pinker, a professor of psychology at Harvard University, and answer the questions below. This essay is adapted from his book *The Better Angels of Our Nature: Why Violence Has Declined*, published by Viking Press. The essay originally appeared in the *Wall Street Journal* on September 24, 2011.

1. Working together as a group—in a paragraph or two—describe the audience you think Pinker was writing for.

2. You'll notice that some words and phrases in the article are underlined. After you've read the article, working in your group, write a definition of each of the underlined words or phrases. Do not look them up in a dictionary; instead, use one of these five strategies for dealing with difficult language:

   a. Derive the meaning from context.

   b. Analyze the parts of the word.

   c. Back up and reread the passage.

   d. Keep reading to see if the writer explains the difficult passage.

   e. Decide the word is not important and just keep reading.

   If you'd like more information about these strategies, see Dealing with Difficult Language (20.9, p. 280).

3. Finally, after you've read the article, go back and highlight each example of evidence or support that you can find. Remember that evidence can be any of the following:

   - Examples
   - Extended examples
   - Stories
   - Interviews
   - Statistics
   - Survey results
   - Analysis of trends
   - Facts
   - Expert testimony

Violence Vanquished

STEVEN PINKER

SEPTEMBER 24, 2011

1   On the day this article appears, you will read about a shocking act of violence. Somewhere in the world there will be a terrorist bombing, a senseless murder, a bloody underline{insurrection}. It's impossible to learn about these catastrophes without thinking, "What is the world coming to?"

2   But a better question may be, "How bad was the world in the past?"

3   Believe it or not, the world of the past was *much* worse. Violence has been in decline for thousands of years, and today we may be living in the most peaceable era in the existence of our species.

4   The decline, to be sure, has not been smooth. It has not brought violence down to zero, and it is not guaranteed to continue. But it is a persistent historical development, visible on scales from underline{millennia} to years, from the waging of wars to the spanking of children.

5   This claim, I know, invites skepticism, underline{incredulity}, and sometimes anger. We tend to estimate the probability of an event from the ease with which we can recall examples, and scenes of underline{carnage} are more likely to be beamed into our homes and burned into our memories than footage of people dying of old age. There will always be enough violent deaths to fill the evening news, so people's impressions of violence will be disconnected from its actual likelihood.

6   Evidence of our bloody history is not hard to find. Consider the genocides in the Old Testament and the crucifixions in the New, the gory underline{mutilations} in Shakespeare's tragedies and Grimm's fairy tales, the British monarchs who beheaded their relatives and the American founders who dueled with their rivals.

7   Today the decline in these brutal practices can be quantified. A look at the numbers shows that over the course of our history, humankind has been blessed with six major declines of violence.

8   The first was a process of pacification: the transition from the anarchy of the hunting, gathering and horticultural societies in which our species spent most of its evolutionary history to the first agricultural civilizations, with cities and governments, starting about 5,000 years ago.

9   For centuries, social theorists like Hobbes and Rousseau speculated from their armchairs about what life was like in a "state of nature." Nowadays we can do better. Forensic archeology—a kind of "CSI: Paleolithic"—can estimate rates of violence from the proportion of skeletons in ancient sites with bashed-in skulls, decapitations

or arrowheads embedded in bones. And ethnographers can tally the causes of death in tribal peoples that have recently lived outside of state control.

10   These investigations show that, on average, about 15% of people in <u>prestate</u> eras died violently, compared to about 3% of the citizens of the earliest states. Tribal violence commonly <u>subsides</u> when a state or empire imposes control over a territory, leading to the various "<u>paxes</u>" (Romana, Islamica, Brittanica and so on) that are familiar to readers of history.

11   It's not that the first kings had a <u>benevolent</u> interest in the welfare of their citizens. Just as a farmer tries to prevent his livestock from killing one another, so a ruler will try to keep his subjects from cycles of raiding and feuding. From his point of view, such squabbling is a dead loss—forgone opportunities to extract taxes, tributes, soldiers and slaves.

12   The second decline of violence was a civilizing process that is best documented in Europe. Historical records show that between the late Middle Ages and the 20th century, European countries saw a 10- to 50-fold decline in their rates of homicide.

13   The numbers are consistent with narrative histories of the brutality of life in the Middle Ages, when highwaymen made travel a risk to life and limb and dinners were commonly enlivened by dagger attacks. So many people had their noses cut off that medieval medical textbooks speculated about techniques for growing them back.

14   Historians attribute this decline to the consolidation of a patchwork of feudal territories into large kingdoms with centralized authority and an infrastructure of commerce. Criminal justice was nationalized, and zero-sum plunder gave way to positive-sum trade. People increasingly controlled their impulses and sought to cooperate with their neighbors.

15   The third transition, sometimes called the Humanitarian Revolution, took off with the Enlightenment. Governments and churches had long maintained order by punishing nonconformists with mutilation, torture and gruesome forms of execution, such as burning, breaking, <u>disembowelment</u>, <u>impalement</u> and sawing in half. The 18th century saw the widespread abolition of judicial torture, including the famous prohibition of "cruel and unusual punishment" in the eighth amendment of the U.S. Constitution.

16   At the same time, many nations began to whittle down their list of capital crimes from the hundreds (including <u>poaching</u>, sodomy, witchcraft and counterfeiting) to just murder and treason. And a growing wave of countries abolished blood sports, dueling, witch hunts, religious persecution, absolute <u>despotism</u> and slavery.

17   The fourth major transition is the respite from major interstate war that we have seen since the end of World War II. Historians sometimes refer to it as the Long Peace. ▶

18   Today we take it for granted that Italy and Austria will not come to blows, nor will Britain and Russia. But centuries ago, the great powers were almost always at war, and until quite recently, Western European countries tended to initiate two or three new wars every year. The cliché that the 20th century was "the most violent in history" ignores the second half of the century (and may not even be true of the first half, if one calculates violent deaths as a proportion of the world's population).

19   Though it's tempting to attribute the Long Peace to nuclear deterrence, non-nuclear developed states have stopped fighting each other as well. Political scientists point instead to the growth of democracy, trade and international organizations—all of which, the statistical evidence shows, reduce the likelihood of conflict. They also credit the rising valuation of human life over national grandeur—a hard-won lesson of two world wars.

20   The fifth trend, which I call the New Peace, involves war in the world as a whole, including developing nations. Since 1946, several organizations have tracked the number of armed conflicts and their human toll world-wide. The bad news is that for several decades, the decline of interstate wars was accompanied by a bulge of civil wars, as newly independent countries were led by <u>inept</u> governments, challenged by <u>insurgencies</u> and armed by the cold war superpowers.

21   The less bad news is that civil wars tend to kill far fewer people than wars between states. And the best news is that, since the peak of the cold war in the 1970s and '80s, organized conflicts of all kinds—civil wars, genocides, repression by autocratic governments, terrorist attacks—have declined throughout the world, and their death tolls have declined even more precipitously.

22   The rate of documented direct deaths from political violence (war, terrorism, genocide and warlord militias) in the past decade is an unprecedented few hundredths of a percentage point. Even if we multiplied that rate to account for unrecorded deaths and the victims of war-caused disease and famine, it would not exceed 1%.

23   The most immediate cause of this New Peace was the demise of communism, which ended the <u>proxy</u> wars in the developing world stoked by the superpowers and also discredited genocidal ideologies that had justified the sacrifice of vast numbers of eggs to make a utopian omelet. Another contributor was the expansion of international peacekeeping forces, which really do keep the peace—not always, but far more often than when adversaries are left to fight to the bitter end.

24   Finally, the postwar era has seen a <u>cascade</u> of "rights revolutions"—a growing revulsion against aggression on smaller scales. In the developed world, the civil rights movement obliterated lynchings and lethal <u>pogroms</u>, and the women's-rights movement has helped to shrink the incidence of rape and the beating and killing of wives and girlfriends.

25   In recent decades, the movement for children's rights has significantly reduced rates of spanking, bullying, paddling in schools, and physical and sexual abuse. And the campaign for gay rights has forced governments in the developed world to repeal laws criminalizing homosexuality and has had some success in reducing hate crimes against gay people.

* * *

26   Why has violence declined so dramatically for so long? Is it because violence has literally been bred out of us, leaving us more peaceful by nature?

27   This seems unlikely. Evolution has a speed limit measured in generations, and many of these declines have unfolded over decades or even years. Toddlers continue to kick, bite and hit; little boys continue to play-fight; people of all ages continue to snipe and bicker, and most of them continue to harbor violent fantasies and to enjoy violent entertainment.

28   It's more likely that human nature has always comprised inclinations toward violence and inclinations that counteract them—such as self-control, empathy, fairness and reason—what Abraham Lincoln called "the better angels of our nature." Violence has declined because historical circumstances have increasingly favored our better angels.

29   The most obvious of these pacifying forces has been the state, with its monopoly on the legitimate use of force. A disinterested judiciary and police can defuse the temptation of exploitative attack, inhibit the impulse for revenge and circumvent the self-serving biases that make all parties to a dispute believe that they are on the side of the angels.

30   We see evidence of the pacifying effects of government in the way that rates of killing declined following the expansion and consolidation of states in tribal societies and in medieval Europe. And we can watch the movie in reverse when violence erupts in zones of anarchy, such as the Wild West, failed states and neighborhoods controlled by mafias and street gangs, who can't call 911 or file a lawsuit to resolve their disputes but have to administer their own rough justice.

31   Another pacifying force has been commerce, a game in which everybody can win. As technological progress allows the exchange of goods and ideas over longer distances and among larger groups of trading partners, other people become more valuable alive than dead. They switch from being targets of demonization and dehumanization to potential partners in reciprocal altruism.

32   For example, though the relationship today between America and China is far from warm, we are unlikely to declare war on them or vice versa. Morality aside, they make too much of our stuff, and we owe them too much money.

33   A third peacemaker has been cosmopolitanism—the expansion of people's parochial little worlds through literacy, mobility, education, science, history, journalism and mass media. These forms of virtual reality can prompt people to take ▶

the perspective of people unlike themselves and to expand their circle of sympathy to embrace them.

34   These technologies have also powered an expansion of rationality and objectivity in human affairs. People are now less likely to privilege their own interests over those of others. They reflect more on the way they live and consider how they could be better off. Violence is often <u>reframed</u> as a problem to be solved rather than as a contest to be won. We devote ever more of our brainpower to guiding our better angels. It is probably no coincidence that the Humanitarian Revolution came on the heels of the Age of Reason and the Enlightenment, that the Long Peace and rights revolutions coincided with the electronic global village.

35   Whatever its causes, the implications of the historical decline of violence are profound. So much depends on whether we see our era as a nightmare of crime, terrorism, genocide and war or as a period that, in the light of the historical and statistical facts, is blessed by unprecedented levels of peaceful coexistence.

36   Bearers of good news are often advised to keep their mouths shut, lest they lull people into <u>complacency</u>. But this prescription may be backward. The discovery that fewer people are victims of violence can thwart cynicism among compassion-fatigued news readers who might otherwise think that the dangerous parts of the world are irredeemable hell holes. And a better understanding of what drove the numbers down can steer us toward doing things that make people better off rather than congratulating ourselves on how moral we are.

37   As one becomes aware of the historical decline of violence, the world begins to look different. The past seems less innocent, the present less sinister. One starts to appreciate the small gifts of coexistence that would have seemed utopian to our ancestors: the interracial family playing in the park, the comedian who lands a zinger on the commander in chief, the countries that quietly back away from a crisis instead of escalating to war.

38   For all the <u>tribulations</u> in our lives, for all the troubles that remain in the world, the decline of violence is an accomplishment that we can <u>savor</u>—and an <u>impetus</u> to cherish the forces of civilization and enlightenment that made it possible.

11.6 Tutorial

Three Types of Appeal: Logos, Ethos, and Pathos

Evidence is certainly essential to supporting your position in an essay, but there is another strategy, another way of thinking about strengthening your argument—*appeals*, an odd word. Think about a politician *appealing* for your vote or a nonprofit *appealing* for donations. In this sense, to appeal is to attempt to persuade, and more than 3,000 years ago, the Greek philosopher Aristotle identified three ways to make appeals to an audience. He called them *logos*, *ethos*, and *pathos*, and we still use these Greek terms today. When you consciously decide to appeal in one of these three ways, you are trying to figure out what sort of an argument will be most likely to convince your reader. It is also possible to use more than one appeal for your audience.

Logos.   If you are using *logos* as your appeal to the reader, you are using reason and logic. In fact, the English word *logic* comes from the Greek word *logos*. Using logic, your goal is to demonstrate to your reader that your argument is sensible and reasonable, that the evidence you present is trustworthy, and that the evidence demonstrates the validity of your thesis.

Ethos.   Using *ethos*, your goal is to convince your reader that you are trustworthy. To accomplish this, you need to convince your reader that you know what you're talking about, that you've "done your homework." It's also important to show the reader you have no ulterior motives, that you have integrity. (The English word *ethical* is derived from *ethos*.) If your reader detects any "stretching" of the truth, any distortion of the facts, or any exaggeration in your reporting of information, your credibility will be undermined, making it less likely that your reader will be persuaded.

Pathos.   When you use *pathos* to convince readers, you are using emotions and feelings. You are trying to convince your readers of the validity of your argument by appealing to their values and beliefs. Giving moving details, designed to appeal more to the readers' hearts than their minds, is one way to employ *pathos*. Appeals to *pathos* may not be as effective as *logos* or *ethos*, but they often succeed when combined with *logos*.

11.7   Tutorial
Avoiding Logical Fallacies

There are ways of arguing that are widely seen as unfair, unethical, or dishonest. These kinds of argument, called *fallacies*, are based on illogical statements, manipulation, or deception and should be avoided. *Ethos*, discussed in Three Types of Appeal above, is impossible to achieve if your reader sees you as untrustworthy.

Common Rhetorical Fallacies

Some of the most common fallacies are described below, and you should avoid using them in your writing as they are more likely to alienate your readers than to convince them.

Ad Hominem. Instead of challenging a person's position, the writer attacks his or her character.

> The senator's proposal for free community college tuition is a terrible idea because she is an elitist, East Coast liberal.

Bandwagon Fallacy. Here, the position is that many people agree with your argument, so your readers should too. However, the majority opinion is not always the right or best one.

> Recent polls show that 60% of Americans want tougher laws on background checks before people buy guns, so you should support the proposal to make background checks mandatory.

Begging the Question. Sometimes called *circular reasoning*, this involves arguing a position simply by stating it again in different words.

> Driving a motorcycle without a helmet is unsafe because it is dangerous.

False Analogy. In this fallacy, the writer compares two things that have some similarities and assumes they are similar in other ways, even if they are not.

> Elections in America are like circuses, so we can't take them seriously.

False Choice. This fallacy assumes that in an argument there are only two choices: the one the writer is proposing or something unacceptable, when, in fact, there are other choices.

> You must resist all gun control laws, or you are against the Second Amendment.

Hasty (or Sweeping) Generalizations. Closely related to stereotyping, this dangerous fallacy makes assertions about everyone belonging to a group because of the characteristics of some people in the group.

> Millennials don't understand what hard work is.

Post Hoc Ergo Propter Hoc. Latin for "After this, therefore because of this." In this fallacy, it is argued that because something happened right after something else, the first event *caused* the second.

> The budget for the Department of the Interior has been reduced by 15%; as a result, the population of wolves in Wyoming, Idaho, and Montana has dropped by 50%.

Slippery Slope.   This is an argument that says that if one thing is done, catastrophic events will inevitably follow.

> If the state passes a 1% tax increase, within five years our taxes will have tripled.

Straw Man.   The writer distorts an opponent's argument into something easily refuted and then argues against that argument instead of the opponent's actual argument.

> The Democrats don't want border security, so to protect the country, we need to elect a Republican Congress next year.

TOPIC 12
Organizing Ideas

This Topic discusses strategies for ensuring that when you write, your ideas are organized to have the maximum impact on the reader.

Navigating Topic 12

The tutorials and presentation listed below provide practical advice on how to logically organize ideas in your academic writing. After each strategy is presented, there is an activity allowing you to practice it. You can work through the entire Topic on your own, learning about all the strategies and practicing them; work on items you've been assigned by your instructor; or choose just the ones you find helpful.

Introduction to Organizing Ideas   63

12.1	Tutorial	Unity	63
12.2	Activity	Evaluating Thesis and Unity	67
12.3	Writing	One Unusual Thing	68
12.4	Activity	Thesis and Unity in One Unusual Thing	69
12.5	Presentation	Chunking and Ordering	69
12.6	Activity	Practice Chunking	69
12.7	Activity	Practice Ordering Ideas	70
12.8	Tutorial	Coherence	70
12.9	Activity	Editing for Coherence	74

Introduction to Organizing Ideas

Topic 12 starts with a discussion of how to ensure your writing is unified by checking that your support directly relates to your thesis statement and making sure you do not change the focus of your thesis as you move through your essay. It continues with an explanation of how to chunk and order ideas to support your argument and finishes with a series of examples of ways to ensure coherence (the smooth flow of ideas) in your essay through the use of logical organization, repetition of key words and pronouns, and the use of transitional words and phrases.

12.1 Tutorial

Unity

Unity is the quality of belonging to a whole. A football team has unity when all the parts—the linemen, the running backs, the defensive team, and even the coaches—are working together as a team. If the backfield thinks the linemen are missing their blocks, or if the offense thinks the defense is missing too many tackles, or if the coaches think the players aren't staying in shape—if the different parts of the team aren't working well together—the team isn't unified (and probably isn't winning a lot of games).

An essay is unified when all the parts work together. An essay has unity problems when parts of the essay do not work well with the other parts and do not support the thesis of the essay.

Unity Problems Caused by Unrelated Material

As an example, an essay might start out with a clear thesis, but then some parts of the essay wander away from that thesis and, in extreme cases, may even begin supporting a different thesis. The essay that follows has these kinds of unity problems.

Is It Possible to "Get Ahead" in America?

It has often been said that "in America, if you work hard you will get ahead," but I believe that <u>most Americans, even if they work hard, will not get ahead</u>.

Here's the thesis.

One important reason many Americans can't work their way out of poverty is our unequal education system. Funding for schools is based on property taxes paid in each local school district. School systems located in poorer areas are underfunded because the property in those areas is of much lower value than property in wealthy suburbs. Lower funding leads to buildings that are often dilapidated, textbooks that are in short supply, and teachers who are paid lower salaries than their counterparts in wealthier areas. In many cases, the most effective teachers in poor schools leave after a few years for the higher salaries in wealthier school districts.

This paragraph provides the first reason that lots of Americans won't get ahead even if they work hard: the education system is unequal.

To make matters worse, many students from truly wealthy families are sent to private schools where they have beautiful surroundings, the best teachers, small class sizes, and access to guidance and counselling services. <u>Many of these kids have grown up in families that put pressure on them to succeed, which leads them to suffer from psychological problems. Depression, bipolar disorder, and even suicide are common among these students. Sometimes their families spend more on therapy and medication than they do on education.</u>

Note that the underlined portion of this paragraph is no longer discussing the thesis of the essay but has wandered into a discussion of unrelated problems experienced by wealthy students.

Young people who grow up in poverty usually don't have the kinds of connections that help them to obtain a good job. Their parents, too often, do not have the kinds of jobs in large corporations or offices where they can help their kids meet people who might hire them. They seldom have older brothers or sisters who can introduce them to people who can give them advice about how to move up in the world. In fact, sometimes, when they do get a job interview at a place where they have a chance of advancement, they are simply unfamiliar with the protocol for such meetings.

This paragraph gives a second argument in support of the thesis: lack of social connections. No unity problem here.

In addition, young people who grow up in lower-income households frequently don't have role models to follow and to receive encouragement from. Many of these young students are the first in their families to attempt to go to college. They, too often, don't know someone who can "teach them the ropes." And frequently they are under pressure to get a job and start supporting a family.

This paragraph gives a third reason to support the thesis: no role models. It supports the thesis.

<u>The belief that all it takes to "get ahead" is hard work results in people thinking that if they haven't gotten ahead, it's their fault: they didn't work hard enough. In fact, there are many causes why, despite hard work, many don't get ahead—an education system that doesn't treat them fairly, the struggle to find the right balance of time and money, a personal crisis, or a personal mistake.</u> **It takes more than hard work to get ahead in America. It takes luck . . . or being born into a middle-class family.**

This paragraph discusses a related issue but does not support the thesis, so it should be deleted, but the bolded sentence could make a powerful end to the essay.

Sometimes these young people give up on college and decide just to try to make it in the workplace. Starting in jobs that don't require a college education, they find, no matter how hard they work, that they just can't get a promotion. Often, they work more and more hours—60 or 70 a week—and they are, nevertheless, barely keeping themselves above water. Then a crisis hits. They become pregnant. They become sick. Their job is eliminated. Suddenly, they're deep in debt with no hope of digging themselves out. They worked hard, but it didn't pay off.

Another paragraph that supports the thesis. Another reason why, even after working hard, some people don't "get ahead."

Unity Problems Caused by a Change of Focus

A different kind of unity problem occurs when writers start out with a good strong thesis and then, as they continue writing, change their mind about the thesis, so that by the end of the essay, they are arguing a different position.

Greg's brief essay, which appears below, illustrates this second kind of unity problem. It is also an essay that needs more development with evidence and examples. (See Development, Support, or Evidence [11.3, p. 48] for more on how to develop and support a thesis.)

> **Strengthen the Drunk Driving Laws!**
>
> Montana needs tougher laws against drunk driving. Everyone know that too many Montanans are being injured or even killed by people who are driving when impaired by alcohol.
>
> A few years ago, my sister was in a crosswalk and was hit by a drunk driver. Margie was in the hospital for six weeks and still suffers from intense pain in her hip. Even though the driver of the other car was convicted of DWI, he was given probation before judgment.
>
> When a jerk in my class in high school was found guilty of driving while intoxicated for the second time, the judge believed the "sob story" his lawyer told and gave him a sentence of only six months, which was then suspended.
>
> When a little girl in my neighborhood was killed by a drunk driver, the judge, who has a reputation for being lenient, sentenced him to "time served."
>
> After reading about these horrific cases, I hope you'll agree that judges in Montana need to start giving tougher sentences for drunk driving.

The clear thesis of this paper appears as the first sentence:

> "Montana needs tougher laws against drunk driving."

But look at the closing sentence, in which the writer seems to intend to restate the thesis in different words:

> "Judges in Montana need to start giving tougher sentences for drunk driving."

The problem is that the writer has changed his mind. He no longer believes that Montana needs "tougher laws," but that the state needs "tougher judges."

So how would you fix this unity problem? The most obvious (but least effective way) would be to change the final sentence so it agrees with the thesis in the first sentence. This would be ineffective because all the examples given in the essay illustrate problems with lenient judges, not lenient laws. Much more effective would be to change the first sentence so it agrees with the last sentence. Then the paper would be unified because the thesis would remain constant from beginning to end, with the evidence in the body of the essay all supporting that thesis.

There is, however, an additional problem with the essay. It doesn't present very convincing evidence to support the thesis. Three brief descriptions of personal experiences are one kind of evidence, but if the writer wants to argue that this is a major problem for the state of Montana, he needs to find evidence on a much larger scale—evidence that these lenient judges are prevalent throughout the state, data showing that large numbers of drunk drivers are getting away with slaps on their wrists, and evidence that some experts have agreed that lenient judges are a large problem.

12.2 Activity
Evaluating Thesis and Unity

Working in your group, read the following essay, identify the thesis, and identify any places where there are unity problems.

Motorcycle Helmets and Individual Freedom

Many states have laws requiring motorcyclists to wear helmets when riding their bikes. These laws violate the principle of individual freedom. Henry David Thoreau wrote in "Civil Disobedience," "That government is best that governs least," and Lincoln is reported to have said, "My freedom to swing my arms ends where your nose begins."

I agree with Thoreau that the government should pass as few laws as possible, thereby maximizing individual freedom. And I agree with Lincoln that we only need laws to prevent one person's freedom from harming another person. The law requiring motorcycle helmets is a violation of these principles and an attack on the individual freedom of Americans.

I recognize that some laws are necessary. We need a law that says I must drive on the right side of the road so I don't crash into people coming from the opposite direction. I understand laws that say I can't fire a weapon in a public place because I could kill or injure someone. I understand laws that require people who own factories to provide necessary safety measures because, if they didn't, they could harm their workers.

But why do we need laws requiring employers to check the immigration status of their employees? These laws don't protect the employees from being harmed by their employer; they are a restriction on the employer's individual freedom. How about laws requiring that I get my children vaccinated? Don't I have individual freedom to make decisions about my own children's health?

Clearly the law requiring motorcycle helmets violates personal freedom. I understand that people think these helmets save lives, and I suppose they do. But if I choose to take chances with my own life, isn't that my choice? If I choose not to wear a helmet and then crash into a tree, I'm the only one who suffers. I haven't done harm to anyone else.

There is nothing more exhilarating than cruising down a highway on a spring afternoon with the wind blowing through my hair. I can smell the flowers blooming along the sides of the road and hear the songs of the birds. It's just not the same experience if I'm wearing a helmet.

I'm fine with the government passing laws requiring me to drive on the right side of the road, to have headlights that work, and to have brakes that work. Those laws are there to prevent me from harming other people. But laws like the helmet law—laws that protect me only from myself—are a gross violation of individual liberty.

12.3 Writing

One Unusual Thing

Write a brief, one-page essay in which you tell your instructor one unusual thing about your family or about your high school. He or she will be reading these papers to get to know each of you but also to begin a discussion of how to make your writing more effective. Please provide concrete examples to back up what you write about your family or school.

12.4 Activity

Thesis and Unity in One Unusual Thing

You may recall that most successful college essays focus on a single idea or main point, which is known as the thesis. The writing assignment in One Unusual Thing (12.3, p. 68) was "to tell your instructor *one* unusual thing about your family or about your high school." In other words, you were asked to write an essay with a thesis: the "one unusual thing" about your family or your high school.

Your instructor will organize the class into groups of three or four and give each group copies of some of the papers your class turned in for that assignment. Work together with your group to decide if each paper is about just "one unusual thing." If a paper discusses two or three different "unusual things," it would not be following the assignment, and it would not have a single, clear thesis. If it starts out discussing a particular "interesting thing," but changes its focus to something different by the end, again, it doesn't have a single, clear thesis. After about twenty minutes, the groups will report out on how well each of the essays is organized.

12.5 Presentation

Chunking and Ordering

To watch this presentation on chunking and ordering, which involves chunking ideas into related groups and ordering those groups to build the body of your essay, go to *Achieve for The Hub*, Topic 12, and open Unit 12.5.

12.6 Activity

Practice Chunking

Here's a brainstormed list on one of the suggested topics from Using Brainstorming to Narrow a Topic (10.4, p. 31)—religion. Chunk these items. In other words, organize them into logical groups or chunks of ideas that are related. Then give each chunk a label.

Is religion dying out?

How does someone choose a religion?

What do most religions have in common?

Religions provide guidance for how to lead a good life.

Definition of religion

What is not a religion?

Do religions have to believe in a god/gods?

Religions provide comfort when people experience tragedy or loss.

What do religions say about other religions?

What do people get out of religion?

Religion helps people to accept death.

Is Alcoholics Anonymous a religion?

Religions provide community and companionship.

Religions can motivate people to go to war.

Religion is the opiate of the people.

Religion motivates people to resist giving in to animal instincts.

How do religions start?

Religions provide support for the needy

12.7 Activity

Practice Ordering Ideas

In Practice Chunking (12.6, p. 69), you grouped brainstormed ideas into logical "chunks" and gave each "chunk" a name.

For this activity, you will decide on the order in which you would like to discuss your "chunks" of ideas in an essay. In the process, you may think of some ideas to add or decide to move some ideas from one "chunk" into another. When you finish, you will have a thoughtful and well-organized plan for an essay, almost an outline.

12.8 Tutorial

Coherence

Coherence is simply the connection of ideas within a piece of writing to make logical sense to the reader and ensure he or she can follow the writer's line of thought. When people read a coherent text, they easily understand the parts, how they fit together, and why they are in the order presented. A piece of writing is not coherent when the reader has trouble following the writer's argument because the ideas do not connect smoothly or obviously.

Three ways to improve the coherence of your writing are logical organization, repetition of key words and pronouns, and the use of transitions.

Logical Organization

One way to ensure coherence is to organize a sequence of ideas in a recognizably logical order—from general to specific, most important to least important (or vice versa), first to last (chronological), near to far (or back to front), bottom to top (or top to bottom), or left to right (or right to left).

General to Specific

Travel can be very educational. You learn all kinds of new information when you visit a place you've never been to before, but you also meet new people with new ways of looking at the world. Most enjoyable, you experience new kinds of food—tastes you never would have sampled at home.

Most Important to Least Important

The primary reason I am going to college is to gain the skills and credentials that will lead to a good job when I graduate. I also want to learn about ideas and people and ways of seeing the world that are different from what I experienced growing up in my hometown of Lawton, Oklahoma. It is also important to me that I understand political issues better. I sometimes listen to debates on television about issues I should care about, but I don't know enough to really have an opinion.

First to Last (Chronological)

When I first came to Lakeland Community College, I felt totally confused. I was supposed to pay my bill in the Bursar's Office, but I didn't even know what a bursar was. When I sat down in my first class and the instructor started explaining the syllabus, her policy on plagiarism, and office hours, I had the vague notion that these things were important, but I didn't really know what they were. Today, after two years at this school, I feel like an expert. I know my way around. In fact, this summer I will be working as a student guide for new students who come to orientation.

Near to Far

Out of my window, I see tree branches crisscrossing the panes of glass. They belong to the maple tree beside the front door, and now, in winter, they are bare except for a few withered brown leaves. Beyond the branches, behind a row of trees, stretches the front lawn, carpeted in snow, and scattered with branches from a recent storm. Far in back to the left, insulated with tarpaper and surrounded by an electric fence is the beehive, warm and still quietly humming despite the subzero temperatures.

Bottom to Top

I live in an eight-story building in downtown Denver. As you approach the building at street level, you'll see a series of small shops—a men's clothing store, a bookstore, a computer store, and, of course, a Starbucks. As you look up, you'll notice seven floors of apartments with large glass windows and little balconies cantilevered out into space. If you lean back and look all the way up to the top, you may get a glimpse of people sitting around in chairs while others swim in the rooftop pool.

Left to Right

It's a small room with slanted ceilings and windows facing south and east. On the left side there is a shelf filled with books, a window hung with glass ornaments and a shell wind chime, and a calendar. In the middle, in front of the south-facing window, is a desk and chair, a computer, a phone, and containers of pens and pencils. On the right side is another desk with drawers full of files and an odd-shaped closet, without a door, lined with shelves jammed with office supplies.

Repetition of Key Words and Pronouns

Coherence in a text can be enhanced by repetition of a key word, the use of synonyms for that word, and the repetition of pronouns referring to that word. In the following text, note the repetition of the term *scientist*, the use of *these experts* as a synonym for the word *scientists*, and the use of the pronoun *they* to refer to the scientists.

Scientists studying the warming of the planet are increasingly worried. They point to the melting of the Arctic ice cap as one alarming development. In a recent study by these scientists, it was announced that the rate of melting in 2012 was nearly four times the rate in 2003. When these experts looked at melting in Antarctica, they found that melting there is contributing more to rising sea levels than previously thought. In addition, other scientists suggest that the warming of the oceans is proceeding at a faster rate than predicted. If nothing is done, these experts predict that sea levels will rise by more than two feet, and 32 to 80 million people will experience coastal flooding within twenty years.

Use of Transitional Expressions

Another way to improve coherence is to use transitional expressions, words and phrases such as *for example*, *as a result*, and *finally*. These expressions serve as signposts, helping the reader follow the text and the connections being made within it. Here's a chart of the most common transitional expressions organized by their function.

To signal sequence	again, also, then, first, second, last, next, before, after
To signal time	later, subsequently, in the meantime, the next day, a week later, after a while, in a few days, within minutes, earlier that day
To signal examples	for example, for instance, specifically, such as, to illustrate, namely, specifically
To signal location	in front of, beside, behind, nearby, next to, adjacent to, below, beyond, elsewhere, to the left, to the right, near, far
To signal summary	hence, in summary, to summarize, in brief, in conclusion, as a result, as I have demonstrated
To signal comparison	in the same way, likewise, similarly, also
To signal contrast	in contrast, on the other hand, however, instead, nevertheless, regardless, but, yet, on the contrary
To signal causation	as a result, therefore, thus, so, accordingly, fortunately, consequently

The following two paragraphs demonstrate how much transitional expressions help make a piece of writing coherent. In Paragraph 1, the transitional expressions have been omitted. Read it first. With a little effort, you should be able to understand what it says. Then read Paragraph 2, in which transitional expressions have been inserted. The difference between these two paragraphs demonstrates how important transitional expressions are to coherence.

Paragraph 1

When Jeanine started her new job as a server at Ciao, a high-end Italian restaurant, she was a little nervous because of her lack of experience. She didn't know how to pronounce many of the Italian words on the menu. The more experienced servers were very helpful. They showed her how to put in a drink order at the bar and how to let the kitchen know if a customer had an allergy. She became more comfortable and more confident. She is one of those experienced servers who help out the newcomers, but she still has trouble pronouncing *bruschetta*.

Paragraph 2

When Jeanine started her new job as a server at Ciao, a high-end Italian restaurant, she was a little nervous because of her lack of experience. For example, she didn't know how to pronounce many of the Italian words on the menu. Fortunately, the more experienced servers were very helpful. For instance, they showed her how to put in a drink order at the bar and how to let the kitchen know if a customer had an allergy. As a result, she became more comfortable and more confident. Today, she is one of those experienced servers who help out the newcomers, but she still has trouble pronouncing *bruschetta*.

12.9 Activity

Editing for Coherence

Working in your group, revise the following essay by making the organization more logical, repeating key words and phrases, and adding transitional words and phrases.

Making Millions

I'm working on becoming a millionaire. It's a good thing I have lots of energy, because I'm going to need it. I'm only twenty-five but I'm handling a lot more than the average young adult. I juggle a 40-hour work week, 15 credit hours of school, and two kids on a daily basis. I'm not talking about your average Monday through Friday 9 to 5 type of job, either. It's more along the lines of 1:00 to 7:00 PM six days a week with a random day off. Oops, I almost forgot. There's one more complication. Sundays offer variety—often in the form of a migraine—with a schedule (for my convenience, of course) of 6:00 to 2:00 AM for those of us who need no sleep before our Monday morning classes. Monday morning, I need even more of it to get up and running.

After school and after work is when I really need a supply of it. Off I go to the Kiddie Academy in Brookdale (or to Hampton if it happens to be Saturday) to pick up my two gregarious children. I have one daughter, Lakia, age 5 (Kindergartener Extraordinaire) and one son, Blake, age 3 (The Accident King). Lakia, while good at heart, already has the curse of the brilliant child—boredom. This requires constant attention and a lot of work on my part. I need to be the source of all things entertaining on an around-the-clock basis or suffer the consequences of her overactive imagination. Even under the most intense supervision, my son Blake is an accident always happening. I thank God that he has "Super Powers" (although I object strongly to calling him Power Ranger Blake [the green one]) that allow him to feel no pain. I have never had to clean up so many spills or take so many trips to the emergency room as I do now. If only *I* had that "no fear" attitude toward doing things that I lost around the time of puberty.

Which brings me to my newly found hobby of returning to school. Amidst and in opposition to, multiple family members' warnings that I was "already too busy to take on any more responsibilities," I started back to school this semester. And I came back with a vengeance. I wasn't going to go to school part-time and have it take forever. I was slow in starting to begin with. So, five classes and 15 credits later, here I am, running a little low on enthusiasm. Besides, my boss was kind enough to let me come to work at one, as opposed to my pre-student hour of noon.

What it takes to be a full-time mom, student, and professional adult is phenomenal. Yet, somehow, I do it (without help) 24/7, 365 days a year with a reasonable amount of sanity. If I could figure out a way to bottle all that stuff—could you imagine the millions I would make?

TOPIC 13
Using Language Powerfully

It's not surprising that good writers carefully edit their writing to ensure there are no errors, that everything is grammatically correct. In this Topic, however, you will be working on a different issue—not just "Is my writing correct?" but also "Have I said this in the clearest, most exact, most powerful way I can?"

Navigating Topic 13

The tutorials listed below provide information about strategies for writing powerfully, and each contains, or is followed by, an opportunity to apply the skills you have just learned. You can work through the entire Topic on your own, learning about all the strategies and practicing them; work on items you've been assigned by your instructor; or choose just the ones you find helpful.

Introduction to Using Language Powerfully 78

13.1	Tutorial	Connotation and Denotation 78
13.2	Activity	Seeing How Concrete Language Works 79
13.3	Tutorial	Using Concrete Language to Bring Writing to Life 80
13.4	Activity	Adding Concrete Language 81
13.5	Activity	Words, Fancy and Plain 82
13.6	Tutorial	Figurative Language 84
13.7	Tutorial	Using a Dictionary to Understand Words 87
13.8	Activity	Using a Dictionary to Select the Right Word 88
13.9	Activity	Determining the Meanings of Confusing Words 89

Introduction to Using Language Powerfully

This Topic focuses on strategies for enhancing your writing by using language more powerfully. Understanding the difference between connotation and denotation; including concrete, sensory details; choosing the right words for the writing occasion; using figurative language; and knowing how to use a dictionary to find the precise word you need and to determine the meanings of confusing words will all help you to communicate more effectively.

13.1 Tutorial

Connotation and Denotation

To use language effectively, you have to be careful to choose words that convey exactly what you mean to say. Take a look at the twelve words or phrases listed below.

mogul	fat cat	well-to-do person
billionaire	wealthy person	moneyed person
tycoon	person of means	loaded
magnate	affluent person	prosperous

In one sense, these words all *mean* the same thing. They all refer to someone who has a lot of money. But, in another sense, their meanings are quite different. If you say someone is *prosperous*, you are implying that they worked hard and earned a lot of money; if you say someone is *moneyed*, it is more likely you are suggesting they were born into wealth. To say someone is a *fat cat* means something very different from saying someone is a *person of means*. Describing someone as *loaded* is not the same as describing them as *wealthy*.

The basic meaning, shared by all these words, is that the persons referred to have a lot of money. This basic meaning of a word is known as its *denotation*. *Connotation* is the term used to refer to the secondary meanings that have come to be associated with words, meanings that often have cultural or emotional overtones. For example, the term *fat cat* is often used to refer to powerful businesspeople or politicians to indicate disapproval of the way they use their wealth or influence, while calling someone a *person of means* is more neutral but can suggest the person is not only wealthy but has inherited money as a result of belonging to the upper class. Saying someone is *loaded* is slang for saying they are *wealthy*: you might use the former when talking to friends but the latter in an academic essay.

When writing, be careful to select words with the precise denotative meaning you want to convey and be sure that any connotative meanings are in line with what you mean to communicate. Also take into account the writing situation: words that are appropriate in informal writing situations, such as emails or letters to friends, are not necessarily the right choice in college writing assignments or workplace writing like memos or reports.

Activity: Explaining Differences in Meaning

Working in your group, write an explanation of the differences in meaning among the following two sets of words.

Set 1

| unusual | bizarre | abnormal |
| odd | weird | unnatural |

Set 2

| articulate | voluble | rambling |
| glib | prolix | verbose |

13.2 Activity

Seeing How Concrete Language Works

Working in your group, read and discuss the following two versions of the same passage. After ten minutes, each group will report out their answers to these two questions:

1. Which is more effective?
2. Why?

Passage 1

On most days, when I enter the Capitol, a train carries me from the building where my office is located through a tunnel lined with flags and seals. The train halts and I make my way, past people, to the elevators that take me to the second floor. Stepping off, I walk around the press who normally gather there, say hello to the Capitol Police, and enter, through double doors, onto the floor of the U.S. Senate.

The Senate chamber is not the most beautiful space in the Capitol, but it is imposing nonetheless. The walls are set off by panels and columns. Overhead, the ceiling is an oval, with an American eagle in its center. Above the visitors' gallery are statues of the nation's first twenty vice-presidents.

Passage 2

On most days, I enter the Capitol through the basement. A small subway train carries me from the Hart Building, where my office is located, through an underground tunnel lined with the flags and seals of the fifty states. The train creaks to a halt and I make my way, past bustling staffers, maintenance crews, and the occasional tour group, to the bank of old elevators that takes me to the second floor. Stepping off, I weave around the swarm of press that normally gathers there, say hello to the Capitol Police, and enter, through a stately set of double doors, onto the floor of the U.S. Senate.

The Senate chamber is not the most beautiful space in the Capitol, but it is imposing nonetheless. The dun-colored walls are set off by panels of blue damask and columns of finely veined marble. Overhead, the ceiling forms a creamy white oval, with an American eagle etched in its center. Above the visitors' gallery, the busts of the nation's first twenty vice presidents sit in solemn repose.

—Barack Obama, *Audacity of Hope,* pages 13–14

13.3 Tutorial

Using Concrete Language to Bring Writing to Life

Abstract language is used to describe ideas and qualities that do not have a physical presence. For example, common abstract terms are words like *democracy*, *sexism*, *success*, *freedom*, *ideal*, or *love*, all of which convey concepts. All of them are open to different interpretations depending on how they are used, by whom, and in what context.

Concrete language refers to specific sensory details—descriptive words related to sight, sound, touch, smell, and taste—that bring writing to life. Examples of these types of words are *black velvet curtains, golden daffodils, knives and forks, sewage fumes, hurricane winds*, and *screeching brakes*, all of which relate to the physical world and can be perceived through the senses.

Here is a paragraph from *The Painted Drum* by Louise Erdrich. The narrator, Faye Travers, who handles estate sales, uses concrete and sensory language to describe an old house she is visiting to assess the contents.

The Tatro house is not grand anymore. The original nineteenth-century home-stead has been renovated and enlarged so many times that its style is entirely obscured. Here a cornice, there a ledge. The building is now a great clapboard mishmash, a warehouse with aluminum-clad storm windows bolted over the old rippled glass and a screen porch tacked darkly across its front. The siding is painted the brown-red color of old blood. The overall appearance is rattling and sad, but the woman who greets me is cheerful enough, and the inside of the house is comfortable, but dim. The rooms are filled with an odor I have grown used to in my work. It is a smell that alerts me, an indefinable scent, really, composed of mothballs and citrus oil, of long settled dust and cracked leather. The smell of old things is what it is. My pulse ticks as I note that even on the ground floor an inordinate number of closets have been added during some period of expansion. Some run the length of whole walls, I estimate, roughly the room's proportions.

Erdrich uses concrete details to describe the look of the house: "nineteenth-century homestead," "[h]ere a cornice, there a ledge," "aluminum-clad storm windows," and siding "painted the brown-red color of old blood," a vivid image. She describes how it smells, an "indefinable scent . . . composed of mothballs and citrus oil, of long settled dust and cracked leather," and how it makes her feel, "my pulse ticks," indicating her rising excitement at the treasures she might find. As you read these descriptive details, you can see and smell and experience what the narrator is seeing, smelling, and experiencing.

Adding these kinds of details to your writing will not only make it more inter-esting for your readers but also make it more accurate and informative. Whether you are telling a story, providing an example, describing a scene, or making a persuasive case, including concrete details will add color and life to your words.

13.4 Activity

Adding Concrete Language

Working in your group, edit the following text to make it more concrete and specific. To do this, you will need to simply "make up" relevant concrete details.

When I got home from work last night, I was exhausted. All I wanted was a quick dinner, a bottle of beer, and an early bedtime. Then I opened the refrig-erator and discovered that the meat I planned to cook had gone bad. Worse yet, my roommate had drunk my last bottle of beer. So off I went to the local store to purchase a few things. Coming out of the store with my supplies, I discovered I had a flat tire. After changing the tire and driving home, I was too tired to cook, so I headed straight to bed.

13.5 Activity
Words, Fancy and Plain

In this activity, you will be asked to think about the word choice that is most effective in a series of writing situations. You will be asked to think about when simple, clear language would work best and when more sophisticated language would be more effective. For most of the following items, there is room for argument about the best answer. In fact, that's the point of this activity: not to get you arguing but to get you thinking about the different options the English language offers.

For each of the items below, working in your group, discuss the pros and cons of the different choices of words used to express the same idea. If your group can agree on which option is the most effective in an item, write a short explanation of why you selected that option. If you cannot agree, write a brief discussion of the strengths and weaknesses of the various choices.

1. You work as a supervising nurse in a large hospital. In a formal letter of reprimand for one of your subordinates who has violated hospital policy, which of the following sentences do you think would be the most effective?

   a. Nurse Baker's behavior on December 18 was dreadful.

   b. Nurse Baker's behavior on December 18 was atrocious.

   c. Nurse Baker's behavior on December 18 was unacceptable.

2. The financial aid office at your school has limited funds available for scholarships for needy students. In a letter you write to that office, which of the following sentences do you think would be the most effective?

   a. For the past four years, my family has been struggling financially since my mother lost her job.

   b. For the past four years, my family has been down on their luck since my mother lost her job.

   c. For the past four years, my family has been impoverished since my mother lost her job.

3. As a teacher of a fourth-grade class, you need to write a note to one of your students. Which of the following sentences do you think would be the most effective?

    a. Please ask one of your parents to write a terse note explaining why you are late for school so often.

    b. Please ask one of your parents to write a short note explaining why you are late for school so often.

    c. Please ask one of your parents to write a brief note explaining why you are late for school so often.

4. In an email to your friends telling them how to get to the location for a picnic, which of the following wordings do you think would be the most effective?

    a. After about a half mile, the trail you are following will split. At this point, take the path to the left.

    b. After about a half mile, the trail you are following will divide. At this point, take the path to the left.

    c. After about a half mile, the trail you are following will bifurcate. At this point, take the path to the left.

5. In a letter asking for a refund from a plumbing company, which of the following sentences do you think would be the most effective?

    a. I am writing to complain about the careless work done by the plumber you sent to my house on June 18.

    b. I am writing to complain about the sloppy work done by the plumber you sent to my house on June 18.

    c. I am writing to complain about the negligent work done by the plumber you sent to my house on June 18.

6. In a letter applying for a summer internship at an accounting firm, which of the following sentences do you think would be the most effective choice?

    a. If I am hired as a summer intern at your firm, I will work hard to make your company's relationship with younger customers better.

    b. If I am hired as a summer intern at your firm, I will work hard to ameliorate your company's relationship with younger customers.

    c. If I am hired as a summer intern at your firm, I will work hard to improve your company's relationship with younger customers.

7. You want to carry a sign supporting your candidate Maggie Sloan when you go to a political rally. Which of the following would be the most effective wording for your sign?

    a. Maggie Sloan has what it takes to be mayor.

    b. Maggie Sloan is eminently qualified to be mayor.

    c. Maggie Sloan will be an outstanding mayor.

8. In your position as executive chef at an upscale restaurant, you are writing a letter to a newly hired cook. Which wording do you think would be the most effective?

   a. Before beginning work with us, please carefully look over the following policies.

   b. Before beginning work with us, please carefully read the following policies.

   c. Before beginning work with us, please carefully peruse the following policies.

9. In a cover letter for a job as a manager at a large department store, which of the following sentences do you think would be the most effective?

   a. In my job at Walmart last summer, I became an expert at handling customers.

   b. In my job at Walmart last summer, I became an expert at customer service.

   c. In my job at Walmart last summer, I became an expert at dealing with customers.

10. In an email to your brother, who is coming to work in the same office where you have been working, which of the following would be the most effective wording?

   a. It is important that you respect the limits on personal messages sent over the office's email system.

   b. It is important that you respect the parameters on personal messages sent over the office's email system.

   c. It is important that you respect the boundaries on personal messages sent over the office's email system.

13.6 Tutorial

Figurative Language

Figurative language uses figures of speech, such as similes, metaphors, and personification, to convey information and ideas in more creative and powerful ways than ordinary language. For example, instead of writing "My professor spoke extremely rapidly," you could use a simile, "My professor talked *as* fast as an auctioneer." By comparing your professor's speech to that of an auctioneer, you create an image for readers that helps them to understand just how quickly your professor talks. Or you could use a metaphor and say, "My professor's words were rapid-fire bullets that ricocheted off the classroom walls." Her words were not literally bullets, but this description conveys the idea that they were fast, loud, and strong. Personification involves attributing human characteristics or emotions to an inanimate object or something non-human, as in this example: My computer is a malevolent intelligence determined to see me fail.

Similes

If someone writes, "When he finally sat down to write his essay, Marcos spent fifteen minutes arranging the items on his desk like a dentist preparing his tools before beginning a root canal," he or she is using a simile. Similes make comparisons using the words *as* or, as in this case, *like*. Similes are effective because they use something most of us are familiar with—in this case, the careful arrangement of a dentist's tools—to explain something we don't know about—how carefully Marcos arranges everything on his desk before beginning writing. Similes are also effective because they are often clever, playful, or even funny—but not always. In this example, the comparison suggests that Marcos is about to embark on a serious project; this is a root canal job, not a cleaning. However, overused, worn-out similes have the opposite effect. Try to avoid such hackneyed similes as *ate like a pig*, *mad as a wet hen*, or *slept like a log*. Try to make fresh, new comparisons in your writing.

Metaphors

A metaphor is a figure of speech that is much like a simile, except that instead of saying X is *like* Y, a metaphor asserts that X *is* Y. Here's an example: "The IRS *is a vulture* circling my meager savings and preparing to swoop down on them." When you use a metaphor like this, you are comparing two dissimilar items that share one characteristic. Although there is not a literal connection, you are making an imaginative one in order to create a memorable image in your reader's mind. In this example, the writer is comparing the IRS to a vulture, suggesting that just as that bird will circle its prey endlessly until it tires or dies, the IRS will never give up, and your savings cannot be protected from it.

Here's another example. In *The Stuff of Thought: Language as a Window into Human Nature*, Steven Pinker writes, "A verb is the chassis of the sentence. . . . It is a framework with receptacles for the other parts—the subject, the object, and various oblique objects and subordinate clauses—to be bolted onto." He doesn't mean a verb literally *is* a chassis. He means that, in a sentence, the verb plays a role much like the role the chassis plays for a car.

One word of caution about metaphors: Once you introduce one into your writing, do not change your mind and switch to a different metaphor as the following example does.

> During the Great Recession, my family became *a ship tossed by violent seas*, but luckily we didn't get *too far over our skis* and do anything foolish.

This writer starts with a metaphor about a ship in rough seas, but switches to a metaphor about skiing, which is confusing for the reader.

Personification

An example of personification appeared in the opening paragraph: "My computer is a malevolent intelligence determined to see me fail." Note that this writer is treating her computer as though it is alive, personifying this inanimate object by suggesting it has the human traits of intelligence and malevolence, or ill will. "My bathroom scale is telling me I need to go on a diet" is another example of personification.

Writers use personification to help readers relate to objects, animals, ideas, or other things, bringing them to life and making them easier to understand or care about. When a journalist talks about a "fire swallowing a forest whole," the reader gets a sense of the enormous destructive power of the flames and the feeling that they are almost alive, choosing their prey. When a novelist writes that "the wasted moon peered through the ragged clouds, too weak to throw a shadow or to reveal the fallen child," she creates a sense of foreboding; the moon, like the child, is weak and powerless.

It is wise to use personification sparingly to make a point, to add depth or color to your writing, or to engage readers with a subject they might not usually relate to.

When to Use Figurative Language

Using figurative language like similes, metaphors, and personification can be fun, both for the writer and for the reader. It can also be powerful and clever. You will most often find it used in works of fiction, such as novels, poems, and plays. Used sparingly in academic papers, it can help readers understand something they aren't familiar with by comparing it to something they are familiar with, help them to perceive something from a different perspective, or bring a dry topic to life. However, figurative language is not always appropriate. In most business writing and in some academic writing, it may seem flowery or pretentious. Also, given the content, it might not be appropriate. In the hard sciences, for example, a lot of writing is very technical, and specific formats must be followed.

There is no formula to help you decide whether or not to use figurative language, but it helps to think about your audience, to consider the context in which you are writing, and even to see what other writing for that audience in that context looks like.

13.7 Tutorial

Using a Dictionary to Understand Words

Writers sometimes find themselves unsure about a word they are thinking about using. One solution to this hesitation is to look the word up in a print dictionary or an online one, such as **dictionary.com** or **merriam-webster.com**. The entries there can help you with spelling, determining the word's part of speech, pronunciation, meaning(s), word origin, and usage. For many words, the dictionary will also suggest synonyms, words with similar meanings that might even more precisely express what you want to say. In an online dictionary, if you click on each of the listed synonyms, you will be taken to a definition of that word, making it easier to decide which word best fits the meaning you are trying to express.

   Below is an annotated sample entry from *The American Heritage Dictionary of the English Language* for the word *periodic*.

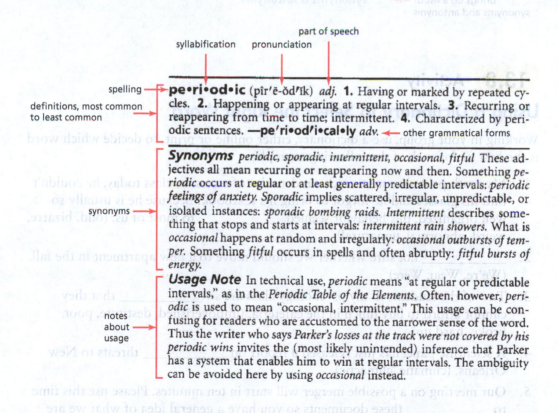

syllabification   pronunciation

part of speech

spelling →

pe•ri•od•ic (pîr′ē-ŏd′ĭk) *adj.* **1.** Having or marked by repeated cy-

definitions, most common to least common →

cles. **2.** Happening or appearing at regular intervals. **3.** Recurring or reappearing from time to time; intermittent. **4.** Characterized by periodic sentences. **—pe′ri•od′i•cal•ly** *adv.* ← other grammatical forms

synonyms →

Synonyms *periodic, sporadic, intermittent, occasional, fitful* These adjectives all mean recurring or reappearing now and then. Something *periodic* occurs at regular or at least generally predictable intervals: *periodic feelings of anxiety. Sporadic* implies scattered, irregular, unpredictable, or isolated instances: *sporadic bombing raids. Intermittent* describes something that stops and starts at intervals: *intermittent rain showers.* What is *occasional* happens at random and irregularly: *occasional outbursts of temper.* Something *fitful* occurs in spells and often abruptly: *fitful bursts of energy.*

notes about usage →

Usage Note In technical use, *periodic* means "at regular or predictable intervals," as in the *Periodic Table of the Elements.* Often, however, *periodic* is used to mean "occasional, intermittent." This usage can be confusing for readers who are accustomed to the narrower sense of the word. Thus the writer who says *Parker's losses at the track were not covered by his periodic wins* invites the (most likely unintended) inference that Parker has a system that enables him to win at regular intervals. The ambiguity can be avoided here by using *occasional* instead.

On the next page is a definition from the *Merriam-Webster Online Dictionary.*

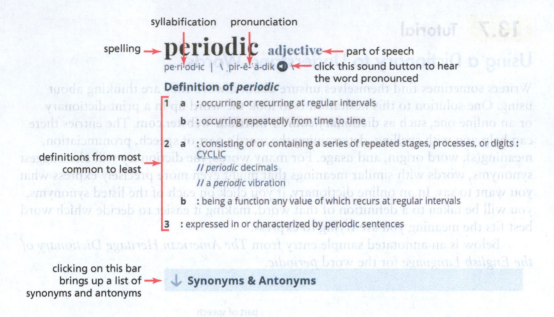

syllabification   pronunciation

spelling → **periodic** **adjective** ← part of speech

pe·ri·od·ic | \ ˌpir-ē-ˈä-dik 🔊 ← click this sound button to hear the word pronounced

Definition of *periodic*

1 **a** : occurring or recurring at regular intervals

    b : occurring repeatedly from time to time

2 **a** : consisting of or containing a series of repeated stages, processes, or digits : CYCLIC

definitions from most common to least →

    // periodic decimals

    // a periodic vibration

    b : being a function any value of which recurs at regular intervals

3 : expressed in or characterized by periodic sentences

clicking on this bar brings up a list of synonyms and antonyms →

↓ **Synonyms & Antonyms**

13.8 Activity

Using a Dictionary to Select the Right Word

Working in your group, use a dictionary, either online or print, to decide which word is the best fit for each of the following examples.

1. My math professor seems to be under a lot of stress. In class today, he couldn't find his glasses and he forgot to bring his textbook. Because he is usually so well organized, this behavior seemed _____ to most of us. (odd, bizarre, weird, abnormal, unnatural)

2. _____ not sure whether we should move to a new apartment in the fall. (We're, Wear, Were)

3. Two of the students in my psychology class are so _____ that they cannot afford to buy lunch in the cafeteria. (impoverished, destitute, poor, broke, hard up)

4. A scientific panel has just released a report on _____ threats to New Orleans. (climatic, climactic)

5. Our meeting on a possible merger will start in ten minutes. Please use this time to _____ these documents so you have a general idea of what we are proposing. (read, skim, peruse, study, review)

6. When you are ready for your interview, simply _____ down the hall to the conference room. (proceed, precede)

7. As soon as I met my fiancé's father, I realized that he was _____. (moneyed, rich, affluent, loaded)

8. The three young boys _____ asked their grandmother if they could have a glass of milk. (respectively, respectfully)

9. I am hoping that the new windows we had installed will _____ our problem with high heating bills. (ameliorate, mollify, solve, reduce)

10. Since my sister has been studying public speaking, she has become much more _____ than she used to be. (verbose, articulate, wordy, garrulous)

13.9 Activity

Determining the Meanings of Confusing Words

This is an activity for you to work on individually, not in a group. When you've finished, you'll have a list of the words that you have found confusing with their correct meanings. Take your time with this activity; do just a few each day.

Listed below are groups of words that some writers confuse. First, read through the list and cross out the words you are sure you know. Then go to work on the remaining words. Look them up in a print dictionary or an online one, and write an explanation of the differences in meaning next to each group. You'll notice there are a few words that are already crossed out. These are not words in formal English, so you should not use them when you want to be formally correct.

accept	except	_____
adapt	adopt	_____
adverse	averse	_____
advise	advice	_____
affect	effect	_____
aggravate	annoy	_____
agree to	agree with	_____
all right	~~alright~~	_____
all together	altogether	_____
allusion	illusion	_____
a lot	~~alot~~	_____

already	all ready	
among	between	
amoral	immoral	
amount	number	
angry at	angry with	
ante-	anti-	
anxious	eager	
anyone	any one	
assure	ensure	insure
awhile	a while	
beside	besides	
between	among	
bring	take	
capital	capitol	
censor	censure	
cite	site	sight
climatic	climactic	
coarse	course	
compare to	compare with	
complement	compliment	
conscience	conscious	
continual	continuous	
could have	~~could of~~	
couldn't care less	~~could care less~~	
council	counsel	
desert	dessert	
different from	different than	
disinterested	uninterested	
elicit	illicit	
emigrate	immigrate	
eminent	imminent	
everyone	every one	

explicit	implicit	_____
farther	further	_____
fewer	less	_____
hanged	hung	_____
hopefully	hopeful	_____
imply	infer	_____
in	into	_____
its	it's	_____
lie	lay	_____
passed	past	_____
precede	proceed	_____
principal	principle	_____
quotation	quote	_____
raise	rise	_____
respectfully	respectively	_____
sensual	sensuous	_____
sit	set	_____
sometime	some time	sometimes _____
supposed to	suppose to	_____
their	there	they're _____
then	than	_____
to	too	two _____
try to	try and	_____
used to	use to	_____
wear	we're	where _____
weather	whether	_____
whose	who's	_____
would have	would of	_____
your	you're	_____

TOPIC 14
Thinking While Writing

Very often, the difference between mediocre writing and excellent writing is the quality of the *thinking* that went into the writing. In this Topic you will explore strategies to make your writing more effective by thinking more broadly and deeply about your subject and thesis.

Navigating Topic 14

The tutorials and presentations listed below provide information about strategies for thinking while writing, and each contains, or is followed by, an opportunity to apply the skills you have just learned. You can work through the entire Topic on your own, learning about all the strategies and practicing them; work on items you've been assigned by your instructor; or choose just the ones you find helpful.

Introduction to Thinking While Writing 93

14.1	**Writing**	One Interesting Thing about You 93
14.2	**Activity**	Class Discussion on Interesting Writing 93
14.3	**Tutorial**	Avoid Proving the Obvious 94
14.4	**Tutorial**	Use Thinking to Find an Interesting Thesis 94
14.5	**Writing**	Who Should Get Reserved Parking? 96
14.6	**Activity**	Thinking about Reserved Parking 96
14.7	**Presentation**	Thinking about Alex's Paper 97
14.8	**Presentation**	Thinking Deeply 98
14.9	**Presentation**	Thinking Broadly 98
14.10	**Writing**	Revising Your Reserved Parking Paper 98

Introduction to Thinking While Writing

This Topic begins by asking you to write a short paper about something interesting about you, and then, in groups, you will look at the papers you and your classmates wrote to see what makes some of the papers more interesting than others. Next, there is advice about how to make your writing more interesting by avoiding obvious topics and thinking carefully about your subject, which is followed by writing assignments related to campus parking. Three narrated presentations demonstrate strategies for thinking deeply and thinking broadly, after which you have the option to revise your essay based on what you've learned.

14.1 Writing

One Interesting Thing about You

Write a one-page essay on one interesting thing about the kind of person you are. Your instructor is the audience for this assignment. He or she will be reading these papers to get to know each of you in the class but also to begin a discussion of how to make your writing more effective. Remember this essay should be around one page long; don't take on too much. Please provide concrete examples to back up what you write about yourself.

14.2 Activity

Class Discussion on Interesting Writing

For this activity, you are going to make use of the papers you and your classmates wrote for the writing activity One Interesting Thing about You (14.1), which asked you to write about one interesting thing about the kind of person you are.

Your instructor will make a numbered list of all the thesis statements in your papers and will organize the class into groups, giving each group a copy of the list. Each group's task is to read over these statements and select the five that seem most likely to produce *interesting* papers. Remember that the assignment was to write about "one *interesting* thing about the kind of person you are."

Study the five you select and attempt to come up with some ideas about what makes a thesis statement interesting. Groups will report out after about twenty minutes.

14.3 Tutorial

Avoid Proving the Obvious

An effective essay argues something interesting and thoughtful. It does not argue something everyone already agrees with. Essays that are written to prove statements like the following are unlikely to be either interesting or thoughtful.

- Drunk driving is a terrible thing.
- Communication is important to a good relationship.
- Child abuse should not be tolerated.
- We should not tolerate racism.
- America must protect itself against terrorism.

Each of these statements is true, but none of them is likely to result in a very good essay. Why not? Because almost everyone already agrees with these statements. They belabor the obvious. They argue a point that is not arguable because almost no one disagrees with them.

To avoid wasting your time making an argument that most people would already agree with, you might want to try this trick. Picture yourself standing in front of your class, reading your thesis out loud and then asking whether anyone disagrees. If you cannot picture more than one or two hands being raised, then you need to find a more interesting thesis.

14.4 Tutorial

Use Thinking to Find an Interesting Thesis

Here are two examples showing how two students have thought their way to a thesis that isn't obvious, that makes a point that everyone doesn't already agree with, and that shows they've really given some thought to their topic. In each of these examples, the basic strategy is the same: simply thinking harder about the topic.

Example 1: Thinking about Helping Children "Get Ahead"

In a sociology class, students were asked to write about some aspect of "parenting." Charlene, a single mother with two young daughters, Carrie and Angel, decided on a draft thesis that it is important for parents to do everything they can to help their children "get ahead." She wanted her daughters' lives to be more comfortable and more successful than hers. She wanted to give them "every advantage" so they wouldn't be "left behind."

Charlene started writing about how she bought books and a computer for Carrie and Angel; enrolled them in a preschool program that she could barely afford; and, when her daughters were old enough for elementary school, moved to a neighborhood in her city that was known for the quality of its schools even though she had to take a second job in order to afford the rent.

As she thought she was almost finished with her essay, she saw a news report on television that bothered her greatly—a report that many wealthy parents had spent millions of dollars to hire a company that would get their children into highly competitive universities. This company bribed athletic coaches to write letters about the children's athletic ability when they had not actually participated in any sports. The company also had contacts inside testing companies that allowed them to alter the children's scores on various tests. They even hired people to take college placement tests for the children.

Charlene was shocked. She knew these parents thought they were simply doing everything they could to help their children "get ahead," but they had clearly gone too far. Charlene began to rethink her essay. While she still thought parents should try to help their children "get ahead," she now recognized that there were also dangers to this approach.

The admissions cheating scandal she had seen on the news illustrated one danger, but Charlene wondered if there were others. She thought about parents she knew who were so eager to help their children that they did their children's homework for them. She thought about a friend of hers who was so determined that her son would get straight A's that she wouldn't allow him to try out for the school play because it would take too much time away from his school work. She thought about parents who put so much pressure on their children that they developed stress-related psychological problems.

After all this thinking, Charlene had arrived at a much more thoughtful and interesting thesis: while it is important for parents to help their children be successful, it is also important to avoid the dangers that can arise when this parenting approach goes too far.

Example 2: Thinking about Drunk Driving

In a criminal justice class, students were asked to write about a current criminal justice issue. One student wrote a wonderful paper about drunk driving that didn't just belabor the obvious. He argued that, while drunk driving is certainly a problem, we are placing all our attention on preventing drunk driving when more people in America are killed each year as a result of speeding. He reported that in 2011, 9,878

Americans died as a result of drunk driving, while 10,001 died in accidents caused by speeding. He wasn't arguing that drunk driving isn't a major problem; he was arguing that speeding is a slightly larger problem that people do not appear to be as upset about. There are no Mothers Against Speeding organizations. No one is tying ribbons on their door handles to protest speeding.

Each of the essays discussed above became more effective when the writer found something interesting and thoughtful to say after thinking more deeply about the topic.

One Word of Caution. Sometimes when students are told to write something that is not obvious, something that everyone doesn't already agree with, they go to the opposite extreme. They write a paper with a thesis that no one could ever agree with and that they have no chance of proving in any reasonable way: "Unicorns really do exist" or "The president is a literal zombie." This kind of farfetched thesis is not what is being suggested here. Instead, you are simply being asked to write a paper that argues something that is not obvious, something that results from doing some real thinking about your topic.

14.5 Writing

Who Should Get Reserved Parking?

Write a short paper, about a page, in which you propose who should get reserved parking spaces at your college or university. Be sure to provide evidence to support your assertions. The audience for this assignment is other students in your class.

14.6 Activity

Thinking about Reserved Parking

The writing assignment for Who Should Get Reserved Parking? (14.5) asked you to do the following.

> Write a short paper, about a page, in which you propose who should get reserved parking spaces at your college or university. Be sure to provide evidence to support your assertions. The audience for this assignment is other students in your class.

Here is what one student, Alex, wrote in response to this assignment:

At this time of year, it is terribly difficult to find a parking place at the college. Several times I have been late to class because I've been driving around looking for a place to park. It would be great to have a reserved parking place, but after discussing this with several of my classmates and thinking about it for a long time, I have decided that the college should provide reserved parking places to the disabled, the faculty, and the college president.

The disabled deserve reserved parking because their lives are hard enough as it is. If disabled students have the courage to attend college, we should do everything possible to make their lives easier. Some disabled students simply could not make it to class if they had to park in the distant lots and make their way in a wheelchair. This should be the highest priority for reserved parking.

If the faculty were not here, there wouldn't be a college. They play the most important role at the college. They teach the classes. If a faculty member doesn't make it to class, then twenty or thirty students suffer. This is why I think faculty should have reserved parking places.

Being the president of a college is a very prestigious position. I know our president worked for more than thirty years before she was promoted to president. If someone has worked his or her way to this position, we should recognize that accomplishment by providing reserved parking.

In conclusion, reserved parking at this college should be given to the disabled, faculty, and the president.

In groups, discuss Alex's paper. What do you think of the *thinking* that went into this essay? Do you think the writer of this paper would want people who work for buildings and grounds to have reserved parking? Why do you think the writer didn't include them? After about ten minutes, the groups will report out.

14.7 Presentation

Thinking about Alex's Paper

To watch this presentation that discusses the thinking that went into Alex's paper in Thinking about Reserved Parking (14.6, p. 410), go to *Achieve for The Hub*, Topic 14, and open Unit 14.7.

14.8 Presentation

Thinking Deeply

To watch this presentation that discusses the deeper thinking that could go into Alex's paper in Thinking about Reserved Parking (14.6, p. 96), go to *Achieve for The Hub*, Topic 14, and open Unit 14.8.

14.9 Presentation

Thinking Broadly

To watch this presentation that discusses the broader thinking that could go into Alex's paper in Thinking about Reserved Parking (14.6, p. 96), go to *Achieve for The Hub*, Topic 14, and open Unit 14.9.

14.10 Writing

Revising Your Reserved Parking Paper

In Who Should Get Reserved Parking? (14.5, p. 96), you wrote a short paper proposing who should get reserved parking spaces at your college. For this assignment, you are going to revise that paper based on what you've learned about thinking deeply and broadly.

TOPIC 15

Revising

B ecause effective revision is so important and takes time, be sure you schedule enough time for a rigorous review once you finish drafting a paper or other piece of writing.

Navigating Topic 15

The tutorials listed below provide information about strategies for revising. You can work through the entire Topic on your own, learning about all the strategies and practicing them; work on items you've been assigned by your instructor; or choose just the ones you find helpful.

Introduction to Revising 100

15.1	Tutorial	Revision Basics 100
15.2	Tutorial	Revising for Assignment, Audience, and Purpose 101
15.3	Tutorial	Backward Outlining 101
15.4	Tutorial	Revising for Thesis and Unity 105
15.5	Tutorial	Revising for Organization 107
15.6	Tutorial	Revising for Support 109
15.7	Tutorial	Revising for Coherence 114
15.8	Activity	Backward Outlining Applied 118
15.9	Tutorial	Reviewing Options for What to Include in an Essay 118
15.10	Tutorial	A Revision Checklist 120

Introduction to Revising

For most writers, revising begins almost as soon they start writing. They are constantly rereading and making changes as they go, but once they have a complete draft, they do a major revision. Revising is what turns average writing into excellent writing. It involves taking a hard look at every element of an essay from the thesis and introduction to the organization of ideas, types of support, and concluding words. Although some revising goes on throughout the process of writing, the most important revision work takes place after a draft has been completed.

Topic 15 provides information about and strategies for revising for audience, purpose, assignment, thesis, unity, support, organization, and coherence. It also discusses using backward outlining as a revision strategy, and it concludes with suggestions for how to make an essay more interesting, along with a revision checklist.

15.1 Tutorial

Revision Basics

When you are ready to revise, you want to be able to stand back from what you've written and view it objectively. Often it is easier to do this if you let some time pass between when you finish a draft and when you start revising it, ideally at least a day or two. However, if you finish your draft late the night before it's due, go to bed and revise it in the morning when you're fresh. If you don't have even that much time, at least get up and have a cup of coffee or take a walk around the block before you start revising. The important thing is to give yourself enough time to switch roles from being the writer of the draft to being an objective reader who can find ways to improve it.

Before you begin revising, it's always a good idea to get some feedback from others. Sometimes your instructor will schedule class time for peer review, a process that allows students to receive feedback on a draft from other students (see Peer Review [8.4, p. 8] for details). Even if no peer review sessions are planned, ask a friend, a brother or sister, or even another student in your class to read over your paper and let you know what works and what could use some improvement.

It's also important to recognize the difference between revision and editing. *Revision* is when you to look at the big issues in what you have written. Does it have a clear thesis? Is it unified? Does it provide enough evidence to support the points it makes? Is it organized effectively? *Editing* is when you look at the sentence-level issues like grammar, punctuation, spelling, and word choice. These are two different activities, and it is best not to try to do them both at the same time. Revise first, and when that is finished, you can more effectively edit for correctness (for more details, see Topic 16: Editing [p. 121]).

Some writers prefer to print out a copy of their draft and revise by marking up that copy and later transferring the changes to the draft on the computer. Others prefer to do their revising directly on the computer. Use whichever approach works best for you.

15.2 Tutorial

Revising for Assignment, Audience, and Purpose

When you are ready to start revising, it's a good idea to read your draft over quickly to refresh your sense of the essay as a whole and then to ask yourself these questions.

1. **What was the assignment your instructor gave for this essay?** What exactly were you asked to do? Does your essay include everything the assignment calls for? Is it the right length? (For more details, see Reading an Assignment [9.1, p. 12].)

2. **Who is the audience for this essay?** Is there more than one? What do they already know? How technical can, or should, you be? Are they likely to agree or disagree with you? Have you written in a style, with a voice, that is appropriate for that audience? (For more details, see Thinking about Audience [9.4, p. 14].)

3. **What is your purpose for writing this essay?** Is it to persuade, explain, express feelings or thoughts, or entertain? Is your purpose to request something, to recommend something, to reassure the audience, or to summarize something? Does the draft you have written really address that purpose? (For more details, see Thinking about Purpose [9.6, p. 17].)

15.3 Tutorial

Backward Outlining

Below is a draft of an essay that will be used throughout this Topic to illustrate the revision process. On the right is a backward outline of the essay. To create the backward outline, the writer simply read each paragraph and jotted down a brief summation of the main point in that paragraph. In this example, these brief statements of each paragraph's main point are displayed to the right of the essay itself. Most writers actually write these statements on a separate sheet of paper or in a separate Word document.

A backward outline like this can be used to improve thesis and unity (see Revising for Thesis and Unity [15.4, p. 105]), ensure logical organization (see Revising for Organization [15.5, p. 107]), and ensure sufficient and appropriate support (see Revising for Support [15.6, p. 109]).

Hard Work and Getting Ahead

1   It has often been said that "in America, if you work hard you will get ahead." This idea is what most people mean by the American Dream. I disagree with this idea. Before I disagree, however, it's probably a good idea to pin down exactly what it is I am disagreeing with.

1. Background

2   When people express this belief in getting ahead in America, I don't think they believe that *everyone* who works hard gets ahead. Surely, they recognize that some people work very hard and, nevertheless, end up living out their lives in grinding poverty. Also, I don't think they believe that everyone who gets ahead worked hard. Surely, they also recognize that some people inherit a fortune or win the lottery and do not need to work much at all. So, I am assuming that advocates of the "hard-work-equals-getting-ahead philosophy" really mean that, even if it isn't true for everyone, it is *generally* true—true for most people. This is what I disagree with. I believe that most Americans, even if they work hard, will not get ahead. I don't believe that the American Dream really exists for most Americans.

2. Introduction with thesis: most Americans, even if they work hard, will not get ahead

3   Young people who grow up in poverty usually don't have the kinds of connections that help them get a good job. Their parents, too often, do not have the kinds of jobs in large corporations or offices where they can help their kids meet people who might hire them. Furthermore, they seldom have older brothers

3. Lack of contacts and familiarity with business behavior

or sisters who can introduce them to people who can give them advice about how to move up in the world. Sometimes, when they do get a job interview at a place where they have a chance of advancement, they are simply unfamiliar with the protocol for such meetings.

4   Another important reason many Americans can't work their way out of poverty, can't achieve the American Dream, is our unequal education system. Funding for schools is based on property taxes paid in each local school district. School systems located in poorer areas are underfunded because the property in that area is of much lower value than property in wealthy suburbs. As a result, funding for schools in poorer neighborhoods will be much less than funding for schools in rich neighborhoods. Bruce Biddle and David Berliner, writing for the Association for Supervision and Curriculum Development website, point out that "a few students from wealthy communities or neighborhoods within generous states attend public schools with funding of $15,000 or more per student per year, whereas some students from poor communities or neighborhoods within stingy or impoverished states attend schools that must make do with less than $4,000 per student per year." Lower funding leads to school buildings that are often dilapidated, textbooks in short supply, and teachers who are paid lower salaries than their counterparts in wealthier areas. In many cases, the most effective teachers in poor schools leave after a few years for the higher salaries in wealthy schools. Things then become even more unequal. Those who went to the better schools do much better on tests and get into the better colleges and universities. The kids from the poor schools are lucky if they get into a regional state university.

4. Funding for our education system favors kids from wealthy families

5   To be fair, however, even though many students from truly wealthy families are sent to private schools where they have beautiful surroundings, the best teachers, small class sizes, and lots of guidance and counseling, they have problems, too. Lots of these kids have grown up in families that put a lot of pressure on them to succeed, so they experience significant stress and frequently have many psychological problems. Depression, bipolar syndrome, and even suicide are common among these students.

5. Wealthy kids go to private schools but feel a lot of stress

6   The belief that all it takes to "get ahead" is hard work results in people thinking that if they haven't gotten ahead, it's their fault. They didn't work hard enough. In fact, there are many causes why, despite hard work, many don't get ahead—an education system that doesn't treat them fairly, the struggle to find the right balance of time and money, a personal crisis, or a personal mistake. It takes more than hard work to get ahead in America. It takes luck or being born into a middle-class family.

6. Belief that hard work = getting ahead leads those born in poverty to blame themselves and not work to change the system

7   I want to be clear about what I mean by "hard work" and "getting ahead." Working hard doesn't have to involve physical labor. In this essay, when I talk about hard work, I mean working as many hours per week as is physically possible, sometimes even at two full-time jobs. It also means that the hard worker works hard at his or her job. They don't goof off, they don't take a lot of breaks, and they seldom call in sick. I also want to clarify what I mean when I talk about "getting ahead." You don't have to be very rich to have gotten ahead. What I mean by getting ahead is doing a little better than your parents did—making a higher salary, living in a nicer house, and having a better education.

7. Defining terms: hard work and getting ahead

8 Sometimes these young people give up on college and decide just to try to make it in the workplace. Starting in jobs that don't require a college education, they find, no matter how hard they work, that they just can't get a promotion. Often they work more and more hours—60 or 70 a week—and they are barely keeping themselves above water.

9 Finally, sometimes young people's chances of "getting ahead" are eliminated because they make a mistake. Seeing how impossible it is to succeed, despite hard work, they decide to try to beat the system by doing something illegal. They steal something, start dealing drugs, get mixed up with a gang, or get hooked on drugs themselves. Suddenly, all their hopes of getting ahead have evaporated.

10 The idea that in America if you work hard, you'll get ahead is both untruthful and harmful. It is untruthful because it ignores the many societal conditions that make it unlikely that people born into poverty will be able to get ahead, and it is harmful because it encourages people to think that if they haven't gotten ahead, it's their own fault and, therefore, they should not question an inequitable system.

8. Many who attempt college give up and then discover they will never make a decent living in the jobs available to non-college grads

9. Some young people make a mistake that gets them in trouble and makes it difficult to get hired in a decent job

10. Conclusion: the idea that in America, if you work hard, you will get ahead, is both untrue and harmful

15.4 Tutorial
Revising for Thesis and Unity

One of the most important revision steps is checking to see whether your draft essay has a clear thesis, whether the thesis at the end of the essay is the same as it was at the beginning—of course, expressed in different words—and whether everything in the paper supports that thesis. (For more details, see Thesis Statements [10.5, p. 32] and Unity [12.1, p. 63].)

Using a Backward Outline to Check on Thesis and Unity

This is the backward outline created in Unit 15.3 (p. 101), which lists the main points in the essay paragraph by paragraph. The two versions of the thesis are underlined.

1. background

2. intro with thesis: <u>most Americans, even if they work hard, will not get ahead</u>

3. lack of contacts and familiarity with business behavior

4. funding for our education system favors kids from wealthy families

5. wealthy kids go to private schools but feel a lot of stress

6. belief that hard work = getting ahead leads those born in poverty to blame themselves and not work to change the system

7. defining terms: hard work and getting ahead

8. many who attempt college give up and then discover they will never make a decent living in the jobs available to non-college grads

9. some young people make a mistake that gets them in trouble and makes it difficult to get hired in a decent job

10. conclusion with restated thesis: <u>the idea that in America, if you work hard, you will get ahead is both untrue and harmful</u>

A backward outline like this makes it easy to check for thesis and unity. The thesis appears in the second paragraph: "most Americans, even if they work hard, will not get ahead." But in the concluding paragraph (10), the thesis is stated this way: "the idea that in America, if you work hard, you will get ahead is both untrue and harmful." In the process of writing the paper, the author came up with an idea that wasn't there when she wrote the second paragraph, so the restated thesis in paragraph 10 adds the idea that the belief that working hard will lead to success is actually harmful.

To ensure that the paper has a single clear thesis, the writer needs to either revise the thesis statement in paragraph 2 or the one in paragraph 10. If the writer changes paragraph 10 by deleting the assertion that the belief that working hard will lead to success causes harm (and perhaps eliminates paragraph 8, which supports that idea), the paper would be unified around a single thesis. However, the idea about "harm" is the most original idea in the essay, so the paper will be stronger if the writer leaves paragraph 10 as it is and inserts the idea of the harm done by that belief to the thesis in paragraph 2. In addition, the writer will need to add more support to paragraph 8, providing evidence that this "harm" really occurs, perhaps even adding two or three new paragraphs.

When the thesis at the end of a draft of an essay is different from the thesis at the beginning, it's usually the result of the writer having done some thinking. In the process of writing the draft, thinking about the topic, and finding evidence, it is not unusual for a writer to end up with a thesis that differs from the original one. Because this difference results from *thinking* about the topic, the thesis at the end, as in this essay on getting ahead, is usually more thoughtful than the one the writer started with, in which case changing the original thesis to agree with the final one is the preferred option.

Now take a look at item 5 in the backward outline above: "wealthy kids go to private schools but feel a lot of stress." The writer, maybe because she has friends at private schools or has read about the issue, included the idea that kids from rich families are under a lot of psychological stress. But it doesn't belong in this paper: this is a paper arguing that it's not true that hard work will lead to "getting ahead," so the paragraph is not relevant and should be deleted.

If you think it will work for you, use backward outlining to help you find and revise problems with thesis and unity. Even if you decide not to use this method when revising, you will still need to make sure your draft essay has a single clear thesis and that everything in the essay supports that thesis.

15.5 Tutorial

Revising for Organization

The tutorial on backward outlining in Unit 15.3 (p. 101) ended with an outline of a draft essay. In Unit 15.4 (p. 105) that outline was modified to eliminate problems with thesis and unity. Below is the backward outline after those revisions were made.

1. background

2. intro with thesis: the belief that most Americans, if they work hard, will get ahead is untrue and even harmful

3. lack of contacts and familiarity with business behavior

4. funding for our education system favors kids from wealthy families

5. ~~wealthy kids go to private schools but feel a lot of stress~~

6. belief that hard work = getting ahead leads those born in poverty to blame themselves and not work to change the system

7. defining terms: hard work and getting ahead

8. many who attempt college give up and then discover they will never make a decent living in the jobs available to non-college grads

9. some young people make a mistake that gets them in trouble and makes it difficult to get hired in a decent job

10. conclusion: the idea that in America, if you work hard, you will get ahead is both untrue and harmful

Now it is time to look at these items and see if there is a way of ordering them that will make the argument easier for the reader to follow. The first thing you might notice is item 7, a paragraph that defines the key terms *hard work* and *getting ahead*. It's a good idea to make sure the reader will understand what the writer means by these terms, but why wait until the seventh paragraph to define them? Moving them up to be closer to the introductory material so they become the third item seems advisable.

In the revised outline below, the definition paragraph that was item 7 has been moved to item 3. Now, paragraphs 1, 2, and 3 are in the right place as introductory material, and paragraph 9, the conclusion, is where it belongs. But what about paragraphs 4 through 8? Are they in the most effective order? Actually, they don't seem to be in any particular order at all. The writer could try arranging them from most important to least, but it's difficult to decide which is most or least important, so chronological order seems like it would work better. Organizing the paragraphs in terms of *when* what they describe would affect an individual—moving from those things that happen to children, to those that impact college students, and finally to those that affect people in the workplace—makes sense. That's what the following revised outline does.

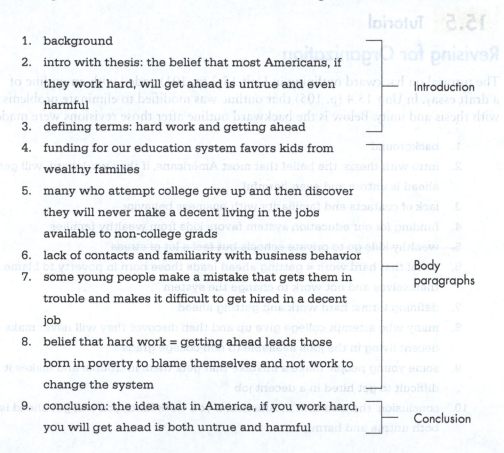

1. background

2. intro with thesis: the belief that most Americans, if they work hard, will get ahead is untrue and even harmful   — Introduction

3. defining terms: hard work and getting ahead

4. funding for our education system favors kids from wealthy families

5. many who attempt college give up and then discover they will never make a decent living in the jobs available to non-college grads

6. lack of contacts and familiarity with business behavior

7. some young people make a mistake that gets them in trouble and makes it difficult to get hired in a decent job   — Body paragraphs

8. belief that hard work = getting ahead leads those born in poverty to blame themselves and not work to change the system

9. conclusion: the idea that in America, if you work hard, you will get ahead is both untrue and harmful   — Conclusion

Now the body paragraphs are in a logical order. Although paragraph 8 has no logical position in the chronological ordering, it is really interesting. Its assertion that the belief that everyone who works hard will get ahead is actually harmful is a thoughtful idea, but it doesn't fit in the chronological order of the other body paragraphs, so putting it last—just before the conclusion—seems like a good solution.

That's how you can use backward outlining to revise the organization of an essay.

15.6 Tutorial

Revising for Support

The tutorial on backward outlining in Unit 15.3 (p. 101) ended with an outline of a draft essay. In Unit 15.4 (p. 105) that outline was modified to eliminate problems with thesis and unity, and in Unit 15.5 (p. 107), it was reorganized to make the writer's argument easier to follow. Below is the backward outline after those revisions were made. In addition, the writer has made notes (in blue handwriting) of places where she will need more evidence to support her assertions.

1. background
2. intro with thesis: the belief that most Americans, if they work hard, will get ahead is untrue and even harmful — Introduction
3. defining terms: hard work and getting ahead
4. funding for our education system favors kids from wealthy families *Lots of evidence for this point, so I could add some more.*
5. many who attempt college give up and then discover they will never make a decent living in the jobs available to non-college grads *Here I have a little evidence. I should add my brother's experience or my friend Josie's. Perhaps I can find some actual statistics about this.* — Body paragraphs
6. lack of contacts and familiarity with business behavior *In this paragraph, I state very general opinions with little evidence to back them up. Need more development here.*

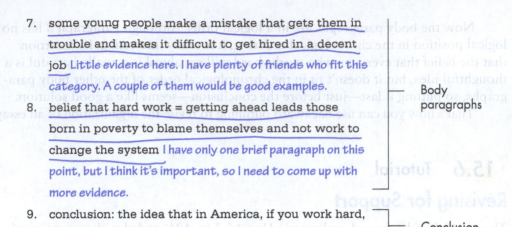

7. some young people make a mistake that gets them in trouble and makes it difficult to get hired in a decent job *Little evidence here. I have plenty of friends who fit this category. A couple of them would be good examples.*

8. belief that hard work = getting ahead leads those born in poverty to blame themselves and not work to change the system *I have only one brief paragraph on this point, but I think it's important, so I need to come up with more evidence.*

9. conclusion: the idea that in America, if you work hard, you will get ahead is both untrue and harmful

Body paragraphs

Conclusion

Topic 11: Developing Ideas (p. 41) discussed different approaches for providing support to back up the opinions you express in an essay with facts, expert opinion, examples, and narratives. When revising, you need to read your draft essay carefully, identifying each place you assert an opinion and asking yourself whether you could provide more evidence to support that opinion.

The underlined items in the outline above are all assertions of the writer's opinions. That's not a problem; making an argument always involves expressing the writer's opinions. However, it would be a problem if any of these opinions appear in the essay without adequate support or evidence. At this point, the writer, having identified the five opinions she asserted in the essay, evaluated the evidence she had provided to support each of them and made notes about where she needed to add more support and what that might consist of. She then revised her essay, as shown below. The new support she added is underlined. Note that the author has included in-text citations for the sources she has added and provided a works cited list at the end of her essay.

Hard Work and Getting Ahead

1 It has often been said that "in America, if you work hard you will get ahead." This idea is what most people mean by the American Dream. I disagree with this idea. Before I disagree, however, it's probably a good idea to pin down exactly what it is I am disagreeing with.

2 When people express this belief in getting ahead in America, I don't think they believe that *everyone* who works hard gets ahead. Surely, they recognize that some people work very hard and, nevertheless, end up living out their lives in grinding poverty. Also, I don't think they believe that everyone who gets ahead worked hard.

Surely, they also recognize that some people inherit a fortune or win the lottery and do not need to work much at all. So, I am assuming that advocates of the "hard-work-equals-getting-ahead philosophy" really mean that, even if it isn't true for everyone, it is *generally* true—true for most people. This is what I disagree with. I believe that most Americans, even if they work hard, will not get ahead. I don't believe that the American Dream really exists for most Americans.

3   Before going any further, I want to be clear about what I mean by "hard work" and "getting ahead." Working hard doesn't have to involve physical labor. In this essay, when I talk about hard work, I mean working as many hours per week as is physically possible, sometimes even at two full-time jobs. It also means that the hard worker works hard at his or her job. They don't goof off, they don't take a lot of breaks, and they seldom call in sick. I also want to clarify what I mean when I talk about "getting ahead." You don't have to be very rich to have gotten ahead. What I mean by getting ahead is doing a little better than your parents did—making a higher salary, living in a nicer house, and having a better education.

4   Another important reason many Americans can't work their way out of poverty, can't achieve the American Dream, is our unequal education system. Funding for schools is based on property taxes paid in each local school district. School systems located in poorer areas are underfunded because the property in that area is of much lower value than property in wealthy suburbs. As a result, funding for schools in poorer neighborhoods will be much less than funding for schools in rich neighborhoods. Bruce Biddle and David Berliner, writing for the ASCD (Association for Supervision and Curriculum Development) website, point out that "a few students from wealthy communities or neighborhoods within generous states attend public schools with funding of $15,000 or more per student per year, whereas some students from poor communities or neighborhoods within stingy or impoverished states attend schools that must make do with less than $4,000 per student per year." Lower funding leads to school buildings that are often dilapidated, textbooks in short supply, and teachers who are paid lower salaries than their counterparts in wealthier areas. In many cases, the most effective teachers in poor schools leave after a few years for the higher salaries in wealthy schools. Sean Reardon at Stanford University, in "School District Socioeconomic Status, Race, and Academic Achievement," has concluded that "the variation in academic achievement among school districts is very large; students in some districts have scores more than 4 grade levels higher than others." Further, Reardon concludes, "This variation is

very highly correlated with the socioeconomic characteristics of families in the local community" (12). Things then become even more unequal. Those who went to the better schools do much better on tests and get into the better colleges and universities. The kids from the poor schools are lucky if they get into a regional state university.

5   Sometimes these young people give up on college and decide just to try to make it in the workplace. In fact, the *Washington Post* reports that more than half of students who start college drop out within six years (Salingo). Starting in jobs that don't require a college education, they find, no matter how hard they work, that they just can't get a promotion. Often they work more and more hours—60 or 70 a week—and they are barely keeping themselves above water. For example, my brother Matt gave up the first semester he attended Hightower Community College and went to work full time as a clerk in a Radio Shack. A year later he was still making minimum wage, so he asked for a raise only to be told that he would not get any raises until he completed an AA degree. Having built up $7,000 in credit-card debt, he took a second job driving for Uber. Three years later he's still in debt and working sixty hours a week. For people in my brother's situation, when a crisis hits, they are completely wiped out. If Matt became sick or was laid off by Radio Shack, he would have no choice but to file for bankruptcy. For people like Matt, hard work doesn't pay off.

6   Young people who grow up in poverty usually don't have the kinds of connections that help them get a good job. Their parents, too often, do not have the kinds of jobs in large corporations or offices where they can help their kids meet people who might hire them. My brother Matt and I grew up in a family where both our parents had low-level jobs in a hotel. When Matt started looking for a job, they didn't know anyone who could help him. Furthermore, these young people seldom have older brothers or sisters who can introduce them to people who can give them advice about how to move up in the world. Sometimes, when they do get a job interview at a place where they have a chance of advancement, they are simply unfamiliar with the protocol for such meetings. My friend Josie was invited for a job interview at a large corporation. When she arrived wearing a casual sweater and pair of slacks, she discovered that everyone was wearing business suits and dresses. She never heard again from that corporation.

7   Finally, sometimes young people's chances of "getting ahead" are eliminated because they make a mistake. Seeing how impossible it is to succeed, despite hard work, they decide to try to beat the system by doing something illegal. They steal something, start dealing drugs, get mixed up with a gang, or get hooked on drugs

themselves. My best friend, Althea, was doing well in high school until her junior year. She started dating a guy who was known for dealing drugs. Soon she joined him in the business. A few months later, they were both arrested, and now Althea has a felony on her record, making it unlikely anyone will hire her for a good job. The guy I was dating in my sophomore year was caught shoplifting in his senior year making it unlikely he'll ever reach his goal of going to law school. All it takes is one mistake, and these kids' hopes of getting ahead have evaporated.

8   The belief that all it takes to "get ahead" is hard work results in people thinking that if they haven't gotten ahead, it's their fault. They didn't work hard enough. My father is a perfect example of this. When he was in his thirties and still working cleaning up rooms in a hotel, he gradually began to see himself as a failure. He blamed himself for not having gotten ahead in America. A few years later, when I started college, I tried to get him to take a few classes too. However, he was so convinced he was a failure that he simply couldn't imagine going back to school. In fact, there are many reasons why, despite hard work, many don't get ahead—an education system that doesn't treat them fairly, the struggle to find the right balance of time and money, a personal crisis, or a personal mistake. It takes more than hard work to get ahead in America. It takes luck or being born into a middle-class family.

9   The idea that in America if you work hard, you'll get ahead is both untruthful and harmful. It is untruthful because it ignores the many societal conditions that make it unlikely that people born into poverty will be able to get ahead, and it is harmful because it encourages people to think that if they haven't gotten ahead, it's their own fault and, therefore, they should not question an inequitable system.

(**NOTE:** Always start the works cited list on a new page.)

Works Cited

Reardon, Sean. "School District Socioeconomic Status, Race, and Academic Achievement." Stanford Center for Educational Policy Analysis, Apr. 2016, https://cepa.stanford.edu/sites/default/files/reardon%20district%20ses%20and%20achievement%20discussion%20draft%20april2015.pdf.

Salingo, Jeffrey. "Why Do So Many Students Drop Out of College? And What Can Be Done About It?" *The Washington Post*, 8 June 2018, https://www.washingtonpost.com/news/grade-point/wp/2018/06/08/why-do-so-many-students-drop-out-of-college-and-what-can-be-done-about-it/?utm_term=.b2a90fd8aa04.

Tutorial

Revising for Coherence

Writers provide coherence in their writing in three ways: implementing a logical organization, repeating key words and phrases, and using transitional expressions. (For more details, see Practice Ordering Ideas [12.7, p. 70] and the tutorial Coherence [12.8, p. 70].)

To revise for the use of key words and phrases, you need to identify them in your essay. Below is the essay "Hard Work and Getting Ahead." As you read, it quickly becomes clear that "working hard," "getting ahead," and "American Dream" are key words or phrases. These words and phrases and others that stand in for "hard work" and "getting ahead" are highlighted in blue. Whether you do this highlighting or not (and you could do it with a highlighter on a paper copy of your draft), once you have decided what your key words and phrases are, you need to check to see whether you have used them and other phrases that stand in for them throughout your paper. In the essay below, note that "hard work" and "getting ahead" are repeated throughout the essay, reminding the reader that these are key ideas. However, "American Dream" is used just three times, all in the first four paragraphs. Noticing this, the writer needs to look for places to use "American Dream" more often in paragraphs 5 through 9 so the reader is reminded that "American Dream" is a key concept.

Transitional expressions are like road signs that help readers understand where they are going, what's coming up next, and how the parts of the essay relate to each other. When the writer of this essay circled all the transitional expressions she could find, she was happy to see she had done a good job with this aspect of coherence. However, she also discovered several places where a transitional word or expression needed to be added to help ideas flow smoothly together. These places are underlined.

Hard Work and Getting Ahead

1   It has often been said that "in America, if you work hard you will get ahead." This idea is what most people mean by the American Dream. I disagree with this idea. Before I disagree, however, it's probably a good idea to pin down exactly what it is I am disagreeing with.

2   When people express this belief in getting ahead in America, I don't think they believe that *everyone* who works hard gets ahead. Surely, they recognize that some people work very hard and, nevertheless, end up living out their lives in grinding poverty. Also, I don't think they believe that everyone who gets ahead worked hard. Surely, they also recognize that some people inherit a fortune or win the lottery and

do not need to work much at all. So, I am assuming that advocates of the "hard-work-equals-getting-ahead philosophy" really mean that, even if it isn't true for everyone, it is *generally* true—true for most people. This is what I disagree with. I believe that most Americans, even if they work hard, will not get ahead. I don't believe that the American Dream really exists for most Americans.

3   Before going any further, I want to be clear about what I mean by "hard work" and "getting ahead." Working hard doesn't have to involve physical labor. In this essay, when I talk about hard work, I mean working as many hours per week as is physically possible, sometimes even at two full-time jobs. It also means that the hard worker works hard at his or her job. They don't goof off, they don't take a lot of breaks, and they seldom call in sick. In addition, I want to clarify what I mean when I talk about "getting ahead." You don't have to be very rich to have gotten ahead. What I mean by getting ahead is doing a little better than your parents did—making a higher salary, living in a nicer house, and having a better education.

4   Another important reason many Americans can't work their way out of poverty, can't achieve the American Dream, is our unequal education system. Funding for schools is based on property taxes paid in each local school district. School systems located in poorer areas are underfunded because the property in that area is of much lower value than property in wealthy suburbs. As a result, funding for schools in poorer neighborhoods will be much less than funding for schools in rich neighborhoods. Bruce Biddle and David Berliner, writing for the ASCD (Association for Supervision and Curriculum Development) website, point out that "a few students from wealthy communities or neighborhoods within generous states attend public schools with funding of $15,000 or more per student per year, whereas some students from poor communities or neighborhoods within stingy or impoverished states attend schools that must make do with less than $4,000 per student per year." Lower funding leads to school buildings that are often dilapidated, textbooks in short supply, and teachers who are paid lower salaries than their counterparts in wealthier areas. In many cases, the most effective teachers in poor schools leave after a few years for the higher salaries in wealthy schools. Sean Reardon at Stanford University, in "School District Socioeconomic Status, Race, and Academic Achievement," has concluded that "the variation in academic achievement among school districts is very large; students in some districts have scores more than 4 grade levels higher than

others." Further, Reardon concludes, "This variation is very highly correlated with the socioeconomic characteristics of families in the local community" (12). <u>When it comes time to go to college</u>, things become even more unequal. Those who went to the better schools do much better on tests and get into the better colleges and universities, <u>but</u> the kids from the poor schools are lucky if they get into a regional state university.

5   <u>Making the problem worse</u>, sometimes these young people give up on college and decide just to try to make it in the workplace. (In fact,) the *Washington Post* reports that more than half of students who start college drop out within six years (Salingo). Starting in jobs that don't require a college education, they find, no matter how hard they work, that they just can't get a promotion. Often they work more and more hours—60 or 70 a week—and they are barely keeping themselves above water. (For example,) my brother Matt gave up the first semester he attended Hightower Community College and went to work full time as a clerk in a Radio Shack. (A year later) he was still making minimum wage, (so) he asked for a raise (only) to be told that he would not get any raises until he completed an AA degree. Having built up $7,000 in credit-card debt, he took a second job driving for Uber. (Three years later) he's still in debt and working sixty hours a week. For people in my brother's situation, when a crisis hits, they are completely wiped out. If Matt became sick or was laid off by Radio Shack, he would have no choice but to file for bankruptcy. For people like Matt, hard work doesn't pay off.

6   <u>Another contributing factor in this sad situation is that</u> young people who grow up in poverty usually don't have the kinds of connections that help them get a good job. Their parents, too often, do not have the kinds of jobs in large corporations or offices where they can help their kids meet people who might hire them. My brother Matt and I, <u>for example</u>, grew up in a family where both our parents had low-level jobs in a hotel. When Matt started looking for a job, they didn't know anyone who could help him. Furthermore, these young people seldom have older brothers or sisters who can introduce them to people who can give them advice about how to move up in the world. Sometimes, when they do get a job interview at a place where they have a chance of advancement, they are simply unfamiliar with the protocol for such meetings. My friend Josie, <u>for instance</u>, was invited for a job interview at a large corporation. When she arrived wearing a casual sweater and pair of slacks, she

discovered that everyone was wearing business suits and dresses. She never heard again from that corporation.

7   Finally, sometimes young people's chances of "getting ahead" are eliminated because they make a mistake. Seeing how impossible it is to succeed, despite hard work, they decide to try to beat the system by doing something illegal. They steal something, start dealing drugs, get mixed up with a gang, or get hooked on drugs themselves. For instance, my best friend, Althea, was doing well in high school until her junior year. She started dating a guy who was known for dealing drugs. Soon she joined him in the business. A few months later, they were both arrested, and now Althea has a felony on her record, making it unlikely anyone will hire her for a good job. Another example is the guy I was dating in my sophomore year. He was caught shoplifting in his senior year, making it unlikely he'll ever reach his goal of going to law school. All it takes is one mistake, and these kids' hopes of getting ahead have evaporated.

8   The belief that all it takes to "get ahead" is hard work results in people thinking that if they haven't gotten ahead, it's their fault. They didn't work hard enough. My father is a perfect example of this. When he was in his thirties and still working cleaning up rooms in a hotel, he gradually began to see himself as a failure. He blamed himself for not having gotten ahead in America. A few years later, when I started college, I tried to get him to take a few classes too. However, he was so convinced he was a failure that he simply couldn't imagine going back to school. In fact, there are many causes why, despite hard work, many don't get ahead—an education system that doesn't treat them fairly, the struggle to find the right balance of time and money, a personal crisis, or a personal mistake. It takes more than hard work to get ahead in America. It also takes luck or being born into a middle-class family.

9   The idea that in America if you work hard, you'll get ahead is both untruthful and harmful. It is untruthful because it ignores the many societal conditions that make it unlikely that people born into poverty will be able to get ahead, and it is harmful because it encourages people to think that if they haven't gotten ahead, it's their own fault and, therefore, they should not question an inequitable system.

(**NOTE:** The works cited list always starts on a new page.)

Works Cited

Reardon, Sean. "School District Socioeconomic Status, Race, and Academic Achievement." Stanford Center for Educational Policy Analysis, Apr. 2016, https://cepa.stanford.edu/sites/default/files/reardon%20district%20ses%20and%20achievement%20discussion%20draft%20april2015.pdf.

Salingo, Jeffrey. "Why Do So Many Students Drop Out of College? And What Can Be Done About It?" *The Washington Post*, 8 June 2018, https://www.washingtonpost.com/news/grade-point/wp/2018/06/08/why-do-so-many-students-drop-out-of-college-and-what-can-be-done-about-it/?utm_term=.b2a90fd8aa04.

15.8 Activity

Backward Outlining Applied

Backward Outlining (15.3, p. 101) is a tutorial that explains how to do backward outlining. Units 15.4 (p. 105), 15.5 (p. 107), and 15.6 (p. 109) explain and show how you could use a backward outline to improve the thesis, unity, organization, and support of a draft essay.

For this activity, make a backward outline of a draft of one of your essays and then use it to revise the thesis, unity, organization, and support of the essay.

15.9 Tutorial

Reviewing Options for What to Include in an Essay

At its most basic, the content of an essay consists of these three components:

- An introduction
- Body paragraphs that provide support for the thesis
- A conclusion

These three components can make a perfectly satisfactory essay, but there are many other components that can make your essay more interesting, more convincing, and more appealing to the reader, as outlined below. When revising an essay, ask yourself whether the inclusion of any of these components would improve your essay.

Ways to Make Essays More Interesting

1. **Add more arguments.**   Just because you've come up with three reasons that support the position you have taken in your thesis, there is no reason to stop thinking. Most essays can be made more convincing if they include more reasons, more arguments, to support the thesis.

2. **Provide definitions of key terms.**   If there are several words or phrases that are central to your argument, you may want to use a paragraph near the beginning of your essay to explain how you will be using them. For example, if you're writing about juvenile delinquency, you may want to explain what that term will mean in your discussion. It's not that you think your reader has never heard of the term; it's just that it has a wide range of meanings, and you want to make clear what you mean when you use the term. Does it, for example, include juveniles who commit murder? How about juveniles who spray paint graffiti?

3. **Recognize negative effects.**   Your thesis may be a good idea, and you may have presented a number of positive outcomes that will result from it, but it is often a good strategy also to admit that there are some negative outcomes that may result. Recognizing these can add to your credibility. They demonstrate that you are knowledgeable enough to be aware of these negatives and honest enough to admit they exist. Of course, it is a good idea if you can also explain why these negatives are less serious than they appear or how they can be mitigated.

4. **Recognize what opponents may say.**   Closely related to recognition of negative effects is the recognition of opponents' arguments, especially if those arguments are well known. Summarize them as objectively as you can and then answer, rebut, or counter them.

5. **Include some history of the topic you're writing about.**   How long has it been an issue? What positions have others taken about it?

6. **Make suggestions for implementation.**   If you are trying to convince your reader to agree with you about some issue, it can be a great idea to include some advice, toward the end of the essay, about what steps will be needed to implement the change you are proposing.

7. **Make a call to action.**   Even stronger than advice about implementation is a call to action, urging the reader not just to begin implementing some change, but to actually commit to some cause.

8. **Include background about who you are and/or why you decided to write about the topic.** Especially if it makes you a more credible author or demonstrates you are an author with a particular viewpoint, it can be very helpful to take a paragraph or two to give the reader some information about who you are and why you are writing about the topic.

15.10 Tutorial
A Revision Checklist

Use the following checklist to ensure that the next time you are revising an essay, you think about every single issue that might require revision.

Assignment, Audience, and Purpose

☐ Does the essay meet the requirements of the assignment?

☐ Is the style of the essay appropriate for the anticipated audience?

☐ Is the essay likely to accomplish the purpose of the essay?

Title and Introduction

☐ If your instructor expects a title, have you supplied one that captures the essence of your essay?

☐ Does your introduction provide useful background information?

☐ Does your introduction include a clear statement of your thesis?

☐ Does your introduction make your reader eager to read your paper?

Thesis

☐ Does your essay have a clear thesis?

☐ Is the thesis at the end of the essay the same as the thesis at the beginning?

☐ Does your thesis assert something interesting and thoughtful?

☐ Do you avoid proving the obvious?

Support, Organization, and Unity

☐ Does everything in the essay support the thesis?

☐ Do you provide convincing evidence to support every assertion in the essay?

☐ Are the main points of the essay organized in a logical order?

☐ Are related ideas in your essay grouped together?

☐ Do you provide transitional phrases to assist the reader in following your argument?

☐ Do you answer arguments you can imagine someone who disagrees with you raising?

Conclusion

☐ Even though worded differently, does the thesis in the conclusion make the same statement as the thesis in the introduction?

☐ Did you avoid introducing any new ideas in the conclusion?

TOPIC 16
Editing

Despite questions being raised about the insistence that everyone write in a single standard version of English, it is still the case that being able to write in conformity with the rules of Standard Written English can be extremely beneficial in college and in the workplace.

Navigating Topic 16

In this Topic, you and your classmates are going to learn those pesky grammar rules in a new way. Instead of *The Hub* giving you a set of rules, you will be given examples of sentences without errors and similar sentences with errors. Working in groups, you will examine these sets and discover the underlying grammar rules for yourselves. Knowledge gained in this way, by discovering it for yourself, stays with you longer than knowledge that is simply spelled out for you. In addition, you will learn this information, these writing conventions, in your own language, expressed in a way that makes sense to you and that is easier for you to remember.

To make what you learn truly useful, you need to have a place where you record it. I suggest that you open and save a Word document in which you record everything you learn as you work on Topic 16. Alternatively, you could use a notebook or journal to record this information.

The grammar topics are listed below. Your instructor will probably organize the class into groups to work on these together. However, if you want to, you can explore the ones that interest you on your own. You should also be aware that a more traditional presentation of grammar rules is available at *Achieve for The Hub* through the search function.

Thinking about Grammar   124

16.1   **Activity**   Good and Bad English   124
16.2   **Presentation**   The Grammar in Your Head   124

Punctuating to Avoid Fragments, Run-Ons, and Comma Splices 124

16.3	Tutorial	What Is a Sentence? 125
16.4	Activity	Fragments 126
16.5	Activity	Correcting Fragments 127
16.6	Activity	What Is an Independent Clause? 128
16.7	Activity	Run-Ons and Comma Splices 128
16.8	Activity	Correcting Run-Ons and Comma Splices 130
16.9	Activity	Correcting Fragments, Run-Ons, and Comma Splices 132
16.10	Activity	Punctuating Independent Clauses 1 133
16.11	Activity	Punctuating Independent Clauses 2 133
16.12	Activity	Punctuating Independent Clauses 3 134
16.13	Activity	Punctuating Independent Clauses 4 135
16.14	Activity	Punctuating Introductory Elements 1 137
16.15	Activity	Punctuating Introductory Elements 2 138
16.16	Activity	Editing an Essay for Punctuation 1 139
16.17	Activity	Editing an Essay for Punctuation 2 141

Using Apostrophes to Show Possession and to Indicate Contractions 144

16.18	Tutorial	Apostrophes 1 (Possessives) 144
16.19	Activity	Apostrophes 2 (Possessives) 145
16.20	Activity	Apostrophes 3 (Possessives) 146
16.21	Activity	Apostrophes 4 (Possessives) 147
16.22	Activity	Apostrophes 5 (Possessives) 148
16.23	Tutorial	Apostrophes 6 (Contractions) 149
16.24	Activity	Contractions versus Possessive Pronouns 149
16.25	Activity	Editing an Essay for Apostrophes 1 151
16.26	Activity	Editing an Essay for Apostrophes 2 153

Ensuring Subject-Verb Agreement 155

16.27	Activity	Subject-Verb Agreement 1 155
16.28	Activity	Subject-Verb Agreement 2 156
16.29	Activity	Subject-Verb Agreement 3 157

16.30	**Activity**	Subject-Verb Agreement 4 (Indefinite Pronouns 1) 158
16.31	**Activity**	Subject-Verb Agreement 5 (Indefinite Pronouns 2 and 3) 159
16.32	**Activity**	Editing an Essay for Subject-Verb Agreement 1 161
16.33	**Activity**	Editing an Essay for Subject-Verb Agreement 2 163

Avoiding Pronoun Reference and Agreement Errors   165

16.34	**Activity**	Pronouns and Antecedents 165
16.35	**Activity**	Vague Pronoun Reference 1 166
16.36	**Activity**	Vague Pronoun Reference 2 167
16.37	**Activity**	Vague Pronoun Reference 3 167
16.38	**Tutorial**	Pronoun Agreement 168
16.39	**Activity**	Correcting Pronoun Errors 172
16.40	**Activity**	Editing an Essay for Pronoun Errors 1 172
16.41	**Activity**	Editing an Essay for Pronoun Errors 2 174

Combining Sentences in Interesting Ways   176

16.42	**Tutorial**	Sentence Combining 176
16.43	**Activity**	Sentence Combining 1 177
16.44	**Activity**	Sentence Combining 2 178
16.45	**Activity**	Sentence Combining 3 179
16.46	**Activity**	Sentence Combining 4 180
16.47	**Activity**	Sentence Combining 5 182

Language and Computers   183

| 16.48 | **Activity** | Computers and Editing 1   183 |
| 16.49 | **Tutorial** | Computers and Editing 2   184 |

Thinking about Grammar

To begin this topic, you will do a little thinking about the concept of grammar in a very general way in Units 16.1 and 16.2.

16.1 Activity

Good and Bad English

You've probably heard people talk about "good English" and "bad English." You may have even used these terms yourself. In this activity, you are being asked to think about the meaning of the terms *good English* and *bad English*.

Working in groups, you will discuss the following questions.

1. What is the difference between "good" English and "bad" English?
2. Why do people consider "bad" English "bad"?
3. Who speaks and writes mostly in "good" English?
4. Why should someone want to become proficient in "good" English?

After about fifteen minutes, your group will be asked to report out its response to each of the questions.

16.2 Presentation

The Grammar in Your Head

To watch a presentation that discusses grammar and how much you already know about it (even if you don't think you know anything), go to *Achieve for The Hub*, Topic 16, and open Unit 16.2.

Punctuating to Avoid Fragments, Run-Ons, and Comma Splices

Punctuation is used to divide sentences into their major parts. Because there is no punctuation in spoken English, the proper use of punctuation sometimes proves difficult for students when they are writing.

16.3 Tutorial

What Is a Sentence?

In the past, you may have been taught this traditional definition of a *sentence*:

> A sentence is a group of words containing a subject and a verb and expressing a complete thought.

If that definition works for you, of course, continue to use it. But it doesn't work for all students—especially the "complete thought" part.

Using a Test Frame

If the traditional definition above does not work for you, try this "test frame" devised by Rei Noguchi, a linguist and English teacher who taught for years at California State University, Northridge:

> A sentence is a group of words that makes sense when placed on the line below:
>
> They refused to believe the idea that _____

Here's how it works. If you have written a group of words and are not sure whether they are a sentence or not, you place the words on the blank line in the test frame and then read the entire sentence, beginning with "They refused to believe," out loud. If that sentence "makes sense," then the group of words is a sentence. If it doesn't "make sense," your group of words is not a sentence.

For example, imagine you have written, "The woman running after the bus." Now you are not sure whether that group of words is actually a sentence, so you place it on the blank line in the "test frame" and then read it out loud: "They refused to believe the idea that the woman running after the bus." Clearly that sentence doesn't "make sense," so your original group of words is not a sentence.

Here's another example. You have written, "She placed it in her refrigerator." To see whether that group of words is a sentence, you place it on the black line in the test frame and then read the entire sentence out loud: "They refused to believe the idea that she placed it in her refrigerator." That sounds fine, so the original group of words is a sentence.

One caution: This method of identifying sentences does not work for questions or commands, as the following examples demonstrate.

> **Question:** Did you finish the homework? (This is a complete sentence.)
>
> They refused to believe the idea that <u>did you finish the homework?</u>
>
> **Command:** Turn off the lights when you come to bed. (This is a complete sentence.)
>
> They refused to believe the idea that <u>turn off the lights when you come to bed</u>.

Activity: Is This a Sentence?

Working in groups, decide whether each of the following is or is not a sentence, using the test frame to make your decision. On the line before each number, enter an S for *sentence* or an N for *not a sentence*.

_____ 1. The woman smoking a cigarette in the parking lot.

_____ 2. I found it in the back seat of my car.

_____ 3. The teacher who gave me a D last semester in math.

_____ 4. When Jorge learned that he had been promoted to manager.

_____ 5. The children cried.

_____ 6. Lashawn knew the answer.

_____ 7. The only question that I missed on the exam.

_____ 8. If Tawanda answers the phone and starts laughing.

_____ 9. Dogs bark.

_____ 10. Saving money is not easy.

16.4 Activity

Fragments

A fragment is usually considered a serious grammatical mistake. The following pairs of items are labeled as either fragments or sentences, with the fragments printed in blue. In Tutorial 16.3 (p. 439), you learned what a sentence is. Now, working in your group, study each of these paired examples and then write a definition of the term *fragment*.

Sentence	✓ I saw the damage to my car.
Fragment	✗ When I saw the damage to my car.

Sentence	✓ I had been studying for a math test.
Fragment	✗ The math test I had been studying for.

Sentence	✓ I love vegetables like Brussels sprouts, broccoli, and asparagus.
Fragment	✗ For example, Brussels sprouts, broccoli, and asparagus.

Sentence	✓ Because Lin was late for class, he had to sit in the front row.
Fragment	✗ Because Lin was late for class.

Sentence	✓ The woman wearing a purple sweater is my psychology teacher.
Fragment	✗ That woman wearing a purple sweater.

NOTE: Write your definition of a *fragment* in a notebook or online file for future reference.

16.5 **Activity**

Correcting Fragments

The following items include fragments. There are usually several ways to correct a fragment. Working in groups, first identify and underline any fragments in each item and then revise the item so that the fragment is eliminated.

1. When I learned Liz was going to be late. I was furious. She has not been on time for a single meeting this year.

2. The fact that Kayla was promoted. Made me determined to work even harder this year. I am going to get the same kind of promotion if I can.

3. The woman who rode to work on her bike and changed clothes in the women's room. She turned out to be a friend of Courtney's. Now she drives a BMW to work every day.

4. I have saved money out of my check every week for two years. Meaning I now can afford a vacation in Europe. When I return in three weeks. I expect to have some money left over.

5. The teacher in the red blouse and the grey skirt. She is the one who gave me an A in physical education. There was only one reason I got an A. The fact that I was never absent or late.

6. The car Sylvester was driving. It used to belong to L'Tanya. He does not know that it was badly damaged in an accident.

7. The binoculars I borrowed from Ms. Patel and then lost on my camping trip. They cost more than a hundred dollars. I will have to pay her back over the next six months.

8. Until Maria learns I won't be pushed around. I will continue to refuse to work with her. She is just too bossy.

9. To hunt for a cat for three weeks and not find him. That was almost more than I could bear. I had given up looking for him, and he just walked into the backyard.

10. The doctor whom Linda has been going to and who also treated my mother. He has an office on Pratt Street. I have an appointment with him next week.

16.6 Activity

What Is an Independent Clause?

In the following sentences, the independent clauses have been underlined. Working in groups, use what you have already learned about sentences to study the following sentences and figure out what an independent clause is. Working together as a group, write a definition of an *independent clause*. Then write an explanation of the difference between an independent clause and a sentence.

1. The phone rang, and my dog started barking.
2. When it rains, my knees ache.
3. Javier tried to solve the puzzle.
4. Raelyn laughed out loud when she heard the news about Earl.
5. Mark graduates in June, and his sister graduates next year.
6. Because of the snow, the parade was cancelled.
7. Paola is buying a new car this afternoon.
8. Riding a bicycle in the city can be dangerous.
9. Jayla made a salad, and Dion roasted a chicken.
10. If Sarah comes to class tomorrow, I will invite her to the party.

16.7 Activity

Run-Ons and Comma Splices

Run-ons and comma splices are serious errors that many teachers find very problematic. In this unit, you will learn to recognize these two errors. In Correcting Run-Ons and Comma Splices (16.8, p. 130), you will learn how to correct them.

In the following groups of sentences, the versions that are run-ons and comma splices are printed in blue. The correct versions are printed in black. Working in your group, study these examples. Then, as a group, write definitions of a *run-on* and a *comma splice*.

Group 1

Correct	✓ I used to live in Seattle. I worked at Boeing.
Run-On	✗ I used to live in Seattle I worked at Boeing.
Comma Splice	✗ I used to live in Seattle, I worked at Boeing.

Group 2

Correct	✓ Matt walked out of the meeting without saying a word. He was angry at the decision the group had made.
Run-On	✗ Matt walked out of the meeting without saying a word he was angry at the decision the group had made.
Comma Splice	✗ Matt walked out of the meeting without saying a word, he was angry at the decision the group had made.

Group 3

Correct	✓ Deon made a delicious lasagna. His wife made an avocado salad.
Run-On	✗ Deon made a delicious lasagna his wife made an avocado salad.
Comma Splice	✗ Deon made a delicious lasagna, his wife made an avocado salad.

Group 4

Correct	✓ All flights to Denver were cancelled. There was a terrible ice storm.
Run-On	✗ All flights to Denver were cancelled there was a terrible ice storm.
Comma Splice	✗ All flights to Denver were cancelled, there was a terrible ice storm.

NOTE: Write your definition of a *run-on* in a notebook or online file for future reference.

NOTE: Write your definition of a *comma splice* in a notebook or online file for future reference.

Correcting Run-Ons and Comma Splices

In Run-Ons and Comma Splices (16.7, p. 128), you learned to recognize run-ons and comma splices within four groups of sentences. In this activity, you will learn how to correct them.

Each of the following groups of sentences begins with a run-on and then a comma splice. These errors, shown in blue, are followed by five correct sentences representing a variety of methods to correct run-ons and comma splices. There are more ways for correcting these errors, but the ones here should give you an idea of the range of options.

Working in your group, make a list of at least five ways to correct run-ons and comma splices. Then see if you can think of one or two additional ways to do so.

Group 1

Run-On	✗ I lived in Seattle in 2008 I worked at Boeing.
Comma Splice	✗ I lived in Seattle in 2008, I worked at Boeing.
Correct	✓ I lived in Seattle in 2008. I worked at Boeing.
Correct	✓ I lived in Seattle in 2008; I worked at Boeing.
Correct	✓ When I lived in Seattle in 2008, I worked at Boeing.
Correct	✓ While living in Seattle in 2008, I worked at Boeing.
Correct	✓ I lived in Seattle in 2008; at that time, I worked at Boeing.

Group 2

Run-On	✗ Matt walked out of the meeting without saying a word he was angry at the decision the group had made.
Comma Splice	✗ Matt walked out of the meeting without saying a word, he was angry at the decision the group had made.
Correct	✓ Matt walked out of the meeting without saying a word. He was angry at the decision the group had made.
Correct	✓ Matt walked out of the meeting without saying a word; he was angry at the decision the group had made.
Correct	✓ Matt walked out of the meeting without saying a word because he was angry at the decision the group had made.

Correct	✓ Angry at the decision the group had made, Matt walked out of the meeting without saying a word.
Correct	✓ Matt was angry at the decision the group had made; as a result, he walked out of the meeting without saying a word.

Group 3

Run-On	✗ Deon made a delicious lasagna his wife made an avocado salad.
Comma Splice	✗ Deon made a delicious lasagna, his wife made an avocado salad.
Correct	✓ Deon made a delicious lasagna. His wife made an avocado salad.
Correct	✓ Deon made a delicious lasagna; his wife made an avocado salad.
Correct	✓ While Deon made a delicious lasagna, his wife made an avocado salad.
Correct	✓ While Deon's wife made an avocado salad, he made a delicious lasagna.
Correct	✓ Deon made a delicious lasagna; meanwhile, his wife made an avocado salad.

Group 4

Run-On	✗ All flights to Denver were cancelled there was a terrible ice storm.
Comma Splice	✗ All flights to Denver were cancelled, there was a terrible ice storm.
Correct	✓ All flights to Denver were cancelled. There was a terrible ice storm.
Correct	✓ All flights to Denver were cancelled; there was a terrible ice storm.
Correct	✓ All flights to Denver were cancelled because there was a terrible ice storm.
Correct	✓ Because there was a terrible ice storm, all flights to Denver were cancelled.
Correct	✓ There was a terrible ice storm; as a result, all flights to Denver were cancelled.

NOTE: Record at least five ways to correct a run-on or comma splice in a notebook or online file for future reference.

Correcting Fragments, Run-Ons, and Comma Splices

In Unit 16.5 (p. 127), you learned to correct fragments, and in Unit 16.8 (p. 130), you learned to correct run-ons and comma splices. In this activity, you will put all that you learned together. In the following sentences, correct all the errors, which include fragments, run-ons, and comma splices.

1. I am getting a blister on my thumb, I will have to quit playing soon.
2. When she made a chocolate cake for my mother. She forgot to add any sugar.
3. The man wearing a plaid jacket. He is my math teacher.
4. When Aryelle opened the newspaper. She saw a picture of her old boyfriend.
5. There was no money in my account, the bank honored my check anyway.
6. Odelia's brother has done many stupid things. Such as getting four tickets for speeding. He also is in trouble for bouncing checks.
7. Because Jordan drank fourteen cans of beer. We had to carry him home.
8. Anthony is trying to run two miles every morning. To lose ten pounds in the next three months.
9. The management at my apartment building does a great job. For example, having the parking lot plowed every time it snows. In addition, they keep the lawn in great shape.
10. I have never been to Las Vegas, I have no intention of going now.
11. The picnic has been called off let's all get together at Rab's house.
12. My father made a phone call, then he drove away without saying a word.
13. I hoped to get a part in the play. Even though I knew my chances were not very good. I thought the director might need an actor with a southern accent.
14. When Dexter got to the parking lot. He realized he had left his book in the classroom.
15. I wanted chocolate chip I got mocha chocolate.
16. I am experiencing some physical problems as I reach my fifties. My knees bother me a lot. Also, shortness of breath when I try to run.
17. Gus ran as hard as he could, he came in third.
18. The cake is delicious I cannot eat another bite.
19. Jessica lost fourteen pounds on her diet, I lost only six.
20. Peaches bought a new computer. Using the money she had won in the lottery.

16.10 Activity

Punctuating Independent Clauses 1

In the following pairs of items, the sentence in black is correct, and the sentence in blue has an error. Study these sentences and figure out which grammar rule they all demonstrate.

Pair 1

✓ Chin lives in Overlea, and his brother lives in Parkville.

✗ Chin lives in Overlea and his brother lives in Parkville.

Pair 2

✓ Drew bought a laptop, but he has not learned how to use it.

✗ Drew bought a laptop but he has not learned how to use it.

Pair 3

✓ Kyesha went to the ocean, and it rained every day.

✗ Kyesha went to the ocean and it rained every day.

Pair 4

✓ Maria works at a bakery, but she is looking for a second job.

✗ Maria works at a bakery but she is looking for a second job.

NOTE: Don't record anything in your notebook or online file until you have completed Unit 16.12 (p. 134).

16.11 Activity

Punctuating Independent Clauses 2

In the following pairs, the sentence in black is correct, and the sentence in blue has an error. Study these sentences and figure out which grammar rule they all demonstrate.

Pair 1

✓ Hector opened his biology book and started to study.

✗ Hector opened his biology book, and started to study.

Pair 2

   ✓ Mary opened the door and let a strange cat into the house.

   ✗ Mary opened the door, and let a strange cat into the house.

Pair 3

   ✓ Oklahoma is a great place to work and to raise children.

   ✗ Oklahoma is a great place to work, and to raise children.

Pair 4

   ✓ My mother has worked hard all her life but has not gotten ahead as a result.

   ✗ My mother has worked hard all her life, but has not gotten ahead as a result.

NOTE: While the second sentence in Pair 4 illustrates the "official" rule, many people disregard the rule and use a comma before the *but* anyhow.

NOTE: Don't record anything in your notebook or online file until you've completed Unit 16.12.

16.12 Activity

Punctuating Independent Clauses 3

Now here are all the sentence pairs from Units 16.10 (p. 133) and 16.11 (p. 133). Sentences printed in black are correct; those printed in blue are incorrect. Study them carefully and figure out what the grammar rule is for these kinds of sentences. You may want to refresh your memory of what an "independent clause" is before you work on these (see Unit 16.6 [p. 128]).

Pair 1

   ✓ Chin lives in Overlea, and his brother lives in Parkville.

   ✗ Chin lives in Overlea and his brother lives in Parkville.

Pair 2

   ✓ Drew bought a laptop, but he has not learned how to use it.

   ✗ Drew bought a laptop but he has not learned how to use it.

Pair 3

✓ Kyesha went to the ocean, and it rained every day.

✗ Kyesha went to the ocean and it rained every day.

Pair 4

✓ Maria works at a bakery, but she is looking for a second job.

✗ Maria works at a bakery but she is looking for a second job.

Pair 5

✓ Hector opened his biology book and started to study.

✗ Hector opened his biology book, and started to study.

Pair 6

✓ Mary opened the door and let a strange cat into the house.

✗ Mary opened the door, and let a strange cat into the house.

Pair 7

✓ Oklahoma is a great place to work and to raise children.

✗ Oklahoma is a great place to work, and to raise children.

Pair 8

✓ My mother has worked hard all her life but has not gotten ahead as a result.

✗ My mother has worked hard all her life, but has not gotten ahead as a result.

NOTE: Record the grammar rule these items demonstrate in a notebook or online file for future reference.

16.13 Activity
Punctuating Independent Clauses 4

The sentences you have been working on in Units 16.10 (p. 133), 16.11 (p. 133), and 16.12 (p. 134) all used the conjunctions *and* or *but*. These are the most frequently used of the *coordinating conjunctions*, but there are others. Here's the complete list.

You might want to use the word FANBOYS, which is spelled with the first letter of all seven, to remember them.

For

And

Nor

But

Or

Yet

So

In the following sentence pairs, the black sentences are correct; the blue ones contain an error. Study these to see whether these five additional conjunctions follow the same grammar rules as *and* and *but*.

Pair 1

✓ In New York most people ride the subway to work, or they take a bus.

✗ In New York most people ride the subway to work or they take a bus.

Pair 2

✓ For breakfast I usually have a bowl of cereal or some scrambled eggs.

✗ For breakfast I usually have a bowl of cereal, or some scrambled eggs.

Pair 3

✓ Negotiations are going to continue all night, for the union has announced a strike for tomorrow morning.

✗ Negotiations are going to continue all night for the union has announced a strike for tomorrow morning.

Pair 4

✓ Nathan studied all weekend for the midterm test in his biology class.

✗ Nathan studied all weekend, for the midterm test in his biology class.

Pair 5

✓ There is an accident on the Expressway this morning, so I am driving through the city.

✗ There is an accident on the Expressway this morning so I am driving through the city.

Pair 6

✓ My daughter has grown so tall that she needs a new bed.

✗ My daughter has grown, so tall that she needs a new bed.

Pair 7

✓ I have applied for more than a dozen jobs, yet I have not been invited for a single interview.

✗ I have applied for more than a dozen jobs yet I have not been invited for a single interview.

Pair 8

✓ We haven't yet received any word from our daughter in Brazil.

✗ We haven't, yet received any word from our daughter in Brazil.

Pair 9

✓ The new café in my neighborhood doesn't serve espresso, nor does the café near my work.

✗ The new café in my neighborhood doesn't serve espresso nor does the café near my work.

Pair 10

✓ Neither the textbook for my math class nor the website explains how to factor polynomials.

✗ Neither the textbook for my math class, nor the website explains how to factor polynomials.

NOTE: Record in a notebook or online file whether the five additional conjunctions in the preceding examples follow the same grammar rules as *and* and *but*.

16.14 Activity
Punctuating Introductory Elements 1

In the following pairs of sentences, the black versions are correct; the blue versions include an error. Study these to see what punctuation rule they illustrate.

Pair 1

✓ When it rains, my knees ache.

✗ When it rains my knees ache.

Pair 2

✓ Because I sprained my ankle, I cannot play tennis this weekend.

✗ Because I sprained my ankle I cannot play tennis this weekend.

Pair 3

✓ If I miss the bus, I will have to wait for an hour.

✗ If I miss the bus I will have to wait for an hour.

Pair 4

✓ Running after the bus, Jamey sprained his ankle.

✗ Running after the bus Jamey sprained his ankle.

Pair 5

✓ In the third drawer from the top, I found my iPhone.

✗ In the third drawer from the top I found my iPhone.

Pair 6

✓ To open a bank account, Susan had to fill out more than a dozen forms.

✗ To open a bank account Susan had to fill out more than a dozen forms.

NOTE: Don't record anything in your notebook or online file until you have completed Unit 16.15.

16.15 Activity

Punctuating Introductory Elements 2

The following pairs of sentences demonstrate one additional complication to the punctuation rule you worked on in Unit 16.14 (p. 137). Study them to determine what this complication is. Again, the black sentences are correct; the blue ones have an error.

Pair 1

✓ When I graduate will be a time for celebrating.

✗ When I graduate, will be a time for celebrating.

Pair 2

✓ Being unemployed can produce much anxiety.

✗ Being unemployed, can produce much anxiety.

Pair 3

✓ To let the dog out without a leash was a big mistake.

✗ To let the dog out without a leash, was a big mistake.

Pair 4

✓ In the top drawer of my dresser is a collection of mismatched socks.

✗ In the top drawer of my dresser, is a collection of mismatched socks.

Pair 5

✓ Taking five courses this semester has been very stressful.

✗ Taking five courses this semester, has been very stressful.

NOTE: What complication to the punctuation rule you identified in Unit 16.14 do these items illustrate? Record your answer in a notebook or online file.

16.16 Activity

Editing an Essay for Punctuation 1

Proofread the following essay and correct any errors you find. These errors will be in the following categories:

- Fragments
- Run-on sentences
- Comma splices
- Errors punctuating two independent clauses joined by *and, but, or, for, so, yet,* or *nor*
- Errors punctuating introductory elements

In some cases, you will be able to correct errors by simply adding or deleting punctuation; in other cases, especially when editing fragments, you may need to do a little rewording of the sentence.

Anticipation Can Kill the Moment

I don't remember my last day of college. It's an odd thing to admit but I don't remember such a major milestone in my life. I don't recall any tearful goodbyes to my favorite professors. Any solemn "see you laters" to my friends and classmates. The whole day is a blank. All the celebration and sadness that I would imagine happened is simply missing from my memory.

For a while, I wondered why this was. After four years of late nights in the library or early mornings working in the dining hall the final day was a dark spot in my memory. All the anticipation of four years of learning, and training for the real world, and I don't remember what I had for breakfast, or if I slept in. It's funny how the most important of days seems to slip by like that, they seem so brief in comparison to the time spent waiting for them. You might miss them if you blink slowly.

What I came to realize, is that many days that held significance in my life were equally blank. My high school graduation, for one. That day was nothing but a commencement speech, as far as I know. Another important day that I can't remember, was my first date, I can't remember picking up my date, taking her home, or anything in between. Similarly, I can't remember the last playoff game I played in high school. I know we lost but I don't know how that happened.

Thinking about all of these days I realized that the thing I remember most about graduating college was fear, I had felt it creeping up on me for the entirety of my final semester. Looking over my shoulder as I filled out job applications and hoped for something to turn up. There's nothing like realizing, after four years of relative safety, that there is nothing standing between you and adulthood. No more years of school, no more time to prepare for jobs, no one to depend on but yourself after you cross the stage. Like all the most important moments in life it's a plunge that has to be taken. A band-aid that has to be ripped off in order to move forward.

So it was for all the other important days I feel I've missed, I remember feeling that fear or anticipation, but not the event itself. I spent so much time worrying about it during the buildup. For my first date, I remember sweating over how much Axe body spray to use, what clothes to wear, and whether the girl liked me or not. For the baseball game I simply wondered if I would play, and for how long, and if we could win it. For graduation my thoughts focused on the future, rather than on the moment I was in. I wondered about where I would work, or if I could even find a job. Worried that I might fail if I ventured out into the world. The anticipation, it seems, killed the moment.

16.17 Activity
Editing an Essay for Punctuation 2

Proofread the following essay and correct any errors you find. These errors will be in the following categories:

- Fragments
- Run-on sentences
- Comma splices
- Errors punctuating two independent clauses joined by *and, but, or, for, so, yet,* or *nor*
- Errors punctuating introductory elements

In some cases, you will be able to correct errors by simply adding or deleting punctuation; in other cases, especially when editing fragments, you may need to do a little rewording of the sentence.

New or Used?

Among the hardest choices of adult life is what kind of car to buy, there are seemingly millions of options to choose from. Whether it's got leather or velour seats, compact or SUV, or any of the dizzying array of colors that manufacturers conjure up. It's not just the looks or the brand that matter while searching there are also seemingly endless places to buy a car, from local shops with a scattering of used vehicles to massive dealerships with parking lots full of options. But underlying all of this is whether to buy new or used and as each has its perks, this can further complicate car buying.

Of course, the first and most important thing to do in a car search is to decide what kind of car you want. This means narrowing down the brands, the makes, and models that you could imagine yourself owning. If you tend to do a lot of sporting activities. Maybe consider a hatchback or an SUV for some extra storage space. If you have a long commute every day, maybe look at compact cars that get good gas mileage. It's essential to think long and hard about what your lifestyle will require, and then to look for that type of car in a brand you trust.

Then you have to make the hard decision of whether to buy new or used. Without a doubt, a new car will be more expensive. No matter how hard you haggle it will end up being thousands of dollars more than older, used models with some mileage on them. In exchange for this upfront cost, though, the car should (theoretically) last for many years, and will include all of the latest technology available. You may also be able to get a warrantee. Which will guarantee free repairs on certain parts of the vehicle for tens of thousands of miles—some brands will even dole out a lifetime warrantee for their vehicles but this is rare. You also have the guarantee that the car has never been in an accident, never had coffee spilled on the seats, and has never had a shaggy dog shed fur all over the rugs.

A used car, sadly, can't always give you that guarantee. Firstly, there's the possibility of a sleazy used-car salesman who sells you an old junker with a promise and a trustworthy smile and the junker breaks down in a cloud of steam and bitter feelings mere weeks later. Many car shops will try to take advantage of first-time car buyers. Selling damaged and even dangerous cars to unsuspecting drivers for new-car money. This often happens in private deals (i.e., a person sells their car to another person without a dealership or auto shop in the middle), but can also happen at less-than-reputable used car lots. A bad deal like this will not always result in injury or a broken-down vehicle, but may simply be a rip-off, used cars are often sold for more than they're worth, which is why it's important to use price-comparison tools like Kelley Blue Book for background research.

Although the consequences of a bad deal can be dire buying a used car means you also have the opportunity to get more than you pay for. Some people buy cars for thousands of dollars less than what they're worth, simply because the owner is trying to get rid of the vehicle at any cost, and a substantial discount in insurance costs. You also avoid the immediate and steep drop in the car's value, which hits the moment you drive a new car off the lot. With a used car you're on the benefiting end of that price drop, and you might end up with a car that's been so well taken care of that it might as well be new. Even last year's model, with practically new features and very few miles on the odometer could be several thousand dollars cheaper used than it was new. To get these deals, is not easy, you have to ask around, this will only work if you have a dealer or another seller whom you trust, who you know won't take advantage of you.

There are a number of different factors that could decide whether you buy new or used, in the end, it will always come down to what you need. If you want a warrantee and a literal carload of new gadgets then maybe a new car is the right way to go. If you want something tried and tested for a bargain price, and are willing to risk some extra maintenance costs in the long run, then a used car might be a better fit. But regardless of which is the right choice for you, it always pays to ask around and find a dealer or a seller who can deliver on your needs. More important than whether you buy a new or a used vehicle will always be whether you trust the person selling it to you.

Using Apostrophes to Show Possession and to Indicate Contractions

Apostrophes can be troublesome because they have two completely different uses in English: to show possession and to indicate contractions.

16.18 Tutorial

Apostrophes 1 (Possessives)

The most common use of apostrophes is to show possession, and most everyone knows that possession is similar to ownership. When you write about "Maggie's car," you mean the car that Maggie owns. When you talk about "my mother's house," you mean the house that your mother owns. However, the use of apostrophes to show possession is much broader than just "ownership." Look at this example:

> We saw Picasso's painting of three musicians in the Museum of Modern Art.

The word *Picasso* is possessive, but Picasso doesn't own that painting; the Museum of Modern Art owns it. Picasso made it. Here are two more examples of a possessive being used to indicate something that someone made:

> Shana's essay was almost five pages long.
>
> Donna's risotto was judged to be the best in the entire city.

Up to this point, you've seen possession used to express two relationships: when someone owns something and when someone has made something. The following sentences contain possessive words expressing other relationships. Working in your group, study each set of sentences and record a brief statement of the kind of relationship being represented by the possessives.

Set 1

Miguel's arm was fractured in the accident.

My car's windshield is cracked.

My school's roof was damaged in the storm.

Kind of relationship: _____

Set 2

LaDawn's sister was hired at the restaurant where I work.

Chris's mother will graduate from college this semester.

Kyle's niece is getting married this weekend.

Kind of relationship: _____

Set 3

Max's forgetfulness has caused him many problems.

Lizzie's thoughtfulness makes her a great friend.

I really enjoy Gillian's sense of humor.

Kind of relationship: _____

Set 4

Jake was not aware of the college's policy on withdrawing from classes.

Toyota's logo looks like a T made out of circles.

Milano's menu is mostly Italian dishes, but there are some American items too.

Kind of relationship: _____

Set 5

Many of today's students are working at least twenty hours a week.

A one-hour's delay would have caused us to miss our connection in Chicago.

This year's tomatoes are larger than ever.

Kind of relationship: _____

NOTE: The possessive word always appears in front of the word being possessed.

16.19 Activity

Apostrophes 2 (Possessives)

Working in your group, underline or highlight the possessive words in the following sentences. Every sentence may not have a possessive word, and some may have two.

1. Marcella's umbrella is bright red.
2. Today's special is meatloaf and mashed potatoes.
3. I grabbed my boss's hand and shook it forcefully.
4. My professor's absence policy was stricter than the college's policy.
5. Several dogs were barking as I walked up the sidewalk.
6. I have often observed my professor's compassion for students.
7. I was very impressed with the soprano's voice.
8. My bicycle's tire was flat.
9. Yesterday's snow was completely melted by this morning.
10. Craig's book's cover had a large coffee stain.

16.20 Activity

Apostrophes 3 (Possessives)

The following groups of sentences demonstrate one rule about the use of apostrophes. Again, the black sentences are correct; the blue ones have an error. Study these examples and figure out the grammar rule they illustrate.

Group 1

✓ Mariel's laptop was stolen from her car.

✗ Mariels laptop was stolen from her car.

✗ Mariels' laptop was stolen from her car.

Group 2

✓ Greg's car is a Volkswagen.

✗ Gregs car is a Volkswagen.

✗ Gregs' car is a Volkswagen.

Group 3

✓ Jan was sitting in her teacher's car.

✗ Jan was sitting in her teachers car.

✗ Jan was sitting in her teachers' car.

Group 4

✓ I found someone's purse in the restroom.

✗ I found someones purse in the restroom.

✗ I found someones' purse in the restroom.

NOTE: Record the grammar rule these items demonstrate in a notebook or online file for future reference.

16.21 Activity

Apostrophes 4 (Possessives)

The following groups of sentences demonstrate a second rule about the use of apostrophes. Again, the black sentences are correct; the blue ones have an error. Study these examples and figure out the grammar rule they illustrate.

Group 1

✓ These two students' essays are excellent examples.

✗ These two students essays are excellent examples.

✗ These two student's essays are excellent examples.

Group 2

✓ My grandparents' house is more than a hundred years old.

✗ My grandparents house is more than a hundred years old.

✗ My grandparent's house is more than a hundred years old.

Group 3

✓ The two candidates' speeches were long and boring.

✗ The two candidate's speeches were long and boring.

✗ The two candidates speeches were long and boring.

Group 4

✓ Three chairs' cushions were stained when Aris spilled a glass of wine.

✗ Three chairs cushions were stained when Aris spilled a glass of wine.

✗ Three chair's cushions were stained when Aris spilled a glass of wine.

NOTE: Record the grammar rule these items demonstrate in a notebook or online file for future reference.

16.22 Activity
Apostrophes 5 (Possessives)

The following groups of sentences demonstrate a third rule about the use of apostrophes. This grammar rule affects only a small group of words, but it's the one that causes students the most trouble. Again, the black sentences are correct; the blue ones have an error. Study these examples and figure out the rule they illustrate.

Group 1

✓ The children's coats were soaking wet, but they didn't seem to mind.

✗ The childrens coats were soaking wet, but they didn't seem to mind.

✗ The childrens' coats were soaking wet, but they didn't seem to mind.

Group 2

✓ The men's names were Jose and Juan.

✗ The mens names were Jose and Juan.

✗ The mens' names were Jose and Juan.

Group 3

✓ My wife asked the server where the women's room was.

✗ My wife asked the server where the womens room was.

✗ My wife asked the server where the womens' room was.

Group 4

✓ The two deer's footprints were clearly visible in the mud.

✗ The two deers footprints were clearly visible in the mud.

✗ The two deers' footprints were clearly visible in the mud.

NOTE: Record the grammar rule these items demonstrate in a notebook or online file for future reference.

Apostrophes 6 (Contractions)

While the most common use for apostrophes is to indicate possession, they are also used to form contractions. Contractions are formed by combining two words into one and leaving out one or more letters. Note that the apostrophe is placed where the letter or letters have been left out, not at the place where the two words are joined.

is not → isn't

she will → she'll

I am → I'm

we had → we'd

can not → can't

Contractions are not appropriate in formal writing. When deciding whether contractions are appropriate in a particular piece of writing, it's a good idea to ask the person you are writing for. Some teachers think apostrophes are inappropriate in college essays; others think they are fine.

Activity: Practice with Contractions

Form contractions with each of the following pairs of words:

they are	it is
he is	who is
could not	are not
had not	did not
you are	have not

Contractions versus Possessive Pronouns

Students frequently create errors in their writing because they confuse contractions and possessive pronouns, especially the ones that are spelled quite similarly. Study the following examples and try to figure out when to use the version with an apostrophe and when to use the one without an apostrophe. The sentences in black are correct. The ones in blue include an error.

After you've studied these examples, write a paragraph in which you explain how to decide when an apostrophe is needed with pronouns like these and when it is wrong to use an apostrophe with them.

Pair 1

✓ I hope it's not too late to sign up for the trip to Washington.

✗ I hope its not too late to sign up for the trip to Washington.

Pair 2

✓ Jill watched as her dog hid its bone under the bed.

✗ Jill watched as her dog hid it's bone under the bed.

Pair 3

✓ I hope you're coming to the movie with us.

✗ I hope your coming to the movie with us.

Pair 4

✓ Juanita saw your sister in the supermarket.

✗ Juanita saw you're sister in the supermarket.

Pair 5

✓ Jamard's parents are selling their house and moving to Florida.

✗ Jamard's parents are selling they're house and moving to Florida.

Pair 6

✓ They're making a new movie about Alexander Hamilton.

✗ Their making a new movie about Alexander Hamilton.

Pair 7

✓ I wonder whose car that is parked in front of my house.

✗ I wonder who's car that is parked in front of my house.

Pair 8

✓ Tamira knows who's driving to the beach this weekend.

✗ Tamira knows whose driving to the beach this weekend.

NOTE: Record the apostrophe rule these items demonstrate in a notebook or online file for future reference.

Editing an Essay for Apostrophes 1

The following essay has errors involving apostrophes. Working in your group, edit the essay to correct these errors.

The Death Penalty

Were all familiar in America with the justice system. Due to the large police presence around the country, its virtually certain that, in some way or another, every single person in the country has had an interaction with law enforcement at some point. Most of us get a speeding ticket here and there, but for the worst offenders—murderers, serial rapists, and the like—the penalty goes all the way up to and including death. The United States is one of the only developed nation's in the world to still allow the death penalty, which raises the question: why? In many cases, the death penalty is not only an inhumane way to treat violence in society, but it can also come out to be more expensive and more time-consuming than comparable rehabilitation programs.

While the death penalty certainly instills fear in many criminals, its never been enough to deter every one of them from committing a heinous crime like murder. So then the question remains, why continue? It solves nothing to kill a murderer—if anything, it only serves to remind us that, as Gandhi once said, "An eye for an eye leaves the whole world blind." It also helps to remember that revenge is not the same as justice, and its' not worth pursuing if the real goal is to prevent future crimes. Families of a murderers' victims may desire to kill the person as payment for their loss, but in reality they only become a little more like the criminal, and in the process another life is taken.

Another more calculating reason to forgo the death penalty is it's extraordinary cost. While an actual execution may not be very expensive, according to a number of recent studies imprisoning death row inmates can be upwards of fifty percent more expensive than for the general prison population.

And then theres the appeal process; most inmates are in a legal fight for their lives right up until the day that theyre killed. That means thousands of hours of legal work for public defenders and prosecutors as inmates work their way through the endless appeals of the American justice system, and those hours are billed directly to the taxpayer's. This compares to roughly two hundred hours of appeals on average for a general population inmate.

And while the drugs often used to execute prisoners are usually cheap, that has not been so in the last couple years. Ohio, Texas, and Oklahoma are just a few of the states that have experienced shortages of the drugs used for lethal injections, which has driven up they're price. Other states' have even considered bringing back the firing squad, although human right's groups are unlikely to be impressed by that proposal.

And then there are the cases where the police, or a prosecutor, or some other office along the way gets it wrong. These are cases where innocent people are sent to their death for crimes they didn't commit. According to a 2014 study, roughly one in twenty-five inmates sentenced to death is innocent—and yet not all of them are able to make their case before their execution is carried out. This amounts to murder by the justice system rather than justice for the victims.

Whether its the cost or the issue of human rights', the death penalty is a holdover from an older era that we could do without. Most countries in the world have done away with it already, leaving the United States as one of only fifty-eight nations that still allow it. Some US states have even banned the practice, such as Massachusetts, New York, and New Mexico. Meanwhile, other states have gone to increasing lengths to keep killing their worst criminals. But rather than trying to erase the problem of violent crime, what we as a society should be doing is working to treat the causes of violence. Treatment, early intervention, and better policing are all more effective ways to try to keep violent crime from occurring—and any of them is more humane than trading life-for-life.

Editing an Essay for Apostrophes 2

The following essay has errors involving apostrophes. Working in your group, edit the essay to correct these errors.

Cooking in the Digital Age

We have a tradition in my family: every Christmas, my mom makes about a dozen small fruitcakes and sends them out to all our relative's households. Some go to New York to my moms sister, some to my dads' family in California, and one travels south to Florida. Its a tradition that weve repeated every year since I was just a little kid.

Every Thanksgiving, after the turkey had been eaten and the leftovers' stashed away for the next week of meals, my mom and I would break out the bowls and measuring cups, the fake maraschino cherries and the candied fruit chunks—and the dreaded figs—and set to work. The fruitcakes would be assembled, the batter would be sampled, and salmonella would be warned of. Then came the wrapping: in order to make a fruitcake properly, it had to sit wrapped in a bourbon-soaked gauze for roughly a month, which not only preserves it but also adds a little zip from the bourbon.

This is the tradition. Every Christmas we cut up the cake and enjoy a few slices (people may cringe, but its' the only genuinely good fruitcake in the known world). It's been this way for decades, ever since my mom got the recipe from my grandmother. But this kind of cooking and passing down of recipes' is falling out of fashion. Since the advent of the internet, family recipes have taken a backseat to quick and easy meals found online, leading more and more young cooks to start at they're phone or they're computer rather than at a cookbook.

A prime example of this trend is Buzzfeed. You might have heard of their news service or social media commentary, but Buzzfeed is also known for it's series of tasty videos. These show time-lapse video's of someone making a certain recipe, often something exotic like a cheeseburger with buns made of fried mac and cheese. The videos are entertainment (and believe me, their as entertaining as they are mouth-watering), but theyre also meant to be instructive. Some episodes will have a guest chef come and teach a new cooking technique, or theyll have a Buzzfeed employees parent come and make their family recipe.

This has become the new norm. The internet is a vast reference book for those who seek tips or recipes or just want to dream about something juicy. Other outlets have gone a similar route to Buzzfeed, and they're videos now take up a great deal of space on everyones' Facebook feed. Its a "thing" for this generation to try out these videos, too; I myself am guilty of using a Buzzfeed recipe to make a "pizza bread boule." (Yes, it's exactly what you're picturing.)

New studies' are showing, however, that millennials are coming into the real world without real-world skills like cooking. In answering the question why that is, the internet cooking craze may be part of the reason. It used to be that you learned a few recipes from someone at home and learned to improvise from there. But now its click, scroll, and read; some site's will even tell you what you can make from the leftover ingredients you find at the back of your fridge. Its' no longer solely a family experience—cooking has become both incredibly accessible and harder to learn properly at the same time.

There are pros and cons to this new way of doing things. On the one hand, not everyone can learn to cook or has someone at home to teach them. For those people, the internet is a welcome helper in the kitchen, where the endless combinations' of ingredients can be an overwhelming place to start. But whats lost are the traditional recipes like my moms' fruitcake, which is not something that will make it's way into a Buzzfeed video anytime soon. Learning to cook at home is learning to cook properly, to improvise and to figure out what combinations work, and to create your own recipes. That creativity may not make it to this generation—though at least well always have mac and cheese buns.

Ensuring Subject-Verb Agreement

Subject-verb agreement errors can greatly diminish the effectiveness of your writing; luckily, they are not that difficult to correct.

16.27 Activity

Subject-Verb Agreement 1

In the following pairs, the sentence in black is correct, and the sentence in blue has an error. Study these sentences and figure out the grammar rule they demonstrate.

Pair 1

✓ One student rides a motorcycle to school.

✗ One student ride a motorcycle to school.

Pair 2

✓ Two students ride motorcycles to school.

✗ Two students rides motorcycles to school.

Pair 3

✓ A tree grows in Brooklyn.

✗ A tree grow in Brooklyn.

Pair 4

✓ Many trees grow in Brooklyn.

✗ Many trees grows in Brooklyn.

Pair 5

✓ Marcia's mother lives in California.

✗ Marcia's mother live in California.

Pair 6

✓ Marcia's parents live in California.

✗ Marcia's parents lives in California.

NOTE: Record the grammar rule these items demonstrate in a notebook or online file for future reference.

16.28 Activity

Subject-Verb Agreement 2

In the following sentence pairs, the sentence in black is correct, and the sentence in blue has an error. Study these sentences and figure out the grammar rule they demonstrate.

Pair 1

✓ An essay is due on Friday.

✗ An essay are due on Friday.

Pair 2

✓ Four essays are required in this course.

✗ Four essays is required in this course.

Pair 3

✓ He is my cousin.

✗ He are my cousin.

Pair 4

✓ They are my best friends.

✗ They is my best friends.

Pair 5

✓ A car was parked in my driveway.

✗ A car were parked in my driveway.

Pair 6

✓ Two cars were parked in my driveway.

✗ Two cars was parked in my driveway.

Pair 7

✓ A police officer was waiting on my porch.

✗ A police officer were waiting on my porch.

Pair 8

✓ Two police officers were waiting on my porch.

✗ Two police officers was waiting on my porch.

NOTE: Record the grammar rule these items demonstrate in a notebook or online file for future reference.

16.29 Activity

Subject-Verb Agreement 3

In the following sentence pairs, the sentence in black is correct, and the sentence in blue has an error. Study these sentences and figure out the grammar rule they demonstrate.

Pair 1

✓ A friend of my parents lives in Denver.

✗ A friend of my parents live in Denver.

Pair 2

✓ A box of cookies was left on my doorstep.

✗ A box of cookies were left on my doorstep.

Pair 3

✓ One of my friends was in a car accident.

✗ One of my friends were in a car accident.

Pair 4

✓ The box of crayons was on sale for ninety-nine cents.

✗ The box of crayons were on sale for ninety-nine cents.

Pair 5

✓ High levels of water pollution are a threat to health.

✗ High levels of water pollution is a threat to health.

Pair 6

✓ Many songs on the top-ten list are ballads.

✗ Many songs on the top-ten list is ballads.

NOTE: Record the grammar rule these items demonstrate in a notebook or online file for future reference.

16.30 **Activity**

Subject-Verb Agreement 4 (Indefinite Pronouns 1)

In the following pairs, the sentence in black is correct, and the sentence in blue has an error. Study these sentences and figure out the grammar rule they demonstrate.

Pair 1

✓ Everyone in my math class is going to pass.

✗ Everyone in my math class are going to pass.

Pair 2

✓ Someone is waiting in your office.

✗ Someone are waiting in your office.

Pair 3

✓ Anyone with a question is invited to attend the meeting.

✗ Anyone with a question are invited to attend the meeting.

Pair 4

✓ Each of the puppies was adorable.

✗ Each of the puppies were adorable.

Pair 5

✓ Either of those sweaters is a good match with that skirt.

✗ Either of those sweaters are a good match with that skirt.

Pair 6

✓ One of these bicycles was stolen.

✗ One of these bicycles were stolen.

Pair 7

✓ Neither of these jobs offers medical insurance.

✗ Neither of these jobs offer medical insurance.

NOTE: Record the grammar rule these items demonstrate in a notebook or online file for future reference.

Indefinite Pronouns 1

You probably noticed that the subject in each of the preceding sentences is a pronoun; in fact, it is a special kind of pronoun known as an *indefinite pronoun*. Below is a list of common indefinite pronouns. Note that these indefinite pronouns are *always singular*. In Activity 16.31, you will encounter other indefinite pronouns that are not always singular.

Always singular			
anybody	everybody	neither/either	one
anyone	everyone	nobody	somebody
anything	everything	no one	someone
each	much	nothing	something

16.31 Activity

Subject-Verb Agreement 5 (Indefinite Pronouns 2 and 3)

In Unit 16.30 (p. 158), you encountered a group of indefinite pronouns that are *always singular*. Here they are again:

Always singular			
anybody	everybody	neither/either	one
anyone	everyone	nobody	somebody
anything	everything	no one	someone
each	much	nothing	something

Indefinite Pronouns 2

In the following sentence pairs, the subjects are all indefinite pronouns, but these are quite different from the ones you were working with in Activity 16.30. As usual, the sentences in black are correct; the sentences in blue have an error. Study these and figure out the grammar rule for this group of indefinite pronouns.

Pair 1

   ✓ Both of my brothers are going to work in my mother's restaurant for the summer.

   ✗ Both of my brothers is going to work in my mother's restaurant for the summer.

Pair 2

   ✓ Many of the patients in this hospital are from other states.

   ✗ Many of the patients in this hospital is from other states.

Pair 3

   ✓ A few of the houses in my neighborhood were damaged by the hurricane.

   ✗ A few of the houses in my neighborhood was damaged by the hurricane.

Pair 4

   ✓ Several of my favorite songs are by Beyoncé.

   ✗ Several of my favorite songs is by Beyoncé.

NOTE: Record the grammar rule these items demonstrate in a notebook or online file for future reference.

There are sixteen pronouns in English that are always singular (see p. 159). The four listed in the box below are the only pronouns in English that are always plural.

Always plural	both	few	many	several

Indefinite Pronouns 3

There is a third group of indefinite pronouns that function in a third way. Study the following groups of sentences, in which those in black are correct and those in blue have an error. Figure out what the grammar rule is for this group of indefinite pronouns. What determines whether the indefinite pronouns in this group are singular or plural?

Group 1

   ✓ All of my cookies are gone.

   ✗ All of my cookies is gone.

   ✓ All of my cake is gone.

   ✗ All of my cake are gone.

Group 2

  ✓ Some of my relatives are living in Florida.

  ✗ Some of my relatives is living in Florida.

  ✓ Some of my essay is about Florida.

  ✗ Some of my essay are about Florida.

Group 3

  ✓ None of the children were absent today.

  ✗ None of the children was absent today.

  ✓ None of the lecture was about grammar.

  ✗ None of the lecture were about grammar.

NOTE: Record the grammar rule these items demonstrate in a notebook or online file for future reference.

Earlier in this activity, you were introduced to the sixteen pronouns that are always singular. Following that, you encountered four pronouns that are always plural. Now you have discovered the six pronouns, listed in the box below, that are sometimes singular and other times plural.

Singular or plural	all any	more most	none	some

16.32 Activity

Editing an Essay for Subject-Verb Agreement 1

Proofread the following essay and correct any errors you find. These errors will all involve subject-verb agreement. To correct these errors, you will need to change the subject so it agrees with the verb or change the verb so it agrees with the subject.

Staying Fit

    Something millions of people struggle with, particularly in the United States, is staying physically fit. There are myriad reasons people worry about their weight, ranging from poor diet to not enough exercise. Because this is such an issue for so many people, it have garnered an enormous number of solutions. Some solutions is based in science and research; however, many more are urban myths or are only meant to sell some product and do nothing to help weight loss or muscle growth.

Weight loss is perhaps the most common reason people diet. Millions of Americans is considered overweight or obese, and the number are rising steadily every year. For these millions, the first answer to their weight problems seem simple: eat less. This has given rise to fad "fasting diets," among other calorie-counting methods. The logic seems sound: if you eat fewer calories, your body will search for more and will begin to burn off whatever fat it has stored already. But recent studies has shown that this is not always the case. Your body often responds the opposite way, storing more fat in anticipation of a longer period without food. So while overeating can lead to weight gain, undereating can also result in weight gain.

Another common weight loss idea is that "cleansing" will help. Hundreds of people do juice cleanses, during which each of them spend a week or two drinking nothing but juices. A carton of these juices are shipped as self-contained diets. In one sense, this is not a bad idea—the juices are healthy enough, and they keep one from eating too much else in the way of calories. However, the fat will not simply melt away in a few weeks as some commercials claim. And other cleanses are completely worthless; many are based on supplement pills, seaweed, kelp, or other substances that a company, like GNC, sell to unsuspecting buyers. They sound healthy, but they can't do what they advertise.

There are also fad workouts that are said to cure obesity. You've probably seen the commercials for P90X or Crossfit; they feature men and women who have the most chiseled muscles a person can get and tell people watching that they, too, could look like this if they join the program. Companies like Bowflex tries to sell new workout machines on a similar premise: working out will make you more fit in a few weeks. Recent studies has shown, however, that working out actually doesn't cause the body to burn a significant number of calories when compared to not working out. The body needs an average of 2,000 calories a day just to do the things we all have to do: breathe, talk, walk, and perform other bodily functions. Workouts burn only an extra few hundred calories, meaning that you can cancel out all your sit ups and deadlifts with one slice of pizza.

Which brings us to the only way to really lose weight: balance. Weight loss solutions is all about the panacea for obesity. But one size will never fit all when it comes to weight loss. There are too many factors—everyone's metabolism is different, everyone's genes will only allow them to be so thin or so broad, and men and women carry fat differently. The most important thing to do to lose weight is to find what works for one's own body. This means eating right and avoiding too much processed food and added sugar, and eating vegetables and fruit for nutrients and fiber. It doesn't have to mean counting calories and working out for two hours a day—it just means finding your balance.

16.33 **Activity**

Editing an Essay for Subject-Verb Agreement 2

Proofread the following essay and correct any errors you find. These errors will all involve subject-verb agreement. To correct these errors, you will need to change the subject so it agrees with the verb or change the verb so it agrees with the subject.

Do We Exist? How Do We Know?

"I think, therefore I am." It's a statement meant to answer the age-old question, "How do we know we exist?" The question of consciousness have bothered philosophers since time has been recorded, asking us to wonder whether or not our world is real, whether or not we are real, and how we can prove it. Though the subject has been probed by many over time, it's only recently that we've seen attempts at a scientific answer. But despite the influx of modern study and thought, an absolute answer still eludes us.

First, a rough definition: Merriam-Webster defines consciousness as "The state of being characterized by sensation, emotion, volition, and thought."

In other words, each of us experience the state of being alive, mentally present, and aware of ourselves. For the sake of not muddying the waters here, we'll leave animals out of this and say that humans are the only beings who fully experience this state (although certain primates and even elephants have been shown to have some basic understanding of self). This is, as far as we can tell, what sets us apart from the rest of the animal kingdom. It's our greatest advantage and the source of all the thought, art, science, and history that we knows today.

Although it was the French philosopher René Descartes who first coined the phrase, "ego cogito, ergo sum" (usually translated to English as, "I think, therefore I am") in the mid-1600s, the idea of higher cognition and the self had already been in existence for millennia. But the focus of early philosophers were often more on the soul than on the mind; for example, Judeo-Christian ideology hones in on the idea of "free will," a gift supposedly given to man by God to separate him from the animals and to allow him to create his own destiny. Similarly, Egyptian and Greek theologies tell of a soul that remains conscious after death, traveling to the underworld to (potentially) live on.

But in modern times, everyone have developed modern perceptions of reality. The age of computers have given rise to a theory that everything we see, the entire universe around us, including our own minds, are all part of an advanced computer simulation being run by a more evolved race of beings. While it may sound like science fiction, it's hard to argue with some of the points the theory makes about our reality. They are perhaps best summarized by the character Morpheus in the first movie of the *Matrix* trilogy: "If real is what you can feel, smell, taste and see, then 'real' is simply electrical signals interpreted by your brain." An advanced enough computer, or artificial intelligence (AI), could (theoretically) hijack the senses the mind relies on and replace the real world with a simulated alternative—or create humans and place us in what we call Earth. What we perceive as consciousness could be no more than an ordered array of 1's and 0's, generated by a hyper-advanced version of Sim City. How would we know the difference?

Stranger still may be the idea of "panpsychism." According to the Stanford Encyclopedia of Philosophy, followers of this theory holds that everything in the world possesses its own brand of consciousness. From humans to animals, all the way down to the grains of sand that cover the beach, everything have some kind of experience. What it's like to be a rock, most of us can never say, but this odd theory tells us that because a rock exists, it has an experience. It may not be able to think like a human, and it most certainly can't tell us what it's like to be itself, but it has the most basic level of consciousness possible. For followers of this odd field, that's enough to say it has some parts of a mind, just not enough to rival our own.

Each of these theories—the soul, the simulation hypothesis, panpsychism— have never been completely proven—and maybe they never will be. Maybe one day neuroscience or some other field will give us the answer to what consciousness is. At the moment, however, scientists can't even agree on exactly when consciousness arises in human beings. It will undoubtedly take more time and further study to discover the origin of human thought. For now, we may just have to accept that Descartes was right: the best way to know that we exist is that we can wonder about whether we do.

Avoiding Pronoun Reference and Agreement Errors

Pronouns are extremely useful words, but errors with them can detract significantly from the effectiveness of your writing.

16.34 Activity

Pronouns and Antecedents

A *pronoun* is a word that takes the place of a noun. In each of the sentences in the following activity, a pronoun is printed in blue. The noun that the pronoun is taking the place of—is standing in for—is called its *antecedent*.

Identifying Antecedents

Working together with your group, identify the antecedent for the pronoun in blue in each of these sentences. Pay particular attention to the last two. They are a little different, but perfectly correct.

1. Our state senator has announced that **he** will retire at the end of next year.
2. Before my sister could finish dinner, **she** remembered to call me.
3. This lasagna will taste great after **it** is baked for an hour.
4. The jury members told the judge **they** wanted to continue deliberating all weekend.
5. My grandparents knew that **they** would be invited to my graduation.
6. Kristin bought a computer from her uncle. **He** fixed it when it broke down.
7. My cousins had a party for the young man who moved in next door. **They** invited everyone in the neighborhood.
8. The book I was reading was about ancient Greece. **It** started with the earliest settlements on the island of Crete.
9. When **she** arrived at work, Imani was surprised to find the office closed.
10. Because **they** live in Hawai'i, my parents don't have any winter clothes.

The pronouns in these sentences work just the way pronouns are supposed to work. Each one is clearly taking the place of a specific noun, its antecedent. Notice that in 6, 7, and 8 the antecedent is actually located in a previous sentence. In 9 and 10, the pronoun comes earlier in the sentence than its antecedent. These are all perfectly correct.

16.35 Activity

Vague Pronoun Reference 1

In Pronouns and Antecedents (16.34, p. 165), you saw the way a pronoun takes the place of a noun, its antecedent. The next set of sentences is a little different. Working in groups, try to identify the antecedent for the pronouns in blue in these sentences. If you cannot identify an antecedent, be prepared to explain why not.

1. Mr. Nowak sent a package to my father when **he** received a promotion.
2. Maria told Christine that **she** had passed the final exam.
3. When Isaiah shook George's hand, **he** never looked at **him**.
4. Helen's brothers never came to see her parents while **they** were on welfare.
5. After Juanita paid the salesclerk, **she** whistled.

This problem—having more than one possible antecedent for a pronoun—is known as *vague pronoun reference*. Revise each of the sentences above to correct this problem.

16.36 Activity

Vague Pronoun Reference 2

In Vague Pronoun Reference 1 (16.35, p. 166), you discovered one kind of error with pronoun reference—a pronoun that has two possible antecedents. In this section, you will discover another. Working in groups, try to identify the antecedent for the pronouns in blue in these sentences. If you cannot identify an antecedent, be prepared to explain why not.

1. In Hawai'i, **they** all live near the ocean.
2. Scott bought a pair of skis, but he has never even tried **it** before.
3. By early April the dogwoods had flowered, and by the middle of May, **they** had fallen to the ground.
4. In New York City, **they** were much friendlier than I expected.
5. At the Department of Motor Vehicles, **they** told me I needed to get a new title to my car.

This problem—a pronoun that simply has no antecedent—is another form of *vague pronoun reference*. Revise each of the sentences above to correct this problem.

16.37 Activity

Vague Pronoun Reference 3

The sentences in this activity are different from any that you've seen so far. Working in groups, try to identify the antecedent for the pronouns in blue in these sentences. If you cannot identify an antecedent, be prepared to explain why not.

1. Actually visiting Jerusalem was something of a disappointment for Sarah. She had dreamed about the trip since she was a child. **This** is what was so disappointing to her.
2. I bought these shoes at Ward's during the spring sale. **This** is why they were so cheap.
3. I got my résumé typed on a word processor, and **after** three interviews, I was hired as a data processor for the Social Security Administration. I really appreciated Maxine's help with **this**.

4. The sky was beginning to get darker, and I had missed the last bus to Washington. **This** was making me very worried.

5. My mother wants to take us to Portland, and my father is hoping that we come to his house in Boston. **This** seems like a very nice offer.

This problem—using the pronoun *this* to refer back to some general idea that is hard to identify—is yet another form of *vague pronoun reference*. Revise each of the sentences above to correct this problem.

16.38 **Tutorial**

Pronoun Agreement

Units 16.34–16.37 explain the concept of pronoun reference, the idea that a pronoun stands for or takes the place of a noun (or occasionally another pronoun), which is called the *antecedent* for that pronoun. Those units also explained that it should always be completely clear what noun or pronoun is the antecedent of each pronoun.

This unit will introduce an additional rule about the use of pronouns. In the following sentences the black versions are correct, and the blue versions contain an error. Study these examples and determine what this additional grammar rule is.

✓ My brother lives in California, but he is coming to visit this weekend.

✗ My brother lives in California, but they are coming to visit this weekend.

✓ My mother owns a convertible, but she never puts the top down.

✗ My mother owns a convertible, but he never puts the top down.

✓ When Bernie Sanders ran for president, he surprised everyone.

✗ When Bernie Sanders ran for president, they surprised everyone.

✓ If people in America work hard, they expect to get ahead.

✗ If people in America work hard, he expects to get ahead.

✓ When my father was in high school, he got straight A's.

✗ When my father was in high school, she got straight A's.

NOTE: Record the grammar rule these items demonstrate in a notebook or online file for future reference.

You probably noticed that in each of the blue sentences, there is a problem involving the pronoun and its antecedent. They don't match up correctly. In some cases, the pronoun is singular and the antecedent is plural; in other cases, it's the other way around and the pronoun is plural and its antecedent is singular. In still others, the pronoun is male, but the antecedent is female, or the other way around. We call this matching of pronouns and their antecedents *agreement*. Pronouns must *agree* with their antecedents in number (singular or plural) and gender.

The errors in the blue sentences above are easy to see. Almost nobody would write those sentences. They are being used simply to introduce the principle of pronoun agreement. In the next group of sentences, however, the blue versions contain errors that are not quite so obvious, errors that some students actually make.

✓ I admire women who can stand up for themselves.

✗ I admire women who can stand up for herself.

✓ My Macintosh was much less expensive than I expected it to be.

✗ My Macintosh was much less expensive than I expected them to be.

✓ Janice is one of those women who will make names for themselves.

✗ Janice is one of those women who will make a name for herself.

In these pairs of sentences you can see that ensuring that pronouns agree with their antecedents can be a little tricky. The third pair is especially difficult. Note that the sentence is saying that there are a number of women who will make names for themselves, so *themselves* refers to *women*, not *Janice*.

A Note about "Singular" *They*

Take a look at the following sentences. As usual, the black sentences are correct, while the blue sentence has an error.

✓ When a student takes an exam, he or she should read the questions carefully.

✓ When a student takes an exam, they should read the questions carefully.

✗ When a student takes an exam, they should read the questions carefully.

Note that the second and third bulleted sentences are identical, but one is black and one is blue. They are marked this way because there is some disagreement about the use of *they* in these sentences. For many years, grammarians have insisted that *they* can only be plural, but, despite the grammarians, the English language, like all languages, is constantly changing. These days, most people find that *he or she* is a little awkward, but they don't want to use just *he* because it ignores the fact that students are just as likely to be female. To avoid being awkward or sexist, they use *they* as a singular pronoun. This change in the language is widely—but not universally—accepted today.

For those writers (and readers) who have accepted the use of *they* as singular, the second bulleted sentence is correct. In deciding whether you are going to use *they* as a singular as well as a plural pronoun, you should think carefully about your audience. If your audience is your instructor in an English class, you might want to ask him or her (or should that be *they?*) if it is permissible to use *they* as a singular pronoun. The following examples illustrate the same issue.

✓ A voter in this country should mark his or her ballot carefully.

✓ A voter in this country should mark their ballot carefully.

✗ **A voter in this country should mark their ballot carefully.**

✓ A member of a jury must make up his or her own mind about the guilt or innocence of the accused.

✓ A member of a jury must make up their own mind about the guilt or innocence of the accused.

✗ **A member of a jury must make up their own mind about the guilt or innocence of the accused.**

You may be surprised to learn that writers have been using this "singular" *they* for hundreds of years. Chaucer used it and so did such respected writers as William Shakespeare, Jane Austen, Thomas Huxley, and Daniel Defoe. The rule that *they* could be used only with a plural antecedent was first announced in the eighteenth century and became widespread in the nineteenth century.

Gender-Neutral Pronouns

In the twenty-first century, a new set of rules is being proposed: the use of *gender-neutral pronouns*. In an age in which it has become widely accepted that the two genders—male and female—do not apply to everyone, an age in which we are becoming aware that people may be transgender or non-binary, various new pronouns have been suggested. Most popular of these new pronouns are those represented by *ze* and *hir*. They correlate with traditional pronouns like this:

Ze talked.	I emailed *hir.*	*Hir* car is blue.	*Ze* talks to *hirself.*
He talked.	I emailed *him.*	*His* car is blue.	*He* talks to *himself.*
She talked.	I emailed *her.*	*Her* car is blue.	*She* talks to *herself.*

While this set of non-gendered pronouns grew out of the LBGTQ community, it turns out they are also useful when a pronoun is needed to refer to an antecedent that has no gender or whose gender is unknown: *someone, angels, robots*, and genderless creatures in science fiction.

Agreement and Indefinite Pronouns

You know that a pronoun must agree with its antecedent in two ways: the pronoun must be singular or plural to match its antecedent, and the pronoun must be male or female (or non-gendered) to match its antecedent. However, many students have difficulty with the idea of pronoun agreement when the antecedent is not a noun but an indefinite pronoun. The following chart lists the most common indefinite pronouns and indicates whether they are singular or plural.

Always singular	anybody anyone anything each either	everybody everyone everything much	neither nobody no one nothing	one somebody someone something
Always plural	both	few	many	several
Singular or plural	all any	more most	none	some

The indefinite pronouns that are always singular are a little confusing because words like *everyone* and *each* seem to be standing for a number of people, and so seem to be plural. That's the hard part. Even though they *seem* to be plural, all the pronouns in the first row of the chart are *always* singular.

In the second row of the chart, the pronouns seem to be plural, and they are, so they're not so hard.

In the third row, singular or plural, things are a little trickier. These pronouns are singular if they are followed by a prepositional phrase ending in a singular noun. They are plural if they are followed by a prepositional phrase ending in a plural noun. Here are some examples that show how this works:

- Most of the songs are from the sixties. (*most* is plural because *songs* is plural)
- Most of the music is from the sixties. (*most* is singular because *music* is singular)
- Some of the books were damaged in the flood. (*some* is plural because *books* is plural)
- Some of the test was very easy. (*some* is singular because *test* is singular)
- Any of the beers in this bar are organic. (*any* is plural because *beers* is plural)
- Any of the wine on this list is too expensive for my budget. (*any* is singular because *wine* is singular)

16.39 Activity

Correcting Pronoun Errors

Working in your group and using what you learned in Units 16.34–16.38, edit the following sentences. All errors will involve vague pronoun reference (16.34–16.37) or pronoun agreement (16.38).

1. When young children are read to, he or she is beginning to learn to read.
2. Before she had time to sit down, Joy Reed asked Melania Trump a question.
3. In New York City, they are voting in a special election this Tuesday.
4. The clerk agreed to refund my father's deposit before he had even asked for it.
5. In this election, they are spending millions of dollars on advertising.
6. Regina paid too much for her microwave, and she really doesn't like to microwave food. This is why she tried to sell the microwave on Craig's List.
7. Reggie and Joshua got into a huge argument last night, so this morning he called to apologize.
8. The football team had committed themselves to playing on Sundays.
9. When a customer wants help with a purchase, they shouldn't have to wait fifteen minutes.
10. A politician has to make promises that sometimes they can't keep.

16.40 Activity

Editing an Essay for Pronoun Errors 1

The following essay contains errors involving vague pronoun reference and pronoun agreement. Working in your group, edit the essay to correct these errors.

Voter Registration

Most countries around the world today are democracies. It's the first time in history that that can be said; the number of democracies only surpassed other forms of government in the twentieth century, making it the dominant method of choosing leadership. But this means that each nation has to choose their representatives, and that means there needs to be a method for doing so: voting. In the United States, a single day each year is set on which people vote for their representatives. But in order to get to the voting booth in the first place, citizens must navigate the voter registration laws in his or her home state. In some places, these processes are so arduous that it is difficult or impossible for people to vote—meaning that some people in this democracy are effectively denied a voice.

The United States has been a democracy since the late 1700s when it won its independence from Great Britain. At the time it was one of the only democracies in the world—and perhaps *the* only one. But while other modern democracies have developed over the last 200 years, the United States has done relatively little to adapt to the changing times. It is an embarrassment. We still use paper ballots, we still bubble in the name of the person we vote for, and we still have to register ourselves to vote.

In some countries, the registration process is streamlined. In Estonia, for example, voter registration is automatic. They send a voter identification card to each citizen and even allows it to be used to vote online because it wants people to vote. This not only makes voting more convenient—as it can literally be done from the comfort of one's own home—but also increases voter turnout. When voting is easier, and even encouraged by policies like automatic voter registration, voter turnout rises dramatically.

Other countries have tried a different approach. Australia, for one, has mandatory voting. The fine is about $20 if you don't cast a ballot, and if you think they won't find you, you'll find you're mistaken rather quickly. The government cross-references addresses, tax records, and any other data about each citizen to ensure that everyone votes or pays their fine. This ensures that the country has a virtually 100% voter turnout each year, ensuring every citizen has a voice in their government.

A more relaxed approach to this process is taken in Sweden, where voting is not compulsory but registration is. Once citizens hit 18, he or she is immediately registered to vote. The same goes for immigrants, who are also registered the moment they become citizens. In Sweden, they really want everyone to vote.

These countries compare starkly with the United States. Each American state has their own registration process, and the wait times to be processed can be weeks or even months. When an American mails in their registration forms, they can take weeks to process them and issue voter ID cards.

Americans also don't get the day off from work to vote; in many countries, Election Day is a national holiday. This is another problem that needs immediate attention. In America, many people can't afford to miss time at their job and therefore won't be able to vote. There is also the issue of voter identification: some states now require a photo ID to vote, and this has become a problem for many low-income, elderly, and minority voters, who do not have easy access to identification. That process, too, costs money and can take weeks to carry out.

Compared to many other countries, America has a very complex voting process. Registering can be slow and arduous, and the process of voting itself can be equally so. Many other countries have set better examples and moved into the twenty-first century with their election practices. Though America has one of the oldest democracies around, it is not the most evolved; with some time and some clear guidance from overseas, however, it one day might be.

16.41 Activity

Editing an Essay for Pronoun Errors 2

The following essay has errors involving vague pronoun reference and pronoun agreement. Working in your group, edit the essay to correct these errors.

Wildlife Refuges

It's easy to forget that wildlife refuges exist; we never really see them, as they occupy a space that most humans never set foot in. Their purpose is to shelter animals from human beings and give them respite from pollution and development. But they also provide access for people who want to see the outdoors as it is meant to be: untouched and undisturbed.

The National Wildlife Refuge System (NWRS) was founded over a hundred years ago by President Theodore Roosevelt as a means to preserve certain wildlife species. He ordered Ethan Hitchcock, his Secretary of the Interior, to start work on refuges before he had even been sworn in. At the time, they had been over-hunting animals and driving many species to dangerously low levels, threatening their survival. The creation of the wildlife refuges not only stabilized many of those populations but also created a massive network where scientists could continue making gains on conservation work. Since then, the refuge system has grown to include hundreds of refuges across the country, protecting thousands of animal species and millions of acres of land. This is why the system of wildlife refuges is so important.

While the refuges' original intent was to preserve wildlife for the sake of sustainable hunting and resource conservation (i.e., fur, feathers, and other products taken from animals), they have evolved into a haven for species protected by the Endangered Species Act. And they have also become test sites for conservation work, places where universities and other interest groups can study animal and plant life. This allows them an undisturbed habitat, where they can test new conservation methods and habitat management techniques.

Refuges are essential territory for biologists, but they're also beneficial for the public. They're a great place to go hunting—and with some species, like turkey or deer, it's essential for some of those herds (or flocks) to be culled. A periodic cull controls populations, allowing for greater competition and biodiversity among species. However, in some refuges, the hunters outnumber the biologists, and they don't respect the other's rights.

Another benefit the public gets to enjoy is the trails and other maintained areas where they can walk and enjoy nature. They provide free, curated access to the outdoors that can be hard to find elsewhere. Some of the best trails in the country are on refuges, and they're free and open to the public at all hours of the day.

Wildlife refuges aren't places we think about very often—in fact, people could be driving through a refuge and not even know it. But despite their place on the periphery, they are essential sites for study and research. They provide easy access to nature not only for those who want to conserve it, but also for people who simply enjoy it. They know how important these refuges are. For access to the outdoors, there is no better place.

Combining Sentences in Interesting Ways

The exercises in this section will give you the opportunity to explore the flexibility of language, discover the many options for expressing a single idea, and the chance to practice the grammar conventions covered earlier in this Topic.

16.42 Tutorial
Sentence Combining

Most students find sentence-combining activities to be fun, perhaps because there are no *correct* answers. The following activities give you a series of short, simple declarative sentences and ask you to combine them into one longer and more complex sentence. They invite you to be inventive, to be playful, and to experiment with different combinations. The only rule is that the one sentence you come up with must include all the information that was in the original short sentences. Of course, you will also need to make sure your sentences are grammatically correct.

Here's an example of how this works:

Short Sentences

Daris is a student in my English class.

Daris gave me a ride this morning.

My car broke down on the interstate.

Possible Combinations

When my car broke down on the interstate this morning, Daris, a student in my English class, gave me a ride.

Daris is a student in my English class, and when my car broke down on the interstate this morning, he gave me a ride.

Daris, who is a student in my English class, gave me a ride when my car broke down on the interstate this morning.

When my car broke down on the interstate this morning, a student named Daris in my English class gave me a ride.

16.43 Activity

Sentence Combining 1

Below are five sets of short, simple sentences. Working with your group, combine each set into one longer and more complex sentence. Make sure your one sentence contains all the information from the set of short sentences.

Set 1

The man is wearing a green sweater.
The man is my uncle.
The man is wearing a red hat.
The man is smoking a cigar.

Set 2

Javier climbed onto his bicycle.
Javier's bicycle was bright green.
Javier grasped the handlebars.
Javier placed his feet on the pedals.
Javier smiled.

Set 3

We went for a hike.
We hiked around Lake Delafield.

It started to rain.

We took shelter in a cabin.

The cabin belonged to Professor Starr.

Set 4

April was sweating profusely.

She clenched her teeth.

April struggled to open the door to her Volkswagen.

Her struggle was desperate.

Set 5

Jasmine had been rude.

Jasmine realized it.

Jasmine made a U-turn.

Jasmine drove back to school.

Jasmine apologized to her teacher.

16.44 Activity

Sentence Combining 2

Below are five sets of short, simple sentences. Working with your group, combine each set into one longer and more complex sentence. Make sure your one sentence contains all the information from the set of short sentences

Set 1

The price of gas has reached three dollars a gallon.

Gerard Bisset's car is seven years old.

Gerard Bisset is my next-door neighbor.

Gerard Bisset is going to buy a Prius.

Set 2

I left my computer in the Parkside Restaurant.

My computer is a Macintosh.

My computer is a laptop.

I had dinner in the Parkside Restaurant last night.

I am not worried.

Set 3

My grandfather was a truly generous man.

My grandfather gave away all his money.

My grandfather left our family impoverished.

Set 4

Benjamin Cardin is a senator from Maryland.

Benjamin Cardin wrote a bill.

The bill would provide more Pell Grants to students.

Benjamin Cardin will be interviewed on Channel 13 tonight.

Set 5

I was listening to my favorite Beethoven symphony.

My favorite Beethoven symphony is the Eroica.

I noticed a woman walking into the room.

She was a woman I did not want to talk to.

She had dumped me for another guy last year.

16.45 Activity

Sentence Combining 3

Below are five sets of short, simple sentences. Working with your group, combine each set into one longer and more complex sentence. Make sure your one sentence contains all the information from the set of short sentences.

Set 1

I like a good cappuccino.

A cappuccino is coffee with lots of warm milk.

A cappuccino usually has whipped cream on top.

I also like a good cold beer.

Set 2

I read a novel this weekend.

The novel was about a totalitarian state.

The novel's title was *1984*.

It was written by George Orwell.

Set 3

I was sitting by a beautiful stream.

I was reading a book.

A woman walked up.

The woman sat down near me.

She was reading the same book I was.

Set 4

I need to go shopping.

I am out of coffee.

I am out of bread.

I am out of eggs.

I am out of money.

I can't go shopping.

Set 5

My daughter started the first grade last week.

She loves going to school.

Two of her best friends are in her class.

Her teacher seems to be very nice.

Her teacher is Ms. Williams.

16.46 Activity

Sentence Combining 4

Below are five sets of short, simple sentences. Working with your group, combine each set into one longer and more complex sentence. Make sure your one sentence contains all the information from the set of short sentences.

Set 1

That man is wearing a bright purple sweater.

That man is wearing an orange shirt.

That man is playing a harmonica.

That man was here yesterday.

I think that man is a busker.

Set 2

Angelique took a deep breath.

She walked to the end of the diving board.

She was wearing a black one-piece swimming suit.

She paused for a full minute.

She launched herself into the air.

She entered the water with almost no splash.

Set 3

Asher was planting irises in his garden.

It started to rain.

Asher refused to stop.

He got all his irises planted.

He got soaking wet.

Set 4

I was waiting for the elevator in the science building.

My English professor walked up.

My English professor was carrying a box of test tubes.

I looked at her more closely.

I discovered she wasn't my English professor.

Set 5

The dancers were waiting for the music to begin.

Their faces looked excited.

Their smiles looked artificial.

They had rehearsed well.

They were ready to perform.

Activity

Sentence Combining 5

Following are five sets of short, simple sentences. Working with your group, combine each set into one longer and more complex sentence. Make sure your one sentence contains all the information from the set of short sentences.

Set 1

> I live in the city.
>
> I am used to lots of noise.
>
> I am used to cars honking.
>
> I am used to the sirens of fire engines.
>
> I probably couldn't sleep in the country.

Set 2

> I made a risotto.
>
> Risotto is one of Donna's favorite dishes.
>
> Donna grilled chicken.
>
> We drank some wine from Italy.
>
> The wine was a Chianti.

Set 3

> At first the crowd was silent.
>
> Then a roar erupted.
>
> People stood up.
>
> People stamped their feet.
>
> Bono came out again.
>
> Bono took a bow.

Set 4

> Arun was studying chemistry.
>
> The phone rang.
>
> Arun answered the phone.
>
> It was his girlfriend.
>
> Arun forgot about chemistry.

Set 5

I applied for a job at the new steak house.

I have an AA degree in culinary arts.

I worked for four years in my parents' restaurant.

My parents owned an Italian restaurant.

I was offered a position as sous chef.

Language and Computers

Here, at the end of Topic 16, you will explore using computers to edit your writing.

16.48 Activity

Computers and Editing 1

Paragraph 1, below, has nine grammar errors that have been underlined. Paragraph 2 is identical to Paragraph 1 except the errors have been corrected. You may want to compare each of the nine underlined errors in Paragraph 1 with the corresponding corrections in Paragraph 2 to make sure you understand what the errors are.

Paragraph 1

Lots of problems for the work force have been solved by the minimum wage. The work force actually has a <u>Government</u> backing the<u>m, and</u> saying <u>its</u> not fair to pay someone pennies when it takes quarters to survive. Before the minimum wage was ena<u>cted busi</u>nesses could pay their employees anything they wanted, sometimes leaving their employees without the money to buy simple necessities such as food, w<u>ater cloth</u>ing, or shoes. This was a very unfair system, exploiting the workers, who had no way to defend themselves. Many of these workers didn't even have a <u>choice, ma</u>ny had families that they supported. If <u>you</u> decided to leave your current job to find a better paying one, <u>you</u> never knew how long it was going to take to find one. Spending every penny they earned just to surv<u>ive, le</u>ft no savings to rely on while they looked for a new job.

Paragraph 2

Lots of problems for the work force have been solved by the minimum wage. The work force actually has a <u>government</u> backing the<u>m and</u> saying <u>it's</u> not fair to pay someone pennies when it takes quarters to survive. Before the minimum wage was enacted, businesses could pay their employees any-thing they wanted, sometimes leaving their employees without the money to buy simple necessities such as food, water, clothing, or shoes. This was a very unfair system, exploiting the workers, who had no way to defend themselves. Many of these workers didn't even have a choice. Many had families that they supported. If they decided to leave their current job to find a better paying one, they never knew how long it was going to take to find one. Spending every penny they earned just to survive left no savings to rely on while they looked for a new job.

Activity: Testing Grammar Checkers

When you're ready to do this activity, type Paragraph 3, below, into a word proces-sor and then run the computer's grammar checker to see what it locates as errors. Compare the grammar checker's list of errors with those in Paragraph 1. How good a job did the grammar checker do?

Paragraph 3

Lots of problems for the work force have been solved by the minimum wage. The work force actually has a Government backing them, and saying its not fair to pay someone pennies when it takes quarters to survive. Before the minimum wage was enacted businesses could pay their employees anything they wanted, sometimes leaving their employees without the money to buy simple necessities such as food, water clothing, or shoes. This was a very unfair system, exploiting the workers, who had no way to defend themselves. Many of these workers didn't even have a choice, many had families that they supported. If you decided to leave your current job to find a better paying one, you never knew how long it was going to take to find one. Spending every penny they earned just to survive, left no savings to rely on while they looked for a new job.

16.49 Tutorial
Computers and Editing 2

Microsoft Word has one simple tool that can be very useful when you are editing your writing: the Find function, usually found on the Edit menu. As you are writing this semester, keep track of the grammar, punctuation, and word choice rules that you have trouble with most often.

When you have finished writing and revising your essay, use the Find function to search for each of the problematic terms. Here's one student's list:

to, too, two

its, it's

's, s'

your, you're

This student first used Find to search for every place she had written *to*. As the computer found each one, she checked to see if it was used correctly. Then she searched for *too* and checked each of those. Next, she searched for *two* and checked each of those. Then she did the same for each of the other terms on her list.

As you saw in Unit 16.48 (p. 183), the computer is not so good at deciding whether something you have written is grammatically correct, but it is infallible at finding every instance of a word or phrase. So I recommend that you use the Find function to locate every place you've used a word or phrase from your list, but then use your own understanding of the rule involved, as you've learned it in this topic, to decide whether you've used the word or phrase correctly.

TOPIC 17

Titles, Introductions, and Conclusions

Topic 17 discusses three brief but important parts of an essay—the title, the introduction, and the conclusion—and provides strategies for ensuring these three components enhance the effectiveness of your essay.

Navigating Topic 17

The tutorials below provide information about how to write titles, introductions, and conclusions, and each is followed by an opportunity to apply the skills you have just learned. You can work through the entire Topic on your own, learning about all the strategies and practicing them; work on items you've been assigned by your instructor; or choose just the ones you find helpful.

Introduction to Titles, Introductions, and Conclusions   186

17.1	Tutorial	Titles 187
17.2	Activity	Writing Titles 189
17.3	Tutorial	Introductory Paragraphs 189
17.4	Activity	Writing Introductory Paragraphs 192
17.5	Tutorial	Closing Paragraphs 193
17.6	Activity	Writing Conclusions 195

Introduction to Titles, Introductions, and Conclusions

Topic 17 opens with a discussion of options for titles, then provides different ways to write an introductory paragraph, and closes with a discussion of strategies for concluding an essay effectively and avoiding several common mistakes.

17.1 Tutorial

Titles

The first thing a reader sees in your essay is the title, so it's important. But coming up with one is probably best left to the end of the writing of the essay. At that point, you'll have a clear idea of what the essay is about and what you want to bring to the reader's attention in the title.

Options for Titles

In coming up with a title, as with everything else you write in an essay, you want to think about the audience you are writing for and the purpose for which you are writing. (For more information, see Thinking about Audience [9.4, p. 14] and Thinking about Purpose [9.6, p. 17].) What will be most effective with your reader? How can you best convey the gist of your paper and indicate your purpose? Of course, there are no easy or automatic answers to these questions. You will need to decide which will work best with the person or people you expect will read what you have written. Here are some useful options.

Option 1: Announce Your Topic or Thesis

At its most straightforward, Option 1 means you simply announce the topic you will be discussing:

"Genetically Modified Organisms"

"Immigration Policy"

"Global Warming"

Notice that these titles tell the topic of the paper, but do not give a hint about what the writer will say about the topic.

A variation on Option 1 is to announce not just your topic, but your thesis.

"Tax Cuts for the Rich Do Not Trickle Down to the Rest of Us"

"Children Are Being Separated from Their Parents at the US Border"

"The Next Five Years Are Our Last Chance to Reverse Global Warming"

Option 2: Capture Your Reader's Attention

If the goal in Option 1 is to announce your topic or your thesis, the goal in Option 2 is entirely different. Under Option 2, the goal is to capture the readers' attention, to make them want to read what you have written, to entice them to read your essay. Wit and whimsy can help here, so you can say something startling or puzzling.

"Unbelievable Development"

"This Doesn't Add Up"

"Until Hell Freezes Over"

Be aware, though, that these puzzling or enticing titles can backfire. Encountering a title that is obviously trying to tease a reader into reading can actually put them off: "I don't like being teased, so I'm not going to read this." The most flagrant and least successful example of this type of title that some students have resorted to over the years is "Sex." Then the first sentence of the paper admits the ruse: "Now that I have your attention, I'd like to talk about gun safety."

Option 3: Entice First; Announce Second

The third option is really a combination of the first two. You start with one of those puzzling, enticing phrases, then you add a semicolon, and then you add a straightforward statement of your topic or your topic and your stance about that topic.

"Until Hell Freezes Over: The Next Five Years Are Our Last Chance to Reverse Global Warming"

"Unbelievable Development: Children Are Being Separated from Their Parents at the US Border"

"This Doesn't Add Up: Tax Cuts for the Rich Do Not Trickle Down to the Rest of Us"

Option 3 might seem like the obvious best choice since it combines the advantages of the first two options. However, it can also lead to long and somewhat clumsy titles. As it turns out, these two-part titles are most commonly used for very scholarly works, especially book-length works.

Now that you know some basic options available to you for a title, you can combine this knowledge with your understanding of your audience to come up with a title for any writing you do.

17.2 Activity
Writing Titles

Working in your group, select one of the following essay options and come up with at least three different titles for it. Be ready to share your writing in about fifteen minutes.

1. An essay for a class in political science in which you will argue that America's right to free and fair elections is threatened by various political acts of the party in power

2. An article to be published in your local newspaper proposing ways to make it safer for bicyclists on public roads

3. An essay for a class in nursing or another health field in which you argue for changes in how nurses or health-care workers are educated

4. A letter to your local congressional representative in which you argue for the need to lower the cost of going to college

5. A letter to the Secretary of Education in which you suggest improvements in the requirements or procedure involved in applying for financial aid

17.3 Tutorial
Introductory Paragraphs

Because getting started on a piece of writing can often be the hardest part, writing the introductory or opening paragraph can sometimes have a paralyzing effect. In this unit you will read about some options that should help you avoid this kind of paralysis. When you do get started, remember to think about who will read what you're writing. Who is your audience? Then write the kind of introduction that will be most effective with that audience. (For more information on audience, see Thinking about Audience [9.4, p. 14].) You will also want to keep in mind your topic and the purpose for which you are writing (see Thinking about Purpose [9.6, p. 17]).

Elements of a Good Introduction

Regardless of which option you choose for organizing your introduction, certain elements are almost always included:

- **A hook.**   A statement, an example, a fact, or a quotation that catches the reader's attention.

- **Background information or history.**   An explanation of the context in which you are arguing your position. What has happened leading up to your proposal? What problems exist that make your proposal necessary? What solutions have been suggested in the past, and why did they fail?

- **Establishment of *ethos*.**   It's important to convince your audience that you can be trusted, that you know what you're talking about, and that you will not exaggerate or dissemble. (For more information on *ethos*, see Three Types of Appeal [11.6, p. 58].)

- **A thesis.**   The position you are taking—the point you are making, your stand on your topic—is your thesis and is customarily stated in an introductory paragraph. (For more information on thesis, see Thesis Statements [10.5, p. 32].)

Types of Introductory Paragraphs

There are many way you can start an essay. Here are several different strategies you can use.

Problem to Solution

One highly effective option for an introductory paragraph is to identify a problem, providing some evidence that the problem exists, offering some discussion of the history of the problem, and finally suggesting a solution to the problem, which becomes the thesis of the essay.

> Americans have always prided themselves on their rugged individualism. We know how to take care of ourselves. We don't need any help, especially from the government. As a result, we have been slow to adopt a system of universal health care. Today we are the only industrialized country in the world not to provide health care for all its citizens. As a result, compared to other industrialized countries, we have the highest infant mortality rates and the lowest life expectancy. It is clear that, when it comes to health care, we need to "get over" our rugged individualism and adopt universal health care.

State Your Support First

It can also be effective to start your introductory paragraph with examples of your evidence, especially if that evidence is powerful. After a brief statement of some of your evidence, you can then end the paragraph with your thesis.

> The United States is the only advanced industrialized nation in the world that does not offer universal health care. If we adopted such a system, there would be less illness, less suffering, and less early mortality for American citizens. Surprisingly, studies show that under universal health care costs would go down as more people receive preventive care. It is time for the United States to adopt a system of universal health care.

Start with an Example or Quotation

Many writers find it effective to begin their opening paragraph with a quotation or a personal example.

> Last year I was laid off, which meant, in addition to having no job, I had no health insurance. There was no way I could afford to see my doctor for the regular physical I have had every year for the previous fourteen years, so I had no idea that I had gall stones. As a result, in the middle of the night, with extreme pain in my right shoulder and back and horrific vomiting, I ended up having major emergency surgery to remove my gall bladder. Had those stones been detected by a simple chest x-ray, a normal part of my annual physical, my gall bladder could have been removed by laparoscopic surgery, a much simpler procedure. Too many Americans are in the same position I was in: unable to afford preventative care because they have no insurance and, as a result, needing much more dangerous and expensive emergency treatment. Something is seriously wrong with health care in this country. In fact, the United States is the only advanced industrialized nation in the world that does not offer universal health care. If we adopted such a system of health care, there would be less illness, less suffering, and less early mortality for American citizens. Surprisingly, studies show that under universal health care costs would go down as more people receive preventive care. It is time for the United States to adopt a system of universal health care.

Start by Exploring Your Evidence

A less straightforward but more interesting way to write an opening paragraph is to forget about the thesis for the time being, and open instead with a paragraph that dives into your most compelling evidence. Then, after a paragraph or more exploring this evidence, provide a clear statement of your thesis.

> The United States is the only advanced country in the world that does not provide universal health care. As a result, Americans have worse health outcomes than the rest of the world in many categories. For example, life expectancy in the United States is 79.3 years, lower than the life expectancy in thirty other industrialized countries. One study has shown that out of 100,000 Americans, 112 will die each year from preventable diseases. In the twelve other countries in the same study, the highest number of preventable deaths was 84. Infant mortality is measured as the number of deaths within one year per 1,000 live births. Infant mortality in the United States is 5.8; the average rate for eleven comparable countries is 3.4. Why is it that the country with the strongest economy, the highest standard of living, and the greatest gross domestic product in the world has such low health outcomes?

After this strong opening paragraph, the writer could include a paragraph stating the thesis and the primary reasons that support it.

State Your Thesis and Support

The most straightforward way to open an essay is to state your thesis and the primary reasons that support the thesis.

> The United States should adopt a system of universal health care for three reasons. First, universal health care will mean less illness, less suffering, and less infant mortality for American citizens. Second, universal health care will actually result in lower overall costs for health care as everyone will receive preventive care. Third, we are the only advanced industrialized nation in the world that does not offer universal health care.

You may have been taught to write an introductory paragraph this way in the past. However, this is not usually very effective either at capturing the reader's interest or providing context for the discussion to follow. It is too predictable and lacks imagination. Whenever you can, use one of the more creative options listed above.

17.4 Activity

Writing Introductory Paragraphs

Working in your group, select one of the following essay topics and write an introductory paragraph for it. It's okay to select the same essay you chose for Writing Titles (17.2, p. 189). Be ready to share your writing in about fifteen minutes.

1. An essay for a class in political science in which you will argue that America's right to free and fair elections is threatened by various political acts of the party in power

2. An article to be published in your local newspaper proposing ways to make it safer for bicyclists on public roads

3. An essay for a class in nursing or another health field in which you argue for changes in how nurses or health-care workers are educated

4. A letter to your local congressional representative in which you argue for the need to lower the cost of going to college

5. A letter to the Secretary of Education in which you suggest improvements in the requirements or procedure involved in applying for financial aid

17.5 Tutorial

Closing Paragraphs

Like guests who take forever to say goodbye and be on their way, a closing paragraph that goes on too long can make readers groan and roll their eyes, and it can leave them feeling much less enthusiastic than they had felt as they were reading the essay. To choose the most effective strategy for your conclusion, be sure you remember who your audience is and what your purpose is for writing. For more information, see Thinking about Audience (9.4, p. 14) and Thinking about Purpose (9.6, p. 17).

Strategies for Effective Conclusions

In the final paragraph of your essay, you want to wrap things up tidily and leave readers remembering the gist of what they have read. Here's a list of ideas to help you accomplish this:

1. Restate your thesis in a fresh and memorable way.
2. Close with a witty, funny, or moving statement.
3. Remind readers of the most powerful facts, examples, or other evidence you have presented.
4. End with a powerful quotation.
5. Conclude by urging readers to take whatever action you have been arguing for.

Examples of Effective Conclusions

This is an introduction from Introductory Paragraphs (17.3, p. 189) that starts with an example. It is followed by two possible conclusions.

Last year I was laid off, which meant, in addition to having no job, I had no health insurance. There was no way I could afford to see my doctor for the regular physical I have had every year for the previous fourteen years, so I had no idea that I had gall stones. As a result, in the middle of the night, with extreme pain in my right shoulder and back and horrific vomiting, I ended up having major emergency surgery to remove my gall bladder. Had those stones been detected by a simple chest x-ray, a normal part of my annual physical, the gall bladder could have been removed by laparoscopy, a much simpler surgery. Too many Americans are in the same position I was in: unable to afford preventative care because they have no insurance and, as a result, needing much more dangerous and expensive emergency treatment. Something is seriously wrong with health care in this country. In fact, the United States is the only advanced industrialized nation in the world that does not offer universal health care. If we adopted such a system of health care, there would be less illness, less suffering, and less early mortality for American citizens. Surprisingly, studies show that under universal health care costs would go down as more people receive preventive care. It is time for the United States to adopt a system of universal health care.

One effective conclusion for an essay starting with the preceding introduction could be this one:

Our society will be more humane and more healthy, and the costs of health care will be reduced, if we move to a system of universal health care. It is important that you add your voice to this movement and support candidates who will work for universal health care. No one should have to undergo an emergency surgery for gall stones.

In this conclusion, the writer summarizes the main points of his argument and then urges the reader to support the cause of universal health care. The paragraph ties the entire essay together by reminding the reader of the writer's emergency surgery.

Here is another effective conclusion for the same introductory paragraph that uses a different strategy:

Dr. Bruce Viadeck, author of more than 150 articles on medical issues has pointed out that "we used to say that the United States shared with South Africa the distinction of being the only industrialized nations without universal health insurance. Now we don't even have South Africa to point to" (16). We are now the only industrialized country in the world that doesn't guarantee health care to all its citizens. This must change.

This writer has decided to use a powerful quotation—one that points to our unique failure as a nation to provide universal health care—to drive home the point of the essay and then concludes with a terse statement that sums up the point of the essay.

Concluding Strategies to Avoid

One way to ensure you draft a strong concluding paragraph is to avoid doing any of the following.

1. Don't bring up anything new, such as an argument or evidence you have not previously discussed.

2. Don't announce what you have done. Don't write things like "In this essay, I have . . ." or "I have proved . . ."

3. Don't include an overused and obvious phrase like "In conclusion . . ." or "As I have said . . ."

4. Don't apologize by saying something like "Even though I am not an expert . . ."

5. Finally, check the "fresh and memorable" way you have restated your thesis. Make sure that even though it is worded differently, it is still making the same point as the thesis you stated earlier in the paper.

17.6 Activity
Writing Conclusions

Working in your group, select one of the following essay topics and write a conclusion for it. It's okay to select the same essay you chose for Writing Titles (17.2, p. 189) or Writing Introductory Paragraphs (17.4, p. 192). Be ready to share your writing in about fifteen minutes.

1. An essay for a class in political science in which you will argue that America's right to free and fair elections is threatened by various political acts of the party in power

2. An article to be published in your local newspaper proposing ways to make it safer for bicyclists on public roads

3. An essay for a class in nursing or another health field in which you argue for changes in how nurses or health-care workers are educated

4. A letter to your local congressional representative in which you argue for the need to lower the cost of going to college

5. A letter to the Secretary of Education in which you suggest improvements in the requirements or procedure involved in applying for financial aid

TOPIC 18
Writing Strategies

The strategies discussed in this Topic are useful in many different writing situations— essay assignments, reports, summaries, fiction and nonfiction writing, book and movie reviews, lab reports, and more—but the focus here is on writing essays. Writers will sometimes write essays that use a single one of these types of writing: an elaborate extended definition might be a three- or four-page essay, for example, or an explanation of the multiple causes of a complex event like the Great Recession of 2008 could easily be an essay all by itself. More commonly, however, although an essay or article may have one overall organizing principle, such as argument, cause and effect, or classification, it will also include several different strategies in order to present information effectively. For example, after an introductory paragraph in an argument essay, a writer might use definition to explain how she will be using several key words. A little later, she might use narration to provide background information about the topic. Further on, she might include a comparison of two possible solutions to the problem being addressed. This weaving back and forth among the various strategies can result in a sophisticated argument that convincingly presents and supports its position.

Navigating Topic 18

The tutorials listed below provide information about these strategies, and each contains, or is followed by, an opportunity to apply the skills you have just learned. You can work through the entire Topic on your own, learning about all the strategies and practicing them; work on items you've been assigned by your instructor; or choose ones you would find helpful.

Introduction to Writing Strategies 198

Argumentation 198

18.1	Tutorial	What Is an Argument? 199
18.2	Activity	What Are the Features of Effective Arguments? 199
18.3	Tutorial	The Features of Effective Arguments 199

18.4	Tutorial	Thinking about Audience and Purpose 200
18.5	Tutorial	How to Answer Counterarguments 200
18.6	Writing	Answering Counterarguments 202
18.7	Tutorial	Three Types of Appeal: *Logos, Ethos,* and *Pathos* 202

Description and Observation 208

| 18.8 | Tutorial | Strategies for Writing Descriptions and Observations 208 |
| 18.9 | Writing | Describing/Observing a Person, Place, Thing, or Event 211 |

Narration 212

| 18.10 | Tutorial | Strategies for Writing Narratives 212 |
| 18.11 | Writing | Narrating an Event 215 |

Process 216

| 18.12 | Tutorial | Strategies for Process Writing 216 |
| 18.13 | Writing | Explaining a Process or How Something Works 218 |

Comparison and Contrast 219

| 18.14 | Tutorial | Strategies for Writing Comparison and/or Contrast 219 |
| 18.15 | Writing | Comparing and/or Contrasting Two Items 223 |

Cause and Effect 223

| 18.16 | Tutorial | Strategies for Writing Cause and Effect 223 |
| 18.17 | Writing | Explaining the Causes or Effects of an Event or Action 226 |

Definition 226

18.18	Tutorial	Strategies for Writing Definitions 226
18.19	Activity	Revising Definitions 229
18.20	Writing	Providing Simple or Extended Definitions 230

Classification 230

| 18.21 | Tutorial | Strategies for Writing Classification 230 |
| 18.22 | Writing | Breaking a Topic into Categories 232 |

Summary   232

18.23	Writing	What Makes a Good Summary? 233
18.24	Activity	Analyzing Summaries 233
18.25	Tutorial	Strategies for Writing a Summary 233
18.26	Writing	Summarizing Baldwin 235

Proposal   238

| 18.27 | Tutorial | Strategies for Writing a Proposal   238 |
| 18.28 | Writing | Making a Proposal to Solve a Problem   241 |

Reflection   241

| 18.29 | Tutorial | Strategies for Writing a Reflection   241 |
| 18.30 | Writing | Reflecting on an Important Experience   242 |

Weaving Strategies into a Strong Essay   243

| 18.31 | Tutorial | Using Multiple Writing Strategies in an Essay   243 |
| 18.32 | Activity | Identifying Multiple Writing Strategies in an Essay   243 |

Introduction to Writing Strategies

This Topic explores several different writing strategies: argumentation, description and observation, narration, process, comparison and contrast, cause and effect, definition, classification, summary, proposal, and reflection. For each strategy, you will find advice about when it might be useful, examples, advice for using it effectively, and an opportunity to practice using it.

Argumentation

An argument is a piece of writing that takes a position on an issue, provides various types of evidence to support that position, and acknowledges and addresses valid counterarguments.

18.1 Tutorial

What Is an Argument?

An argument is simply a piece of writing that takes a position on an issue and provides evidence to support that position. In fact, it is sometimes suggested that all writing is argument.

In college courses, argument essays are typically three or four pages long, but sometimes, especially if they involve significant research, they can be much longer. They can also be much shorter: an argument could be as short as a single paragraph. The crucial factor is that an argument takes a position on an issue.

The following sections explore many of the features of effective arguments.

18.2 Activity

What Are the Features of Effective Arguments?

Working in your group, make a list of the features necessary for an effective argument. To help you get started, one feature is *an argument takes a position and expresses it in a clear and arguable thesis.*

18.3 Tutorial

The Features of Effective Arguments

In order to be effective, an argument should meet the following criteria.

- **It takes a position.**   The primary feature of an effective argument is that is takes a stand, a position, on an issue about which reasonable people may disagree. This position is clearly stated as a thesis, usually near the beginning of an essay. (For more information, see Thesis Statements [10.5, p. 32].) Keep in mind that the point of an argument is not simply to state something that is true; the point is to convince the reader that it is true.

- **It provides support for that position.**   This support can take many forms: examples, statistics, facts, reasons, expert opinion, and more. Remember that an argument has to convince the reader, so ask yourself whether you think your reader would be convinced by the evidence you have provided. If not, what kinds of additional support do you need to incorporate? (See Topic 11: Developing Ideas [p. 41] for more on types of support and how to find them.)

- **It provides necessary background information.** Sometimes this information explains why the issue is important, or it might define important terms or provide some history of how the issue has evolved over time.

- **It responds to opposing arguments.** An effective argument acknowledges that not everyone agrees with the position the essay has taken. The essay will summarize opposing arguments fairly and politely and then will explain why they are not convincing. Perhaps the evidence supporting the opposition is flawed in some way. Perhaps the opposing argument has overlooked important parts of the argument. Perhaps the opposing argument makes some valid points, but these do not outweigh the arguments in the essay.

18.4 Tutorial

Thinking about Audience and Purpose

Before starting any writing task, most people find it helpful to think about their audience and purpose. Thinking about your audience will help you to write in an appropriate style, determine what technical terms you will need to explain, decide how much background information or history to include, and what tone to use. It will also help you to select the kind of evidence that your audience will find most convincing. For more information about audience, see Thinking about Audience (9.4, p. 14).

Thinking about your purpose—what you want to achieve as a result of your writing—will focus your work and help you to decide how to organize and present your argument. For additional details on purpose, see Thinking about Purpose (9.6, p. 17).

18.5 Tutorial

How to Answer Counterarguments

In most cases, when writing an argument, your audience is not those who agree with you. Why would you try to convince those who already agree with you? Instead, your argument will be most effective if it is aimed at those who are undecided on the issue you are addressing. They can be convinced. What about those who are totally opposed to your position? Some of them may be persuadable, but most of your energy should be aimed at the middle group—those whose minds are not made up and therefore might be open to a different point of view.

Your arguments to support your thesis, supported by reasoning, evidence, and facts, should work well with the undecided group. But think for a moment about why they might be "undecided." In many cases, they are undecided because they are aware of counterarguments, arguments that oppose the position you are supporting. At first glance, it might seem that your best strategy is to ignore these counterarguments. Why bring up arguments that undermine your position? You can always hope your audience isn't aware of these arguments.

Here's the problem with that strategy. If you ignore them, your audience may conclude you are either not well informed or you are biased or not fair-minded. Ignoring counterarguments will make your writing less effective.

Identifying and Refuting Counterarguments

You can develop a list of counterarguments in three ways.

1. Conduct good research, which will probably unearth some of these arguments.

2. Talk to someone (or several people) who disagrees with your position and listen carefully to the arguments he or she makes.

3. Imagine yourself in an argument with someone who holds the opposite position from yours. What arguments would he or she be making?

Once you have identified counterarguments, you need to refute them—prove them to be inaccurate, false, or weak—using any one of several strategies.

- Challenge the authenticity of the evidence, the data supporting the opposing view, if you have reason to suspect it is inaccurate or untrue.

- Produce evidence supporting your position that is stronger than the evidence supporting the opposing view.

- If an opposing view relies on pathos (an appeal to emotion, not facts), point out that the opposing view is based primarily on emotion and not on solid evidence.

- Critique the character or expertise of people making the opposing view if there is evidence that they are not reliable, truthful, or certified experts in the field.

- Point out that the negative consequences that will result from the opposing position outweigh any positive results.

- If an opposing point cannot be refuted, concede it and argue that your other points far outweigh that one opposing point.

18.6 Writing

Answering Counterarguments

The reasons for refuting counterarguments and strategies for doing so are discussed in How to Answer Counterarguments (18.5, p. 200).

Your instructor will assign this activity as part of the process of writing one of the essays that conclude each reading/writing project in Part 1 of *The Hub*.

Assignment.   Write a short paper—less than a page—in which you state several of the arguments that opponents of your position might take and then write your answer to each of these counterarguments.

18.7 Tutorial

Three Types of Appeal: *Logos, Ethos,* and *Pathos*

As long ago as the fourth century BC, the Greek philosopher Aristotle identified three types of argument, which he named *logos, ethos,* and *pathos.* These three strategies are usually referred to as appeals. Think about a politician *appealing* for your vote or a nonprofit *appealing* for donations. In this sense, to appeal is to attempt to persuade by adopting a strategy likely to succeed with the audience.

- **Arguments based on *logos*** appeal to the head. They are based on evidence, reasoning, and logic. In fact, the English word *logic* is derived from *logos.* Arguments based on *logos* often make use of facts, quotations from experts, statistics, survey and poll results, interviews, and charts and graphs. Usually these kinds of factual evidence are tied together by sound reasoning which can explain the causes, the results, the benefits, or the side effects of the factual evidence.

- **Arguments based on *ethos*** have the goal of winning the reader's confidence in the writer. To accomplish this, writers include information that establishes their credibility or expertise by mentioning their credentials, awards they have won, or honors they have received. They also make clear the values and beliefs that underlie their arguments. Another way of gaining the reader's confidence is to write in a way that is clearly fair, a way that avoids mean-spirited personal attacks or distortions of the truth, and that recognizes it is possible for reasonable people to disagree about an issue.

- **Arguments based on *pathos*** appeal to the readers' feelings, to their heart. Frequently, writers appeal to their readers' hearts by telling a story, especially a moving one, that includes, for example, details about the suffering of people enduring an oppressive political regime, the injustices a certain group is experiencing as a result of societal bigotry, or the sacrifices parents or family members are making to care for an ill child or ailing elder.

Sometimes writers are hesitant to use and readers are alienated by emotional arguments, but they also can be extremely effective, especially when writers think about their audience and only use emotional arguments that are likely to succeed with that audience. Sometimes a purely logical argument, especially one with an avalanche of factual evidence, can overwhelm or bore the reader. And, if writers spend too much time explaining how many honors they have received and how much they are committed to their values, they may discover they have alienated their audience.

The most effective writing is often a combination of all three types of argument—logical, ethical, and emotional. In the following essay, written by an older student in one of my classes a few years ago, the writer skillfully weaves all three appeals together to make his point. Included below is just the body of Kevin's essay; in its final form, it would also include a works cited list.

Gifted and Talented Programs: More Harm Than Good?

KEVIN TURNER

1   My granddaughter called me a couple of years ago with big news. "I've been selected for gifted and talented," she announced with excitement and joy in her voice. I shared her joy; I was elated to hear how excited she was as she got ready for the sixth grade. But I also felt a contradictory emotion: I felt guilty for feeling such elation. I had for years had serious reservations about gifted and talented programs and any other programs that separate kids according to our perceptions of their abilities.

Kevin begins his essay with an appeal to the reader's feelings by discussing his own feelings (*pathos*).

2   I want to be clear. There are good arguments on both sides of this issue. Those who support "gifted and talented" programs have some powerful reasons for their support.

In this paragraph, he tries to win the reader's confidence by demonstrating he understands both sides of the argument (*ethos*).

3   Some point out, for example, that <u>our society needs to provide challenging curricula to the most talented students, those who will grow up to lead the country, to discover new treatments for diseases, and to produce art and music that challenge our souls. In a gifted and talented program, these students can be challenged to think more deeply and more creatively. They can experience the thrill of learning concepts they never thought they could understand. They can hone their thinking, writing, and speaking skills as they challenge and are challenged by other top students. Our nation will benefit in the future from the "gifts" and "talents" of these students.</u>

4   A second argument for "gifted and talented" programs is that <u>bright students, like my granddaughter, are too often bored in traditional classrooms with a range of students from those struggling to understand the material to those ready for more challenging material. A conscientious teacher will usually "teach to the middle," which means those students at the "top" will seldom be challenged and will frequently be bored. It was disheartening when my granddaughter told me one summer that she hated reading because the books she was assigned in school were too easy.</u>

5   My daughter was overcome with joy and pride that her daughter would be in the "gifted and talented" program. She, like most parents, wants what's best for her child. <u>I understand that and love seeing her excitement about her daughter's success.</u> So, I have tried, unsuccessfully so far, to explain to her why I have such reservations about the program.

6   I point out that <u>our system for identifying these bright students is seriously flawed. A multiple-choice test of arithmetic skills or reading</u>

Using reasoning, here Kevin argues that students will benefit from these programs and so will the nation (*logos*).

Again, an appeal to logic or reasoning (*logos*).

In this paragraph, the author combines an appeal to feelings (joy and pride) with more effort at showing he is being fair (*pathos* and *ethos*).

Here Kevin uses logic to argue that the system for judging students is unfair (*logos*).

comprehension doesn't measure a student's "gifts" or "talents." It, more likely, measures the child's socioeconomic background. Those who grow up in families struggling with poverty are less likely to have access to books. Those whose single mothers have to work two jobs are less likely to have had the experience of learning to add and subtract at home. When they are tested for entrance to a selective program, sometimes as early as the age of four or five, the test will favor children from more affluent homes.

7   This bias is exacerbated in many large cities where wealthier parents are paying for tutoring services to make sure their children get into "gifted and talented" kindergartens. According to Leslie Brody, writing in *The Wall Street Journal*, a tutorial service in New York "charges $100 to $400 an hour for private sessions" and clients can receive "15 to 40 hours of tutoring over four to six months," resulting in fees of thousands of dollars (Brody).

In this paragraph, he is using facts combined with reasoning (*logos*).

8   Because the testing system favors children from more affluent families, the demographics of the students who qualify for "gifted and talented" kindergarten in New York City are heavily skewed against Black and Latinx students. According to "Making the Grade II," a 2019 report by the New York School Diversity Advisory Group, Latinx children made up 41% of all kindergartners in New York City in 2018, but were only 10% of the students judged to be qualified for the "gifted and talented" programs. Black children were 24% of all kindergartners but only 8% of those who qualified for "gifted and talented" kindergarten (26).

More facts and logic to argue that there is racial bias in gifted and talented programs (*logos*).

9   To me, the most compelling reason to oppose "gifted and talented" programs is that they undermine the American Dream, the idea that in

this country everyone who is willing to work hard can achieve success. The illusory state of that dream is manifest in the enormous gap between the wealthy and the rest of us. In 2019, a report by the Federal Reserve Board entitled "Introducing the Distributional Financial Accounts of the United States" presented shocking statistics about the wealth gap in America. "In 2018," according to the Fed's report, "the top 10% of U.S. households controlled 70 percent of total household wealth, up from 60 percent in 1989." The report also notes that "the bottom 50% of the wealth distribution experienced . . . a fall in total wealth share from 4 percent in 1989 to just 1 percent in 2018" (Batty et al. 26). Not only has there been a large gap between the wealth of the top 10% and everyone else, but that gap is growing wider.

More facts and logic to argue that gifted and talented programs exacerbate the wealth gap and undermine the American Dream (logos).

10   Many factors contribute to this gap, but it is hard to deny that one factor is programs like "gifted and talented." Whatever gaps exist when four- and five-year-olds arrive in kindergarten are exacerbated by a system that results in mostly children from affluent backgrounds being placed into a program designed to help them advance faster.

Here he uses reasoning to argue his point (logos).

11   I fully recognize that those who support "gifted and talented" programs have good arguments to support their position. I completely understand the pride and joy of parents like my daughter when her daughter was accepted into such a program. I don't blame parents for wanting what's best for their children. And I recognize that programs for bright students have produced very talented scientists and entrepreneurs, very

Again, Kevin assures the reader of his fairness, his recognition of the arguments on the other side (ethos).

creative artists and composers, and very productive engineers and architects, all of whom contribute greatly to making America the richest and most powerful nation on Earth. Those are positive results of our educational system, at least partially as a result of programs like "gifted and talented."

12   However, those same programs also contribute to the vast and growing gap between the wealthy and the rest of us in our society. Having to choose between these two goals, I have decided that I would rather live in a country in which wealth is more evenly distributed, a country in which the American Dream is a reality, even if that country is less rich and less powerful.

Kevin ends with a reasoned explanation of why he comes down where he does on this issue (*logos*).

Rogerian Argument: A Different Way of Arguing

Up to this point, the discussion has focused on a certain kind of argument, sometimes called "classical argument." In classical argument, the writers (or speakers) are trying to convince their audience to agree with their view, their position, or what they are proposing. This is the way most of us construct arguments most of the time.

But it is not the only way to argue. The psychologist Carl Rogers has proposed an alternative. Instead of viewing the goal of an argument to be to "win," to convince the reader to agree with your position, the goal of Rogerian argument is to reach common ground, to come to agreement. Rogerian arguments tend to avoid staking out an "either/or" analysis but to search instead for areas of "both/and." Instead of viewing the rhetorical terrain as offering either a "win" or a "loss," Rogerians try to find grounds on which the writer and the audience can both "win." Rogerian arguments show respect for the views of those who disagree and seek to understand the reasons for their disagreement.

The following chart illustrates the typical organization for a classical and a Rogerian argument.

Classical Argument	Rogerian Argument
1. Introduction with thesis statement	1. Introduction pointing out a problem and how both writer and reader are affected by the problem
2. Background information	2. An attempt, in neutral and respectful language, to present the reader's position
3. Evidence and argument	3. A presentation, again in fair and reasonable language, of the writer's position
4. Response to opposing views	4. A closing paragraph in which the writer suggests where the reader could move toward the writer's position and why
5. Conclusion	

In most academic and business writing, the classical form of argument is expected, but, when thinking about your audience, you may identify situations in which the Rogerian argument format would be more effective. It is often used in tense situations to get people from opposing sides of an issue to better understand each other's positions and, perhaps, find some common ground.

Description and Observation

Writers use description to provide readers with a vivid picture of a person, a thing, or a place. Description is an important element of observations, writing assignments that ask you to provide a detailed description of an event, room, person, place, or performance.

18.8 Tutorial

Strategies for Writing Descriptions and Observations

This tutorial starts with a discussion of basic description and then discusses how you can use descriptive writing in an observation.

Writing Descriptions

It is important when writing descriptions to provide concrete details—the color, shape, size, or appearance of people, places, and things—but it is also possible to enhance a description by including sensory details about smell, taste, touch, or sound (see Using Concrete Language to Bring Writing to Life [13.3, p. 80]). Descriptions are usually easier for readers to process if they are organized in a logical order—for example, from bottom to top, left to right, or near to far. Refer to Coherence (12.8, p. 70) for a discussion and examples of types of logical organization.

The following is a well-written description of a character in the novel *The Magician's Assistant* by Ann Patchett.

> Mr. Howard Plate was big like his sons, with hair that might have been red when he was their age and now was that colorless sandy brown that red hair can become. But it was his face that drew attention, the way it was fine on one side and collapsed on the other, as if he had been hit very hard and the shape of the fist in question was still lodged beneath his left eye. It had the quality of something distinctly broken and poorly repaired. The bad light cast by the living room lamps threw a shadow into the cave of his cheek, where a random interlacing of scars ended and began. (pp. 205–206)

Writing Observations

Many writing situations call for an observation, or a detailed description of something—an event, a room, a person, a place, or a performance—a type of writing that can be useful in many situations, as shown in these examples:

1. An organization you belong to has asked you to visit a room to see if it is appropriate for a guest speaker your group invited to give a lecture.

2. You and your neighbors have become concerned about a dangerous intersection and want to propose to your local government that steps be taken to make it safer.

3. You have become frustrated by the amount of time it takes to purchase your textbooks at the campus bookstore at the beginning of the semester.

Each of these situations calls for a written document, perhaps a proposal, and that document will include some description.

How to Prepare for and Write an Observation

Here are some guidelines for writing a useful, focused observation.

1. Before visiting the site you are going to observe, you need to make some decisions:
   - What is the purpose of the observation?
   - What kinds of information will be useful for that purpose?

- How much time will you need for the observation?
- Will the time of day or the day of the week make a difference in what you will observe?

2. When making the actual observation, you will need to take careful notes. One good system for doing this is to use a double-entry notebook or pad of paper. Draw a line down the center of the page. On the left, record the actual details you see; on the right, record your thoughts or reactions to those details.

3. The most important feature of an observation is the presence of clear, concrete detail, detail that supports the purpose of the observation.

The two paragraphs below are descriptions of a lecture hall that the writer is observing as a possible site for a guest lecture. The highlighting indicates the different focus in each paragraph.

Paragraph 1

The Humanities Lecture Hall seats 175 people in chairs that provide pull-up desks for taking notes. The lights over the seating area can be dimmed leaving the stage brightly lit. The lectern on the stage has a microphone built in and a small light to illuminate the speaker's notes. The room is equipped with a powerful projector and a large screen that are controlled from the lectern.

Paragraph 2

The Humanities Lecture Hall is an attractive room whose walls are covered by beautiful walnut panels. The seats are covered in an attractive red, yellow, and blue material. The American and state flags hang on either side of the stage. The carpeting in the room is a red and yellow pattern which matches the seat coverings.

Both paragraphs contain concrete details, but the details in paragraph 1 will be helpful to the group trying to decide whether to book the lecture hall, while the details in paragraph 2 will not. The writer of paragraph 1 focused on details relevant to the hall as a possible site of a guest lecture: the number of seats with pull-up desks, the quality of the lighting, the presence of a well-equipped lectern, and easy access to a screen and projector. The writer of paragraph 2 seems to have forgotten the purpose of the observation and instead has focused on details of the hall's decoration.

It is important to organize your written observation in a logical fashion. Notice that paragraph 1 is organized spatially, beginning by reporting on the seating area, then moving to the speaker's lectern, and ending with the projection system available to the speaker.

Sometimes, instead of organizing an observation spatially, it will be more useful to organize it temporally—that is, according to time. Paragraph 3 was written as part of a letter urging improvements in the college bookstore's procedures during the first week of classes. Note the highlighted time-related phrases that help organize the observation for the reader.

Paragraph 3

I observed the check-out procedures at the bookstore on the first day of classes this semester, September 3, 2019, from 8:00 in the morning when the bookstore opened to noon. At 8:00, 43 students were in line waiting for the bookstore to open. In the first half hour, I was surprised to see that only two of the four cash registers were available for use. Employees, who I believe could have been staffing the other two registers, were actually unpacking boxes of books and placing them on the shelves. At 9:00, I asked twelve students as they purchased their books how long they had waited to be checked out. All twelve reported they had arrived at the bookstore at 7:30 and had gotten in the check-out line at about 8:15. Each hour for the remainder of the morning, I questioned twelve students about their wait time to be checked out. At 10:00, the bookstore opened the other two cash registers. The twelve students I questioned at that time had been waiting in the check-out line for an hour and a half or more. At 11:00, the twelve students had waited more than two hours. Again, at 12:00, the twelve students had waited more than two hours.

18.9 Writing

Describing/Observing a Person, Place, Thing, or Event

In a short paper—less than a page is plenty—complete one of the following assignments.

1. **Describe one of the following.** Be sure to provide plenty of concrete and sensory detail and to organize your description in a logical order.
   - Your kitchen
   - Your bedroom
   - The place where you work
   - Someone in your family
   - Your favorite possession

2. **Observe one of the following situations.** Decide on the kinds of information that would be useful to find out in order to achieve the stated purpose and the best time of day to make your observations.

- **Situation:** A family tradition

  Purpose: What makes it successful?

- **Situation:** Everyday use of cell phones

  Purpose: The impact of cell phones on face-to-face interactions

- **Situation:** A live performance you have attended

  Purpose: Why was it a success or a failure?

See Using Concrete Language to Bring Writing to Life (13.3, p. 80) for more on types of descriptive language, and see Coherence (12.8, p. 70) for examples of types of logical organization.

Narration

Human beings have been telling stories since the beginning of time. Narration is just a technical name for telling stories, and it is one of the most common and most useful writing strategies. Narration can not only make your writing more interesting, but it can also provide persuasive support for your thesis.

18.10 Tutorial

Strategies for Writing Narratives

Normally when we write narration, we organize the content in chronological order—*first this happened, then this*—and so forth. Occasionally, writers may want to vary from this strictly chronological order. For example, a writer might tell the end of a story first and then go back to the beginning to explain how that ending came about. Seldom are narratives written to stand alone; more commonly, they are one part of a larger piece of writing.

So, if you were writing an essay arguing that your city needs to invest in safer bike lanes, your essay would probably contain facts and statistics about safety and the annual number of accidents involving bikes. However, you might also include a narrative about the time you were badly injured when a car struck you as you were riding across an intersection even though you had the right of way.

If you were writing an essay arguing that the federal effort to aid Puerto Rico after Hurricane Maria was inadequate, you would want to report on the damage to the island, the number of lives lost, and the effects on people and institutions of months without electricity. You would also want to report on how the amount of federal assistance to Puerto Rico compared to the assistance provided to Florida after Hurricane Michael and to the Carolinas after Hurricane Florence. But in addition to all this factual information, you might want to narrate the story of your mother's struggle to survive Maria with the highway to her village washed away and no electricity for more than six months. Narration can be a powerful way to provide support to your thesis.

Features of Effective Narrative Writing

In the book *The Immortal Life of Henrietta Lacks*, Rebecca Skloot mixes scientific reporting with the telling of very human stories. Below she narrates the events that occurred when Henrietta Lacks's cancer cells were first delivered to a lab at Johns Hopkins Hospital, where they would start their journey toward playing a major role in medical research.

Excerpt from Chapter 4, "The Birth of Hela"

Mary followed Margaret's sterilizing rules meticulously to avoid her wrath. After finishing her lunch, and before touching Henrietta's sample, Mary covered herself with a clean white gown, surgical cap, and mask, and then walked to her cubicle, one of four airtight rooms George had built by hand in the center of the lab. The cubicles were small, only five feet in any direction, with doors that sealed like a freezer's to prevent contaminated air from getting inside. Mary turned on the sterilizing system and watched from outside as her cubicle filled with hot steam to kill anything that might damage the cells. When the steam cleared, she stepped inside and sealed the door behind her, then hosed the cubicle's cement floor with water and scoured her workbench with alcohol. The air inside was filtered and piped in through a vent on the ceiling. Once she'd sterilized the cubicle, she lit a Bunsen burner and used its flame to sterilize test tubes and a used scalpel blade, since the Gey lab couldn't afford new ones for each sample.

Only then did she pick up the pieces of Henrietta's cervix—forceps in one hand, scalpel in the other—and carefully slice them into one-millimeter squares. She sucked each square into a pipette, and dropped them one at a time onto chicken-blood clots she'd placed at the bottom of dozens of test tubes. She covered each clot with several drops of culture medium, plugged the tubes with rubber stoppers, and labeled each one as she'd labeled most cultures they grew: using the first two letters of the patient's first and last names.

After writing "HeLa," for *Henrietta* and *Lacks,* in big black letters on the side of each tube, Mary carried them to the incubator room that Gey had built just like he'd built everything else in the lab (37–38).

This narrative illustrates many of the features of effective narrative writing.

1. *The author is using narrative to make a point.* By detailing all the steps Mary took to prepare to work with the HeLa cells, Skloot is illustrating the great care taken to sterilize the work space before culturing them and the process involved. Good narrative is usually shaped to convey a particular point of view or to make a point.

2. *Skloot uses transitional expressions or time-related phrases throughout to help the reader keep track of the sequence of events (highlighted in blue).* Narratives are usually organized in chronological order—now one event happened, then this, and so on. However, they can jump around, for instance, first telling what is occurring now, and then providing the backstory, what happened before this event.

3. *There is at least one human character with a name, Mary, to provide human interest.* Narratives usually center around a person or persons.

4. *The narrative is filled with concrete details that help us see the lab and that establish Skloot's expertise as a writer.* She knows the names of things.

The passage is repeated below, this time with these vivid concrete details highlighted.

Excerpt from Chapter 4, "The Birth of Hela"

Mary followed Margaret's sterilizing rules meticulously to avoid her wrath. After finishing her lunch, and before touching Henrietta's sample, Mary covered herself with a clean white gown, surgical cap, and mask, and then walked to her cubicle, one of four airtight rooms George had built by hand in the center of the lab. The cubicles were small, only five feet in any direction, with doors that sealed like a freezer's to prevent contaminated air from getting inside. Mary turned on the sterilizing system and watched from outside as her cubicle filled with hot steam to kill anything that might damage the cells. When the steam cleared, she stepped inside and sealed the door behind her, then hosed the cubicle's cement floor with water and scoured her workbench with alcohol. The air inside was filtered and piped in though a vent on the ceiling. Once she'd sterilized the cubicle, she lit a Bunsen burner and used its flame to sterilize test tubes and a used scalpel blade, since the Gey lab couldn't afford new ones for each sample.

Only then did she pick up the pieces of Henrietta's cervix—forceps in one hand, scalpel in the other—and carefully slice them into one-millimeter squares. She sucked each square into a pipette, and dropped them one at a time onto chicken-blood clots she'd placed at the bottom of dozens of test tubes. She covered each clot with several drops of culture medium, plugged the tubes with rubber stoppers, and labeled each one as she'd labeled most cultures they grew: using the first two letters of the patient's first and last names.

After writing "HeLa," for *Henrietta* and *Lacks*, in big black letters on the side of each tube, Mary carried them to the incubator room that Gey had built just like he'd built everything else in the lab (pages 37–38).

You can, of course, use narration at any point in an essay where it will help support your thesis, but you should also consider using narration as a way of opening or concluding your essay.

18.11 Writing

Narrating an Event

For this assignment, you are going to write a short piece of narration, a page would be plenty, in which you tell the story of an event you have experienced. Don't take on too much—don't try to tell the story of your first *year* in college; pick an event you can narrate in a page.

Choose one of the following to write about.

1. Your experience registering for classes for the first time
2. The first time you met someone you are now in a relationship with
3. What you do when you first wake up on a typical morning
4. A time when you were pulled over by a police officer
5. A time when you were really surprised
6. A time when you learned a lesson
7. A topic of your own choice

Be sure your story makes a point, includes many concrete and sensory details to illustrate it, and uses transitional expressions or time-related phrases to organize it. (See Using Concrete Language to Bring Writing to Life [13.3, p. 80] and Coherence [12.8, p. 70] for discussion and examples of types of logical organization.)

Process

18.12 Tutorial

Strategies for Process Writing

When writers find themselves needing to explain how to do something or how something works, they often use process writing. Process writing is usually organized chronologically: *First*, you do this. *Next* you do that. In process writing, it is important to keep your audience in mind. How much detail do you need to explain the process so your reader will understand it? Can you use technical terms? If so, do you need to provide definitions of them? Are you writing for a general audience or for people already familiar with your subject?

▲ Figure 1   Peter Adams

How to Do Something

The following paragraph explains how to chop an onion.

> To chop an onion, you first need a little terminology. The sort of messy end of the onion, where there are hairy strands left from the root, is called the root end. The opposite end is called the stem end. You need to identify this root end of the onion before doing any cutting. Now cut the onion in half making sure your cut passes through the root end, leaving half of the root end on each half. For now, you can set aside one of the two halves. Next, cut away the stem end (not the root end) and then peel away and discard the outer layer or two of the onion. Your next step is to make a series of slices lengthwise, being careful not to slice through the root end. Now make three or four horizontal slices starting at the stem end and stopping before you reach the root end. Finally, make a series of cuts at a 90 degree angle to the horizontal cuts, and watch as the beautiful uniform diced pieces of onion appear.

Of course, many times explaining a process will be clearer if you present it as a numbered list. Illustrations can help as well.

1. To chop an onion, you first need a little terminology. The sort of messy end of the onion, where there are hairy strands left from the root, is called the root end. The opposite end is called the stem end. You need to identify this root end of the onion before doing any cutting.

2. Now cut the onion in half making sure your cut passes through the root end, leaving half of the root end on each half. For now, you can set aside one of the two halves.

3. Next, cut away the stem end (not the root end) and then peel away and discard the outer layer or two of the onion.

4. Your next step is to make a series of slices lengthwise, being careful not to slice through the root end (Figure 1).

5. Now make three or four horizontal slices starting at the stem end and stopping before you reach the root end (Figure 2).

6. Finally, make a series of cuts at a 90 degree angle to the horizontal cuts, and watch as the beautiful uniform diced pieces of onion appear (Figure 3).

 ▲ Figure 2   Peter Adams   ▲ Figure 3   Peter Adams

How Something Works

While explaining how to do something (as in the example above) is the most common use for process writing, the same chronological organization can be used to explain how something works, as the following paragraph illustrates.

How Impeachment of the President Works

The impeachment process begins in the House of Representatives, when any member files charges. These charges are forwarded to the Judiciary Committee, which investigates, usually by holding hearings and listening to witnesses. If a majority of the committee agrees, Articles of Impeachment are submitted to the full House for consideration. If a simple majority of those present and voting agrees, the House appoints managers to present the impeachment charges to the Senate. The Senate conducts a trial based on the impeachment charges. In the case of presidential impeachment, the Chief Justice of the Supreme Court presides. Conviction by the Senate requires a two-thirds vote by those present and results in removal from office.

18.13 Writing
Explaining a Process or How Something Works

Write a short paper—around a page—in which you either explain a process for doing something or explain how something works using one of the following topics.

Explaining a Process

1. How to attach a word-processed document to an email
2. How to find a movie you want to watch, download it, and watch it
3. How to use an application like Google Maps to download directions to someplace you would like to go
4. How to request an incomplete grade for a course
5. How do to another task of your choosing

Explaining How Something Works

6. How a constitutional amendment is passed
7. How a recall of a product is processed
8. How the Most Valuable Player for the American or National Baseball League is selected
9. How the winner of the Nobel Peace Prize is determined
10. How something else of your choosing is done

Comparison and Contrast

Writers often compare and/or contrast two items, people, places, or ideas in order to identify differences or similarities between them, make a recommendation about one of them, explain how they produce different outcomes, or justify different treatments of them.

18.14 Tutorial

Strategies for Writing Comparison and/or Contrast

When you *compare*, you discuss similarities; when you *contrast*, you focus on differences. It is often useful to compare and/or contrast things: two buildings, two cities, two proposals, two ideas, even two people. For instance, if you were recommending which of two candidates for a job should be hired, your recommendation could be based on comparing their qualifications and work experiences. If you were trying to explain why two approaches to the same problem produced such different results, it might be useful to contrast the methods and research involved in designing both.

It is also possible to do both—to discuss the similarities and the differences between two or more subjects. For example, if you were trying to explain why two patients should receive quite different treatments for apparently similar illnesses, you might compare and contrast their symptoms, physical conditions, and histories, as well as the possible treatment options. Although comparing and/or contrasting two items can be very useful, comparing and/or contrasting more than two is, of course, also perfectly valid, but more difficult. Whether you are focusing on similarities or differences or both, it is important to discuss all the points of similarity or difference for both, or all, subjects, giving equal attention to each.

There are two commonly used ways of organizing comparison and/or contrast writing: the point-by-point method and the subject-by-subject method. While the examples given below are paragraphs, it is also possible to use these methods for organizing longer pieces of comparison and/or contrast writing, even for entire essays, as noted in the text that follows the examples.

Point-by-Point Method

Read the following paragraph in which Timothy Noah compares two writers who had a profound influence on how Americans view opportunity and upward mobility.

The writers were Horatio Alger Jr. and James Truslow Adams. Alger wrote *Ragged Dick* (1868), *Luck and Pluck* (1869), and other dime novels for boys about getting ahead through virtue and hard work. To call these books popular would be an understatement: fully 5 percent of all the books checked out of the Muncie, Indiana, public library between November 1891 and December 1902 were authored by Alger. Adams was a more cerebral fellow who wrote books of American history, one of which (*The Epic of America*, 1931) introduced the phrase "the American dream" to our national discourse. Writing at the start of the Great Depression, Adams envisioned not "a dream of motor cars and high wages merely," but rather "a dream of a social order in which each man and each woman shall be able to attain to the fullest stature of which they are innately capable, and be recognized by others for what they are, regardless of the fortuitous circumstances of birth or position." Born a half century apart, neither Alger nor Adams could claim to have risen from the bottom. Both were born into well-established families whose American roots dated to the early seventeenth century. Alger could trace his lineage to three Pilgrims who in 1621 sailed to Plymouth Plantation on the *Fortune*, the second English ship to arrive there. Adams—no relation to the presidential Adamses—was descended from a man who arrived in Maryland in 1638 as an indentured servant and within three years possessed 185 acres. Alger's father was a Unitarian minister, Adams's a stockbroker. Both fathers were men of good breeding and education who struggled to make ends meet but were able—at a time when well over 90 percent of the population didn't finish high school—to obtain higher education for their sons. Alger went to Harvard, and Adams went to Brooklyn Polytechnic and, briefly, Yale. Both sons initially followed their fathers into the ministry and finance, respectively, before becoming full-time writers.

To understand the point-by-point method of organization, let's analyze how Noah's paragraph is organized using Chart 1 (p. 221). Noah basically tells us that there are five ways that the lives of Horatio Alger and James Adams were similar. He then addresses each point for both subjects. His first point is that both Alger and Adams were influential writers. Then he says they both came from well-established families. He observes that while both men's fathers were well-educated, they struggled financially. He next reports that despite these financial struggles, both men's fathers were able to get their sons into good colleges. Finally, he notes that both men initially entered their fathers' professions, but then became writers.

In an essay, a writer could discuss the same points listed here in greater detail, taking each one and writing a paragraph about each subject in relation to that point. For a more in-depth essay, she might write several paragraphs that discuss the two subjects in relation to each point made about them.

Chart 1: Point by Point

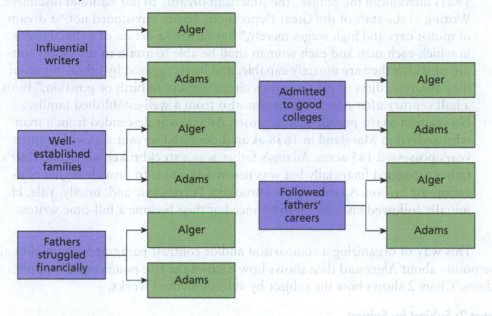

Subject-by-Subject Method

To illustrate the second method of organizing a comparison and/or contrast paragraph, the subject-by-subject method, let's look at a different arrangement of Noah's paragraph.

> The first of these two writers was Horatio Alger Jr. who wrote *Ragged Dick* (1868), *Luck and Pluck* (1869), and other dime novels for boys about getting ahead through virtue and hard work. To call these books popular would be an understatement: fully 5 percent of all the books checked out of the Muncie, Indiana, public library between November 1891 and December 1902 were authored by Alger. Born in 1832, Alger could not claim to have risen from the bottom. He was born into a well-established family whose American roots dated to the early seventeenth century and could trace his lineage to three Pilgrims who in 1621 sailed to Plymouth Plantation on the Fortune, the second English ship to arrive there. Alger's father, a Unitarian minister, was of good breeding and education and struggled to make ends meet but was able—at a time when well over 90 percent of the population didn't finish high school—to obtain higher education for his son, who went to Harvard. Alger initially followed his father into the ministry, before becoming a full-time writer. Similarly, James Truslow Adams was a more cerebral fellow who wrote books of American history, one of which (*The Epic of America*,

1931) introduced the phrase "the American dream" to our national discourse. Writing at the start of the Great Depression, Adams envisioned not "a dream of motor cars and high wages merely," but rather "a dream of a social order in which each man and each woman shall be able to attain to the fullest stature of which they are innately capable, and be recognized by others for what they are, regardless of the fortuitous circumstances of birth or position." Born a half century after Alger, Adams was also from a well-established family. No relation to the presidential Adamses, Adams was descended from a man who arrived in Maryland in 1638 as an indentured servant and within three years possessed 185 acres. Adams's father was a stockbroker who, like Alger's father, struggled financially but was nevertheless able to provide higher education for his son. Adams went to Brooklyn Polytechnic and, briefly, Yale. He initially followed his father into finance but then became a full-time writer.

This way of organizing a comparison and/or contrast paragraph first makes all five points about Alger and then shows how each of the five points equally applies to Adams. Chart 2 shows how the subject-by-subject method works.

Chart 2: Subject by Subject

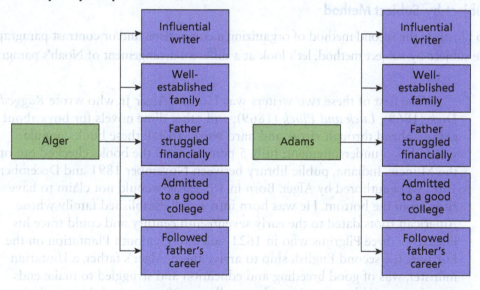

In an essay, a writer could take several paragraphs to discuss the points about Alger and several more to discuss the same points, in the same order, about Adams. He might add paragraphs between the two discussions and again after them analyzing what the writer learned about the similarities between the two subjects and the conclusions he reached about them.

Comparing and/or Contrasting Two Items

Write a short paper—no more than a page—in which you compare two items from one of the listings below. Once you make your choice, you might do a little brainstorming to see how many points of similarity or difference you can come up with for the two. This should help you decide which of the two ways of organizing—point-by-point or subject-by-subject—will work best.

1. Two places you have lived
2. Two candidates for political office
3. The cuisine of two cultures
4. Two vacation spots you have visited
5. Two careers you are considering
6. Three sports you like to play or watch (Comparing and/or contrasting *three* items is more demanding. Try this one if you are feeling up for a challenge.)

Cause and Effect

It is often useful in understanding the world around us to explore what were the causes of something that has happened or to explore what will be the effects of taking a certain action.

Strategies for Writing Cause and Effect

Very often in our complex world, things happen that leave us wondering why. A train derails and scores of people are injured. Why did the train derail? What were the *causes* of the accident? A bad signal? Weather conditions? Operator error? A combination of these factors? What were the consequences, or *effects*? Were passengers injured? Did toxic chemicals spill from a tanker? Were people living close to the accident site impacted?

On the other hand, sometimes institutions consider making changes, and we want to know what will happen if they do. Your city is thinking about closing several schools, for example. What will happen if they do? What will be the *effects*? Will students have to travel further to get to class? Will class sizes increase? Will teachers lose their jobs? Or will there be benefits, such as new buildings with modern equipment, smaller classes, and easier access for low-income students? In thinking about why the city might be considering closing schools, you might think about *causes*: the outdated buildings that cost more to maintain than they are worth, the classrooms designed for a different teaching model than the one now in use, or the lack of public transportation for students coming from other parts of the city. In both cases, you are thinking about causes and effects. It is one important way we understand the world, and it is one useful writing strategy. Sometimes, as in the examples below, the cause-and-effect strategy is used to organize a single paragraph, but quite often it is used to organize longer pieces of writing, including, at times, entire essays.

Causes and effects occur in many combinations. One cause can lead to a single effect or multiple effects: a windstorm can cause significant tree damage and little else, or it can bring down trees, which block roads and fall on power lines, cutting off electricity. Several causes can lead to one effect or several different effects: only attending some classes, doing little studying, and not preparing for a test can lead to an F, but together they can also lead to a failing overall grade, academic suspension, and having to repeat a semester of study. Causes and effects can also occur in related chains, with a cause leading to an effect leading to a cause and so on: you leave early for a job interview and slip on the ice the landlord has not yet salted and sprain your wrist; the ER is busy, so you do not get seen for over two hours and arrive late for your appointment; you have not had time to review your notes or organize your thoughts, so you go in feeling unprepared; you receive a call later that day saying you did not get the job. If only you had not left early that morning.

One word of caution: You should not assert that a cause-and-effect relationship exists when you are not sure that an event, or series of events, has resulted in a particular effect or effects. For example, you wore your "lucky" jeans to school today and you got an A on a test. You may be tempted to argue that your A on the test was caused by the "lucky" jeans, even though there was probably no connection. So, as you think about your topic, be careful to check that there is in fact a direct causal relationship between the events and results you discuss.

The following paragraph asserts that three causes resulted in one effect, that the candidate lost the election. The diagram that appears after the paragraph represents how the effect was the result of three different causes.

My candidate for Congress lost the election even though everyone thought she would win. Now that the race is over, we can see that she assumed she would have strong support in the city, so she didn't really campaign very hard there; she ended up losing the city vote by 8 percent. She also didn't start fundraising until two months before the primary and never had sufficient money to pay for enough television ads. In addition, her decision to support restrictions on the use of fertilizers because they damage the water supply cost her heavily among rural voters.

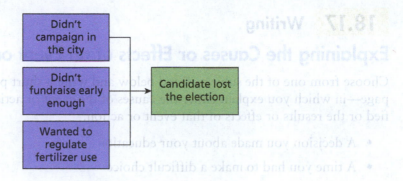

Now let's look at a paragraph that analyzes the effects of a particular action or cause.

The company where I work has decided to allow its employees to work on flextime, which means we can choose whether to work from 8:00 to 4:00, from 9:00 to 5:00, or from 10:00 to 6:00. This flexible scheduling has greatly improved employee morale. In addition, people are not constantly leaving the company for a different job the way they were before flextime. The number of applications for job openings has also doubled. Most important to management, productivity is up 18 percent over a year ago.

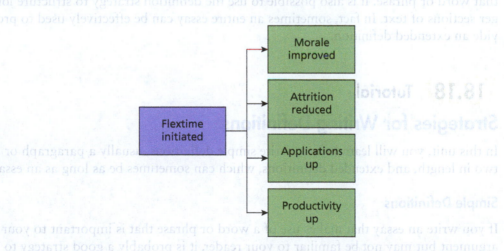

In this example, one cause, allowing flextime, resulted in four positive effects: improved morale, reduced attrition, increased applications for job openings, and improved productivity.

Explaining the Causes or Effects of an Event or Action

Choose from one of the subjects listed below and write a short paper—less than a page—in which you explain either the causes of the event or action you have identified or the results or effects of that event or action.

- A decision you made about your education
- A time you had to make a difficult choice
- A time someone helped you in a significant way
- A mistake you made
- A time you experienced bad luck

Definition

Providing a definition of a key word or phrase is a useful strategy, especially in the beginning of an essay. It will ensure that the reader understands how you are using that word or phrase. It is also possible to use the definition strategy to structure longer sections of text. In fact, sometimes an entire essay can be effectively used to provide an extended definition.

18.18 Tutorial

Strategies for Writing Definitions

In this unit, you will learn how to write simple definitions, usually a paragraph or two in length, and extended definitions, which can sometimes be as long as an essay.

Simple Definitions

If you write an essay that makes use of a word or phrase that is important to your argument but may not be familiar to your reader, it is probably a good strategy to provide a definition of that term near the beginning of the paper. You may even need to define more than one term.

Before discussing *how* to define a word, it may be useful to think for a minute about *why* you might want to define it. The first and most obvious reason is because you are using a word that your reader is unlikely to be familiar with. For example:

- You are writing for a general audience about economic issues and want to use the term *arbitrage*.

- You are writing about bird watching to an audience not familiar with birds and you use the term *raptor*.

- You are writing about medical issues to an audience of nonmedical professionals and you need to use the term *keratosis*.

A second reason you might want to define a word you are using is to ensure your readers understand your particular definition of the word. For example, if you will be using the term *juvenile delinquency* in a paper, you may decide to define it because you want to make clear exactly what you mean by it. You might explain, "In this essay, I will be using the term *juvenile delinquency* to refer to serious criminal acts, not misdemeanors and not minor vandalism, performed by people under the age of eighteen." Note that you are not trying to suggest that your way of defining the term is the only correct way to define it; you are merely making clear that *in this essay* this is how you will be using the term.

Defining a word at the most basic level consists of two steps:

1. Placing the word in a broad category
2. Identifying the features of the word that distinguish it from other members of that broad category

This process can be quite straightforward:

A dermatologist is a doctor who specializes in treating ailments of the skin.

Baseball is a sport played with bats and balls on a diamond-shaped field.

Other times it becomes a little more complicated:

A bird is an animal that has feathers and can fly.

The problem here is that kiwis, ostriches, and emus are all birds that don't fly. A more careful definition could be this:

> A bird is an animal that has feathers and wings.

Notice that this definition also solves the problem raised by bats and flying insects. They don't have feathers.

The definitions above are fairly brief; each is just a sentence. But in college writing it is often useful to provide a more extended definition, as here:

> A raptor is a bird that hunts and feeds on living animals or carrion. Raptors typically have a hooked beak, strong legs, and feet with sharp talons. Common species of raptors include hawks, eagles, owls, and falcons. Most raptors have excellent eyesight. Birds with long straight beaks like herons and egrets are not considered raptors.

Note that after the one-sentence definition, this writer has included other information about what is and what is not a raptor.

Extended Definitions

Sometimes defining a term is both complicated and important. For example, defining exactly what *plagiarism* is can be important to students who need to understand the concept in order to avoid any violation of the rules prohibiting it. Many instructors include a lengthy definition of the term in their syllabi. Many writing textbooks devote pages to explaining and giving examples of what is and what is not plagiarism. In an extended definition, after giving a concise definition of a term, you might include examples of what does and what does not fit the definition, reasons for defining the term just the way you have, and even an explanation of the word's history.

Guidelines for Writing a Definition

Depending on the term you are defining and your reason for defining it, you may use some or all of the following strategies for writing a definition.

- Place the term in the broad category to which it belongs.
- Explain the features that most examples of the term possess.
- Explain how it is different from other members of that category.

- Give examples of the term.
- Explain what the term is *not*: providing contrasting examples can help develop a clearer picture of your meaning.
- Use language and examples with which your audience is likely to be familiar.
- Discuss the origin of the term and how its definition has changed over time.
- Begin with a straightforward statement: A(n) _____ is a(n) _____ that has _____.

Do not do the following:

- Begin with a phrase like any of the following:

    - My definition of _____ is _____.
    - _____ means _____.
    - _____ means different things to different people.
    - _____ is when _____.
    - _____ is something that _____.

- Use the word being defined in the explanation of what it means.

18.19 Activity

Revising Definitions

Below are six definitions. Working in your group, use the guidelines at the end of Strategies for Writing Definitions (18.18) to revise each one to make it more effective.

1. A **recession** means a lot of people are out of work because companies are laying off workers. Recessions can be mild or strong and may even lead to depressions. Also, recessions can be caused by governments spending more money than they have.
2. My definition of the term **medical clinic** is a place where people go when they are sick or injured. Clinics are located in cities and in smaller towns. They always have at least one doctor and many additional support staff.
3. **Obscenity** is something vulgar or disgusting such as a word or event or act.
4. A **socialist** is someone who supports socialism.
5. A **catastrophe** is when something truly terrible happens.
6. A **lie** means a statement that is far from the truth.

18.20 Writing

Providing Simple or Extended Definitions

Write a simple definition of four of the words or phrases in the following list or an extended definition—at least a page—of one of them.

- lie
- art
- fake news
- delayed gratification
- fact
- freedom of speech
- happiness
- word (This one is quite hard; give it some extra time and effort.)
- success

Classification

When writing about a large, complex topic, it is frequently useful to break it down into smaller parts, or categories, that are easier to understand, and then use the information about the parts to help explain the whole.

18.21 Tutorial

Strategies for Writing Classification

Many times, writing about a complex topic can be made easier and more effective if the topic is divided into smaller parts, especially if the parts call for different treatments or different responses. This strategy is often used to write a paragraph or two in a longer essay, but it is sometimes used to organize an entire essay.

At its simplest, classification divides things into just two categories: books are either fiction or nonfiction, athletes are either professional or amateur, and living things are either animal or vegetable. But often it is more helpful to divide things into several categories. Automobiles are either gasoline fueled, diesel fueled, electric, or hybrid. Nonflowing bodies of water can be oceans, seas, lakes, ponds, bays, gulfs, or fjords. Literature traditionally consisted of prose, poetry, or drama, but many today would add at least biography, autobiography, and creative nonfiction. Food can be classified according to the country of origin: Italian food, South African food, Chinese food, and so forth.

Classification is a particularly useful strategy if you want to say something different about the items in different categories within one larger topic. The paragraph below, for instance, divides victims in a mass casualty incident (the larger topic) into three categories and explains how different treatment is allocated to each of these categories.

In a mass casualty incident such as an earthquake, hurricane, or terrorist attack, when medical personnel first arrive on the scene, patients are divided into three categories: those who will die regardless of treatment (Group 1), those who may live if treated quickly (Group 2), and those who will live even if not treated (Group 3). Because doctors' primary responsibility is to save lives, when the victims are many and the providers are few, all resources are focused on Group 2. When more medical personnel and resources become available, palliative care (reduction of pain and suffering) is administered to Group 1. When resources are plentiful, Group 3 will also be treated. During this time, patients are constantly monitored in case their condition changes and they need to be moved to a different group.

Guidelines for Effective Classification

Use classification:

- When you are writing about a complex subject and breaking it down into a small number of categories will make it easier for the reader to understand the content.

- When each of the categories requires a different treatment or response.

Once you decide to write a classification, consider the following guidelines.

- **Select the categories according to a consistent principle of classification.** For example, it would be inconsistent to classify mattresses as twin, double, queen, king, and foam: the first four categories relate to size while the last one refers to content. Choose a principle of classification that is suitable for your purpose and includes most, if not all, items that would be considered important parts of the larger topic you are discussing.

- **Make sure the categories make sense and serve a purpose.** Classifying students as pursuing certain disciplines such as science and technology, liberal arts, social sciences, and business allows a college to specify different required courses for each category. Classifying students according to the number of brothers and sisters they have does not serve any useful purpose in this context.

- **Make sure the categories are able to accommodate all possible examples.**   Classifying students according to their method of traveling to college using the categories bus, subway, car, truck, and motorcycle would not account for students who walk to school or ride a bicycle.

- **Decide how to classify examples that fit into more than one category.**   If you classify literary texts into fiction, poetry, and drama, where do you place a play that is written in poetic form? One solution would be to add a category labeled *mixed*.

- **Give some thought to the most effective order of presentation of your categories.**   One order might be to present the categories with the most members first and those with fewer members last. Another order could be to present the categories that need attention urgently first and those that need attention less urgently later.

18.22   Writing
Breaking a Topic into Categories

Write a short paper—a half page is plenty—in which you break one of the following topics into smaller categories. State the principle of classification you chose and why.

1. Types of government
2. Sports
3. College courses
4. Diseases
5. Bosses
6. Professors
7. Historical military conflicts
8. Games

Summary

Being able to write an effective summary in which you concisely restate the main points of a reading, novel, movie, lecture, textbook passage, or other longer piece of content will help you in many college courses as well as in the workplace.

18.23 Writing

What Makes a Good Summary?

You probably have a sense of what it means to write a summary. You write something short that briefly states the main content of something longer that you have read.

For this assignment, you will try your hand at summary writing. Your instructor will assign a text for you to read. After you've read it and perhaps made some notes, write a short paper—a half page is plenty—in which you summarize the text.

18.24 Activity

Analyzing Summaries

Your instructor will distribute to each group a set of summaries that were submitted for a recent assignment. Your group's task is to read over the summaries and make two lists: one of what you found that worked well in one or more of the summaries and one of the weaknesses or mistakes you found in one or more of the summaries. After a half hour or so, the groups will report out on their lists.

18.25 Tutorial

Strategies for Writing a Summary

Being able to write a summary is a crucial skill in college and beyond. After reading a complex article or chapter, you may find it helpful to write a paragraph or so in which you record the main ideas from what you read. After listening to a lecture or a discussion, you may want to take a few minutes to summarize the most important points, which can help with your understanding of the class and your memory of it. After watching a movie, a play, or even a YouTube video, you may want to summarize the experience for later recall.

In the workplace, you may be asked to interview a candidate for a job and write a summary of what you learned from the interview. In your first job, it would not be unusual for you to be asked to investigate a complex topic like whether an office should switch to digital record keeping or not and to write a summary of your findings.

The ability to gather together a complex body of information and ideas and present the most important points in a coherent, concise piece of writing is an important skill. In a summary of a written text, it is often, but not always, possible to locate the author's main point (often referred to as a *thesis*) and the ideas that support it. But many times, texts, especially excerpts from longer pieces, do not include a single clear thesis. In these cases, it is up to you as the reader to figure out what you think the major idea or ideas are. In summarizing an event, a batch of data, or a visual image, it will almost always be up to you to decide what the main points are.

Writing a Good Summary

Before writing a summary, carefully read the text. Annotate as you read, and review your notes as you prepare to write. Be sure that you understand what the writer is saying and how his or her ideas connect to each other. Reread or ask for help if you do not, as you cannot write an effective summary unless you fully comprehend what the writer is saying.

As you write, keep in mind the following guidelines for writing a good summary.

1. **A good summary should be much shorter than the text or content being summarized.** It should be usually a quarter to a third of the length of the original if it is a short text (e.g., 1–3 pages). It could be longer if you are summarizing an entire novel, a movie, or a large amount of information.

2. **A good summary should include only the major ideas from what is being summarized.** For a longer piece, it would include the thesis and the major supporting ideas. A good summary does not include less important supporting details.

3. **A good summary should be written in your own words.** Restate or paraphrase key terms, concepts, or ideas. Use quotations very sparingly, if at all, and if you do, use quotation marks. Do not simply plug your own words into the structure of the text you are summarizing. Summarize using your own structure.

4. **A good summary should not include your own ideas or opinions.** Summarize what you have read or observed and do not include your own ideas, opinions, or information from other sources.

5. **A good summary should clearly state the source that is being summarized.** The introductory sentence should note the author and title of a reading (or, for example, the director and title of a movie) and should use appropriate in-text citation (see MLA In-Text Citations [23.2, p. 338] or APA In-Text Citations [24.2, p. 374] for details).

Summarizing Baldwin

Below you will find James Baldwin's essay "On Being 'White' . . . and Other Lies." For this assignment, write a summary of the essay. If you need to refresh your understanding of what makes a good summary, refer to Strategies for Writing a Summary (18.25, p. 233).

On Being "White" . . . and Other Lies

JAMES BALDWIN

James Baldwin (1924–1987) is best known as the author of six novels including *Go Tell It on the Mountain* (1953) and *Giovanni's Room* (1956). He also wrote essays that explored race, racism, homophobia, the immigrant experience, and whiteness. "On Being 'White' . . . and Other Lies" first appeared in the magazine *Essence* in 1984. In this essay he's questioning the racial category "white" by pointing out it was only invented as a category when Europeans came to America.

1   The crisis of leadership in the white community is remarkable—and terrifying—because there is, in fact, no white community.

2   This may seem an enormous statement—and it is. I'm willing to be challenged. I'm also willing to attempt to spell it out.

3   My frame of reference is, of course, America, or that portion of the North American continent that calls itself America. And this means I am speaking, essentially, of the European vision of the world—or more precisely, perhaps, the European vision of the universe. It is a vision as remarkable for what it pretends to include as for what it remorselessly diminishes, demolishes or leaves totally out of account.

4   There is, for example—at least, in principle—an Irish community: here, there, anywhere, or, more precisely, Belfast, Dublin and Boston. There is a German community: both sides of Berlin, Bavaria and Yorkville. There is an Italian community: Rome, Naples, the Bank of the Holy Ghost and Mulberry Street. And there is a Jewish community, stretching from Jerusalem to California to New York. There are English communities. There are French communities. There are Swiss consortiums. There are Poles: in Warsaw (where they would like us to be friends) and in Chicago (where because they are white we are enemies). There are, for that matter, Indian restaurants and Turkish baths. There is the underworld—the poor (to say nothing of those who intend to become rich) are always with us—but this does not describe a community. It bears terrifying witness to what happened to everyone who got here,

▶

and paid the price of the ticket. The price was to become "white." No one was white before he/she came to America. It took generations, and a vast amount of coercion, before this became a white country.

5   It is probable that it is the Jewish community—or more accurately, perhaps, its remnants—that in America has paid the highest and most extraordinary price for becoming white. For the Jews came here from countries where they were not white, and they came here, in part, because they were not white; and incontestably in the eyes of the Black American (and not only in those eyes) American Jews have opted to become white, and this is how they operate. It was ironical to hear, for example, former Israeli prime minister Menachem Begin declare some time ago that "the Jewish people bow only to God" while knowing that the state of Israel is sustained by a blank check from Washington. Without further pursuing the implication of this mutual act of faith, one is nevertheless aware that the Black presence, here, can scarcely hope—at least, not yet—to halt the slaughter in South Africa.

6   And there is a reason for that.

7   America became white—the people who, as they claim, "settled" the country became white—because of the necessity of denying the Black presence, and justifying the Black subjugation. No community can be based on such a principle—or, in other words, no community can be established on so genocidal a lie. White men—from Norway, for example, where they were Norwegians—became white: by slaughtering the cattle, poisoning the wells, torching the houses, massacring Native Americans, raping Black women.

8   This moral erosion has made it quite impossible for those who think of themselves as white in this country to have any moral authority at all—privately, or publicly. The multitudinous bulk of them sit, stunned, before their TV sets, swallowing garbage that they know to be garbage, and—in a profound and unconscious effort to justify this torpor that disguises a profound and bitter panic—pay a vast amount of attention to athletics: even though they know that the football player (the Son of the Republic, *their* sons!) is merely another aspect of the money-making scheme. They are either relieved or embittered by the presence of the Black boy on the team. I do not know if they remember how long and hard they fought to keep him off it. I know that they do not dare have any notion of the price Black people (mothers and fathers) paid and pay. They do not want to know the meaning, or face the shame, of what they compelled—out of what they took as the necessity of being white—Joe Louis or Jackie Robinson or Cassius Clay (aka Muhammad Ali) to pay. I know that they, themselves, would not have liked to pay it.

9   There has never been a labor movement in this country, the proof being the absence of a Black presence in the so-called father-to-son unions. There are, perhaps, some niggers in the window; but Blacks have no power in the labor unions.

10   Just so does the white community, as a means of keeping itself white, elect, as they imagine, their political (!) representatives. No nation in the world, including England, is represented by so stunning a pantheon of the relentlessly mediocre. I will not name names—I will leave that to you.

11   But this cowardice, this necessity of justifying a totally false identity and of justifying what must be called a genocidal history, has placed everyone now living into the hands of the most ignorant and powerful people the world has ever seen: And how did they get that way?

12   By deciding that they were white. By opting for safety instead of life. By persuading themselves that a Black child's life meant nothing compared with a white child's life. By abandoning their children to the things white men could buy. By informing their children that Black women, Black men and Black children had no human integrity that those who call themselves white were bound to respect. And in this debasement and definition of Black people, they debased and defamed themselves.

13   And have brought humanity to the edge of oblivion: because they think they are white. Because they think they are white, they do not dare confront the ravage and the lie of their history. Because they think they are white, they cannot allow themselves to be tormented by the suspicion that all men are brothers. Because they think they are white, they are looking for, or bombing into existence, stable populations, cheerful natives and cheap labor. Because they think they are white, they believe, as even no child believes, in the dream of safety. Because they think they are white, however vociferous they may be and however multitudinous, they are as speechless as Lot's wife—looking backward, changed into a pillar of salt.

14   However—! White being, absolutely, a moral choice (for there are no white people), the crisis of leadership for those of us whose identity has been forged, or branded, as Black is nothing new. We—who were not Black before we got here either, who were defined as Black by the slave trade—have paid for the crisis of leadership in the white community for a very long time, and have resoundingly, even when we face the worst about ourselves, survived, and triumphed over it. If we had not survived and triumphed, there would not be a Black American alive.

15   And the fact that we are still here—even in suffering, darkness, danger, endlessly defined by those who do not dare define, or even confront, themselves—is the key to the crisis in white leadership. The past informs us of various kinds of people—criminals, adventurers and saints, to say nothing, of course, of popes—but it is the Black condition, and only that, which informs us concerning white people. It is a terrible paradox, but those who believed that they could control and define Black people divested themselves of the power to control and define themselves.

Proposal

In school, in your neighborhood, or in your workplace, if you want to innovate, to correct injustices, to improve efficiency, or, generally, to make things better, you need to be able to write an effective proposal.

18.27 Tutorial

Strategies for Writing a Proposal

If you want to innovate, to correct injustices, to improve efficiency, or, generally, to make things better, you need to be able to write an effective proposal. For example, you might want to do one of the following.

- Sway your English teacher to give more time for revising essays.

- Prompt your local government to provide more lighting in your neighborhood.

- Convince the place you work to provide more employee parking.

- Persuade the federal government to improve the FAFSA application.

Each of these would require that you write a proposal.

How to Write a Successful Proposal

A proposal must have two essential components: an argument that there is a problem and a proposed solution to that problem. To fully explain both, you need to do the following.

1. **State the problem.**   You need to state clearly what the problem you are addressing is and present evidence to support the idea that it is a problem. You might give examples of how the problem has affected people or even how it could affect the audience you are writing for. It is also useful to provide background information about the problem. What is the history of the problem? What attempts have been made to address it in the past? With what results? What are the causes of the problem? Is it getting worse? Sometimes this background information works best at the beginning of the proposal, but more often, it is more effective after you've explained what the problem is.

2. **Present a solution.**   You need to provide a clear statement of the solution you are proposing. What is it? Who would have to do it? How much would it cost? How would it work? Once you've clearly explained your solution to the problem, you need to present evidence that it is feasible, that it is a realistic proposal. Then you need to present evidence that, once enacted, your proposal

will solve the problem or, at least, reduce the severity of the negative effects the problem causes.

3. **Address objections to your solution.** You need to think about why some people might object to your proposed solution and explain how their objections are not valid. Point out that it won't cost as much as they claim. Clarify that the negative side effects can be avoided. If they argue that your solution has already been tried and found to be ineffective, explain why it wasn't tried correctly or how the situation has changed so that now it will be effective.

   Sometimes those who oppose a solution don't criticize the proposed solution, but instead argue that a different solution would be more effective. You need to find out about any alternative solutions and evaluate them so that you can confidently argue that other solutions won't work, won't work as well, or will have too many harmful side effects.

4. **Make a strong argument.** You will want to close your proposal with a strong argument for immediate action on your proposal.

In the following proposal, LaShawna Williams includes each of the components suggested above.

A Proposal to Substitute a Discussion Board for the Chat Room

1 Dear Professor Jenkins, I want to bring to your attention a problem that is causing many students great difficulty. Your requirement that we join a chat room on line for an hour every Sunday afternoon at 5:00 is having consequences you may not be aware of.

Clear statement of the problem

2 Many of us work on weekends to support our going to school. I am a cook at a restaurant on Saturdays and Sundays. I have to arrive by 3:00 to begin my prep work for dinner. I try to access your chat room on my cell phone at 5:00, but often we are simply too busy. I know that four of my classmates are having similar conflicts with their Sunday jobs.

Examples of how the problem is causing harm

3 While I can use my cell phone to access the chat room, three of my classmates that I know of don't own cell phones and, of course, don't own computers. They depend on computers in the

writing center or in the library to access your website. The problem is that the library and writing center are not open on Sundays.

4   When we registered for your class, the schedule indicated the class meets on Monday, Wednesday, and Friday from 10:15 to 11:05. We built our class schedules and our work schedules around these times. Now we learn that we also are required to participate in the class chat room every Sunday afternoon, creating considerable hardship.

Background information about the problem

5   I would like to propose a solution to this problem which will still allow you to interact with us and read our thoughts about the readings in the course online, but will not cause the hardships for many of us that the Sunday afternoon chat room is causing. I propose that, instead of the chat room at a certain hour on Sundays, you establish a discussion board that we are required to post on at least six times each week.

Clear statement of the solution

6   There is a discussion board available in Blackboard, so there is no expense to the college, to you, or to the students. We could have the same kind of conversations you are calling for in the chat room, but there would not be a specific time we had to join the conversation. Just like with a chat room, you will be able to monitor the conversation, ask us questions, clear up misunderstandings, and evaluate our performance. Last semester, I was in a class that required us to participate in a discussion board, and it was quite successful. There was much more participation by the class than we are getting in the chat room.

Evidence the solution is feasible and will address the problem

7   I know that you have announced that if we miss three chat room conversations, we can write an extra essay and be graded on that. This, however, is not nearly as good a solution as the discussion board I am proposing. First, it feels more like punishment than participation. Second, it means

Argument that the proposed solution is superior to an alternative solution

we do not benefit from the experience of being part of a discussion.

8   I urge you to announce at our next class meeting that we are switching to the discussion board format instead of the Sunday chat room.

Strong argument for immediate action

Thanks for considering my proposal,
LaShawna Williams

18.28   Writing

Making a Proposal to Solve a Problem

Think of a problem at your school, at your workplace, or in your town or city. Then think of a solution to that problem. Finally, think of the person to whom you could write to propose a solution.

Write a proposal to that person. One or two pages would be plenty, but if you need more to make your case, a longer paper is fine too. Refer to Strategies for Writing a Proposal (18.27, p. 238) for more information on how to write a successful proposal.

Reflection

Reflective writing asks you to think back, to "reflect," on an experience—an essay you have written, a major change in your life, a time when you weren't successful at something you wanted to do—and to examine how you now think and feel about that experience.

18.29   Tutorial

Strategies for Writing a Reflection

Reflective writing is different from most writing you do in college. It asks you to examine your feelings. It asks you to think about the effects an experience has had on you. What have you learned? How have you changed? How will you be different in the future?

Reflective writing is useful in many ways. After you've been working on a project for days or even weeks, it can be very helpful to take a minute to think back over the time you spent on that project: What did you learn? What mistakes did you make? What did you do really well? It can also be useful to examine your feelings about the experience. Do you feel satisfied? Eager to get on to the next project? Disappointed? Relieved? How will you be different in the future as a result of this experience? How can you benefit from the experience going forward? What mistakes will you know how to avoid in the future?

In this course you are asked to reflect on your experience writing essays, but the process of writing down your reflections can be helpful in many other situations as well: you can reflect on a reading, a group activity, or a video. After you have a job interview, it can be very useful to write a short reflection about the experience. When a relationship ends, reflection can be a big help in getting over it and moving on. Even after making a mistake in your life—breaking a law, doing something cruel or thoughtless to someone, or cheating on some task at work or at school—reflective writing can help you learn and move on from these experiences.

18.30 Writing

Reflecting on an Important Experience

Think of an experience you have had in the past couple of years. This could be a project you worked on in school or it could involve a job, a program you volunteered for, a family event of some kind, or an athletic endeavor. Almost any experience that you can remember fairly clearly will work, but it should not have been a quick event that was over in a few minutes. Try to pick something in which you invested considerable time and effort. Then write a short paper—a page or so—reflecting on this experience.

- **Report on what you learned.** What were the most important or most useful ideas you encountered? What mistakes did you make? Was there some part of the experience that you are proud of? Do you have any regrets?

- **Describe how you now feel about the experience.** Are you disappointed? Satisfied? Proud? Relieved? Eager to get on with some new experience?

- **How will you be different in the future?** What did you learn that will make a difference for you in the future? How will you be different?

Weaving Strategies into a Strong Essay

After discussing the writing strategies covered in this topic separately, in this final section you will see how they can be woven together into a powerful essay.

18.31 Tutorial

Using Multiple Writing Strategies in an Essay

In this Topic a series of writing strategies have been discussed that are most often woven together to create a coherent and convincing essay. Although you might be writing a predominantly cause-and-effect, comparison/contrast, process, or argument essay, you will find that you need to use other strategies to flesh out your paper. Before you start drafting, consider your subject, audience, purpose, and assignment. Then review the strategies discussed in this Topic and think about which strategy, or strategies, would work best for your assignment. If you are making an argument, for example, you might consider including the following.

- a paragraph or two defining one or more terms critical to that argument

- a narrative paragraph that provides some historical context for the issue

- a lengthy description of a place important to the argument

- several paragraphs that strengthen the overall argument by focusing on the positive effects that would result from taking the action proposed in the thesis

18.32 Activity

Identifying Multiple Writing Strategies in an Essay

The process of weaving various writing strategies together in a longer essay is a very effective way to organize a compelling essay, as Steven Pinker does in the excerpt below, which comes from his introduction to a book on language. The several references to later chapters refer to the rest of the book.

Working in your group, identify as many different writing strategies used by Pinker in this excerpt as you can.

Words and Worlds

STEVEN PINKER

Steven Pinker, an experimental psychologist, was born in Montreal, Canada. He earned a bachelor's degree in experimental psychology from McGill University and a doctorate from Harvard. He has taught at Stanford and MIT and is currently the Johnstone Family Professor in the psychology department at Harvard. After early research on language development in children, he went on to focus on the cognitive, genetic, and neurobiological underpinnings of language. He has authored ten books and received nine honorary doctorates.

1   On September 11, 2001, at 8:46 A.M., a hijacked airliner crashed into the north tower of the World Trade Center in New York. At 9:03 A.M. a second plane crashed into the south tower. The resulting infernos caused the buildings to collapse, the south tower after burning for an hour and two minutes, the north tower twenty-three minutes after that. The attacks were masterminded by Osama bin Laden, leader of the Al Qaeda terrorist organization, who hoped to intimidate the United States into ending its military presence in Saudi Arabia and its support for Israel and to unite Muslims in preparation for a restoration of the caliphate.

2   9/11, as the happenings of that day are now called, stands as the most significant political and intellectual event of the twenty-first century so far. It has set off debates on a vast array of topics: how best to memorialize the dead and revitalize lower Manhattan; whether the attacks are rooted in ancient Islamic fundamentalism or modern revolutionary agitation; the role of the United States on the world stage before the attacks and in response to them; how best to balance protection against terrorism with respect for civil liberties.

3   But I would like to explore a lesser-known debate triggered by 9/11. Exactly how many events took place in New York on that morning in September?

4   It could be argued that the answer is one. The attacks on the building were part of a single plan conceived in the mind of one man in service of a single agenda. They unfolded within a few minutes of each other, targeting the parts of a complex with a single name, design, and owner. And they launched a single chain of military and political events in their aftermath.

5   Or it could be argued that the answer is two. The north tower and south tower were distinct collections of glass and steel separated by an expanse of space, and they were hit at different times and went out of existence at different times. The amateur video that showed the second plane closing in on the south tower as the north tower billowed with smoke makes the twoness unmistakable: in those horrifying moments, one event was frozen in the past, the other loomed in the future. And another

occurrence on that day—a passenger mutiny that brought down a third hijacked plane before it reached its target in Washington—presents to the imagination the possibility that one tower or the other might have been spared. In each of those possible worlds a distinct event took place, so in our *actual* world one might argue, there must have been a pair of events as surely as one plus one equals two.

6   The gravity of 9/11 would seem to make this entire discussion frivolous to the point of impudence. It's a matter of mere "semantics," as we say, with its implication of picking nits, splitting hairs, and debating the number of angels that can dance on the head of a pin. But this book is about semantics, and I would not make a claim on your attention if I did not think that the relation of language to our inner and outer worlds was a matter of intellectual fascination and real-world importance.

7   Though "importance" is often hard to quantify, in this case I can put an exact value on it: three and a half billion dollars. That was the sum in dispute in a set of trials determining the insurance payout to Larry Silverstein, the leaseholder of the World Trade Center site. Silverstein held insurance policies that stipulated a maximum reimbursement for each destructive "event." If 9/11 comprised a single event, he stood to receive three and a half billion dollars. If it comprised two events, he stood to receive seven billion. In the trials, the attorneys disputed the applicable meaning of the term *event*. The lawyers for the leaseholder defined it in physical terms (two collapses); those for the insurance companies defined it in mental terms (one plot). There is nothing "mere" about semantics!

8   Nor is the topic intellectually trifling. The 9/11 cardinality debate is not about the facts, that is, the physical events and human actions that took place that day. Admittedly, those have been contested as well: according to various conspiracy theories, the buildings were targeted by American missiles, or demolished by a controlled implosion, in a plot conceived by American neoconservatives, Israeli spies, or a cabal of psychiatrists. But aside from the kooks, most people agree on the facts. Where they differ is in the *construal* of those facts: how the intricate swirl of matter in space ought to be conceptualized by human minds. As we shall see, the categories in this dispute permeate the meanings of words in our language because they permeate the way we represent reality in our heads.

9   Semantics is about the relation of words to thoughts, but it is also about the relation of words to other human concerns. Semantics is about the relation of words to reality—the way that speakers commit themselves to a shared understanding of the truth, and the way their thoughts are anchored to things and situations in the world. It is about the relation of words to a community—how a new word, which arises in an act of creation by a single speaker, comes to evoke the same idea in the rest of a population, so people can understand one another when they use it. It is

about the relation of words to emotions: the way in which words don't just point to things but are saturated with feelings, which can endow the words with a sense of magic, taboo, and sin. And it is about words and social relations—how people use language not just to transfer ideas from head to head but to negotiate the kind of relationship they wish to have with their conversational partner.

10   A feature of the mind that we will repeatedly encounter in these pages is that even our most abstract concepts are understood in terms of concrete scenarios. That applies in full force to the subject matter of the book itself. In this introductory chapter I will preview some of the book's topics with vignettes from newspapers and the Internet that can be understood only through the lens of semantics. They come from each of the worlds that connect to our words—the worlds of thought, reality, community, emotions, and social relations.

11   Let's look at the bone of contention in the world's most expensive debate in semantics, the three-and-a-half-billion-dollar argument over the meaning of "event." What, exactly, is an event? An event is a stretch of time, and time, according to physicists, is a continuous variable—an inexorable cosmic flow, in Newton's world, or a fourth dimension in a seamless hyperspace in Einstein's. But the human mind carves this fabric into discrete swatches we call events. Where does the mind place the incisions? Sometimes, as the lawyers for the World Trade Center leaseholder pointed out, it encircles the change of state of an object, such as the collapse of a building. And sometimes, as the lawyers for the insurers pointed out, it encircles the goal of a human actor, such as a plot being executed. Most often the circles coincide: an actor intends to cause an object to change, the intent of the act and the fate of the object are tracked along a single time line, and the moment of change marks the consummation of the intent.

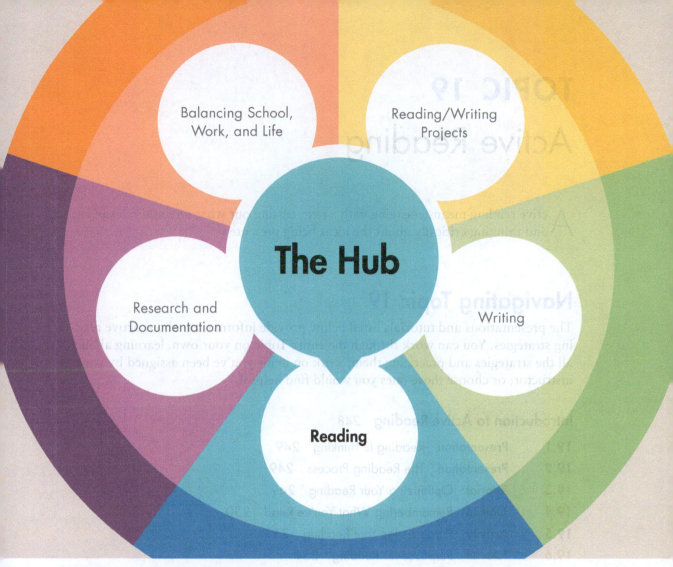

The Hub

Balancing School, Work, and Life

Reading/Writing Projects

Research and Documentation

Writing

Reading

3 Reading

Topic 19   Active Reading   248
Topic 20   Reading Strategies   259
Topic 21   Critical Reading   287

Students in college, particularly students in English courses in college, can expect to be required to read challenging texts regularly. Part 3 is a collection of advice, activities, readings, and videos that will help you as you encounter these college-level texts.

TOPIC 19
Active Reading

Active reading means engaging with a text, teasing out what an author is saying, and thinking critically about the ideas being presented.

Navigating Topic 19

The presentations and tutorials listed below provide information about active reading strategies. You can work through the entire Topic on your own, learning about all the strategies and practicing them; work on items you've been assigned by your instructor; or choose those ones you would find helpful.

Introduction to Active Reading   248

19.1	Presentation	Reading Is Thinking	249
19.2	Presentation	The Reading Process	249
19.3	Tutorial	Optimizing Your Reading	249
19.4	Tutorial	Remembering What You've Read	250
19.5	Activity	Purposes for *Your* Reading	251
19.6	Tutorial	Purposes for Reading	251
19.7	Tutorial	Constructing Meaning	252
19.8	Activity	Constructing Mike Rose's Meaning in "'Grit' Revisited"	253

Introduction to Active Reading

Topic 19 begins with two presentations on concepts that are essential to being a successful active reader: the first emphasizes that reading is thinking, and the second describes how effective readers use a process that involves pre-, during-, and after-reading strategies. It then provides information on remembering what you've read, purposes for reading, and how to construct meaning from texts.

19.1 Presentation
Reading Is Thinking

To watch this presentation, which discusses the importance of thinking, questioning, and extracting meaning from a text as you read, go to *Achieve for The Hub*, Topic 19, and open Unit 19.1.

19.2 Presentation
The Reading Process

To watch this presentation, which discusses the different strategies effective readers use before, during, and after reading to get the most out of a text, go to *Achieve for The Hub*, Topic 19, and open Unit 19.2.

19.3 Tutorial
Optimizing Your Reading

Reading takes concentration, so it makes sense to read when and where you can focus best. This differs from person to person. Some people need the absolute quiet of a library carrel, while others read most effectively listening to music or sitting in a coffee shop. The following are some suggestions for optimizing your reading.

- **Find the right place for you to read.** If even the smallest noise distracts you, find a quiet place where you won't be disturbed. This could be the library, a secluded bench on campus, or your apartment or dorm room when your roommates are in classes. If you do better when there's some background sound, play music, try a lounge in your dorm, or go to a coffee shop.

- **Try to read in the same place and at the same time.** Block out time on your calendar for reading and list your assignments and their due dates. Developing a routine of reading in the same place at the same time will help you to focus and become a more concentrated reader.

- **Choose times to read when you are most alert.** Some people find they can concentrate best in the morning while others prefer to read in the evening. Whatever time works best for you, plan to read your most difficult assignments first, when you have the most stamina and focus.

- **Avoid distractions.**   In today's world, you are always connected to other people via smart phone, email, instant messenger apps, Facebook, Instagram, SnapChat, Twitter, and WhatsApp. In order to concentrate, you need to turn all social media off. Resist checking for messages, updates, or breaking news until after you've finished reading.

- **Break reading assignments into chunks.**   Reading assigned in college can sometimes be dry or difficult to read. Break an assignment into manageable chunks, maybe the content between two major headings, and stop after each section to check that you've understood what you've read. Write a brief summary of the main points or create a diagram or timeline that helps you to organize what you've learned. For challenging readings, break the text into even smaller parts and reread if necessary.

- **Build in breaks and reward yourself for completing assignments.**   At the end of a long section or several smaller ones, take five minutes to stretch your legs or get coffee. Reward yourself for completing an assignment by going for a walk, eating lunch with a friend, or checking your social media.

19.4   Tutorial

Remembering What You've Read

Many readers worry that they won't be able to remember what they have read. A wonderful teacher named Cris Tovani has written a book called *I Read It, But I Don't Get It*. In it she describes the experiences of many readers who struggle to read a book, an essay, or a chapter in a text but who, when they finish, don't remember what they read and, therefore, have concluded that they are not good readers.

David Bartholomae and Anthony Petrosky in an influential book about reading and writing, *Facts, Artifacts, and Counterfacts*, point out that a reader who literally memorized an entire text and could recite it back word for word might not have actually understood the text. One can imagine a computer that could read a text out loud, word for word, but no one would claim that the computer had actually "read" the text.

For now, you should be less concerned about "remembering" the text. Instead, think of reading as an act of thinking, of understanding, of comprehending, of engaging with the text. Approached this way, the point of reading is not to remember everything you read, but to understand the important ideas you learned and the conclusions that you developed during the process of reading. Topic 20: Reading Strategies (p. 259) provides a number of techniques that will assist you in doing this more effectively, such as annotating, keeping a journal, summarizing, and playing the believing and doubting game.

19.5 Activity

Purposes for *Your* Reading

Not only do writers have a purpose for their writing, but readers usually read with a purpose.

Working in your group, make a list of the different kinds of reading the members of your group do. Then list what the purpose is for each different kind of reading, as illustrated in the following chart.

Kind of Reading	Purpose for Reading
A letter from a friend	To learn what they are doing, thinking
A recipe for something you plan to cook in the future	To make a shopping list of ingredients

19.6 Tutorial

Purposes for Reading

We read for many different purposes: to find out when the next bus leaves campus, to find a recipe for a special meal, to locate sources for a research paper, to learn what's happening in the world of politics, or to solve a mystery in a crime novel. A list of some of the many purposes we have for reading might look like this:

- Reading to learn new information

- Reading to understand a difficult concept

- Reading to evaluate and critique different perspectives on a topic

- Reading for practical purposes (e.g., how to change brake fluid or build a set of shelves)

- Reading for a class assignment

- Reading to find specific information in a book, article, or online text

- Skimming to get a general sense of a text

- Scanning to find specific information (e.g., the date of a historical event)

- Reading for pleasure

The way we read is often determined by the purpose for which we are reading, and these variations in purpose require the use of different reading techniques, as can be seen in the following examples.

1. You are reading an email to determine the location of an important sales meeting. You scan the document looking for the conference room number.

2. You are reading a novel for pleasure. You read attentively but in a relaxed manner, savoring the pleasure of the experience.

3. You are reading a letter from a company to which you have applied for a job. You read fairly quickly, skimming the document to find the place where the company says whether you are invited for an interview or not.

4. You are reading a textbook about the causes of the War of 1812 in preparation for a test. You read slowly with great focus, annotating the text, making notes to help you understand and remember the details, summarizing important events, and creating and answering questions you think your instructor might ask.

5. You are previewing a challenging article in a scholarly journal before you dive in for a detailed read. You read the abstract, title, headings, and first and last paragraphs; note the name of the author; review any graphic aids, such as charts and graphs; and consider how difficult the article will be to read and how much time you will need.

6. You are reading a half dozen articles on global warming to see if any of them discuss the effect of rising sea levels in Florida, a topic you are writing about. You preview each and then skim through those that sound promising, looking for more specific information.

Notice how your reading techniques will change depending on your purpose. It's a good idea, before you start reading anything, to think for a minute about the purpose of your reading and to adjust your approach to match that purpose.

19.7 Tutorial

Constructing Meaning

Sometimes the meaning of a text is fairly obvious. Sometimes authors state what they mean to say in the first paragraph, even in the first sentence. But at other times, writers aren't so direct. Sometimes the reader has to construct the meaning by reading carefully, weighing the evidence, evaluating the reasoning, and comparing what the text says with the reader's own experiences.

For example, two groups of students read a section of Rebecca Skloot's book *The Immortal Life of Henrietta Lacks* that describes Lacks's experience going to Johns Hopkins Hospital in Baltimore for treatment of what turned out to be cervical cancer.

The book tells us that Lacks was admitted to the "colored" ward of the hospital, her tissues were used for medical research without her permission or knowledge, and, after her death, her surviving husband and children were tricked into signing an agreement to allow the hospital to perform an autopsy on her body. On the other hand, the book tells us that Hopkins was founded to provide health care for the poor, that Hopkins provided Lacks all the therapy for cervical cancer that medicine at that time had at its disposal, and that Hopkins didn't make any money from Lacks's cells.

Asked to write a brief statement summing up what the passage said about Johns Hopkins Hospital, the students in the first group wrote, "Johns Hopkins was a racist organization." The students in the second group wrote, "The good that Hopkins did for medical science far outweighed the racism it was also guilty of."

When asked why the two groups had arrived at such different "meanings" from the text, a woman in the second group, made up of four African American women, after much hesitation, volunteered an observation: "Group 1 is all white. I think they were afraid that if they didn't come down hard on the racism, we black students would jump all over them." At this point, one of the women in the first group suggested that the women in the second group were all studying to be nurses. It turned out three of the four were in the nursing program.

The point here is not that one group or the other had the "right answer." The point is that the meaning of a text is not something lying quietly on the page waiting to be discovered and underlined. The meaning of a text is something to be constructed by the reader. When readers carefully and thoughtfully read a text, weigh the evidence given, examine the assumptions underlying the text, evaluate the reasoning, and compare it all with their own experiences and thoughts, they are able to *construct* a meaning from the text.

The kind of reading that will allow you to engage with a challenging text and construct a meaning after reading that text is what we mean by active reading. In Topic 20: Reading Strategies (p. 259), you will be introduced to a number of different strategies to help you read this way.

19.8   Activity

Constructing Mike Rose's Meaning in "'Grit' Revisited"

Read the following excerpt from Mike Rose's blog. When you've finished reading it, working with your group, decide what the passage means. What is Rose saying? What's his point? Write your group's decision about the meaning of the essay in a sentence or two.

A word of warning: The meaning of this excerpt is fairly subtle. You will need to pay attention to details, weigh the evidence, and do some thinking in order to decide what the passage means.

"Grit" Revisited: Reflections on Our Public Talk about Education

MIKE ROSE

1   One of the many frustrating things about education policy and practice in our country is the continual search for the magic bullet—and all the hype and trite lingo that bursts up around it. One such bullet is the latest incarnation of character education, particularly the enthrallment with "grit," a buzz word for perseverance and determination. . . .

2   In a nutshell, I worry about the limited success of past attempts at character education and the danger in our pendulum-swing society that we will shift our attention from improving subject matter instruction. I also question the easy distinctions made between "cognitive" and "non-cognitive" skills. And I fear that we will sacrifice policies aimed at reducing poverty for interventions to change the way poor people see the world.

3   In this post, I would like to further explore these concerns—and a few new ones—by focusing on "grit," for it has so captured the fancy of our policy makers, administrators, and opinion-makers.

4   Grit's rise to glory is something to behold, a case study in the sociology of knowledge. If you go back ten or so years, you'll find University of Pennsylvania psychologist Angela Duckworth investigating the role of perseverance in achievement. This idea is not new in the study of personality and individual differences, but Duckworth was trying to more precisely define and isolate perseverance or persistence as an important personality trait via factor analysis, a standard statistical tool in personality psychology. Through a series of studies of high-achieving populations (for example, Penn undergraduates, West Point cadets, Spelling Bee champions), Duckworth and her colleagues demonstrated that this perseverance quality might be distinct from other qualities (such as intelligence or self-control) and seemed to account for between 1.4 to 6.3 percent of all that goes into the achievements of those studied. (Later studies would find several higher percentages.) These findings suggest that over ninety percent of her populations' achievements are accounted for by other personal, familial, environmental, and cultural factors, but, still, her findings are important and make a contribution to the academic study of personality—and support a commonsense belief that hard work over time pays off.

5   It is instructive to read Duckworth's foundational scholarly articles, something I suspect few staffers and no policy makers have done. The articles are revealing in their listing of qualifications and limitations: The original studies rely on self-report

questionnaires, so can be subject to error and bias. The studies are correlational, so do not demonstrate causality. The exceptional qualities of some of the populations studied can create problems for factor analysis. Perseverance might have a downside to it. The construct of perseverance has been studied in some fashion for over a century.

6   But Duckworth and her colleagues did something that in retrospect was a brilliant marketing strategy, a master stroke of branding—or re-branding. Rather than calling their construct "perseverance" or "persistence," they chose to call it "grit." Can you think of a name that has more resonance in American culture? The fighter who is all heart. The hardscrabble survivor. *True Grit.* The Little Train That Could.

7   Grit exploded. *New York Times* commentators, best-selling journalists, the producers of *This American Life*, Secretary of Education Arne Duncan, educational policy makers and administrators all saw the development of grit as a way to improve American education and, more pointedly, to improve the achievement of poor children who, everyone seemed to assume, lacked grit.

8   I'll get to that last part about poor kids in a moment, but first I want to ask some questions few policy makers are asking. What is an education suitable for a democracy? What kind of people are we trying to develop? What is our philosophy of education? With these questions in mind, let's consider some items taken from the two instruments Duckworth and colleagues have used in their studies. The items are listed under grit's two subscales, the factors that comprise grit:

Consistency of Interests Subscale:

- New ideas and projects sometimes distract me from previous ones.
- I have been obsessed with a certain idea or project for a short time but later lost interest.
- I often set a goal but later choose to pursue a different one.

Perseverance of Effort Subscale:

- Setbacks don't discourage me.
- I finish whatever I begin.
- I have achieved a goal that took years of work.

These items are answered on a five-point scale:

- Very much like me
- Mostly like me

▶

- Somewhat like me

- Not much like me

- Not like me at all

9   Let me repeat here what I've written in every other commentary on grit. Of course, perseverance is an important characteristic. I cherish it in my friends and my students. But at certain ages and certain times in our lives, exploration and testing new waters can also contribute to one's development and achievement. Knowing when something is not working is important as well. Perseverance and determination as represented in the grit questionnaires could suggest a lack of flexibility, tunnel vision, an inability to learn from mistakes. Again, my point is not to dismiss perseverance but to suggest that perseverance, or grit, or any quality works in tandem with other qualities in the well-functioning and ethical person. By focusing so heavily on grit, character education in some settings has been virtually reduced to a single quality, and probably not the best quality in the content of character. The items in the grit instruments could describe the brilliant surgeon who is a distant and absent parent, or, for that fact, the smart, ambitious, amoral people who triggered the Great Recession. (Macbeth with his "vaulting ambition" would score quite high on grit.) Education in America has to be about more than producing driven super-achievers. For that fact, a discussion of what we mean by "achievement" is long overdue.

10   But, of course, a good deal of the discussion of grit doesn't really involve all students. Regardless of disclaimers, the primary audience for our era's character education is poor kids. As I and a host of others have written, a focus on individual characteristics of low-income children can take our attention away from the structural inequalities they face. Some proponents of character education have pretty much said that an infusion of grit will achieve what social and economic interventions cannot.

11   Can I make a recommendation? Along with the grit survey, let us give another survey and see what the relationship is between the scores. I'm not sure what to call this new survey, but it would provide a measure of adversity, of impediments to persistence, concentration, and the like. It, too, would use a five-point response scale: "very much like me" to "not much like me." Its items would include:

- I always have bus fare to get to school.

- I hear my parents talking about not having enough money for the rent.

- Whenever I get sick, I am able to go to a doctor.

- We always have enough food in our home.

- I worry about getting to school safely.

- There are times when I have to stay home to care for younger brothers or sisters.

- My school has honors and Advanced Placement classes.

- I have at least one teacher who cares about me.

12   My guess is that higher impediment scores would be linked to lower scores on the grit survey. I realize that what grit advocates want is to help young people better cope with such hardship. Anyone who has worked seriously with kids in tough circumstances spends a lot of time providing support and advice, and if grit interventions can provide an additional resource, great. But if as a society we are not also working to improve the educational and economic realities these young people face, then we are engaging in a cruel hoax, building aspiration and determination for a world that will not fulfill either.

13   The foundational grit research primarily involved populations of elite high achievers—Ivy League students, West Point cadets, National Spelling Bee contestants—and people responding to a Positive Psychology website based at the University of Pennsylvania. It is from the latter population that the researchers got a wider range of ages and data on employment history.

14   I was not able to find socioeconomic information for these populations, but given what we know generally about Ivy League undergraduates, West Point cadets, etc., I think it is a safe guess that most come from stable economic backgrounds. (In one later study, Duckworth and colleagues drew on 7–11 grade students at a "socioeconomically and ethnically diverse magnet public school" where 18% of the students were low-income—that's some economic diversity, but not a school with concentrated disadvantage.) It is also safe to assume that the majority of the people who are interested in Positive Psychology and self-select to respond to an on-line questionnaire have middle-class employment histories with companies or in professions that have pathways and mechanisms for advancement. So the construct of grit and the instruments to measure it are largely based on populations that more likely than not are able to pursue their interests and goals along a landscape of resources and opportunity. This does not detract from the effort they expend or from their determination, but it does suggest that their grit is deployed in a world quite different from the world poor people inhabit.

15   It is hard to finish what you begin when food and housing are unstable, or when you have three or four teachers in a given year, or when there are few people around who are able to guide and direct you. It is equally hard to pursue a career with consistency when the jobs available to you are low-wage, short-term and vulnerable, and have few if any benefits or protections. This certainly doesn't mean that

▶

people who are poor lack determination and resolve. Some of the poor people I knew growing up or work with today possess off-the-charts determination to survive, put food on the table, care for their kids. But they wouldn't necessarily score high on the grit scale.

16   Personality psychology by its disciplinary norms concentrates on the individual, but individual traits and qualities, regardless of how they originate and develop, manifest themselves in social and institutional contexts. Are we educators and policy makers creating classrooms that are challenging and engaging enough to invite perseverance? Are we creating opportunity for further educational or occupational programs that enable consistency of effort? Are we gritty enough to keep working toward these goals without distraction over the long haul?

TOPIC 20
Reading Strategies

Being able to understand, question, connect, and respond to texts is crucial to success in college and beyond. The strategies discussed in this Topic are tools you can use to deepen your reading comprehension.

Navigating Topic 20

The tutorials for this Topic are shown below, and each contains, or is followed by, an opportunity to apply the skills you have just learned. You can work through the entire Topic on your own, learning about all the strategies and practicing them; work on items you've been assigned by your instructor; or choose those ones you would find helpful.

Introduction to Reading Strategies 260

20.1	Tutorial	Activating Schema 260
20.2	Tutorial	Previewing a Text 261
20.3	Activity	Previewing *The Stuff of Thought*, Steven Pinker 264
20.4	Activity	Previewing a Website 268
20.5	Activity	Previewing Other Students' Essays 269
20.6	Tutorial	Annotation Explained 269
20.7	Activity	Annotating a Text 273
20.8	Tutorial	Keeping a Reading Journal 274
20.9	Tutorial	Dealing with Difficult Language 280
20.10	Activity	Decoding Difficult Language 283
20.11	Tutorial	Believing and Doubting 283
20.12	Activity	Reading as a Believer and Doubter 284
20.13	Tutorial	Creating Timelines and Family Trees 284

Introduction to Reading Strategies

In this Topic, different strategies are presented to help you read challenging texts: activating schema, previewing, annotating, keeping a reading journal, dealing with difficult language, reading as a believer and doubter, and creating graphics to understand complex texts.

20.1 Tutorial

Activating Schema

"Activating schema" sounds quite intimidating. In fact, all it means is connecting what you already know to new information you are about to learn. After previewing a text (discussed in Unit 20.2, p. 261), take a few minutes to think about what you already know about the topic of the reading. Whatever the topic, you probably have some information about it based on your own experiences, books or articles you've read, TV shows or movies you've watched, radio news or podcasts you've listened to, or social media you follow. For example, if you're reading a chapter on infectious diseases for a health class, you might think of recent news items about outbreaks of measles in New York City, the flu epidemic at your college last year that knocked you out for a week, or the hygiene precautions you have to take at your food service job to prevent the transmission of bacteria and viruses.

Thinking about what you already know about a subject has two significant benefits: it can make new information easier to understand, and it can help you to remember what you learn because you can connect it to information with which you are already familiar.

As you preview, ask questions and try to answer them. Take the titles and subtitles of chapters and ask yourself what you already know about the issues they will discuss. In a chapter on human populations in an environmental science text, for instance, there might be headings for the number of people the earth can support, factors that influence the size of human populations, the slowing population growth in China, and the increasing population growth in India. What have you heard, read, or seen about population growth and its effects on the environment? Brainstorm a list of everything you already know. Think about news items or documentaries you've watched that talk about decreasing natural resources, increasing pollution, and animal extinctions related to population growth and human activities. When reading a chapter in an economics text that talks about the positive and negative impacts of businesses moving into or out of communities, think about your personal experiences. Maybe you live in an economically depressed area that people are leaving because they cannot find work. What has that meant for your town or city? Or maybe you live somewhere like Seattle, which has become one of the fastest-growing cities in the country, leading to housing shortages and significantly higher rents. Taking a few minutes to think about what you already know will make you a more effective reader and improve your retention of new information.

Activity: Activating Your Schema for Dishonest Numbers

First decide what the article is about. What topic does it discuss? Then activate your schema by discussing what you already know about that topic.

20.2 Tutorial
Previewing a Text

The tutorials Thinking about Audience (9.4, p. 14) and Thinking about Purpose (9.6, p. 17) discuss how writers can benefit from an awareness of the purpose and the audience for their writing. Similarly, readers are better prepared to understand a text if they start with an awareness of who the writer is and who the writer's audience is. In addition, readers benefit from being aware of the writer's topic and purpose.

When you set out to read a book, an article, an essay, a blog, a web page—when you set out to read any text—your strategy may be simply to dive in, to start reading at the beginning and plow your way through to the end. With the limited time in most of our busy lives, simply diving in can seem like the quickest way to get something read.

Most experienced readers, however, have found that taking a few minutes before diving in to get a sense of what it is they are about to read actually saves them time and makes their reading more effective. This does not mean you need to spend hours previewing and predicting; just a few minutes will be very helpful when you start to read. Four steps for effectively previewing a text are given below. Every text is different, so not all of the steps will apply to all texts, but consider as many of them as you can.

Step 1: Preview the Text

Preview the text by doing the following.

- Take a look at the title.
- If the text is a book, look over the front and back covers and the table of contents, if there is one.

- If the text has headings for different parts, read them.

- If the text starts with an abstract or executive summary, read it.

- Skim any introductory material.

- Read the opening paragraph.

- Read the first sentence of each paragraph if the reading is quite short; read the first paragraph under each heading if the passage is longer.

- Read the final paragraph.

- Take a look at any illustrations, charts, tables, or videos if the text is online.

- Note how the author uses font design (bold, italic, or underlined) and color to signal meaning or relationships (e.g., bolding a word often indicates that a definition is to follow or that the word is a key term and important to know).

- Look to see if there are citations, endnotes, or a works cited list.

- Check to see how long the text is.

- Try listing everything you can remember without looking back at the text.

Step 2: Analyze the Rhetorical Situation

As long ago as classical Greece—300 BC or so—thinkers have been aware that four important components exist for every text: the *author* of the text, the *audience* for the text, the *topic* the text is about, and the *purpose* of the text. You don't need to remember the term *rhetorical situation*, which is made up of these four elements, but thinking about author, audience, topic, and purpose should be part of your previewing and predicting process.

1. **Author.** Besides the name of the author, what else can you learn about him or her? What evidence is there that the author really has some expertise about the subject? What biases might the author have? Is the author part of an organization? A corporation? What else has the author written?

2. **Audience.** Whom does it appear that the author intended to be the reader or readers of this text? Whom was he or she addressing? Were there other, secondary, audiences?

3. **Topic.** What is this text about?

4. **Purpose.** What does it appear that the author intended or, at least, hoped would happen as a result of this piece of writing? What did the author want the effect of this text to be on its audience?

Step 3: Predict What the Text Is About

If you take a few minutes to think about a text after you preview it, you will gain important information that will help you read it more effectively. While not every text will reveal answers to all of the following questions, every text will provide answers to some of them.

1. Based on your preview, can you predict what position, if any, the author takes on the subject?

2. Based on the headings, what kind of information do you think the author is going to provide in each section?

3. How is the text organized? Is it presenting an argument? Does the author discuss the causes and/or effects of an event? Is it comparing or contrasting people, ideas, or things? Recognizing how authors organize their writing can provide clues to what they might discuss and can help you predict their main idea(s) about the subject.

4. Does the author seem to make any assumptions about the subject? How might this affect the conclusions he or she reaches?

5. Does the author appear to be biased? How might this affect his or her writing on the subject?

Step 4: Think about Yourself in Relation to the Text

As well as previewing, considering the rhetorical situation, and predicting what a particular text might be about, ask yourself some questions about the topic and your reasons for reading about it. Any background information, or prior knowledge, you already have about a subject will help you read more effectively. If the topic is immigration, for example, do you have friends, relatives, or family members who recently came to the United States? Were your grandparents immigrants? What have you read, heard, or seen on the topic of immigration recently?

Actively thinking about what you already know has several benefits: it gets you thinking about what you're going to read, it helps you understand the text better as you read, and it assists you in remembering what you have read because you can connect the new information you learn to what you already know. In addition, knowing *why* you are reading will focus your attention and help you identify the most relevant points made by the writer.

Here are some useful questions you can ask yourself:

- How much do I already know about the topic?

- Have I had any experiences that are related to this topic? Do I know anyone who has?

- Have I read other texts (newspapers, articles, textbooks, novels) about this same topic?

- Have I seen any movies, documentaries, YouTube videos, or TV programs about this topic or heard about it on the radio or in podcasts?

- How do I feel about the text's stand on the topic?

- What is my purpose for reading this text?

- How similar or different am I from the intended audience for the text?

- How difficult will the text be to read?

- How much time will I need to read it?

There's lots to think about here, and all this is supposed to happen before you even start reading! Most students are really pressed for time, and it probably seems like doing all this "previewing" is just too time-consuming, but give it a try. You might not always have time to run through all these questions, but you can do some of them. After a couple of trial runs, you'll find out which are most useful to you, and for longer readings for which you have more time, you should be able to do most of these.

In the long run, you'll find that previewing will actually save you time because it will make the process of reading easier. You will get more out of the reading because you will have prepared yourself to be an engaged reader.

20.3 Activity

Previewing *The Stuff of Thought*, Steven Pinker

The tutorial Previewing a Text (20.2, p. 261) introduced the idea of previewing a text and predicting what it might be about. You may want to review that material before beginning this activity.

Here you will be putting previewing and predicting skills into practice using content from the cover and back page of Steven Pinker's bestseller *The Stuff of Thought*, reproduced below. Following that are a brief biography of Pinker, the title page and table of contents from the book, and an excerpt from the Preface.

Working in your group, study these materials as you would if you were previewing the book before starting to read it. Then answer as many of the following questions as you can.

1. What do I know, or what can I learn, about the author?
2. What do I know, or what can I learn, about the publisher of the text?

3. What audience was this text intended for? How similar or different am I from this audience?

4. What is the purpose of this text? What does it seem the author hopes to accomplish by it?

5. How well does what I know match what the writer seems to expect the reader to know?

6. What assumptions lie behind the argument in the text?

7. What do the chapter headings suggest about the content of the book?

8. How long is this text?

9. How difficult will this be to read?

10. Does it seem that I will agree or disagree with the text?

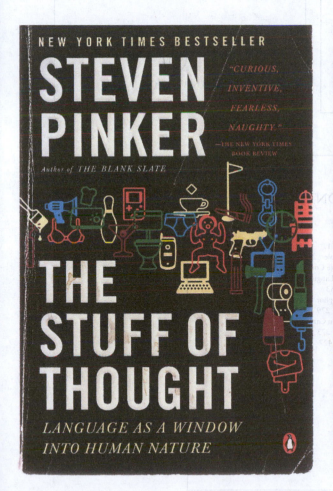

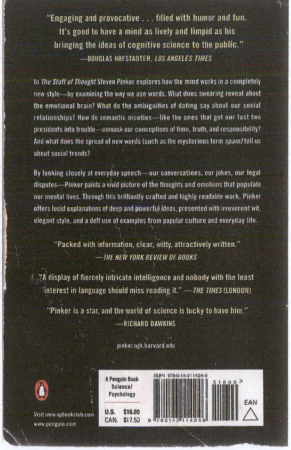

ABOUT THE AUTHOR

Steven Pinker is the Johnstone Family Professor of Psychology and Harvard College Professor at Harvard University. He is the author of seven books, including *The Language Instinct*, *How the Mind Works*, *Words and Rules*, and *The Blank Slate*. He lives in Boston and Truro, Massachusetts.

STEVEN PINKER

The Stuff of Thought

*Language as a Window
into Human Nature*

PENGUIN BOOKS

CONTENTS

Preface   vii

1   Words and Worlds   1
2   Down the Rabbit Hole   25
3   Fifty Thousand Innate Concepts (and Other
      Radical Theories of Language and Thought)   89
4   Cleaving the Air   153
5   The Metaphor Metaphor   235
6   What's in a Name?   279
7   The Seven Words You Can't Say on Television   323
8   Games People Play   373
9   Escaping the Cave   427

Notes   441
References   459
Index   483

PREFACE

1   There is a theory of space and time embedded in the way we use words. There is a theory of matter and a theory of causality, too. Our language has a model of sex in it (actually, two models), and conceptions of intimacy and power and fairness. Divinity, degradation, and danger are also ingrained in our mother tongue, together with a conception of well-being and a philosophy of free will. These conceptions vary in their details from language to language, but their overall logic is the same. They add up to a distinctively human model of reality, which differs in major ways from the objective understanding of reality eked out by our best science and logic. Though these ideas are woven into language, their roots are deeper than language itself. They lay out the ground rules for how we understand our surroundings, how we assign credit and blame to our fellows, and how we negotiate our relationships with them. A close look at our speech—our conversations, our jokes, our curses, our legal disputes, the names we give our babies—can therefore give us insight into who we are.

2   That is the premise of the book you are holding, the third in a trilogy written for a wide audience of readers who are interested in language and mind. The first, *The Language Instinct*, was an overview of the language faculty: everything you always wanted to know about language but were afraid to ask. A language is a way of connecting sound and meaning, and the other two books turn toward each of those spheres. *Words and Rules* was about the units of language, how they are stored in memory, and how they are assembled into the vast number of combinations that give language its expressive power. *The Stuff of Thought* is about the other side of the linkage, meaning. Its vistas include the meanings of words and constructions and the way that language is used in social settings, the topics that linguists call semantics and pragmatics.

                                                *   *   *

3   As in my other books on language, the early chapters occasionally dip into technical topics. But I have worked hard to make them transparent, and I am confident that my subject will engage anyone with an interest in what makes us tick.

> Language is entwined with human life. We use it to inform and persuade, but also to threaten, to seduce, and of course to swear. It reflects the way we grasp reality, and also the image of ourselves we try to project to others, and the bonds that tie us to them. It is, I hope to convince you, a window into human nature.

20.4 Activity

Previewing a Website

The tutorials Thinking about Audience (9.4, p. 14) and Thinking about Purpose (9.6, p. 17) explain how a *writer* can benefit from awareness of his or her audience and purpose for writing. Similarly, a *reader* is better prepared to understand a text if he or she starts with an awareness of who the writer is, the audience for whom he or she is writing, and his or her subject and purpose.

The tutorial Previewing a Text (20.2, p. 261) suggested that when you need to read a text—an article, a book, a chapter, even a website—you should preview it first, which will save you time and make your reading more effective.

Now you're going to apply some of those same previewing techniques to the website **mesotheliomabook.com.** In your group, examine the website and then analyze the rhetorical situation.

1. **Examine the website.**
   - What is the site called?
   - Who is the owner and/or sponsor of the website? Is it a commercial site (.com)? A nonprofit site (.org)? An educational site (.edu)? A governmental site (.gov)?
   - Who is the author of the information you are reviewing?
   - What appears to be the purpose of the site? To provide information about mesothelioma, to sell a product, to raise money, to make a political statement, or something else?
   - How current is the site?
   - Are there any illustrations, charts, tables, or associated videos?

2. **Analyze the rhetorical situation.**
   - **Author.** You don't simply want to find out the name of the author. What else can you learn about him or her? What evidence is there that the author really has some expertise about the subject? What biases might the author have, and how can you tell? Is the author part of an organization? A corporation? What else has the author written?

- **Audience.** Whom does it appear that the author intended to be the reader or readers of this text? Whom was he or she addressing? Were there other, secondary, audiences?
- **Topic.** What is this website "about"? What seems to be its main focus? Does the author take a stand on this focus?
- **Purpose.** What does it appear that the author intended or, at least, hoped would happen as a result of this piece of writing? What did the author want the effect of this text to be on its audience? How can you tell?

20.5 Activity

Previewing Other Students' Essays

For this activity, you will need a draft of a paper you are working on. Your instructor will organize the class into pairs. Then do the following.

1. Exchange draft essays with your partner.
2. Read the title or any headings in the paper and the first paragraph. Do not read the entire essay.
3. Predict what the rest of the essay will be like.
4. If your prediction is not accurate, work with your partner to figure out why it isn't. Did your partner write a title and/or first paragraph that did not fit well with the rest of the paper, or did you misunderstand the title and/or first paragraph?

20.6 Tutorial

Annotation Explained

Effective readers often read with a pencil (or pen) in hand. As they read, they are also writing—right on the text itself. The very process of writing while reading, called *annotation*, almost automatically increases how carefully and thoughtfully you read. Annotating while reading helps you to slow down and think about what you are reading, to decide whether you agree or not with the writer, to ask questions, and to think of examples from your own experience in addition to those in the text. It is a powerful tool for improving how well you understand a text and can be extremely helpful when you return to the text later.

Careful readers often use a highlighter to mark the sections of the text they are annotating. If you like to use a highlighter as you read, don't stop, but try to avoid two common errors: highlighting too much of the text or too little. Too much results in highlighting that is almost useless; it indicates that everything is important, so it's hard to distinguish what are the most significant points the author is making. Too little highlighting can indicate the reader found little of interest in the text, which can result from not understanding the text, or missed some of the main points. Ideally, you want to highlight just the main points, and sometimes important supporting details, so that you can easily find this information later when you are working on an essay or studying for an exam.

Some readers use different colors of highlighting to indicate different kinds of information: for example, blue for important facts, yellow for the main points in the text, and pink for words the reader doesn't know.

Some Reasons to Annotate

Annotations can be used for many different purposes, both alone and in conjunction with highlighting:

1. To mark something important
2. To comment on something you disagree with
3. To mark a reference to another text or book that you'd like to read
4. To add a thought of your own
5. To paraphrase a complicated sentence or short passage to ensure you understand it
6. To mark something you don't understand
7. To mark something you want to think about
8. To question the logic of a section of the text
9. To mark a powerful example
10. To add an example of your own to support the writer's argument
11. To add an example of your own that refutes the writer's argument
12. To summarize a section of text
13. To make a connection to another section of the text
14. To make a connection to something else you have read
15. To make a connection to something you have experienced
16. To remind yourself to follow up on something later

Activity: Explaining Annotations

Below is a text annotated by a thoughtful reader. Next to each annotation is a letter in a yellow circle. Working in your group, explain the reason for each of these annotations.

I first learned about HeLa cells and the woman behind them in 1988, thirty-seven years after her death, when I was

A *Look this up*

Prologue: The Woman in the Photograph

B *was the original photo in color?*

There's a photo on my wall of a woman I've never met, its left corner torn and patched together with tape. She looks straight into the camera and smiles, hands on hips, dress suit neatly pressed, lips painted deep red. It's the late 1940s and she hasn't yet reached the age of thirty. Her light brown skin is smooth, her eyes still young and playful, oblivious to the tumor growing inside her—a tumor that would leave her five children motherless and change the future of medicine. Beneath the photo, a caption says her name is "Henrietta Lacks, Helen Lane, or Helen Larson."

C *is she African-American?*

No one knows who took that picture, but it's appeared hundreds of times in magazines and science textbooks, on blogs and laboratory walls. She's usually identified as Helen Lane, but often she has no name at all. She's simply called HeLa, the code name given to the world's first immortal human cells—*her* cells, cut from her cervix just months before she died.

D *Can cells really be immortal?*

E

Her real name is Henrietta Lacks.

I've spent years staring at that photo, wondering what kind of life she led, what happened to her children, and what she'd think about cells from her cervix living on forever—bought, sold, packaged, and shipped by the trillions to laboratories around the world. I've tried to imagine how she'd feel knowing that her cells went up in the first space missions to see what would happen to human cells in zero gravity, or that they helped with some of the most important advances in medicine: the polio vaccine, chemotherapy, cloning, gene mapping, in vitro fertilization. I'm pretty sure that she—like most of us—would be shocked to hear that there are trillions more of her cells growing in laboratories now than there ever were in her body.

There's no way of knowing exactly how many of Henrietta's cells are alive today. One scientist estimates that if you could pile all HeLa cells ever grown onto a scale, they'd weigh more than 50 million metric tons—an inconceivable number, given that an individual cell weighs almost nothing. Another scientist calculated that if you could lay all HeLa cells ever grown end-to-end, they'd wrap around the Earth at least three times, spanning more than 350 million feet. In her prime, Henrietta herself stood only a bit over five feet tall.

F *wonder why Henrietta is called by her first name, Defler by his last*

I first learned about HeLa cells and the woman behind them in 1988, thirty-seven years after her death, when I was sixteen and sitting in a community college biology class. My instructor, Donald Defler, a gnomish balding man, paced at the front of the lecture hall and flipped on an overhead projector. He pointed to two diagrams that appeared on the wall behind him. They were schematics of the cell reproduction cycle, but to me they just looked like a neon-colored mass of arrows, squares, and circles with words I didn't understand, like "MPF Triggering a Chain Reaction of Protein Activations."

F — wonder why Henrietta is called by her first name, Defler by his last

I was a kid who'd failed freshman year at the regular public high school because she never showed up. I'd transferred to an alternative school that offered dream studies instead of biology, so I was taking Defler's class for high-school credit, which meant that I was sitting in a college lecture hall at sixteen with words like *mitosis* and *kinase inhibitors* flying around. I was completely lost.

G — can't follow this, why was she in college

"Do we have to memorize everything on those diagrams?" one student yelled.

Yes, Defler said, we had to memorize the diagrams, and yes, they'd be on the test, but that didn't matter right then. What he wanted us to understand was that cells are amazing things: There are about one hundred trillion of them in our bodies, each so small that several thousand could fit on the period at the end of this sentence. They make up all our tissues—muscle, bone, blood—which in turn make up our organs.

H — like the way she said this

I

Under the microscope, a cell looks a lot like a fried egg: It has a white (the *cytoplasm*) that's full of water and proteins to keep it fed, and a yolk (the *nucleus*) that holds all the genetic information that makes you *you*. The cytoplasm buzzes like a New York City street. It's crammed full of molecules and vessels endlessly shuttling enzymes and sugars from one part of the cell to another, pumping water, nutrients, and oxygen in and out of the cell. All the while, little cytoplasmic factories work 24/7, cranking out sugars, fats, proteins, and energy to keep the whole thing running and feed the nucleus—the brains of the operation. Inside every nucleus within each cell in your body, there's an identical copy of your entire genome. That genome tells cells when to grow and divide and makes sure they do their

J — cute

K — can sugar be plural?

jobs, whether that's controlling your heartbeat or helping your brain understand the words on this page.

All it takes is one small mistake anywhere in the division process for cells to start growing out of control, he told us. Just *one* enzyme misfiring, just *one* wrong protein activation, and you could have cancer. Mitosis goes haywire, which is how it spreads.

important

what is culture?

"We learned that by studying cancer cells in culture," Defler said. He grinned and spun to face the board, where he wrote two words in enormous print: HENRIETTA LACKS.

20.7 Activity

Annotating a Text

In Annotation Explained (20.6, p. 269), you read how and why effective readers annotate the texts they are reading. For this activity, your instructor will provide a text for you to annotate. Listed below are some of the most common purposes for annotations.

1. To mark something important
2. To comment on something you disagree with
3. To mark a reference to another text or book that you'd like to read
4. To add a thought of your own
5. To paraphrase a complicated sentence or short passage to ensure you understand it
6. To mark something you don't understand
7. To mark something you want to think about
8. To question the logic of a section of the text
9. To mark a powerful example
10. To add an example of your own to support the writer's argument
11. To add an example of your own that refutes the writer's argument
12. To summarize a section of text
13. To make a connection to another section of the text
14. To make a connection to something else you have read
15. To make a connection to something you have experienced
16. To remind yourself to do something later

Keeping a Reading Journal

If all you want from reading a text is a general sense of what it is about, then a good strategy would be to read quickly, not pausing to think or analyze what you've been reading. But at other times, you will have a different motive: you will be reading because you want to really understand what the text has to say. For this kind of reading, many people find it helpful to slow down and take notes on what they're reading, and one good approach to this kind of reading is to record your thoughts in a reading journal.

Whether you use a notebook, a composition book, or just a plain piece of paper, all you need to do to turn it into a reading journal is draw a line down the center of the page. If you want, you can label the left side something like "Ideas from Text" and the right side "My Thoughts about the Ideas." If you want to do this journaling on a computer, just open a Word document and insert a table with two columns.

A brief excerpt, "Words and Worlds," from an extremely interesting but challenging book by Harvard psychology professor Steven Pinker, *The Stuff of Thought*, appears below. This is not a book you can read quickly and get much out of. It requires slow, deliberate reading and thinking, the kind of reading assisted by keeping a reading journal, so it will be used to illustrate what a reading journal looks like. Following the excerpt, you will find one student's writing journal for this text. The numbers in the writing journal correspond to the numbered underlined passages in the text.

Words and Worlds

STEVEN PINKER

1   On September 11, 2001, at 8:46 A.M., a hijacked airliner crashed into the north tower of the World Trade Center in New York. At 9:03 A.M. a second plane crashed into the south tower. The resulting infernos caused the buildings to collapse, the south tower after burning for an hour and two minutes, the north tower twenty-three minutes after that. The attacks were masterminded by Osama bin Laden, leader of the Al Qaeda terrorist organization, who hoped to intimidate the United States into ending its military presence in Saudi Arabia and its support for Israel and to unite Muslims in preparation for a restoration of the caliphate.

2   9/11, as the happenings of that day are now called, stands as **1** the most significant political and intellectual event of the twenty-first century so far. It has set

off debates on a vast array of topics: how best to memorialize the dead and revitalize lower Manhattan; whether the attacks are rooted in ancient Islamic fundamentalism or modern revolutionary agitation; the role of the United States on the world stage before the attacks and in response to them; how best to balance protection against terrorism with respect for civil liberties.

3   But I would like to explore a lesser-known debate triggered by 9/11. Exactly how many events took place in New York on that morning in September?

4   It could be argued that the answer is one. The attacks on the building were part of a single plan conceived in the mind of one man in service of a single agenda. They unfolded within a few minutes of each other, targeting the parts of a complex with a single name, design, and owner. And they launched a single chain of military and political events in their aftermath.

5   Or it could be argued that the answer is two. The north tower and south tower were distinct collections of glass and steel separated by an expanse of space, and they were hit at different times and went out of existence at different times. The amateur video that showed the second plane closing in on the south tower as the north tower billowed with smoke makes the twoness unmistakable: in those horrifying moments, one event was frozen in the past, the other loomed in the future. And another occurrence on that day—a passenger mutiny that brought down a third hijacked plane before it reached its target in Washington—presents to the imagination the possibility that one tower or the other might have been spared. **2** In each of those possible worlds a distinct event took place, so in our *actual* world one might argue, there must have been a pair of events as surely as one plus one equals two.

6   The gravity of 9/11 would seem to make this entire discussion **3** frivolous to the point of impudence. It's a matter of mere "semantics," as we say, with its implication of picking nits, splitting hairs, and debating the number of angels that can dance on the head of a pin. But this book is about semantics, and I would not make a claim on your attention if I did not think that **4** the relation of language to our inner and outer worlds was a matter of intellectual fascination and real-world importance.

7   Though "importance" is often hard to quantify, in this case I can put an exact value on it: three and a half billion dollars. That was the sum in dispute in a set of trials determining the insurance payout to Larry Silverstein, the **5** leaseholder of the World Trade Center site. Silverstein held insurance policies that stipulated a maximum reimbursement for each destructive "event." If 9/11 comprised a single event, he stood to receive three and a half billion dollars. If it comprised two events, he stood to receive seven billion. In the trials, the attorneys disputed the applicable meaning of the term *event*. The lawyers for the leaseholder defined it in physical terms (two

▶

collapses); those for the insurance companies defined it in mental terms (one plot). There is nothing "mere" about semantics!

8   Nor is the topic intellectually trifling. The 9/11 cardinality debate is not about the facts, that is, the physical events and human actions that took place that day. Admittedly, those have been contested as well: according to various conspiracy theories, the buildings were targeted by American missiles, or demolished by a controlled implosion, in a plot conceived by American neoconservatives, Israeli spies, or a cabal of psychiatrists. But aside from the kooks, most people agree on the facts. Where they differ is in the *construal* of those facts: how **6** the intricate swirl of matter in space ought to be conceptualized by human minds. As we shall see, **7** the categories in this dispute permeate the meanings of words in our language because they permeate the way we represent reality in our heads.

9   **8** Semantics is about the relation of words to thoughts, but it is also about the relation of words to other human concerns. Semantics is about the relation of words to reality—the way that speakers commit themselves to a shared understanding of the truth, and the way their thoughts are anchored to things and situations in the world. It is about the relation of words to a community—how **9** a new word, which arises in an act of creation by a single speaker, comes to evoke the same idea in the rest of a population, so people can understand one another when they use it. It is about the relation of words to emotions: the way in which words don't just point to things but are saturated with feelings, which can endow the words with a sense of magic, taboo, and sin. And it is about words and social relations—how **10** people use language not just to transfer ideas from head to head but to negotiate the kind of relationship they wish to have with their conversational partner.

10   A feature of the mind that we will repeatedly encounter in these pages is that **11** even our most abstract concepts are understood in terms of concrete scenarios. That applies in full force to the subject matter of the book itself. In this introductory chapter I will preview some of the book's topics with vignettes from newspapers and the Internet that can be understood only through the lens of semantics. They come from each of the worlds that connect to our words—the worlds of thought, reality, community, emotions, and social relations.

11   Let's look at the bone of contention in the world's most expensive debate in semantics, the three-and-a-half-billion-dollar argument over the meaning of "event." What, exactly, is an event? **12** An event is a stretch of time, and time, according to physicists, is a continuous variable—an inexorable cosmic flow, in Newton's world, or a fourth dimension in a seamless hyperspace in Einstein's. But **13** the human mind carves this fabric into discrete swatches we call events. Where does the mind

place the incisions? Sometimes, as the lawyers for the World Trade Center leaseholder pointed out, it encircles the change of state of an object, such as the collapse of a building. And sometimes, as the lawyers for the insurers pointed out, it encircles the goal of a human actor, such as a plot being executed. Most often the circles coincide: an actor intends to cause an object to change, the intent of the act and the fate of the object are tracked along a single time line, and the moment of change marks the consummation of the intent.

* * *

12 The 9/11 cardinality debate highlights another curious fact about the language of thought. In puzzling over how to count the events of that day, it asks us to treat them as if they were objects that can be tallied, like poker chips in a pile. The debate over whether there was one event or two in New York that day is like a disagreement over **14** whether there is one item or two at an express checkout lane, such as a pair of butter sticks taken out of a box of four, or a pair of grapefruits selling at two for a dollar. The similar ambiguity in tallying events is one of the many ways in which space and time are treated equivalently in the human mind, well before Einstein depicted them as equivalent in reality.

13 As we shall see in Chapter 4, the mind categorizes matter into **15** discrete things (like a *sausage*) and continuous stuff (like *meat*), and it similarly categorizes time into discrete events (like *to cross the street*) and continuous activities (like *to stroll*). With both space and time, the same mental zoom lens that allows us to count objects or events also allows us to zoom in even closer on what each one is made of. In space, we can focus on the material making up an object (as when we say *I got sausage all over my shirt*); in time, we can focus on an activity making up an event (as when we say *She was crossing the street*). This cognitive zoom lens also lets us pan out in space and see a collection of objects as an aggregate (as in the difference between *a pebble* and *gravel*), and it allows us to pan out in time and see a collection of events as an iteration (as in the difference between *hit the nail* and *pound the nail*). And in time, as in space, we mentally place an entity at a location and then shunt it around: we can *move a meeting from 3:00 to 4:00* in the same way that we move a car from one end of the block to the other. And speaking of an *end*, even some of the fine points of our mental geometry carry over from space to time. **16** *The end of a string* is technically a point, but we can say *Herb cut off the end of the string*, showing that an end can be construed as including a snippet of the matter adjacent to it. The same is true in time: the *end of a lecture* is technically an instant, but we can say *I'm going to give the end of my lecture now*, construing the culmination of an event as including a small stretch of time adjacent to it.

▶

14   As we shall see, **17** language is saturated with implicit metaphors like EVENTS ARE OBJECTS and TIME IS SPACE. Indeed, space turns out to be a conceptual vehicle not just for time but for many kinds of states and circumstances. Just as a meeting can be moved from 3:00 to 4:00, a traffic light can go from green to red, a person can go from flipping burgers to running a corporation, and the economy can go from bad to worse. Metaphor is so widespread in language that it's hard to find expressions for abstract ideas that are *not* metaphorical. What does the concreteness of language say about human thought? Does it imply that even our wispiest concepts are represented in the mind as hunks of matter that we move around on a mental stage? Does it say that **18** rival claims about the world can never be true or false but can only be alternative metaphors that frame a situation in different ways? Those are the obsessions of Chapter 5.

Ideas in the Text	My Thoughts about the Ideas
1. 9/11 was the most significant event of this century so far	That "so far" seems very ominous. It implies that worse events are ahead of us.
2. in each of those possible worlds	This is hard to follow. I think he's saying that because, in our imaginations, either plane could have been prevented from striking its target, we are forced to consider, even in the actual world where both towers were struck, that there were two events.
3. frivolous to the point of impudence	I guess that's very frivolous.
4. the relation of language to our inner and outer worlds was a matter of intellectual fascination and real-world importance	Hmmm. Inner and outer worlds? The world in our minds and the world we actually live in?
5. the leaseholder of the World Trade Center	Was the leaseholder just renting the towers? Odd. I would expect the person with the insurance would be the owner.
6. the intricate swirl of matter in space	I don't get this. Is he talking about some kind of nebula or something? What does this have to do with anything?

Ideas in the Text	My Thoughts about the Ideas
7. the categories in this dispute permeate the meanings of words in our language because they permeate the way we represent reality in our heads	These "categories in this dispute" I think refers to whether there was one event or two. What does he mean about the way we represent reality in our heads?
8. semantics is about the relation of words to thoughts	I think words simply stand for thoughts. The word "chair" stands for the thought we have of a thing that is a chair
9. a new word, which arises in an act of creation by a single speaker	Interesting. I wonder how a new word gets into the language spoken by millions of people?
10. people use words to negotiate the kind of relation they want to have with others	Interesting. I wish he had said more about this.
11. even our most abstract concepts are understood in terms of concrete scenarios	I wonder what he means by this.
12. an event is a stretch of time	So far, so good. I get this. Makes sense.
13. the human mind carves this fabric into discrete swatches we call events	Still okay, although I don't see why he decides to call time a fabric.
14. whether there is one item or two in an express checkout line	A great example of how hard it is to count the number of events.
15. the mind classifies things into discrete things (like a *sausage*) and continuous stuff (like *meat*)	Isn't this the same as the distinction between count and non-count nouns?
16. the end of a piece of string compared to the end of a lecture	The end is technically the end, except when it also includes stuff just before the end.
17. language is saturated with implicit metaphors like EVENTS ARE OBJECTS and TIME IS SPACE	This seems to be a major point.
18. rival claims about the world can never be true or false but can only be alternative metaphors that frame a situation in different ways	So here's the answer to the World Trade Center legal argument, but he doesn't tell who actually won in court!

Dealing with Difficult Language

Readers frequently have difficulty when they are reading and bump into a word or phrase that they don't know. The most common strategy for dealing with an unfamiliar word is "to look it up in a dictionary." Now this is not a bad strategy; in fact, sometimes it is very good advice, but "looking it up in a dictionary" is only one of a number of available strategies.

In fact, in many situations it is not the best strategy. When you interrupt your reading to consult a dictionary, it's easy to lose track of the meaning of the text you've been reading. If you encounter a number of unfamiliar words that you look up, you can end up having read an entire passage with little idea of what it meant. To avoid these interruptions to the flow of your reading, you can first use one or more of the following strategies when you encounter unfamiliar words or phrases:

- Derive the meaning from context.
- Analyze the parts of the word.
- Back up and reread the passage.
- Keep reading to see if the writer explains the difficult passage.
- Decide the word is not important and just keep reading.

If all else fails, or if knowing a precise definition of a word is crucial to understanding a text, use a dictionary.

Use Context Clues

Suppose you came across the following sentence in something you were reading:

> She grabbed her portmanteau, which she had packed the night before, and left for the train station.

Chances are, you are not familiar with the word *portmanteau*, but, from the rest of the sentence, it would not be hard to guess that it must be some kind of a suitcase. It is often possible to work out the meaning of a word by carefully reading not only the sentence in which it appears but those that immediately precede or follow it. Basically, you infer from the information provided what a word or term means.

There are several other strategies like this that you can use to figure out the meaning of a word from its context. Authors often include words with similar or opposite meanings close to more challenging words to provide clues to their meanings; textbook authors place important terms in bold or italics and follow them with definitions; and writers often use punctuation to indicate they are about to provide a definition or explanation of a term, introducing it with a colon, setting it off with commas or dashes, or placing it in parentheses.

By the way, figuring out the meaning of a word from its context often gives you only a general sense of the word. For instance, using the example above, a *portmanteau* is actually a large suitcase, usually made of leather, and opening into two halves of equal size. You would never figure out all that detail from the context, but in most cases recognizing that it was a type of suitcase would be all you needed to understand what you were reading.

Use Word Parts

Another strategy that can be useful in figuring out what an unfamiliar word means without "looking it up" is to break it into its parts. Consider the following sentence:

> Karina's essay was filled with polysyllabic words.

If you are unfamiliar with the word *polysyllabic*, you may be able to figure out its meaning by breaking it into parts. You've probably encountered the prefix *poly-* in other words. Do you remember what a polygon is? It's a two-dimensional figure with many sides. How about polygamy? It means being married to multiple partners. By now, it seems clear that *poly-* means *many*, and as the second half of the word is fairly close to *syllable*, a polysyllabic word is apparently a word with many syllables.

Being familiar with word parts, the building blocks of words, can be useful, especially if you are studying in the sciences. Words can contain one or more of the following parts: roots, prefixes, and suffixes. Roots are the core of words and carry their basic meaning. Prefixes are added to the beginning of root words to change their meaning; for example, adding the prefix *un-* to the word *happy* creates *unhappy*, which means the opposite of the original word. Suffixes are placed at the ends of root words and can change their part of speech; for example, adding *-less* to the root word *clue* changes the word from a noun to an adjective, *clueless*. Suffixes can also change the root word's tense; for example, adding *-ed* to the root word *raid* changes it from the present to the past tense, *raided*.

No one expects you to memorize word parts, but if you do a quick search of the internet you will find all sorts of charts listing roots, prefixes, and suffixes with their meanings, which you can download or print out for easy reference. Many scientific terms are built from word parts, and familiarizing yourself with the most common ones, such as *bio-*, *geo-*, *mono-*, or *-itis*, can help you to make sense of terms as you read.

Reread the Passage

Another strategy when you encounter a word or phrase that you don't understand is to back up and reread the passage. Sometimes the meaning will become clearer on a second reading.

Keep Reading

A different strategy is to keep reading. Often writers, realizing they have used a term some readers may not know, will explain the term in the next sentence or even later in the same sentence.

Decide the Word Is Not Important

Sometimes it is perfectly acceptable to decide that a word is not going to be important, at least in the text you're reading, and you can move on without worrying about what it means. Suppose you were reading a mystery novel and came across this sentence:

> The murdered woman was wearing a cerise sweater.

Does it matter what color *cerise* is? Probably not. You will likely be able to follow the action of the novel just fine even though you're not sure of the color of the woman's sweater. But what if, later in the novel, you find out that a suspect had tiny fragments of cerise-colored thread under his fingernails? Now does it matter what color *cerise* is? Actually, it does not. It is important to remember that the victim's sweater was cerise, but it doesn't really matter what color that is. (By the way, *cerise* is a bright or dark red. It comes from the French word for *cherry*.)

Use a Dictionary

Some readers are interested in expanding their vocabulary when they read. If you fit into this group, it is probably still better not to interrupt your reading to look up words unless knowing the meaning of a particular word is crucial to understanding the text. Instead, underline or circle each word whose meaning you guess at from the context. After you've finished reading the text, you can go back, look up all the words you marked, and write their definitions either in the margin beside them or in a log you keep of new words. (Note that online dictionaries are quick and easy to use and provide lots of useful information, including the option to hear how a word is pronounced. It's worth bookmarking a site, such as dictionary.com or merriam-webster.com, for easy reference.)

Decoding Difficult Language

Here is a list of six strategies that you can use when you encounter words you are not familiar with. These strategies are discussed in detail in Dealing with Difficult Language (20.9, p. 280).

1. Derive the meaning from context.
2. Analyze the parts of the word.
3. Back up and reread the passage.
4. Keep reading to see if the writer explains the difficult passage.
5. Decide the word is not important and just keep reading.
6. Look the word up in a dictionary or on your phone.

Your instructor will assign a reading that includes some challenging words. Working in your group, identify the words you have difficulty with. Make a list with three columns as shown in the following example. Then use one or more of the six strategies to figure out the meaning of each word. Save using a dictionary as a last resort.

Challenging Words	Meaning of Words	Strategy or Strategies Used
multifarious	having many parts	word parts
laminated	made of thin layers bonded together	dictionary
restitution	giving back something that had been wrongfully taken away	general context

20.11 Tutorial

Believing and Doubting

The believing and doubting game is an approach to engagement with a text that was developed by Peter Elbow at the University of Massachusetts. It's a wonderful way for getting us, as readers, to engage more deeply with a text.

At its heart, the believing and doubting game simply asks you to read a text two different ways. It asks you to read it once as a "believer," someone who agrees with the author and is reading because you want to understand exactly what the author's point is and why the author came to that conclusion. Then it asks you to read the text a second time from the point of view of a skeptic, someone who doubts that the central argument of the text is correct. This time you are reading to find flaws in the argument, weaknesses in the logic, and reasons to refute the conclusions. Many readers find this approach leads them into a deeper understanding of the text.

One way to use this approach is to write two short—less than a page—summaries of a text. In the first, you write as a believer, someone who agrees with the author, and you focus on the points you agree with. In the second, you write as a doubter, someone who is trying to explain why you disagree with the argument.

20.12 Activity

Reading as a Believer and Doubter

In Believing and Doubting (20.11, p. 283), you read about a strategy that helps you to think deeply about a text as you read it. Now you will try out this approach to engaging with a text using an article supplied by your instructor.

Read the article once as a believer, someone who is in agreement with the author. Don't allow any doubts or disagreements to creep in while you read as a believer. Then write a "believer's summary" in which you summarize the article briefly, emphasizing the points you agree with. Try to limit this summary to a half page.

When you've finished that, read the article again, this time as a doubter, someone who disagrees with the author. Then write a second brief summary in which you focus on the points you disagree with. Again, a half page is plenty.

20.13 Tutorial

Creating Timelines and Family Trees

When reading longer and more complicated works, it is sometimes helpful to keep track of what you're reading and thinking by using creating graphic organizers, such as timelines and family trees.

Timelines

If you're reading a narrative text, one that is telling a story or describing how events happened over time, it may be helpful to create a timeline. Here's an example of what such a timeline might look like.

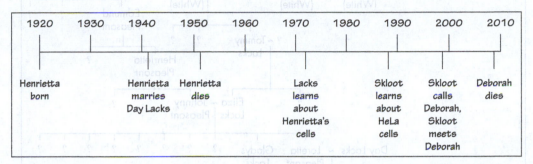

| 1920 | 1930 | 1940 | 1950 | 1960 | 1970 | 1980 | 1990 | 2000 | 2010 |

Henrietta born — Henrietta marries Day Lacks — Henrietta dies — Lacks learns about Henrietta's cells — Skloot learns about HeLa cells — Skloot calls Deborah, Skloot meets Deborah — Deborah dies

Peter Adams

The student who constructed it was reading *The Immortal Life of Henrietta Lacks*. Early in the book, she learned that the main character, Henrietta Lacks, was born in 1920. Realizing that this book was going to cover events that took place over a number of years, she decided to construct a timeline in which she could post the major events in the story. She marked Henrietta's birth in 1920 at the left end of the timeline and 2010, the date the book was published, at the right end. Then she made a vertical mark for every ten years. As she read the book, she marked major events on the timeline.

The student did all this on a piece of plain paper, although she might have created a similar graphic using a computer. A timeline like this is especially helpful when you are reading a text that doesn't present information in chronological order but skips backward and forward in time, as *The Immortal Life of Henrietta Lacks* does.

Family Trees

If you are reading a text—especially a full-length book—with lots of characters, creating a family tree can help you keep their names straight and see the relationships between the different family members. *The Immortal Life of Henrietta Lacks* includes seven generations of one very large family, so making a family tree seemed to be a good strategy to another student. Here is his tree.

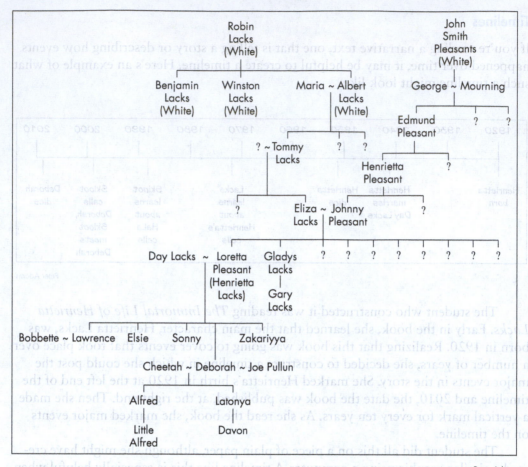

Peter Adams

These family trees can be very messy. Sometimes you discover that you haven't left yourself enough room for all the branches of a family, so you have to start over on a blank sheet. Often, there are several families who interact with each other, so you have to find a way to match up the generations and who married whom. Despite their potential messiness, though, in a book with lots of characters, family trees can be extremely helpful in keeping track of everyone.

TOPIC 21
Critical Reading

Being a critical reader means reading thoughtfully—evaluating the assertions in a text, the support for those assertions, the assumptions underlying them, and the expertise and reliability of the author.

Navigating Topic 21

The tutorials for critical reading are listed below, and each is followed by an opportunity to apply the skills you have just learned. You can work through the entire Topic on your own, learning about all the strategies and practicing them; work on items you've been assigned by your instructor; or choose those ones you would find helpful.

Introduction to Critical Reading   287

21.1   Tutorial   How to Evaluate the Author and Source of a Text   288

21.2   Activity   Evaluating the Author and Source of a Text   289

21.3   Tutorial   Distinguishing among Facts, Statements Most Experts Agree On, and Opinions   290

21.4   Activity   Recognizing Facts, Statements Most Experts Agree On, and Opinions   292

21.5   Activity   Evaluating Evidence   293

21.6   Tutorial   How to Make Inferences   295

21.7   Activity   Making Inferences   297

21.8   Tutorial   Recognizing Assumptions and Biases   298

21.9   Activity   Recognizing Assumptions and Biases in Three Passages   300

Introduction to Critical Reading

In this Topic, you will learn ways to evaluate the author and source of a text, distinguish between facts and opinions, make inferences, and recognize assumptions and biases, all important critical reading skills.

21.1 Tutorial

How to Evaluate the Author and Source of a Text

As you preview, read, and think about what you have read, two crucial factors to keep in mind are the author and the source. Evaluating them is something you usually do when previewing a text (see 20.2, p. 261), but as you dive into reading and as you pause at various points to think about what you have read, you should keep in mind what you have learned about the author and the source of the text.

Evaluating the Author

For most texts you read, the author's name will appear at the top of the text or, sometimes, at the end. Occasionally, there will be a brief biography. But sometimes there will be no biographical information. In these cases, or even if there is a biography, it is a good idea to take a few more minutes to search for the author on Google or another search engine and see what you can learn about him or her.

To evaluate authors, look for evidence of their expertise:

- Do they have a credential or degree that indicates they are qualified to discuss the topic?
- Have they published other relevant works?
- Have they won any awards?
- Does their job give them access to relevant knowledge?
- Do other authors you have been reading refer to them?

If the source reveals little or no information about the author, this may be an indication that he or she is not really an expert.

Evaluating the Source

If the text you're about to read is a chapter or an article in a book, take a look at who edited or published the book. If the article is in a journal or magazine, look into who publishes the journal or magazine and what other articles appear in it. If the text is on a website, see what you can learn about who owns the website. All this information about the source of the text will help you better understand and evaluate it. As you evaluate sources, ask these questions:

- Has the publisher, print or digital, published or posted material by other authors whom you recognize as having expertise in the subject? If yes, it increases the source's credibility.

- Is the source sponsored by a reputable organization—a university, a major foundation, or a government agency? If so, that adds to its credibility and that of the writers it publishes.

- Does the source provide references or documentation to support the legitimacy of the content it is providing? If it does not, be wary.

- Does the source appear to publish material that seems biased? If yes, that doesn't mean you should ignore it, but do be aware of the bias if you use the material.

- Is the content in the source current? For many subjects, especially those relating to science, technology, medicine, and other rapidly changing fields, information becomes outdated quickly, so you want to make sure the source is providing the most current data.

- Is the source well-written and the content presented in a logical, well-organized fashion? This question relates more often to online sources. Anyone can post information on the internet. Legitimate, professional sources take time to edit their content, check the credentials of the writers whose work they host or present, and provide a well-organized homepage. If the content is inaccurate or poorly written, if links are broken, if navigation is difficult, and if you cannot find out information about the publisher, look for more reliable alternatives. If it is not possible to learn much about the publisher of a text or owner of a website, that may be an indication that the source is not reliable.

21.2 Activity

Evaluating the Author and Source of a Text

For a college essay on the controversy over vaccinations for children, working in your group, search for each of the articles listed below (typing their titles into your browser), and evaluate the author and source for each of them. Be prepared to report out on what you learned about both the author and the source for each one. (If you cannot find a site using its title, there is an updated list of URLs available at https://bit.ly/33IIHtf.)

1. "Vaccines: The Myths and the Facts," no author given
2. "Childhood Vaccines: Tough Questions, Straight Answers," Mayo Clinic Staff
3. "MMR Vaccination and Autism," Andrew J. Wakefield

21.3 Tutorial

Distinguishing among Facts, Statements Most Experts Agree On, and Opinions

The activity Evidence and Assertions (11.2, p. 43) illustrates the relationship between facts (evidence) and opinions (assertions) from the point of view of the *writer*. It is also important that *readers* recognize this relationship and are able to distinguish between facts and opinions. It's even more important for readers to recognize that many ideas that are expressed as if they are facts are merely opinions masquerading as facts.

What Are Facts?

Exactly what is a fact? How can you recognize what is factual in what you read? It has often been said that facts are not arguable. Facts are statements that have been proven to be true. Facts are what the experts agree is true. Some factual statements satisfy these definitions without any difficulty. The capital of California is Sacramento. Mt. Everest is the highest mountain in the world. English 101 is a required course at most colleges.

But sometimes statements that appear to be facts need to be carefully stated. For example, "Water boils at 212°" would seem to be a fact, but those who live at high elevations like Denver know that water boils at a lower temperature at higher elevations. The *fact* is "Water boils at 212° at sea level." The statement that "Native Americans' primary food source was the bison" needs to be examined carefully. It turns out to be true for Native Americans in the Plains states but not true in many other parts of what came to be the United States.

It's also the case that what were considered to be facts can change. As recently as the early 2000s, it was a fact that there were nine planets in our solar system. However, in 2006, the International Astronomical Union decided that Pluto is not a planet; it is too small. Today, the fact is that there are eight planets in our solar system. For years, scientists have agreed that the earliest members of the human genus to use stone tools were *Homo habilis*, who evolved around 2.8 million years ago.

But in 2015, stone tools and fossils of early humans were discovered in Kenya that are 3.3 million years old. So the facts about when humans began using tools have also changed.

As a reader, you should carefully examine and think deeply about statements that authors clearly intend that you will accept as facts. Make sure the "fact" is worded carefully so that it is true and that it is currently considered a fact, that experts haven't learned new information that modified what used to be factual.

How Do We Decide Whether the Experts Agree?

On the one hand, there are issues, such as whether boys should be allowed to play football because of the risks of concussion and whether tax cuts for the wealthy will "trickle down" and benefit everyone, about which experts disagree. Statements where there is significant disagreement among experts cannot be considered to be facts. On the other hand, it is unreasonable to insist that something is not a fact unless there is 100 percent agreement about it by every expert in the world; statements about which the vast majority of experts agree can safely be understood to be facts.

Where should we draw the line? How great must the agreement be in order for something to actually be considered a fact? Perhaps the answer to these questions is that, as a reader, you could accept opinions on which a great many experts agree as evidence, just not quite as strong as actual facts. You may also find it useful to investigate the experts who don't agree. Are they legitimate experts? What reasons do they give for their disagreement? Do you find their reasons to make sense?

A word of caution, however: Do not confuse the generally agreed on opinions of a large number of experts with the many statements cluttering the current public discourse that are not agreed to by most experts. Fake news, exaggeration, hyperbole, and even outright lies are not the same as the well-reasoned, evidence-based opinions of experts in a particular field.

How Should Readers Respond to Conclusions, Claims, and Opinions?

It is a *fact* that college tuition has gone up faster than inflation for years, and it is a *fact* that the cost of textbooks has increased dramatically. Further, it is a *fact* that other fees at colleges have gone up at a steep rate. But it is *not* a fact that college is too expensive. That last statement is an *opinion*. It is based on facts, but it is an assertion that someone might make after thinking about the facts, which doesn't make it a fact. Someone else might look at the same set of facts and reach a different conclusion. Still others might know of a different set of facts that could be used to argue that college is not too expensive.

There is, of course, nothing wrong with writers making assertions of their opinions, but as a critical reader, you need to make sure that such assertions are actually supported by convincing evidence. When reading a text that makes an assertion followed by factual evidence or a text that presents a series of facts and then makes an assertion based on those facts, it's a good idea to stop and think about the conclusions the authors have reached. Do they seem reasonable? Could the same facts lead to a different conclusion? Are enough facts presented to justify the conclusion? These kinds of analysis can lead to a more insightful reading of the text, and being able to distinguish between facts and opinions is essential to this kind of analysis.

Finally, some alternative vocabulary. You've been reading about the differences between facts and opinions. What about *conclusions, assertions,* and *claims*? These terms are usually used to mean the same thing as *opinions*. In any case, as a reader, if you encounter statements that you would consider fitting any of these categories, you should carefully examine the evidence provided to support them.

21.4   Activity

Recognizing Facts, Statements Most Experts Agree On, and Opinions

Distinguishing among Facts, Statements Most Experts Agree On, and Opinions (21.3, p. 290) discussed the difference among (1) facts, (2) statements about which almost all experts agree, and (3) opinions (sometimes called *conclusions, claims,* or *assertions*). It is important for readers to be able to distinguish among these three types of statements because opinions without factual evidence to support them should be given little credence.

Working with your group, decide whether the following statements are facts, statements about which almost all experts agree, or opinions.

1. The cost of health care is increasing too much.
2. The cost of health care has risen every year for the past forty years.
3. More Democrats support gun safety laws than Republicans.
4. More lives are lost to speeding drivers every year than to drunk drivers.
5. Every parent should have their children vaccinated against childhood diseases.
6. Immigration takes jobs away from American workers.
7. A lower percentage of immigrants are arrested for criminal behavior than the percentage of American citizens.

8. Completing a college degree improves the chances of economic success in America.

9. Medical costs are too high in America.

10. Women in government are less likely to support going to war than men.

21.5 Activity

Evaluating Evidence

Distinguishing among Facts, Statements Most Experts Agree On, and Opinions (21.3, p. 290) discussed the difference between facts, statements most experts agree on, and opinions. Here, you're going to think about evaluating the facts or evidence a writer provides to support his or her opinions.

Imagine that your college needs to know, on average, how many students eat in the cafeteria each week. This information will be used for budgeting purposes. Below are reports written by three different student employees who were assigned this task. Working in your group, read each of the three reports, evaluate the evidence that supports the assertion made in each one, and decide which report is most convincing.

Report 1

At this college, on average, 1,578 students eat in the cafeteria each week. To arrive at this number, I sat in the cafeteria each day for a week and counted the number of students in the cafeteria. Below are my totals for the week. The cafeteria is closed on weekends.

Monday: 310
Tuesday: 330
Wednesday: 301
Thursday: 349
Friday: 288

Report 2

At this college, on average, 1,316 students eat in the cafeteria each week when classes are in session. To arrive at this number, I sat in the cafeteria each day for a week in September, December, January, and March and counted the number of students in the cafeteria. Below is my data for each month.

September		December		January		March	
Mon.	310	Mon.	285	Mon.	192	Mon.	301
Tue.	330	Tue.	301	Tue.	186	Tue.	244
Wed.	301	Wed.	280	Wed.	228	Wed.	289
Thu.	349	Thu.	338	Thu.	199	Thu.	260
Fri.	88	Fri.	275	Fri.	165	Fri.	143
Totals	1,578		1,479		970		1,237

I arrived at the figure of 1,316 students each week by averaging the four weekly totals I had observed.

Report 3

At this college, an average of 845 students eat in the cafeteria each week when classes are in session. At first, I thought I would sit in the cafeteria for a week at several different times during the academic year and count the number of students in the cafeteria. Then I realized two things: first, to do this would be extremely time-consuming and boring, and, second, it would be inaccurate. Not all students in the cafeteria are eating; many are there simply to do homework while waiting for their next class.

Faced with this realization, I asked the cafeteria manager if the cash registers recorded the number of students who paid for food each week. When she said, "Yes," I asked if she could give me a copy of those weekly totals for a year. She said, "Sure." All I had to do was average the weekly totals she gave me to arrive at an accurate average number of students who ate in the cafeteria each week when classes were in session.

Below are the totals produced by the cash registers for one complete year:

January	Week 1	764		March	Week 1	928
	Week 2	770			Week 2	919
	Week 3	759			Week 3	908
	Week 4	803			Week 4	Spring break
February	Week 1	965		April	Week 1	889
	Week 2	971			Week 2	891
	Week 3	954			Week 3	868
	Week 4	949			Week 4	860

May	Week 1	869			Week 2	985
	Week 2	858			Week 3	976
	Week 3	840			Week 4	969
	Week 4	No classes		**October**	Week 1	962
June	Week 1	No classes			Week 2	965
	Week 2	619			Week 3	957
	Week 3	625			Week 4	956
	Week 4	625		**November**	Week 1	950
July	Week 1	618			Week 2	954
	Week 2	611			Week 3	948
	Week 3	No classes			Week 4	946
	Week 4	623		**December**	Week 1	943
August	Week 1	629			Week 2	941
	Week 2	622			Week 3	931
	Week 3	618			Week 4	No classes
	Week 4	609			**Total**	**36,327**
September	Week 1	980		**Average weekly total: 36,327 ÷ 34 = 845**		

21.6 Tutorial

How to Make Inferences

We all make inferences every day. We look out the window and infer from the gray sky and looming clouds that it's going to rain. We encounter backed up traffic on a usually quiet road and think about possible causes: an accident, roadwork, or maybe dangerous driving conditions if there is snow or freezing rain. To make these inferences, we use clues in what we see or hear and draw conclusions about them based on our knowledge and previous experiences.

Writers do not always directly state their point. Sometimes they rely on the reader to piece together their message from the information they provide. To make an inference when you read a text, you have to think about what you already know about the subject, notice the details and language the writer uses, add up the facts he or she provides, and combine all these to come up with an idea of what the text means.

Guidelines for Making Inferences

- Carefully read the text and make sure you understand the main ideas and details the writer presents.

- Consider the author's purpose for writing. Who might be his or her audience?

- Look for details that provide clues to what the author is saying, especially any that seem unusual.

- Look at everything the author has said and think about what point these facts and details, taken together, seem to be making. Why were these specific details included and not others?

- Evaluate the author's choice of language. What is the overall tone of the text? What does this suggest to you?

- Think about what you already know about the subject. Does what the writer says fit with the information you already have? Have you had experiences that would help you understand his or her point?

- Finally, once you have made your inference, reread to check that it fits all the evidence in the text. Consider whether other conclusions could be made based on the evidence. Is there additional evidence in the text or from other sources that would confirm your hypothesis or cause you to revise it?

Making an Inference

Let's look at an example, a text written by a young college professor about a class he is teaching:

> Before I could even get to my classroom, I had to pass through a metal detector and wait as a heavy metal gate slammed shut behind me and another one opened in front of me. When I arrived in my classroom, right away I saw that only about a dozen of my twenty students were there. I asked where everyone else was, and one young man replied, "Eight of us are on 'lock down.'"

To make an inference about this passage, you first have to read it carefully. Then you should notice details like the *metal detector*, the *heavy metal gates*, and the fact that eight students are on "*lock down*." When you add up these details, you realize he's in a prison. But he's a professor, so what's he doing in prison? Ah, he's teaching a class to inmates. You've made an inference. The text didn't exactly say the professor is teaching in a prison, but by noticing the details, connecting them to what you already know, and thinking about them, you inferred that he must be teaching a class in a prison.

So that's what's meant by making an inference—reading a text, noticing the details, and, using your own knowledge, coming up with meaning that wasn't directly expressed in words but nevertheless can be inferred.

21.7 Activity

Making Inferences

Working in your group, see what inferences you can make from reading each of the two passages below.

Passage 1: Excerpt from *Better: A Surgeon's Notes on Performance*

This passage comes from Dr. Atul Gawande's book about what is involved in providing good patient care.

In 1847, at the age of twenty-eight, the Viennese obstetrician Ignac Semmelweis famously deduced that, by not washing their hands consistently or well enough, doctors were themselves to blame for childbed fever. Childbed fever, also known as puerperal fever, was the leading cause of maternal death in childbirth in the era before antibiotics (and before the recognition that germs are the agents of infectious disease). It is a bacterial infection most commonly caused by *Streptococcus,* the same bacteria that causes strep throat—that ascends through the vagina to the uterus after childbirth. Out of three thousand mothers who delivered babies at the hospital where Semmelweis worked, six hundred or more died of the disease each year—a horrifying 20 percent maternal death rate. Of mothers delivering at home, only 1 percent died. Semmelweis concluded that doctors themselves were carrying the disease between patients, and he mandated that every doctor and nurse on his ward scrub with a nail brush and chlorine between patients. The puerperal death rate immediately fell to 1 percent—incontrovertible proof, it would seem, that he was right. Yet elsewhere, doctors' practices did not change. Some colleagues were even offended by his claims; it was impossible to them that doctors could be killing their patients. Far from being hailed, Semmelweis was ultimately dismissed from his job.

Passage 2: Excerpt from *Outliers: The Story of Success*

This passage is an excerpt from Malcolm Gladwell's book, which explores some of the complex factors that contribute to the success of people like Bill Joy, who created

UNIX and Java computer languages; Bill Gates, founder of Microsoft; and John Lennon of *The Beatles*.

Exhibit A in the talent argument is a study done in the early 1990s by the psychologist K. Anders Ericsson and two colleagues at Berlin's elite Academy of Music. With the help of the Academy's professors, they divided the school's violinists into three groups. In the first group were the stars, the students with the potential to become world-class soloists. In the second were those judged to be merely "good." In the third were students who were unlikely to ever play professionally and who intended to be music teachers in the public school system. All of the violinists were then asked the same question: over the course of your entire career, ever since you first picked up the violin, how many hours have you practiced?

Everyone from all three groups started playing at roughly the same age, around five years old. In those first few years, everyone practiced roughly the same amount, about two or three hours a week. But when the students were around the age of eight, real differences started to emerge. The students who would end up the best in their class began to practice more than everyone else: six hours a week by age nine, eight hours a week by age twelve, sixteen hours a week by age fourteen, and up and up, until by the age of twenty they were practicing—that is, purposefully and single-mindedly playing their instruments with the intent to get better—well over thirty hours a week. In fact, by the age of twenty, the elite performers had each totaled ten thousand hours of practice. By contrast, the merely good students had totaled eight thousand hours, and the future music teachers had totaled just over four thousand hours.

21.8 Tutorial

Recognizing Assumptions and Biases

As discussed in How to Make Inferences (21.6, p. 295), it is important to look beyond the words in the texts you read for a deeper level of meaning. Careful reading can help you to accurately infer from clues in a text the unstated assumptions and biases of the author. Recognizing the assumptions and biases authors bring to what they write, as well as the ones you bring to the text as you read what they say, will help you to better understand, evaluate, and comment on the written material you encounter in college.

Assumptions

All of us make assumptions. In most parts of America, if you want to ask someone where the nearest gas station is, you don't start by asking, "Do you speak English?" Even though there are many people in America, even many American citizens, who don't speak English, when we approach someone on the street to ask directions, we *assume* they speak English.

When we walk into a store to buy a hot dog and a Coke, most of us *assume* that we can pay with a credit card. When we sign up for a course in a college, we *assume* that the course will be taught by someone with some expertise in the subject. When our doctor prescribes a medicine for us to take, we *assume* that the medicine is safe and may alleviate the problem we are taking it for. We assume all the time. There's nothing wrong with making assumptions; in fact, they make modern life possible.

However, when you are reading, it is often a good idea to take a few minutes to ask yourself what assumptions lie behind the text, not because there is something inherently "wrong" with assumptions, but because you need to decide whether you agree that the assumptions the author of the text is making are reasonable, whether or not you share them. For example, maybe you are reading an article by an author who believes in mandatory sentencing for drug offenders and bases his argument for increased government funding to build more prisons on it. If you believe that drug treatment programs are a more effective response to substance-related crimes, you might not accept this writer's assertions because you do not agree with his basic assumption. However, before dismissing his ideas, you should look for the evidence he uses to support his argument and compare it with the evidence you are basing your ideas on.

Understanding the assumptions underlying an argument and deciding whether you share these assumptions will help you decide whether you agree with the conclusions reached by the writer.

Recognizing Your Own Assumptions

In addition, it is important to be aware of one's own assumptions. We all have ways of thinking about the world that we learn from our families, communities, or religious and political institutions. These ways of thinking can be so familiar that we don't even recognize that we have them. We don't question them. But in order to fully evaluate the assumptions of an author, a reader must also be aware of and evaluate his or her own assumptions about the topic being discussed. Maybe you disagree with a writer because he or she is not supporting what you believe to be true. Are you sure your assumptions are correct? What evidence do you have to support them? Once you become more aware of the assumptions that underpin your thinking, you will be better able to recognize and evaluate those of the people you read.

Biases

Sometimes it is suggested that we should not read or rely on writers who are biased. We should look for writers who are even-handed and present both sides of an argument equally. In reality, the situation is more complicated than that. First, almost everyone is biased. It's next to impossible to find a writer who isn't. The fact that a writer is producing a piece of writing with a thesis means he or she has a bias in favor of that thesis. Second, we as readers often are not aware of an author's bias unless we make it a priority to be aware of it. We should read any given piece of writing "with a grain of salt," questioning the writer's assertions and evaluating skeptically the evidence presented.

Here are three ways to identify a writer's bias:

1. Investigate the author's biographical information, either located with the article or available on the internet. If the author works for an organization with a known bias or writes regularly for publications with a known bias, that can be a good indication of his or her bias.

2. Look for evidence of bias in the text itself. Does the writer use "loaded language"? For example, does the writer label those who disagree with his or her position as "immature," "stupid," or "narrow-minded"? Does the writer use demeaning adjectives to describe those with alternative viewpoints, adjectives like "so-called," "self-proclaimed," or "ill-informed"? Or does the writer use "loaded" verbs, such as "spewed," "would have you believe," and "whined"?

3. Ask yourself if the writer demonstrates an awareness that there are reasonable arguments on other sides of the issue. If not, this can indicate bias and a point of view that does not encompass all the relevant information on the subject.

Evaluating Your Own Biases

Just as with assumptions, it is important to be aware of your own biases in order to identify and evaluate the biases of writers. For instance, are you prejudiced in favor of or against particular groups of people, politicians, institutions, books, movies, and so on? Would your particular biases make it hard for you to entertain opposing views? Can you put your point of view aside so that you can fairly assess a different perspective, weighing the evidence provided to see if the alternative argument has merit?

21.9 Activity

Recognizing Assumptions and Biases in Three Passages

Working in your group, analyze any assumptions or biases in the following passages. Be prepared to report your group's analysis after about a half hour.

1. **Gun Control. Now.**

   Sutherland Springs, Texas. Las Vegas. Orlando. Sandy Hook. Columbine. Red Lake, Minnesota. Essex, Vermont. Lancaster. Aurora. Virginia Tech. How many more innocent victims must die at the hands of an antiquated and oft-misinterpreted amendment? Enough.

   It's time to stop the violence.

   Gun control doesn't have to mean no guns. I'm not suggesting we take guns away. I'm suggesting we put tighter controls on acquiring and owning them.

   Gun show loopholes must be stopped. Ammunition should not be sold online. Mandatory wait periods should be enforced, during which time a thorough background check, psychological and medical evaluation, and character references should be completed.

   From the MoveOn.org website
   https://petitions.moveon.org/sign/gun-control-now-1

2. **Medicare for All**

   The U.S. spends more on health care per person, and as a percentage of gross domestic product, than any other advanced nation in the world, including Australia, Canada, Denmark, France, Germany, Japan, New Zealand and the United Kingdom. But all that money has not made Americans healthier than the rest of the world. Quite simply, in our high-priced health care system that leaves millions overlooked, we spend more yet end up with less.

   Other industrialized nations are making the morally principled and financially responsible decision to provide universal health care to all of their people—and they do so while saving money by keeping people healthier. Those who say this goal is unachievable are selling the American people short.

   Americans need a health care system that works for patients and providers. We need to ensure a strong health care workforce in all communities now and in the future. We need a system where all people can get the care they need to maintain and improve their health when they need it regardless of income, age or socioeconomic status. We need a system that works not just for millionaires and billionaires, but for all of us.

   From the Bernie Sanders website
   https://berniesanders.com/issues/medicare-for-all/

3. Stop Animal Abuse

Every day in countries around the world, animals are fighting for their lives. They are enslaved, beaten, and kept in chains to make them perform for humans' "entertainment"; they are mutilated and confined to tiny cages so that we can kill them and eat them; they are burned, blinded, poisoned, and cut up alive in the name of "science"; they are electrocuted, strangled, and skinned alive so that people can parade around in their coats; and worse.

The abuse that animals suffer at human hands is heartbreaking, sickening, and infuriating. It's even more so when we realize that the everyday choices we make—such as what we eat for lunch and the kind of shampoo we buy—may be directly supporting some of this abuse. But as hard as it is to think about, we can't stop animals' suffering if we simply look the other way and pretend it isn't happening.

Animals are counting on compassionate people like you to give them a voice and be their heroes by learning about the issues they face and taking action. Each of us has the power to save animals from nightmarish suffering—and best of all, it's easier than you might think. If you're ready to join the millions of other compassionate people who are working to create a kinder, better world for animals, please read on to learn how animals suffer in the food, animal experimentation, entertainment, clothing and pet-trade industries. Together, we can make a difference.

From the PETA website
https://www.peta.org/issues/

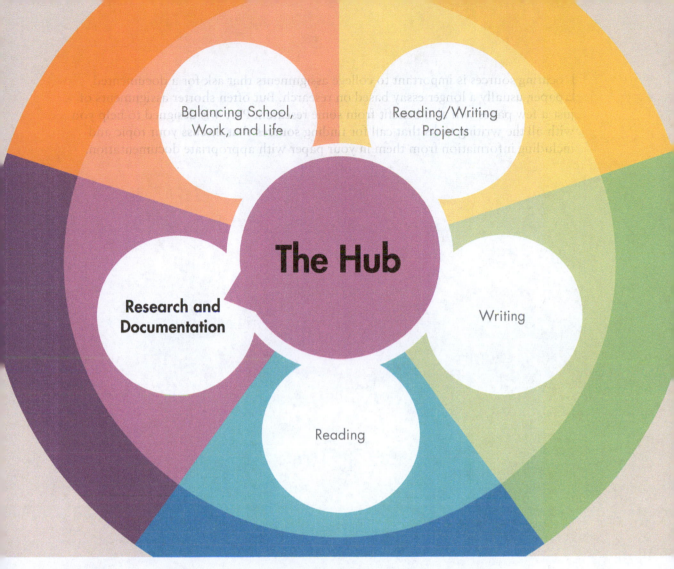

The Hub

Balancing School,
Work, and Life

Reading/Writing
Projects

Research and
Documentation

Writing

Reading

4 Research and Documentation

Topic 22   Research   287
Topic 23   MLA Documentation   336
Topic 24   APA Documentation   373

ocating sources is important to college assignments that ask for a documented paper, usually a longer essay based on research. But often shorter assignments of just a few pages will also benefit from some research. Part 4 is designed to help you with all the writing tasks that call for finding sources that discuss your topic and including information from them in your paper with appropriate documentation.

TOPIC 22
Research

Topic 22 provides information, advice, and suggestions about how to go about doing the kinds of research that are required in many college courses.

Navigating Topic 22

The tutorials listed below provide information about useful research strategies, and each contains, or is followed by, an opportunity to apply the skills you have just learned. You can work through the entire Topic on your own, learning about all the strategies and practicing them; work on items you've been assigned by your instructor; or choose those ones you would find helpful.

Introduction to Research   305

22.1	**Writing**	Thinking about the Research Process 306
22.2	**Tutorial**	The Research Process 306
22.3	**Activity**	Choosing Relevant Steps in the Research Process 308
22.4	**Presentation**	Finding Sources Online 312
22.5	**Tutorial**	Finding Sources in the Library 312
22.6	**Activity**	Evaluating Sources 317
22.7	**Tutorial**	Notetaking 319
22.8	**Tutorial**	Quoting and Paraphrasing 321
22.9	**Activity**	Quoting and Paraphrasing Shaughnessy 327
22.10	**Tutorial**	Conducting Interviews 328
22.11	**Tutorial**	Conducting Surveys 330
22.12	**Writing**	Questions about Plagiarism 332
22.13	**Tutorial**	Avoiding Plagiarism 332
22.14	**Tutorial**	Synthesis 334

Introduction to Research

Topic 22 begins with information on the research process and continues by providing instruction and strategies on how to find and evaluate sources online and in the library, take notes, quote and paraphrase, conduct interviews and surveys, avoid plagiarism, and synthesize sources.

22.1 Writing

Thinking about the Research Process

Think about the last time you had to write a paper that included doing research, or, if you've never been asked to write such a paper, try to imagine yourself writing one. For this assignment, make a list of the steps you took or that you might take if you had to write a paper that included at least some research.

22.2 Tutorial

The Research Process

Below is a list of all the steps that *might* be involved in writing a paper involving research. Of course, not all of these will be involved in every project, but steps 1, 3, 10, 14, 16, 18, 19, 20, and 21 are essential to any research project you work on (and have been underlined in the following checklist), so make sure you complete them. Exactly which steps are necessary in a specific project will depend on many factors: how much time you have, what kind of paper you are asked to write, how much research is expected for the paper, what the assignment is, and more.

Checklist for Steps in the Research Process

Keep in mind that this is a very complete list, and you would use only those steps appropriate for your specific assignment. All of them are useful, though, in different situations, so read through them carefully.

Getting Started

☐ 1. Read and analyze the assignment (see Terms for Writing Assignments [28.2, p. 436] for more details).

☐ 2. Analyze the rhetorical situation (see The Rhetorical Situation [9.3, p. 13]).

---

3. <u>Think about how much time you have for the project and set deadlines for each step.</u>

4. Focus on a topic you are interested in and want to write about. Sometimes it is more appropriate to start with a question about the topic, which will help you focus your research. For example, if the topic is to explore a cause or causes of the Civil War, you might ask, "What was the role of states' rights in the American Civil War?" "How did westward expansion impact the debate on slavery?" "Why did the election of Abraham Lincoln antagonize the southern states?" These questions are sometimes called "research questions."

5. Brainstorm some tentative ideas about your topic or question (see Invention Strategies [10.1, p. 22]).

Researching Your Subject

6. Decide what kind of research you are going to do. Online? Library? Both? Interviews? Surveys? Combinations of these?

7. **Online and library research:** Explore various potential sources in the library or online. You are not yet doing the kind of detailed reading you will need to do later; you are just "browsing around," getting a feel for what kind of sources are out there, and you are thinking about how to narrow, revise, or clarify the topic you plan to research (see Using Brainstorming to Narrow a Topic [10.4, p. 31]). During this exploratory phase, many of the books, articles, or websites you find will include references or links to related sources. Allow yourself to follow links and references that look interesting. Make brief, informal notes about sources that seem particularly interesting. Make sure you record enough information to find these promising sources again. (See Finding Sources Online [22.4, p. 312] and Finding Sources in the Library [22.5, p. 312].)

8. **Interviews:** If you are going to interview anyone, set up an appointment and make a list of questions. (See Conducting Interviews [22.10, p. 328].)

9. **Surveys:** If you are going to use a survey, draft the questionnaire, try it out on a few people, and revise it as needed. Decide how you will find people to survey, distribute the surveys, and compile results. (See Conducting Surveys [22.11, p. 330].)

Focusing Your Research

10. <u>Decide on a focused topic to research and begin thinking about a thesis.</u>

11. Return to the most promising sources and evaluate them. (See Evaluating Sources [22.6, p. 317].)

12. When possible, print or copy the resources that seem most useful.

□ 13. Annotate the copies you made or make notes of those you could not copy. Be sure to include bibliographic information. (See Notetaking [22.7, p. 319].)

Drafting Your Paper

□ 14. <u>Develop a thesis. (See Thesis Statements [10.5, p. 32].)</u>

□ 15. Make an outline or informal plan for the paper.

□ 16. <u>Write a first draft.</u>

□ 17. Do additional research if needed.

□ 18. <u>Revise the paper, which might involve writing several drafts. (See Revising [Topic 15, p. 99].)</u>

□ 19. <u>Check to make sure you have documented all the material you quoted, paraphrased, or summarized with in-text citations. (See MLA In-Text Citations [23.2, p. 338] and APA In-Text Citations [24.2, p. 374].)</u>

□ 20. <u>Proofread and edit the paper.</u>

□ 21. <u>Submit the final paper.</u>

22.3 Activity

Choosing Relevant Steps in the Research Process

Below you will find a list of all the steps presented in The Research Process (22.2, p. 306) that *might* be involved in writing a research paper. In that section, it was pointed out that not all of these will be involved in every project. Exactly which steps are necessary will depend on many factors: how much time you have, what kind of paper you are asked to write, how much research is expected for the paper, what the assignment is, and many more. However, this very complete list is worth thinking about before you start a research project, as you can then select just the steps necessary for your project.

Checklist for Steps in the Research Process

Getting Started

□ 1. Read and analyze the assignment (see Terms for Writing Assignments [28.2, p. 436] for more details).

□ 2. Analyze the rhetorical situation (see The Rhetorical Situation [9.3, p. 13]).

□ 3. Think about how much time you have for the project and set deadlines for each step.

☐ 4. Focus on a topic you are interested in and want to write about. Sometimes it is more appropriate to start with a question about the topic, which will help you focus your research. For example, if the topic is to explore a cause or causes of the Civil War, you might ask, "What was the role of states' rights in the American Civil War?" "How did westward expansion impact the debate on slavery?" "Why did the election of Abraham Lincoln antagonize the southern states?" These questions are sometimes called "research questions."

☐ 5. Brainstorm some tentative ideas about your topic or question (see Invention Strategies [10.1, p. 22]).

Researching Your Subject

☐ 6. Decide what kind of research you are going to do. Online? Library? Both? Interviews? Surveys? Combinations of these?

☐ 7. **Online and library research:** Explore various potential sources in the library or online. You are not yet doing the kind of detailed reading you will need to do later; you are just "browsing around," getting a feel for what kind of sources are out there, and you are thinking about how to narrow, revise, or clarify the topic you plan to research question (see Using Brainstorming to Narrow a Topic [10.4, p. 31]). During this exploratory phase, many of the books, articles, or websites you find will include references or links to related sources. Allow yourself to follow links and references that look interesting. Make brief, informal notes about sources that seem particularly interesting. Make sure you record enough information to find these promising sources again. (See Finding Sources Online [22.4, p. 312] and Finding Sources in the Library [22.5, p. 312].)

☐ 8. **Interviews:** If you are going to interview anyone, set up an appointment and make a list of questions. (See Conducting Interviews [22.10, p. 328].)

☐ 9. **Surveys:** If you are going to use a survey, draft the questionnaire, try it out on a few people, and revise it as needed. Decide how you will find people to survey, distribute the surveys, and compile results. (See Conducting Surveys [22.11, p. 330].)

Focusing Your Research

☐ 10. Decide on a focused topic to research and begin thinking about a thesis.

☐ 11. Return to the most promising sources and evaluate them. (See Evaluating Sources [22.6, p. 317].)

☐ 12. When possible, print or copy the resources that seem most useful.

☐ 13. Annotate the copies you made or make notes of those you could not copy. Be sure to include bibliographic information. (See Notetaking [22.7, p. 319].)

Drafting Your Paper

☐ 14. Develop a thesis. (See Thesis Statements [10.5, p. 32].)

☐ 15. Make an outline or informal plan for the paper.

☐ 16. Write a first draft.

☐ 17. Do additional research if needed.

☐ 18. Revise the paper, which might involve writing several drafts. (See Revising [Topic 15, p. 99].)

☐ 19. Check to make sure you have documented all the material you quoted, paraphrased, or summarized with in-text citations. (See MLA In-Text Citations [23.2, p. 338] and APA In-Text Citations [24.2, p. 374].)

☐ 20. Proofread and edit the paper.

☐ 21. Submit the final paper.

For this activity, working in your group, select one of the following three assignments. Then decide which of the steps listed above you would definitely have to do in order to write the assigned essay.

Assignment 1: Evolution of Thinking on Delayed Gratification

For this assignment, you will write an academic essay suitable for an English composition class in which you discuss the evolution of thinking over the past fifty years about delayed gratification. You will need to explain Walter Mischel's contribution in his famous "Marshmallow Experiment," then explore more recent thoughts on the subject, and, finally, present your own thoughts about the issue. The audience for this essay is your English composition instructor.

You must include information from at least six articles by quoting, paraphrasing, or summarizing relevant passages. When you do this, be sure to provide appropriate citations for any words you quote, paraphrase, or summarize from the websites and to include a works cited list or list of references at the end of your essay.

The essay is due one week from today.

Assignment 2: Freedom of Speech

For this assignment, you will write a ten- to twelve-page academic essay on a topic related to freedom of speech in America. In your essay, you will discuss what freedom of speech means in America through your focus on a specific topic like one of the following:

- The origins of the principle of freedom of speech at the time the country was forming

- Reservations about freedom of speech when it was proposed

- Changes in the principle of freedom of speech over time

- Threats to free speech over the years

- Controversies that have arisen involving free speech

- How the American version of free speech is different from that of other countries

- A topic of your choosing

Think of this essay as writing that would be appropriate in a college course on history, political science, law, or English composition. Your audience for this essay will be your instructor for that course.

Once you've settled on a topic to write about, you will need to do some research. Locate at least six articles or books that discuss your topic. Once you have your articles, write a brief evaluation of each using the questions that follow. Include these evaluations when you turn in your essay.

1. Who was the author(s)? What can you find out about the author(s)? What level of expertise does the author have on the subject?

2. Where was the article published? What kind of journal, book, or website did it appear in, and is that source reliable, accurate, and up-to-date?

3. Does the author or the publisher of the article have a particular bias? Does that bias make the article less valuable as a resource?

4. Who seems to be the audience this article was intended for?

5. Does the article provide convincing evidence to support its thesis?

Be sure to provide appropriate citations for any words you quote, paraphrase, or summarize from the websites and to include a works cited list or list of references at the end of your essay.

This assignment is due in six weeks.

Assignment 3: Taking a Position on the Minimum Wage

For this assignment, you are going to write a three- to four-page essay to convince government officials in your city or state of your position on the minimum wage. You will visit seven websites addressing the issue of raising the minimum wage—five are listed below and two you will find. You will evaluate each of the websites using the questions listed in Assignment 2. Finally, you will recommend what the minimum wage should be in your city or state based on the research you have done. Be sure to provide appropriate citations for any words you quote, paraphrase, or summarize from the websites and include a works cited list or list of references at the end of your essay.

Here are the five websites. Remember: You need to locate two more that also address the effect of raising the minimum wage on employment. You can access these sites by typing their titles into your browser. (If you cannot find a site using its title, there is an updated list of URLs available at https://bit.ly/33IIHtf.)

1. "Increase in Minimum Wage Kills Jobs," Employment Policies Institute
2. "Minimum Wage and Job Loss: One Alarming Seattle Study Is Not the Last Word," Arindrajit Dube, *New York Times*
3. "New Minimum Wage Hikes Set to Kill Jobs in 2018," Brendan Pringle, *Washington Examiner*
4. "The Controversial Study Showing High Minimum Wages Kills Jobs, Explained," Jeff Guo, *Vox*
5. "Study: Seattle's $15 Minimum Wage WORKED," David Pakman, *HuffPost*

22.4 Presentation
Finding Sources Online

To watch this presentation, which discusses how to locate useful and relevant sources through online research, go to *Achieve for The Hub*, Topic 22, and open Unit 22.4.

22.5 Tutorial
Finding Sources in the Library

Research, whether in the library or on the web, has two phases: a "browsing" phase and a "focused" phase. In the browsing phase, you have a general topic you know you want to explore, but you also know that the topic will probably need to be narrowed, focused, or even abandoned. Further, you often have no more than a fuzzy idea about what you are going to argue about the topic or what your thesis will be.

During the browsing phase, you are educating yourself about the topic and getting a feel for the issues, discovering what the main arguments seem to be, and locating "experts," authors referred to over and over in the sources you find. You're not so much looking for material to include in your paper as finding what's out there, although you should be jotting down bibliographic information you come across that looks promising so you can find the source later if you need to.

When you discover a shelf in the library that has a book or two that look useful, explore other books on that same shelf to see if they are also on your topic. When you find an article in a journal that seems important to your topic, look for references to other articles either in a bibliography or perhaps included within the article itself. Again, as you browse, either make notes or make copies of pages so you can locate this material during the focused phase of research.

Once you have a good feel for the topic you have been exploring and have identified the main arguments about it, discovered some "experts," and narrowed, focused, or even revised your topic, you are ready for phase two: the focused phase. At this point, you should have begun to formulate a thesis, with the understanding that it may change considerably as you continue researching and writing.

The second phase is organized around a narrowed topic and a tentative thesis (see How to Use Invention Strategies to Select a Topic [10.3, p. 30] and Thesis Statements [10.5, p. 32]). Now you will be searching the library focusing primarily on two types of materials: books and periodicals (journals and magazines). Because the tools and methods for searching for these two are quite different, we will discuss them one at a time.

Locating Books

The library catalog is your tool for locating books. Today, most libraries' catalogs are computerized, which not only means books are much easier to find but also means you can, in most cases, do your search from home. If you are not familiar with accessing your college's catalog, there are two ways you can become familiar with the process. The first is through a library orientation session. Many college writing classes will schedule a day to meet in the library for such an orientation. Be sure to attend that session. A second way to become familiar is to visit the library and ask a reference librarian to help you get started.

Once you have accessed the library's catalog, you are ready to begin searching for books. The most obvious way into the college's collection of books is to search by *subject* using the topic you have focused on. For example, imagine that you are going to write about the atomic bombing of Hiroshima during World War II, and you have focused on the specific topic of the ethical justification for the bombing. Each college library's catalog web page will look slightly different, but the procedures for locating materials will usually work in a similar way to the following example.

On the search page, begin by choosing to search by title, typing the word "Hiroshima" into the search box, and clicking the Search button.

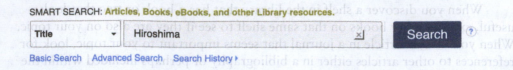

The catalog search engine returns results as follows (only the first two are shown):

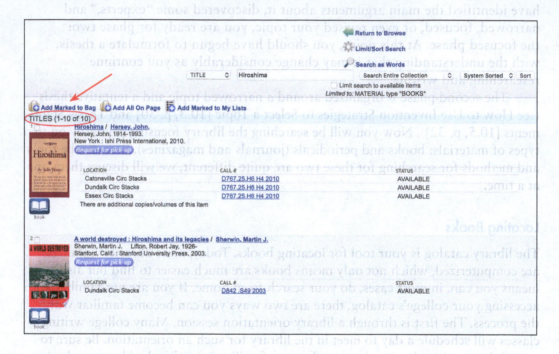

You can see, in the item circled in red, that the library owns ten books with "Hiroshima" in the title. Ten is too many for you to read or even to skim for this assignment, so you need to find a way to narrow down the list. Study the titles to find the books that seem most closely related to your working thesis. Also look for authors who were referred to frequently while you were in the browsing phase.

Locating Articles in Journals and Magazines

It is important that you understand the difference between journals and popular magazines. The following chart will help you with this distinction.

Journals	Magazines
Journals usually have the word *journal* in their title.	Magazines usually do not have the word *journal* in their title.
Articles in journals usually include citations and lists of references.	Magazine articles seldom have citations or lists of references.
Journals are seldom glossy and seldom have full-color illustrations.	Magazines are usually glossy with full-color illustrations.
Journals are usually found in libraries.	Some magazines may be found in libraries, but more often they're available by subscription or at a newsstand.
The authors of journal articles are usually identified by academic credentials.	Magazine articles are usually written by journalists.
Journal articles often begin with a summary or abstract.	Magazine articles usually do not include a summary or abstract.

For most research you do in college, you will be expected to use scholarly sources, although for some topics, some audiences, and some contexts, popular magazines and newspapers may be appropriate.

Most libraries, especially those on college and university campuses, have powerful tools that allow you to locate articles on almost any topic you might want to write about: databases. Many students use Google to search for articles, but there are good reasons why searching using your library's databases is a better choice.

Benefits of Library Databases versus Google

1. **Google will find thousands of articles but does not evaluate the expertise of their authors.** Using Google you'll get a list that includes excellent scholarly articles intermixed with the websites of high school students, blogs by conspiracy theorists, and people trying to sell a gimmick or a cure. Using Google Scholar will produce a list that is more scholarly but doesn't have some of the other benefits of using a library database that are discussed below.

2. **Many of the sources you locate with Google or Google Scholar will charge a fee if you want to access an article.** Most libraries pay a license fee in order for their students to access the sources listed in the databases for free.

3. **When you find articles from a library database that look useful for the paper you are writing, in most cases you can download the paper directly to your computer.** If you later quote from the article, you can cut and paste from the article directly into your paper ensuring that you quote accurately. If you need a paper copy, you can print one from your computer.

4. **Most library databases can be accessed from home.** Sometimes students decide to use Google because they can access it from home, not realizing that they can also access their college library from home. You may want to ask a reference librarian or perhaps your English teacher to show you how to do this.

Many students use Google to search for articles. If you choose to do this, use Google Scholar. Simply open Google, type "Google Scholar" in the search box, and hit Enter. Clicking on the words "Google Scholar" at the top of the page opens the search engine.

Using Library Databases

There are two different types of library databases for periodicals: general and specialized.

General Databases

General databases provide access to a wide range of scholarly journals as well as articles from reputable magazines and newspapers. They can be a good place to start your research if you haven't yet developed your focus or if you have chosen a topic but are not sure what discipline it belongs to. Some of the most widely used general databases are listed below. Your reference librarian can help guide you to the ones that will be most useful for the task you are working on.

- **Academic Search Premier** is a major database that includes general and scholarly sources in the humanities, education, social sciences, computer science, engineering, languages, linguistics, arts, literature, and ethnic studies.

- **JSTOR** provides access to more than 12 million academic journal articles, books, and primary sources; however, JSTOR does not include *current* issues.

- **Lexis/Nexis Academic** provides full-text news, business, and legal publications. It also provides transcripts of television and radio broadcasts and includes national and international sources.

- **ProQuest** includes dissertations and theses, e-books, newspapers, periodicals, historical collections, and governmental and cultural archives estimated to include more than 125 billion digital pages.

Specialized Databases

Specialized databases are preferable once you have a focused topic to search for and when you are confident about the discipline or disciplines where most scholarship on your topic takes place. Most libraries offer large numbers of these specialized databases. Your reference librarian can help guide you to the ones that will be most useful for the topic you are working on. A small sample is listed below.

- **Arts and Humanities Database** covers the arts, archeology, architecture, anthropology, classics, history, philosophy, and modern languages.

- **Medline** includes articles on biomedical and health topics used by health care professionals.

- **MLA International Bibliography** covers scholarship on all aspects of modern languages and literature. More than 70,000 sources are added annually, allowing access to very recent scholarship as well as articles dating back to the 1880s.

- **Social Science Index** covers social science disciplines including anthropology, communication, criminology, economics, education, political science, psychology, social work, and sociology.

22.6 Activity

Evaluating Sources

Two research assignments are listed below. After each assignment, several possible resources (books, blogs, articles, or websites) are listed. Working in your group, view the material provided or visit the website for each of these resources and decide how good a source it would be for a college research paper. Then compile a list of what the group viewed as the strengths and weaknesses of each source you evaluated. The following questions should help you evaluate these sources, as well as others you locate as you research papers.

Questions for Evaluating Sources

- Who is the author(s)? What can you find out about the author(s)? How expert is the author on the subject?

- Where was the article published? (What kind of journal, book, or website?) Who published the book?

- When was the article or book published?

- What can you find out about the organization or company that published it?

- Who seems to be the audience this article or book was intended for?

- Does this article or book add anything new to the argument?

Assignment 1: Exploring Mistakes Made during the Vietnam War

You are writing a research paper for a history class about the mistakes the United States made during the Vietnam War, and you find the following sources. Evaluate them using the questions above. Locate the first three sources using the search terms provided. (If you find that any of the search terms provided do not work, there is a list of URLs available at https://bit.ly/33IIHtf.) Search for the final three sources on Amazon.com, where you can read the back covers.

- An article entitled "The Vietnam War in Hindsight" (Type the entire title into your browser, followed by "Brookings Institute.")
- A book entitled *Against the Vietnam War* (Type "Against the Vietnam War Google Books" into your browser.)
- A blog post entitled "Why Did the U.S. Lose the Vietnam War?" (Type "Why Did the U.S. Lose the Vietnam War? Slate blog" into your browser.)
- A book entitled *Vietnam Insights*

The Vietnam War—was it a civil war or an invasion? Was Ho Chi Minh a communist or nationalist? Did the United States lose this war? These are but a few of the questions presented and examined in *Vietnam Insights: Logic of Involvement and Unconventional Perspectives*, by James M. Griffiths. In cogent and readable form the author focuses on the foreign policies and factors that created the logic for U.S. participation in Vietnam, often presenting a side not widely disseminated before.

Vietnam is still having an effect on U.S. foreign policy. This volume is a valuable contribution to understanding this war that still haunts us.

JAMES M. GRIFFITHS is a Vietnam veteran who served with the Eleventh Armored Cavalry Regiment in 1968 and 1969. Mr. Griffiths has taught high-school history for more than twenty years. His first book, *Vietnam Insights*, is based on the research he has done in order to teach the story of Vietnam to his students. Mr. Griffiths is a resident of Michigan for whom writing this book has fulfilled a lifelong goal.

- A book entitled *Vietnam: An Epic Tragedy, 1945–1975*

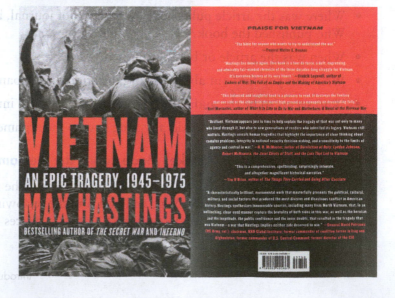

- A book entitled
  *Argument Without
  End*

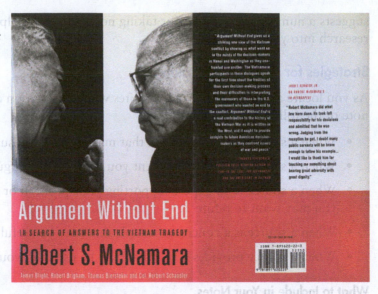

Argument Without End
IN SEARCH OF ANSWERS TO THE VIETNAM TRAGEDY
Robert S. McNamara
James Blight, Robert Brigham, Thomas Biersteker and Col. Herbert Schandler

Assignment 2: Evaluating the Affordable Care Act

You are writing a research paper about the Affordable Care Act (Obamacare) and find the following sources. Evaluate them using the questions above. (Locate the sources using the search terms provided. If these search terms do not work, there is a list of URLs available at https://bit.ly/33IIHtf.)

- The official government site for signing up for healthcare provided under the Affordable Care Act (Type "healthcare.gov" into your browser.)

- An article entitled "Why So Many Insurers Are Leaving Obamacare" in *The Atlantic* (Type the entire title into your browser, followed by "The Atlantic.")

- An article entitled "Overwhelming Evidence That Obamacare Caused Premiums to Increase Substantially" in *Forbes* (Type "overwhelming evidence Obamacare premiums Forbes" into your browser.)

22.7 Tutorial

Notetaking

Much of the writing you do in college involves research, whether you are writing a lengthy formal research paper or you are writing a fairly short essay in which you want to include information or perhaps a quotation or two from some experts on your topic. An essential skill for effective research is effective notetaking. This section suggests a number of strategies for taking notes that will help you incorporate research into your writing.

Strategies for Effective Notetaking

As you locate articles, books, and websites with information about your topic, take note of the following:

- When a source has information that may be useful in supporting your thesis
- When a source makes a statement you may want to argue against
- When a source is an expert supporting your position or advocating a position you may want to refute
- When a source is a concrete example that may be useful in your paper
- When a source provides a fact that may be useful in your paper

What to Include in Your Notes

You will want to include four pieces of information in each note you take.

1. A subject heading that indicates what the note is about
2. Information about the source of the note. This information will be important when you construct a works cited list or list of references. It will also make it easier for you to find the source again if you need to. Be sure to record the following:
   a. Title of the source
   b. Name of the author(s)
   c. Name of the translator(s) or editor(s)
   d. Version or edition
   e. Volume and issue numbers for periodicals
   f. Publisher
   g. Date of publication
   h. Page number for print sources or URL for online sources

   Most sources won't include *all* these pieces of information, so include only the elements that are relevant and available for an acceptable citation.

3. A summary, paraphrase, or quotation of the ideas or information in the source. Be sure to indicate in the note what is summary, what is paraphrase, and what is quotation. (See Strategies for Writing a Summary [18.25, p. 233] and Quoting and Paraphrasing [22.8, p. 321].)
4. Your response to the information

How to Record Your Notes

There are at least four ways to record these notes.

1. **On 3 × 5 or 4 × 6 inch cards.** This is a little more labor intensive than digital options. It requires care to make sure quotations are accurate, and it doesn't provide the context for the relevant content or quotation. It does allow for the notes to be arranged in the order they will appear in the paper. Some writers even tack them on a bulletin board to arrange them.

2. **In a paper journal.** This option has all the disadvantages of note cards. In addition, it is not easy to arrange notes in any order.

3. **In a series of word processing documents.** If you are using the library, this requires you to have a laptop. For online sources, it is very convenient and accurate, as online source material can be copied and pasted right into word processing documents. Notes are easy to arrange in order and to organize in files. In most cases, a large chunk of text can be copied and then the part to be used simply highlighted, allowing the writer to see the relevant content or quotation in its original context.

4. **By photocopying each article or page from a book and writing the source information somewhere on that copy.** Photocopying costs money. You do end up with the entire page on which the relevant information or potential quotation appears, allowing you to see it in context. However, it is a little awkward, but not impossible, to arrange this type of material in order.

Each of these options has advantages and disadvantages. You should use the notetaking method that works best for you.

22.8 Tutorial

Quoting and Paraphrasing

The point of doing research is to find sources—books, articles, interviews, reports, studies, or other texts—that include facts, expert opinion, examples, or other forms of support for the thesis you will be arguing in your essay. Once you have located these kinds of support you will include them in your essay in one of three ways: quotations, paraphrases, or summaries. In this unit, we discuss quoting and paraphrasing. Summarizing is discussed in Strategies for Writing a Summary (18.25, p. 233).

Quotations

When you quote a source, you reproduce the words exactly as they appear in the source document, placing them inside quotation marks. Using a quotation is an effective strategy in the following situations:

- When the author's language is particularly powerful or vivid and would not be as effective if paraphrased
- When the author's language is so technical it is important to report it exactly as it was written
- When the author is highly respected and you think his or her exact words will be more convincing than your own

When quoting from a source, accuracy is essential. You must reproduce the source's words exactly, with exceptions that will be discussed below. Short quotations should be incorporated directly into your text. If you are following MLA style, short means four typed lines or less. If you are following APA style, short means forty words or fewer. Long quotations should be set off in block style.

Short Quotation

According to the Chicana writer Gloria Anzaldúa, "Chicano Spanish is a border tongue which developed naturally" (*Borderlands* 77).

Long Quotation

Even though community colleges are often seen as opening the door to higher education for a large number of students who would not have even considered going to college sixty or seventy years ago, it has not always opened that door as widely as we would hope. Rebecca Cox, in her important book *The College Fear Factor*, points this out:

> [T]he community college has also had a winnowing effect, in functioning as an obstacle to students who enter with the intention of transferring and earning a bachelor's degree. The high attrition rates—within individual courses and across various degree programs—suggest that students face barriers that divert them from accomplishing their goals (3).

Framing Quotations

The way you frame the quotations in your essays will make the quotations more effective. This framing (underlined in the following examples) usually, but not always, comes before the quoted material and consists of introductory information that provides context for the quotation that follows.

> Noted sociologist Annette Lareau, in her major study of child rearing in American families, cautions us that she "was struck by how hard parents try, how much effort they put into each day as they pursue their lives" (*Unequal Childhoods* 360).
>
> In her influential book *Grit*, MacArthur fellow Angela Duckworth explains what grit really is: "Grit is about working on something you care about so much that you're willing to stay loyal to it" (54).
>
> So far in this essay, I have given several reasons why change is so difficult to bring about in higher education. Cheryl Hyman, former president of Chicago City Colleges, suggests another reason when she claims that if there is one thing "educators don't want to hear, it's that education should be run more like a business" (*Reinvention* 30).

Note that in the framing material each example includes two pieces of information:

- The name of the person being quoted (Annette Lareau, Angela Duckworth, and Cheryl Hyman)

- Some information to explain why this person has expertise ("Noted sociologist," "MacArthur fellow" and writer of an "influential book," and "former president of Chicago City Colleges")

Sometimes it's also useful to explain in the framing material how the quoted material relates to the essay itself. In the third example, taken from an essay exploring how difficult it is to make changes in higher education, the framing material explains that the quotation from Hyman will provide yet another reason for why it is so difficult.

One additional feature of the materials these authors have chosen to frame their quotations is the verbs they use: *cautions*, *explains*, and *claims*. Notice how much more information these verbs provide than more ordinary verbs that might have been used, such as *says* or *writes*. *Cautions* tells the reader that not only did Lareau write these words but that they say something that calls into question what we might believe about families from different socioeconomic strata. In the second example, *explains* signals that the quotation has something to say that could clear up any confusion the reader might have about grit. Finally, *claims* signals that the writer of the essay is not completely convinced that Hyman is right about faculty attitudes.

Here is a list of more expressive verbs for introducing quotations. Try using some of them the next time you include a quotation in your writing.

Expressive Verbs		
acknowledges	declares	observes
admits	denies	opposes
advises	discusses	points out
agrees	emphasizes	replies
argues	explains	reports
asserts	hypothesizes	responds
believes	implies	reveals
claims	insists	suggests
concludes	interprets	thinks
confirms	objects	

In the previous examples, the framing material was placed in front of the quoted material. The following examples illustrate that this is not the only way of positioning framing material.

> "India is named for the Indus River, along whose fecund banks a great urban civilization flourished more than four thousand years ago," writes historian Stanley Wolpert in the opening chapter of his monumental *New History of India*.

> "Greek drama grew out of religious ritual," argues Moses Hadad in his introduction to *Greek Drama*, "and was presented as part of a religious cult."

Exceptions to Word-for-Word Quoting

This section on quotations began by saying "you reproduce the words exactly as they appear in the source document." However, there are two primary exceptions to this rule: (1) using ellipses to exclude irrelevant words in quoted material and (2) adding words to explain an author's meaning.

Using Ellipses to Indicate Omitted Words.   Sometimes you want to include some words from one long sentence, or maybe two adjacent sentences, and not include the words between them that are not relevant to your point. *As long as you do not change the author's original meaning*, it is acceptable to omit some words in a quotation. If you decide to do this, indicate the omission with an ellipsis (three spaced periods). In the following example, unnecessary words have been deleted from the original text by Paul Tough. Note the ellipses this writer has used to indicate where these words from the original have been omitted. He has also maintained the author's original meaning.

Original

"What matters most in a child's development, they say, is not how much information we can stuff into her brain in the first few years. What matters, instead, is whether we are able to help her develop a very different set of qualities, a list that includes persistence, self-control, curiosity, conscientiousness, grit, and self-confidence" (Tough, *How Children Succeed*, xv).

Quotation

Education writer Paul Tough insists that what "matters most in a child's development . . . is not how much information we can stuff into her brain in the first few years. What matters, instead, is whether we are able to help her develop . . . persistence, self-control, curiosity, conscientiousness, grit, and self-confidence" (*How Children Succeed*, xv).

Adding Words of Explanation. Sometimes, it is necessary to add words to quoted text in order to explain what a writer is saying. To add words to the original text, enclose the added words in brackets. Note in the example below how the words in brackets have been inserted into the original text that is being quoted to make its meaning clearer to the reader.

Original

You can trace its contemporary rise, in fact, to 1994, when the Carnegie Corporation published *Starting Points: Meeting the Needs of Our Youngest Children,* a report that sounded an alarm about the cognitive development of our nation's children. The problem, according to the report, was that children were no longer receiving enough cognitive stimulation in the first three years of life, in part because of the increasing number of single-parent families and working mothers—and so they were arriving in kindergarten unready to learn. The report launched an entire industry of brainbuilding "zero-to-three" products for worried parents. Billions of dollars' worth of books and activity gyms and Baby Einstein videos and DVDs were sold.

Quotation

According to education writer Paul Tough, "The [Carnegie] report [*Starting Points: Meeting the Needs of Our Youngest Children*] launched an entire industry of brainbuilding 'zero-to-three' products for worried parents."

Paraphrases

When you use your own words to express an author's ideas fairly and accurately, you are paraphrasing. Being able to express someone else's ideas accurately is one way to ensure that you understand them. Use a paraphrase in these situations:

- To help you think through an author's ideas
- To record ideas that you might want to use in an essay
- To show a reader that you have understood an idea
- When the language in the source is not particularly effective
- When the source language doesn't fit well with your language

When you decide to paraphrase, it is important that you faithfully represent the thought in the source in your own words. Unlike summaries, paraphrases are usually about the same length as the original source, sometimes longer, as you are basically translating someone else's language into your own. You might include a word or two from the original source in quotation marks, but most of the wording should be your own, written in your style. As well as rewording, you might want to reorganize the material you are paraphrasing, breaking complicated sentences in the original into shorter ones. In addition, you must include the name of the author and title of the source in your paraphrase and/or provide an in-text citation.

Reproduced below is the original text from Richard Reeves' *Dream Hoarders*, where he argues that the upper middle class in America is leaving everyone else behind and exploiting a variety of advantages in order to do so. An unacceptable paraphrase follows it. It does not mention or cite the passage it refers to, and it uses much of the language of the original, with just a few words changed. The words that come from the original that are still used in this unacceptable paraphrase are underlined. Because they are not placed inside quotation marks, they are actually plagiarized. (The important topic of plagiarism is discussed in detail in Avoiding Plagiarism [22.13, p. 332].)

> **Original**
>
> Americans have historically lauded education as the great equalizer, allowing individuals to determine their own path in life regardless of background. But if this was ever true, it certainly is not today. Postsecondary education in particular has become an "inequality machine." As more ordinary people have earned college degrees, upper middle-class families have simply upped the ante. Postgraduate qualifications are now the key to maintaining upper middle-class status (11).

Unacceptable Paraphrase

Richard Reeves, from the Brookings Institution, has argued that <u>historically, Americans have</u> praised <u>education as the great equalizer</u>, making it possible for everyone to follow <u>their own path regardless of background</u>. If this was true in the past, <u>it certainly is not</u> these days. College has especially helped to encourage inequality. <u>As more people earn college degrees</u>, the <u>key</u> to getting a job that provides a <u>middle-class</u> lifestyle has become a <u>post-graduate degree</u>.

Below is an acceptable paraphrase. Notice that only a few words from the original text are retained in this paraphrase, and they are placed within quotation marks to make it clear that they are Reeves's words. Notice, also, that just like with quotations, paraphrases are usually framed with material like "In his book *Dream Hoarders*, Richard Reeves from the Brookings Institute makes the point that," which identifies the author, his credentials, and the source of the paraphrased material.

Acceptable Paraphrase

In his book *Dream Hoarders*, Richard Reeves from the Brookings Institute makes the point that in the past Americans considered education to be the best route for people from all levels of society to pursue their choice of career. Whether this was ever true or not, he says that these days higher education "has become an inequality machine," because as more regular people have graduated with bachelor's degrees, wealthier people have now made master's and doctoral degrees necessary requirements for higher-paying jobs (11).

22.9 Activity

Quoting and Paraphrasing Shaughnessy

In this activity, you will use the following short passage from Mina Shaughnessy's book *Errors and Expectations: A Guide for the Teacher of Basic Writing* to practice quoting and paraphrasing. Shaughnessy was teaching at City University of New York in the 1990s and was present as "open admissions" transformed her school and many more, and hers was one of the earliest books to address the teaching of students who arrive in colleges and universities with less-than-college-ready writing skills. The following passage is from the first page of her book:

> Toward the end of the sixties and largely in response to the protests of that decade, many four-year colleges began admitting students who were not by traditional standards ready for college. The numbers of such students varied from college to college as did the commitment to the task of teaching them.

Practice Quoting

In an essay you are writing for an education class, you want to make the point that "open admissions" might have resulted in major transformations at some colleges, but it had little effect at others. Working in your group, write a sentence or two in which you quote from the Shaughnessy passage to make that point.

Practice Paraphrasing

Working in your group, make the point that "open admissions" might have resulted in major transformations at some colleges, but it had little effect at others. Write this in a sentence or two, paraphrasing Shaughnessy's passage.

In both cases, make sure you provide an effective frame for the material you quote or paraphrase.

22.10 Tutorial
Conducting Interviews

When thinking about how to provide evidence to support your thesis in a paper, don't overlook the possibility of interviewing an expert. Quoting the words of someone with direct experience can provide strong support for your argument, as in the following scenarios.

- For an essay on a fairly recent military event, you might interview a cousin or uncle who served in Vietnam, Afghanistan, or Iraq.

- For an essay on civil rights, you might interview someone who took part in the sit-ins in the South in 1960 or the march on Washington in 1963 or a person who has recently experienced a violation of his or her civil rights.

- In making decisions about your program of study and future career, you might interview someone working in the field you are considering.

- In the workplace, you might interview someone in the Human Relations Office for a report or a proposal concerning personnel issues.

- For your marketing or sales department, you might interview customers about their perceptions of your company's products or procedures.

Checklist for Steps for Conducting Interviews

Follow these steps for setting up and conducting an interview.

Scheduling an Interview

- ☐ Identify someone to interview.
- ☐ Once your subject has agreed to be interviewed, establish a time and place for the interview as well as an understanding of how long the interview will last.
- ☐ Send an email or note confirming the time and place.
- ☐ Ask your subject if he or she minds being taped.

Planning for an Interview

- ☐ Write down your questions in advance. Think about what you want to know from the subject and write questions that will produce that information.
- ☐ Prioritize your questions.
- ☐ On the page of questions you plan to use, leave plenty of space after each one to record the subject's responses.
- ☐ Be sure to ask questions identifying the subject and determining his or her exact position, job, or role.
- ☐ Consider including questions that will elicit a story ("Tell me about the time . . .") or allow for an open response "So, how did you feel about . . . ?" Asking questions that produce a simple yes or no answer will not provide you with much information.
- ☐ Make sure you have materials for taking notes.
- ☐ Make sure your recording device is working.

Conducting an Interview

- ☐ Respect the subject's time. Arrive promptly and conclude within the time-frame you established.
- ☐ Note the date, time, and place of the interview.
- ☐ Take notes even if you are also recording.
- ☐ Be careful to distinguish in your notes between quotations, paraphrases, and summaries.
- ☐ If your subject provides useful responses to an early question and you want to continue that line of inquiry, do not feel you must get to all the questions you prepared.

Following Up on an Interview

☐ Flesh out your notes as soon as possible after the interview. The longer you wait, the harder it will be for you to accurately recall what was said.

☐ If you are not sure of what the person said or meant, contact him or her and ask. It is important that you provide accurate information.

☐ Send a thank-you note or email to the interviewee.

22.11 Tutorial

Conducting Surveys

Surveys are a useful way to gather evidence for an essay, but they take some time to construct, to administer, and to interpret. A good place to start is to clearly define what it is you want to learn from your survey. If you were writing a paper about the attention paid to politics by people under 30 years old as compared to those 30–50 years old, conducting a survey to try to measure those differences would be a logical approach.

Developing Survey Questions

Once you know what it is you hope to learn, you can begin writing questions for your survey. These questions will be of two types: questions to determine information about the person completing the survey (respondents) and questions to learn their attitude or behavior about a specific topic or issue.

Questions about Respondents.   For most surveys, you will want to know some basic information about the people you are surveying. What this consists of will vary depending on your focus. In a survey about the attention paid to politics by different age groups, for example, you would certainly need to ask respondents their age. You might also want to know their race, their gender, where they live, and even their party affiliation, although you should bear in mind that the more questions you ask, the more likely it is that fewer people will complete the survey.

Survey Questions.   When you create survey questions, there are some principals you should follow.

1. Keep your survey short. The longer it is, the less likely people are to complete it.

2. Keep in mind that people are less likely to answer questions that request a written response than questions that require yes/no, multiple choice, or ratings answers.

3. Only ask questions directly relevant to your goal. Every question should count.

4. Write questions clearly, so there is no confusion about what you are asking.

5. Only ask one question at a time. Reread your questions to check that you have not asked two questions in one, which can confuse respondents and lead to misleading results. If you have, determine if both are important and, if so, make them into two separate questions.

6. Do not word questions so that they lead people to answer them in a certain way. Questions should be unbiased in order to elicit an accurate response.

7. Include response scales when asking questions. Although asking binary (yes/no, true/false) questions is good for eliciting some kinds of information, using response scales allows people to provide an indication of how strongly they feel about a topic. So if you want to know more about how a person feels about an issue, instead of option (a) below, use option (b).

    a. True or False? Do politicians ever tell the truth?

    b. To what extent do you think politicians tell the truth?

       Not at all/Rarely/Sometimes/Often/Always

8. Test your survey on classmates, friends, or family members before using it. They will help you to spot errors, point out confusing questions, and may suggest corrections or even new questions. Revise based on their feedback.

As an example, for an essay on attention to politics, interview questions like the following are likely to produce useful evidence.

1. Circle the item below that most closely represents how often you read a newspaper.

   | Never | 1–2 times a week | 3–4 times a week |
   | 5–6 times a week | Every day | |

2. Circle the item below that most closely represents how often you watch television news.

   | Never | 1–2 times a week | 3–4 times a week |
   | 5–6 times a week | Every day | |

3. Did you vote in the most recent election?

   Yes   No

4. What is the last name of the current governor of your state?

   | Mitchel | Gregory | Tomlinson | Hernandez | Williams |

5. Have you attached a political bumper sticker to your car in the past year?

   Yes   No

Conducting a Survey

Once you have created your survey, you are ready to go to work on getting it into the hands of respondents. You may just sit down somewhere on campus and ask passersby to fill out the survey. If you have access to a mailing list, you can mail the survey out. If you have access to a list of emails, you can email it out, or you can use an online survey site like SurveyMonkey to host your survey.

To make sure your survey results are credible, you must make sure your survey includes a representative sample of respondents. For example, if you interview students in the parking lot, your sample would not be representative because you are omitting students who take a bus to school. Take these steps to ensure that your survey is representative:

1. Survey as large a group as you can.

2. Think of groups of people who have not been included in your survey and figure out a way to make sure they are included.

3. If you have access to a list of names and emails that is too large, randomize your choice of names by selecting, for example, only every twentieth name.

4. When you have compiled a list, check to see if it is representative, for example, by seeing whether men and women are equally represented.

Finally, you need to compile the results and determine how they fit into your essay.

22.12 Writing

Questions about Plagiarism

As you read Avoiding Plagiarism (22.13), make a list of questions you have about the topic.

22.13 Tutorial

Avoiding Plagiarism

Sometimes plagiarism seems like a very complicated and scary concept, but it doesn't need to be. If you plagiarize, you use the words and ideas of another person without giving them credit; you use them as though they are your own words. In American colleges and universities, plagiarism is considered a very serious academic offense and can result in failing grades or even more serious consequences.

Use Quotation Marks and Document Your Sources

Avoiding plagiarism is really simple: if you use the exact words of another writer, you must place them in quotation marks and provide an in-text citation that links to a works cited or references list; if you use the ideas of another writer you must give him or her credit and document the source. You cannot pretend that someone else's words or ideas are your own.

Hardly anyone has trouble understanding the first part: if you use someone else's words in something you're writing, you must put those words in quotation marks (see Quoting and Paraphrasing [22.8, p. 321] for more details). That part's easy, but then you also must provide a citation—a note in parentheses after the quoted words that tells readers where the quoted words came from so they can find the original source if they're interested. There are several systems for formatting these citations, two of which are discussed in detail in *The Hub*: MLA In-Text Citations (23.2, p. 338) and APA In-Text Citations (24.2, p. 374). Make sure you know which citation system your audience expects.

The definition of plagiarism above also discusses using someone else's *ideas*; that's the part that is sometimes harder to grasp. If, while doing research for a writing project, you read an article or a book in which the author makes a really good point that supports your thesis and if you take that idea and express it in your own words, you must *still* give the author credit for the idea. You must make it clear that the idea you are expressing, even if you express it completely in your own words, is an idea you got from another writer.

When you quote another writer's words exactly, you indicate that the words came from someone else by placing them inside quotation marks, but you don't use quotation marks if you are expressing someone else's ideas in your own words when you paraphrase or summarize. In these cases, you must indicate where the idea came from at the beginning of your paraphrase or summary and include an in-text citation after it that links to a works cited or references list, just as you do when you are quoting. As noted earlier, information on two of these documentation styles, MLA and APA, are available in *The Hub* in Topic 23 (MLA, p. 336) and Topic 24 (APA, p. 374).

Note that these principles apply not only to print sources but also to online sources, handwritten documents, spoken words, and even the words of other students.

Here's another important distinction. It is plagiarism if you use someone else's words or ideas without giving them credit through quotation marks and citations. However, if you make an error in the format of your citation, that is not plagiarism. It may be an error that affects your instructor's evaluation of your essay, but it is not plagiarism.

22.14 Tutorial

Synthesis

A well-written essay that uses sources doesn't just present them as a laundry list: "Cunningham says this," "Nguyen says that," and "Marcos says something else." Instead, it weaves them together, points our similarities and disagreements, and compares the methods they use to reach their conclusions. This process of weaving sources into a single conversation, called *synthesis*, can improve the effectiveness of your research.

How to Synthesize Sources

Synthesis is a skill we all practice in our daily lives. Imagine you are looking for a work study job, for example. You might talk to friends and classmates who work in various on-campus venues and ask them what they like and dislike about their jobs, the advantages and disadvantages of each. After thinking about what they all have to say, and taking into account your class schedule, past work experiences, and time limitations, you make a decision that working evenings in the library is your best option. If you're buying a new sound system, you might read *Consumer Reports*, research options on the internet, and talk to friends whose systems you like. Pulling together all this information and taking into account your preferences and needs is how you reach a decision about what to purchase.

In college, synthesis involves researching to locate a variety of sources on the topic you are going to write about, reading them carefully, comparing what they have to say, and then coming to your own conclusion about the issue. In fact, the goal of a research paper is not only to explain what other people have said or think about an issue and how they agree or disagree with each other but to come up with your own ideas about the subject.

In order to synthesize, keep the following in mind as you compare sources.

- What points do different sources agree on?

- What points do different sources disagree on?

- How are the sources different from each other? For example, are they looking at the same or different data, populations, time periods, solutions, and so on?

- How do the different sources support their positions? What types of evidence do they use, and how reliable and convincing is it?

- How do the sources treat the topic? Are they serious, providing significant support for their ideas, or are they expressing personal opinions with little hard evidence to support them?

Once you have a good idea of what your sources are saying, you need to think about what your position is on the issue. Are there sources that support your opinion? Are there ones that do not support your position but make a compelling argument you will need to counter? Once you know what you want to say, use synthesis to create a unified conversation among your sources and yourself.

Examples of Synthesis

Here are some examples of how a writer might synthesize sources in a paper.

1. A writer points out the agreement between two sources, but also acknowledges the differences between their analyses.

    > Slowinski and Smith agree that the current procedure for applying for financial aid is flawed, but they disagree on what the flaws are.

2. A writer points out that two sources agree on some but not all steps to solve a problem.

    > Gomez and Brown agree on three steps that could be taken to curb pollution, but they disagree on the fourth.

3. A writer points out that several sources reached similar conclusions even though the subjects they studied were quite different.

    > Based on studies of three different populations—farm workers in California, college students in Iowa, and hotel employees in the Hilton system—Stevens, Allen, and Crivello reach nearly identical conclusions.

4. A writer, while admitting there is disagreement about solutions to a problem, points to three sources' agreement on what the problem is.

    > Even though they disagree about the solutions we should enact, all three economists I have quoted agree that the extreme wealth gap in America between the very affluent and everyone else is a serious problem.

5. A writer instead of synthesizing two or three sources, synthesizes one source with her own views.

    > Fitzgerald's argument comes to the same conclusion that I have, but for very different reasons.

TOPIC 23
MLA Documentation

In English and in some humanities classes, you may be asked to use the MLA (Modern Language Association) system for documenting sources. These guidelines follow those set forth in the *MLA Handbook*, 8th edition (2016).

Navigating Topic 23

The tutorials listed below provide information about MLA in-text citations, works cited lists, and formatting for papers. You can work through the entire Topic on your own, learning about all the strategies and practicing them; work on items you've been assigned by your instructor; or choose those ones you would find helpful.

Introduction to MLA Style 336

23.1	Tutorial	Documenting Sources in MLA Style 337
23.2	Tutorial	MLA In-Text Citations 338
23.3	Tutorial	MLA Works Cited List 334
23.4	Tutorial	MLA-Style Formatting 359

Introduction to MLA Style

Rather than thinking of the MLA guidelines simply as rules to be followed, think of them as guidelines for participating in an academic community—a community in which the exchange and extension of ideas require a system. Even though the new guidelines present a system for citing many different kinds of sources, they don't cover everything, and at times you will find that you have to think critically to adapt the guidelines to the source you are using.

Topic 23 provides you with an overview of the MLA style plus guidelines for how to correctly cite and document sources using in-text citations and a works cited list. In addition, it contains information on how to correctly format a paper using MLA style.

Documenting Sources in MLA Style

There are often several possible ways to cite a source in the list of works cited. Think carefully about your context for using the source so you can identify the pieces of information that you should include and any other information that might be helpful to your readers. The first step is to identify elements that are commonly found in works that writers cite.

Author and Title

The first two elements, both of which are needed for many sources, are the author's name and the title of the work. Each of these elements is followed by a period.

> Author. Title.

Containers

The next step is to identify elements of what MLA calls the "container" for the work—any larger work that contains the source you are citing. The context in which you are discussing the source and the context in which you find the source will help you determine what counts as a container in each case. Some works are self-contained; if you watch a movie in a theater, the movie title is the title of your source, and you won't identify a separate container title. But if you watch the same movie as part of a DVD box set of the director's work, the container title is the name of the box set. Thinking about a source as nested in larger containers may help you to visualize how a citation works. (Also see Figure 1.)

Figure 1: Basic container information

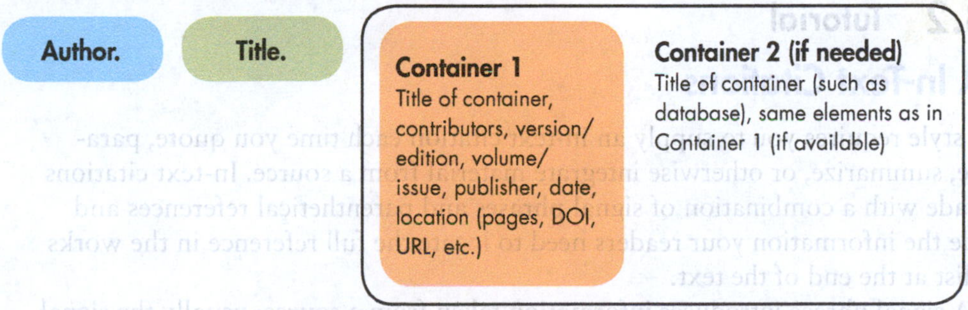

> Author. Title.
>
> **Container 1**
> Title of container, contributors, version/edition, volume/issue, publisher, date, location (pages, DOI, URL, etc.)
>
> **Container 2 (if needed)**
> Title of container (such as database), same elements as in Container 1 (if available)

The elements you may include in the "container" part of your citation include, in order, the title of the container; the name of contributors such as editors or translators; the version or edition; the volume and issue numbers; the publisher; the date of publication; and a location such as the page number, DOI, permalink, or URL. These elements are separated by commas, and the end of the container is marked with a period.

Most sources won't include *all* these pieces of information, so include only the elements that are relevant and available for an acceptable citation. If your container is itself a part of some larger container, such as a database, simply add information about the second container after the first one. You will find many examples of how elements and containers are combined to create works cited entries on pages in the MLA Works Cited List section. The General Guidelines for the Works Cited List also provide details about the information required for each element.

Works Cited Entry (one container)

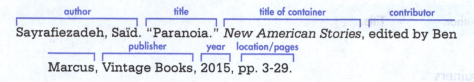

author | title | title of container | contributor
Sayrafiezadeh, Saïd. "Paranoia." *New American Stories*, edited by Ben

publisher | year | location/pages
Marcus, Vintage Books, 2015, pp. 3-29.

Works Cited Entry (two containers)

author | title
Coles, Kimberly Anne. "The Matter of Belief in John Donne's Holy Sonnets."

title of container 1 | volume, number | date | pages | title of container 2
Renaissance Quarterly, vol. 68, no. 3, Fall 2015, pp. 899-931. *JSTOR*,

location (DOI)
doi:10.1086/683855.

23.2 Tutorial
MLA In-Text Citations

MLA style requires you to supply an in-text citation each time you quote, paraphrase, summarize, or otherwise integrate material from a source. In-text citations are made with a combination of signal phrases and parenthetical references and include the information your readers need to locate the full reference in the works cited list at the end of the text.

A signal phrase introduces information taken from a source; usually the signal phrase includes the author's name. Parenthetical references include at least a page number (except for unpaginated sources, such as those found on the web). The list of works cited provides publication information about the source. There is a direct connection between the signal phrase and the first word or words in the works cited entry.

Sample Citation Using a Signal Phrase

In his discussion of Monty Python routines, Crystal notes that the group relished "breaking the normal rules" of language (107).

Sample Parenthetical Citation

A noted linguist explains that Monty Python humor often relied on "bizarre linguistic interactions" (Crystal 108).

Works Cited Entry

Crystal, David. *Language Play*. U of Chicago P, 1998.

Directory to MLA In-Text Citation Models

1. Author named in a signal phrase 339
2. Author named in a parenthetical reference 340
3. Digital or nonprint source 340
4. Two authors 340
5. Three or more authors 340
6. Organization as author 341
7. Unknown author 341
8. Two or more works by the same author 341
9. Two or more authors with the same last name 341
10. Indirect source (author quoting someone else) 341
11. Multivolume work 341
12. Work in an anthology or a collection 342
13. Government source 342
14. Entire work 342
15. Two or more sources in one citation 342
16. Personal communication or social media source 342
17. Literary work 342
18. Sacred text 343
19. Encyclopedia or dictionary entry 343
20. Visual 343
21. Legal source 343

Guidelines for In-Text Citations

1. Author named in a signal phrase Ordinarily, introduce the material being cited with a signal phrase that includes the author's name.

Lee claims that his comic-book creation Thor was actually "the first regularly published superhero to speak in a consistently archaic manner" (199).

2. Author named in a parenthetical reference When you do not mention the author in a signal phrase, include the author's last name before the page number(s), if any, in parentheses. Do not use punctuation between the author's name and the page number(s).

The word *Bollywood* is sometimes considered an insult because it implies that Indian movies are merely "a derivative of the American film industry" (Chopra 9).

3. Digital or nonprint source Give enough information in a signal phrase or in parentheses for readers to locate the source in your list of works cited—at least the author's name or title. If the source lacks page numbers but has numbered paragraphs, sections, or divisions, use those numbers with the appropriate abbreviation in your parenthetical citation. Do not add such numbers if the source itself does not use them.

Digital Source without Stable Page Numbers

As a *Slate* analysis has noted, "Prominent sports psychologists get praised for their successes and don't get grief for their failures" (Engber).

Digital Source with Numbered Pages

Julian Hawthorne points out that his father and Ralph Waldo Emerson, in their lives and their writing, "together . . . met the needs of nearly all that is worthy in human nature" (ch. 4).

4. Two authors Name both authors in a signal phrase or in parentheses.

Gilbert and Gubar point out that in the Grimm version of "Snow White," the king "never actually appears in this story at all" (37).

5. Three or more authors Use the first author's name followed by *et al.* ("and others") in either a signal phrase or parentheses.

Similarly, as Belenky et al. assert, examining the lives of women expands our understanding of human development (7).

6. Organization as author Give the group's full name in a signal phrase; in parentheses, abbreviate common words in the name.

> The American Diabetes Association estimates that the cost of diagnosed diabetes in the United States in 2012 was $245 billion.

> The cost of diagnosed diabetes in the United States in 2012 was estimated at $245 billion (Amer. Diabetes Assn.).

7. Unknown author Use the full title, if it is brief, in your text—or a shortened version of the title in parentheses.

> One analysis defines *hype* as "an artificially engendered atmosphere of hysteria" (*Today's* 51).

8. Two or more works by the same author Mention the title of the work in the signal phrase or include a short version of the title in the parentheses.

> Gardner shows readers their own silliness in his description of a "pointless, ridiculous monster, crouched in the shadows, stinking of dead men, murdered children, and martyred cows" (*Grendel* 2).

9. Two or more authors with the same last name Include the author's first and last name in the signal phrase or first initial and last name in the parentheses.

> One approach to the problem is to introduce nutrition literacy at the K–5 level in public schools (E. Chen 15).

10. Indirect source (author quoting someone else) Use the abbreviation *qtd. in* to indicate that you are using a source that is cited in another source.

> As Arthur Miller says, "When somebody is destroyed everybody finally contributes to it, but in Willy's case, the end product would be virtually the same" (qtd. in Martin and Meyer 375).

11. Multivolume work In the parenthetical citation, note the volume number first and then the page number(s), with a colon and one space between them.

> Modernist writers prized experimentation and gradually even sought to blur the line between poetry and prose, according to Forster (3: 150).

12. Work in an anthology or a collection Use the name of the author of the work, not the editor of the anthology, but use the page number(s) from the anthology.

> In "Love Is a Fallacy," the narrator's logical teachings disintegrate when Polly declares that she should date Petey because "[h]e's got a raccoon coat" (Shulman 391).

In the list of works cited, the work is alphabetized under Shulman, the author of the story, not under the name of the editor of the anthology.

> Shulman, Max. "Love Is a Fallacy." *Current Issues and Enduring Questions*, edited by Sylvan Barnet and Hugo Bedau, 9th ed., Bedford/St. Martin's, 2011, pp. 383-91.

13. Government source Your in-text citation should include the name of the country as well as the name of the agency responsible for the source (as given in the works cited entry). As for an organization as author, use common abbreviations in parentheses.

> To reduce the agricultural runoff into the Chesapeake Bay, the United States Environmental Protection Agency has argued that "[h]igh nutrient loading crops, such as corn and soybean, should be replaced with alternatives in environmentally sensitive areas" (26).

14. Entire work Use the author's name in a signal phrase or a parenthetical citation.

> Pollan explores the issues surrounding food production and consumption from a political angle.

15. Two or more sources in one citation List the authors (or titles) in alphabetical order and separate them with semicolons.

> Economists recommend that employment be redefined to include unpaid domestic labor (Clark 148; Nevins 39).

16. Personal communication or social media source Use the name of the author as given in the works cited list.

> According to @grammarphobia, the expression *if you will* "had a legitimate usage" before it became "empty filler."

17. Literary work Because literary works are often available in many different editions, cite the page number(s) from the edition you used followed by a semicolon; then give other identifying information that will lead readers to the passage in any edition. Indicate the act and/or scene in a play (e.g., 37; sc. 1). For a novel, indicate the part or chapter (e.g., 175; ch. 4).

> In utter despair, Dostoyevsky's character Mitya wonders aloud about the "terrible tragedies realism inflicts on people" (376; bk. 8, ch. 2).

For a poem, cite the part (if there is one) and line(s), separated by a period.

> Whitman speculates, "All goes onward and outward, nothing collapses, / And to die is different from what anyone supposed, and luckier" (6.129-30).

If you are citing only line numbers, use the word *line(s)* in the first reference (e.g., lines 21-22) and the line numbers alone in subsequent references (e.g., 34-36). For a verse play, give only the act, scene, and line numbers, separated by periods (e.g., 4.2.148-49).

18. Sacred text Give the title of the work as in the works cited entry, followed by the book, chapter, and verse (or their equivalent), separated with periods. Common abbreviations for books of the Bible are acceptable in a parenthetical reference.

> He ignored the admonition "Pride goes before destruction, and a haughty spirit before a fall" (*New Oxford Annotated Bible*, Prov. 16.18).

19. Encyclopedia or dictionary entry An entry in a reference work will be listed under the entry's title. Either in your text or in your parenthetical citation, mention the word or entry, enclosing it in quotation marks. Omit the page number if the reference work arranges entries alphabetically.

> The term *prion* was coined by Stanley B. Prusiner from the words *proteinaceous* and *infectious* and a suffix meaning *particle* ("Prion").

20. Visual To cite a visual that has a figure number in the source, use the abbreviation *fig.* and the number in place of a page number in your parenthetical citation: (Manning, fig. 4). If you refer to the figure in your text, spell out the word *figure*. To cite a visual that does not have a figure number in the source, use the visual's title or a description in your text and cite the author and page number as for any other source. Each visual that appears in your project should include a caption with the figure or table number (see p. 364) and information about the source.

21. Legal source For a legislative act (law) or court case, name the act or case either in a signal phrase or in parentheses. Italicize the names of cases but not the names of acts.

> The Jones Act of 1917 granted US citizenship to Puerto Ricans.

> In 1857, Chief Justice Roger B. Taney declared in *Dred Scott v. Sandford* that blacks, whether enslaved or free, could not be citizens of the United States.

MLA Works Cited List

An alphabetized list of works cited, which appears at the end of your project, gives publication information for each of the sources you have cited.

Directory to MLA Works Cited Models

GENERAL GUIDELINES FOR LISTING AUTHORS

1. Single author   347
2. Two authors   347
3. Three or more authors   348
4. Organization or group author   348
5. Unknown author   348
6. Author using a pseudonym (screen name)   348
7. Multiple works by the same author   348
8. Multiple works by the same group of authors   348

ARTICLES AND OTHER SHORT WORKS

9. Article in a magazine   349
10. Article in a journal   349
11. Article in a daily newspaper   349
12. Editorial in a newspaper   350
13. Letter to the editor   350
14. Review   350

BOOKS AND OTHER LONG WORKS

15. Basic format for a book   350
16. Author with an editor or translator   351
17. Editor   351
18. Work in an anthology or a collection   351
19. Multiple works from the same anthology or collection   351

20. Edition other than the first   351
21. Multivolume work   351
22. Encyclopedia or dictionary entry   351
23. Sacred text   352
24. Foreword, introduction, preface, or afterword   352
25. Book with a title in its title   352
26. Book in a series   352
27. Republished book   352
28. More than one publisher named   353
29. Graphic narrative or illustrated work   353

ONLINE SOURCES

30. Entire website   353
31. Short work from a website   353
32. Online book   353
33. Entire blog   353
34. Entry or comment in a blog   354
35. Email   354
36. Tweet   354
37. Posting on a social networking site   354

VISUAL, AUDIO, MULTIMEDIA, AND LIVE SOURCES

38. Work of art or photograph   354
39. Cartoon or comic strip   355
40. Advertisement   355

41.	Map or chart 355		51.	Lecture or public address 357
42.	Musical score 355		52.	Personal interview 357
43.	Sound recording 355			
44.	Film or video 356		**OTHER SOURCES**	
45.	Supplementary material accompanying a film 356		53.	Government publication 357
			54.	Legal source 358
46.	Radio or television program 356		55.	Pamphlet 358
47.	Radio or television interview 356		56.	Dissertation 358
48.	Podcast 356		57.	Published proceedings of a conference 358
49.	Short online audio segment or video 357		58.	Published interview 358
50.	Live performance 357		59.	Personal letter 358

General Guidelines for the Works Cited List

In the list of works cited, include only sources that you have quoted, summarized, or paraphrased in your project. MLA's guidelines are applicable to a wide variety of sources. At times you may find that you have to adapt the guidelines and models in this section to source types you encounter in your research.

Organization of the List

The elements, or pieces of information, needed for a works cited entry are the following:

- The author (if a work has one)
- The title
- The title of the larger work in which the source is located (MLA calls this a "container")—a collection, a journal, a magazine, a website, and so on
- As much of the following information as is available about the source and the container, listed in this order:
  - Editor, translator, director, performer
  - Version
  - Volume and issue numbers
  - Publisher or sponsor
  - Date of publication
  - Location of the source: page numbers, DOI, URL, and so on

Not all sources will require every element. For more information on identifying and organizing source elements, see Unit 23.1 (p. 337). See specific models in this section for more details.

Authors

- Arrange the list alphabetically by authors' last names or by titles for works with no authors.
- For the first author, place the last name first, a comma, and the first name. Put a second author's name in normal order (first name followed by last name). For three or more authors, use *et al.* after the first author's name.
- Spell out *editor, translator, edited by,* and so on.

Titles

- In titles of works, capitalize all words except articles (*a, an, the*), prepositions, coordinating conjunctions, and the *to* in infinitives—unless the word is first or last in the title or subtitle.
- Use quotation marks for titles of articles and other short works.
- Italicize titles of books and other long works, including websites.

Publication Information

- MLA does not require the place of publication for a book publisher.
- Use the complete version of publishers' names, except for terms such as *Inc.* and *Co.*; retain terms such as *Books* and *Press*. For university publishers, use *U* and *P* for *University* and *Press*, respectively.
- For a book, take the name of the publisher from the title page (or from the copyright page if it is not on the title page). For a website, the publisher might be at the bottom of a page or on the *About* page. If a work has two or more publishers, separate the names with slashes.
- If the title of a website and the publisher are the same or similar, use the title of the site but omit the publisher.

Dates

- For a book, give the most recent year on the title page or the copyright page. For a web source, use the copyright date or the most recent update date. Use the complete date as listed in the source.

- Abbreviate all months except May, June, and July and give the date in inverted form: 13 Mar. 2018.

- If the source has no date, give your date of access at the end: Accessed 24 Feb. 2018.

Page Numbers

- For most articles and other short works, give page numbers when they are available in the source, preceded by *p.* (or *pp.* for more than one page).

- Do not use the page numbers from a printout of a source.

- If an article does not appear on consecutive pages, give the number of the first page followed by a plus sign: 35+.

URLs and DOIs

- Give a permalink or a DOI (digital object identifier) if a source has one. (See item 10.)

- If a source does not have a permalink or a DOI, include a URL (omitting the protocol, such as http://). (See item 9.)

- For a library's subscription database, such as Academic ASAP, that does not provide a permalink or a DOI, include only the basic URL for the database home page. (See the last example in item 9.)

- For open databases and archives, such as Google Books, give the complete URL for the source. (See item 32.)

General Guidelines for Listing Authors

Alphabetize entries in the list of works cited by authors' last names (or by title if a work has no author). The author's name is important because citations in the text refer to it and readers will therefore look for it to identify the source in the list.

1. Single author Give the author's last name, followed by a comma, then give the first name, followed by a period.

> Cronin, David.

2. Two authors List the authors in the order in which the source lists them. Reverse the name of only the first author.

> Stiglitz, Joseph E., and Bruce C. Greenwald.

3. Three or more authors List the author whose name appears first in the source followed by *et al.* (Latin for "and others").

> Lupton, Ellen, et al.

4. Organization or group author When the author is a corporation, a government agency, or some other organization, begin with the name of the organization.

> Human Rights Watch.

> United States, Government Accountability Office.

5. Unknown author Begin with the work's title. Titles of short works are put in quotation marks. Titles of long works are italicized.

Article or Other Short Work

> "California Sues EPA over Emissions."

Book, Entire Website, or Other Long Work

> *Women of Protest: Photographs from the Records of the National Woman's Party.*

Television Program

> "Fast Times at West Philly High."

6. Author using a pseudonym (screen name) Use the author's name as it appears in the source, followed by the author's real name in parentheses, if you know it.

> Atrios (Duncan Black).

> JennOfArk.

7. Multiple works by the same author Alphabetize the works by title, ignoring the article *A*, *An*, or *The* at the beginning. Use the author's name for the first entry only. For subsequent entries, use three hyphens followed by a period.

> Coates, Ta-Nehisi. *The Beautiful Struggle: A Father, Two Sons, and an Unlikely Road to Manhood.* Spiegel and Grau, 2008.

> ---. *Between the World and Me.* Spiegel and Grau, 2015.

8. Multiple works by the same group of authors Alphabetize the works by title. For the first entry, use the authors' names in the proper form (see items 1–4). Begin subsequent entries with three hyphens and a period. The three hyphens must stand for the same names(s) as in the first entry.

Agha, Hussein, and Robert Malley. "The Arab Counterrevolution." *The New York Review of Books*, 29 Sept. 2011, www.nybooks.com/articles/2011/09/29/arab-counterrevolution/.

---. "This Is Not a Revolution." *The New York Review of Books*, 8 Nov. 2012, www.nybooks.com/articles/2012/11/08/not-revolution/.

Articles and Other Short Works

9. Article in a magazine Use the complete date given in the source.

Butler, Kiera. "Works Well with Others." *Mother Jones*, Jan./Feb. 2008, pp. 66-69.

Leonard, Andrew. "The Surveillance State High School." *Salon*, 27 Nov. 2012, www.salon.com/2012/11/27/the_surveillance_state_high_school/.

Sanneh, Kelefa. "Skin in the Game." *The New Yorker*, 24 Mar. 2014, pp. 48-55.

Sharp, Kathleen. "The Rescue Mission." *Smithsonian*, Nov. 2015, pp. 40-49. *OmniFile Full Text Select*, web.b.ebscohost.com.ezproxy.bpl.org/.

10. Article in a journal Give the volume number and issue number for all journals.

Bryson, Devin. "The Rise of a New Senegalese Cultural Philosophy?" *African Studies Quarterly*, vol. 14, no. 3, Mar. 2014, pp. 33-56, asq.africa.ufl.edu/files/Volume-14-Issue-3-Bryson.pdf.

Coles, Kimberly Anne. "The Matter of Belief in John Donne's Holy Sonnets." *Renaissance Quarterly*, vol. 68, no. 3, Fall 2015, pp. 899-931. *JSTOR*, doi:10.1086/683855.

Matchie, Thomas. "Law versus Love in *The Round House*." *Midwest Quarterly*, vol. 56, no. 4, Summer 2015, pp. 353-64.

11. Article in a daily newspaper

Salsberg, Bob. "Children's Wellness Initiative Unveiled." *Daily Hampshire Gazette*, 30 July 2019, pp. 1+.

Wolfers, Justin, et al. "1.5 Million Missing Black Men." *The New York Times*, 20 Apr. 2015, nyti.ms/1P5Gpa7.

12. Editorial in a newspaper Add the word *Editorial* after the title (and before any database information).

> "Lunar Landing a Shining Moment with Local Ties." *Daily Hampshire Gazette*, 20 July 2019, p. A6. Editorial.

> "The Road toward Peace." *The New York Times*, 15 Feb. 1945, p. 18. Editorial. *ProQuest Historical Newspapers: The New York Times*, search .proquest.com/hnpnewyorktimes.

13. Letter to the editor

> Starr, Evva. "Local Reporting Thrives in High Schools." *The Washington Post*, 4 Apr. 2014, wpo.st/7hmJ1. Letter.

14. Review Name the reviewer and the title of the review, if any, followed by the words *Review of* and the title and author or director of the work or performance reviewed. Then add information for the publication in which the review appears.

> O'Hehir, Andrew. "Aronofsky's Deranged Biblical Action Flick." Review of *Noah*, directed by Darren Aronofsky. *Salon*, 27 May 2014, www.salon.com/2014/03/27/noah_aronofskys_deranged_biblical _action_flick/.

> Spychalski, John C. Review of *American Railroads—Decline and Renaissance in the Twentieth Century*, by Robert E. Gallamore and John R. Meyer. *Transportation Journal*, vol. 54, no. 4, Fall 2015, pp. 535-38.

> Walton, James. "Noble, Embattled Souls." Review of *The Bone Clocks* and *Slade House*, by David Mitchell. *The New York Review of Books*, 3 Dec. 2015, pp. 55-58.

Books and Other Long Works

15. Basic format for a book For most books, supply the author name(s); the title and subtitle, in italics; the name of the publisher; and the year of publication. If you have used an e-book, give the e-reader type at the end of the entry.

> Wohlleben, Peter. *The Hidden Life of Trees*. William Collins, 2016. Kindle.

> Levs, Josh. *All In: How Our Work-First Culture Fails Dads, Families, and Businesses—and How We Can Fix It Together*. HarperCollins, 2015.

16. Author with an editor or translator

Ullmann, Regina. *The Country Road: Stories*. Translated by Kurt Beals, New
Directions Publishing, 2015.

17. Editor

Wall, Cheryl A., editor. *Changing Our Own Words: Essays on Criticism,
Theory, and Writing by Black Women*. Rutgers UP, 1989.

18. Work in an anthology or a collection
Begin with the name of the author of the
selection, not with the name of the anthology editor.

Sayrafiezadeh, Saïd. "Paranoia." *New American Stories*, edited by Ben
Marcus, Vintage Books, 2015, pp. 3-29.

19. Multiple works from the same anthology or collection
Provide an entry for the
entire anthology and a shortened entry for each selection. Alphabetize the entries by
authors' or editors' last names.

Eisenberg, Deborah. "Some Other, Better Otto." Marcus, pp. 94-136.

Marcus, Ben, editor. *New American Stories*. Vintage Books, 2015.

Sayrafiezadeh, Saïd. "Paranoia." Marcus, pp. 3-29.

20. Edition other than the first

Walker, John A. *Art in the Age of Mass Media*. 3rd ed., Pluto Press, 2001.

21. Multivolume work
Include the total number of volumes at the end of the
citation. If the volumes were published over several years, give the inclusive dates of
publication. If you cite only one of the volumes, include the volume number before
the publisher and give the date of publication for that volume.

Stark, Freya. *Letters*. Edited by Lucy Moorehead, Compton Press, 1974-82. 8 vols.

Stark, Freya. *Letters*. Edited by Lucy Moorehead, vol. 5, Compton Press,
1978. 8 vols.

22. Encyclopedia or dictionary entry

"House Music." *Wikipedia*, 16 Nov. 2015, en.wikipedia.org/wiki/
House_music.

Robinson, Lisa Clayton. "Harlem Writers Guild." *Africana: The Encyclopedia of the African and African American Experience*, 2nd ed., Oxford UP, 2005.

23. Sacred text Give the title of the edition of the sacred text (taken from the title page), italicized; the editor's or translator's name (if any); and publication information. Add the name of the version, if there is one, before the publisher.

The Oxford Annotated Bible with the Apocrypha. Edited by Herbert G. May and Bruce M. Metzger, Revised Standard Version, Oxford UP, 1965.

Qur'an: The Final Testament (Authorized English Version) with Arabic Text. Translated by Rashad Khalifa, Universal Unity, 2000.

24. Foreword, introduction, preface, or afterword Begin with the author of the book part, the part title (if any), and a label for the part. Then give the title of the book, the author or editor preceded by *by* or *edited by*, and publication information. If the part author and book author are the same, use only the last name with the book title.

Sullivan, John Jeremiah. "The Ill-Defined Plot." Introduction. *The Best American Essays 2014*, edited by Sullivan, Houghton Mifflin Harcourt, 2014, pp. xvii-xxvi.

25. Book with a title in its title If the book title contains a title normally italicized, do not italicize the title within the book title. If the book title contains a title normally placed in quotation marks, retain the quotation marks and italicize the entire title.

Lethem, Jonathan. *"Lucky Alan" and Other Stories*. Doubleday, 2015.

Masur, Louis P. *Runaway Dream: Born to Run and Bruce Springsteen's American Vision*. Bloomsbury, 2009.

26. Book in a series After the publication information, list the series name as it appears on the title page.

Denham, A. E., editor. *Plato on Art and Beauty*. Palgrave Macmillan, 2012. Philosophers in Depth.

27. Republished book After the title of the book, cite the original publication date, followed by the current publication information.

de Mille, Agnes. *Dance to the Piper*. 1951. Introduction by Joan Acocella, New York Review Books, 2015.

28. More than one publisher named If the book was published by two or more publishers, separate the publishers with a slash, and include a space before and after the slash.

> Hornby, Nick. About a Boy. Riverhead / Penguin Putnam, 1998.

29. Graphic narrative or illustrated work Begin with the author or illustrator who is most important to your research. List other contributors after the title, labeling their contribution. If the author and illustrator are the same, cite the work as you would cite a book.

> Stavans, Ilan, writer. *Latino USA: A Cartoon History*. Illustrated by Lalo
> Arcaraz, Basic Books, 2000.

> Weaver, Dustin, illustrator. *The Tenth Circle*. By Jodi Picoult, Washington
> Square Press, 2006.

Online Sources

30. Entire website If the website does not have an update date or publication date, include your date of access at the end (see the first example in item 31).

> Glazier, Loss Pequeño, director. *Electronic Poetry Center*. State U of New
> York at Buffalo, 2019, epc.buffalo.edu/.

31. Short work from a website

> Bali, Karan. "Kishore Kumar." *Upperstall.com*, upperstall.com/profile/
> kishore-kumar/. Accessed 2 Mar. 2016.

> Enzinna, Wes. "Syria's Unknown Revolution." *Pulitzer Center on*
> *Crisis Reporting*, 24 Nov. 2015, pulitzercenter.org/projects/
> middle-east-syria-enzinna-war-rojava.

32. Online book After the book publication information, include the title of the site in italics, the year of online publication, and the URL for the work.

> Euripides. *The Trojan Women*. Translated by Gilbert Murray, Oxford UP,
> 1915. Internet *Sacred Text Archive*, 2011, www.sacred-texts.com/cla/
> eurip/troj_w.htm.

33. Entire blog Cite a blog as you would an entire website (see item 30).

> Kiuchi, Tatsuro. *Tatsuro Kiuchi: News & Blog*, tatsurokiuchi.com/. Accessed 3
> Mar. 2016.

> Ng, Amy. *Pikaland*. Pikaland Media, 2015, www.pikaland.com/.

34. Entry or comment in a blog Cite a blog post as you would a short work from a website (see item 31). If you are citing a comment, list the screen name of the commenter, and use the label *Comment on* before the title of the blog post.

Edroso, Roy. "Going Down with the Flagship." *Alicublog*, 24 Feb. 2016,
alicublog.blogspot.com/2014/04/friends-in-high-places.html.

trex. Comment on "Going Down with the Flagship," by Roy Edroso.
Alicublog, 24 Feb. 2016, alicublog.blogspot.com/2016/02/going-down
-with-flagship.html#disqus_thread.

35. Email

Thornbrugh, Caitlin. "Coates Lecture." Received by Rita Anderson,
20 Oct. 2018.

36. Tweet Give the text of the entire tweet in quotation marks, using the writer's capitalization and punctuation. Follow the text with the date and time noted on the tweet, and end with the URL.

@John Cleese. "Yes, I am still indeed alive, contrary to rumour, and
am performing the silly walk in my new app (link: http://www
.thesillywalk.com) thesillywalk.com." *Twitter*, 30 July 2019,
twitter.com/JohnCleese.

37. Posting on a social networking site Cite as a short work from a website (see item 31). Use the text accompanying the post as the title, in quotation marks, if such text is available. If the post has no title or text, use the label *Post*.

kevincannon. "Portrait of Norris Hall in #Savannah, GA—home (for a few
more months, anyway) of #SCAD's sequential art department."
Instagram, Mar. 2014, www.instagram.com/p/lgmqk4i6DC/.

Visual, Audio, Multimedia, and Live Sources

38. Work of art or photograph Cite the artist's name, the title of the artwork or photograph, italicized; the date of composition; and the institution and the city in which the artwork is located. For works located online, include the title of the site and the URL of the work. For a photograph, use the label *Photograph* at the end if it is not clear from the source.

Bronzino, Agnolo. *Lodovico Capponi*. 1550-55, Frick Collection, New York.

Hura, Sohrab. *Old Man Lighting a Fire*. 2015, *Magnum Photos*,
www.magnumphotos.com/C.aspx?VP3=SearchResult
&ALID=2K1HRG681B_Q.

39. Cartoon or comic strip

Flake, Emily. *The New Yorker*, 13 Apr. 2015, p. 66. Cartoon.

Munroe, Randall. "Heartbleed Explanation." *xkcd.com*, xkcd.com/1354/.
Comic strip.

40. Advertisement

Ameritrade. *Wired*, Jan. 2014, p. 47. Advertisement.

Toyota. *The Root*. Slate Group, 28 Nov. 2015, www.theroot.com.
Advertisement.

41. Map or chart
Cite as a short work within a longer work. If the title does not identify the item as a map or chart, add *Map* or *Chart* at the end of the entry.

"Australia." *Perry-Castañeda Library Map Collection*, U of Texas, 1999,
www.lib.utexas.edu/maps/australia/australia_pol99.jpg.

California. Rand McNally, 2002. Map.

42. Musical score

Beethoven, Ludwig van. Symphony no. 5 in C minor, op. 67. 1807. *Center
for Computer Assisted Research in the Humanities*, Stanford U, 2000,
scores.ccarh.org/beethoven/sym/beethoven-sym5-1.pdf.

43. Sound recording
Begin with the name of the person or group you want to emphasize. For a single work from an album or collection, place the title in quotation marks and the album or collection in italics. For a long work, give the title, italicized; the names of pertinent artists; and the orchestra and conductor (if relevant). End with the manufacturer and the date.

Bach, Johann Sebastian. *Bach: Violin Concertos*. Performances by Itzhak
Perlman and Pinchas Zukerman, English Chamber Orchestra,
EMI, 2002.

Sonic Youth. "Incinerate." *Rather Ripped*, Geffen, 2006.

44. Film or video If you cite a particular person's work, start with that name. If not, start with the title of the film; then name the director, distributor, and year of release. Other contributors, such as writers or performers, may follow the director.

> Downey Jnr., Robert, performer. *Avengers: Endgame.* Directed by Anthony
> and Joe Russo, Walt Disney Studios Motion Pictures, 2019.
>
> Scott, Ridley, director. *The Martian.* Performances by Matt Damon, Jessica
> Chastain, Kristen Wiig, and Kate Mara, Twentieth Century Fox, 2015.

45. Supplementary material accompanying a film Begin with the title of the feature, in quotation marks, and the names of any important contributors. End with information about the film, as in item 44, and about the location of the supplementary material.

> "Sweeney's London." Produced by Eric Young. *Sweeney Todd: The Demon
> Barber of Fleet Street*, directed by Tim Burton, DreamWorks, 2007, disc 2.

46. Radio or television program If you are citing a particular episode or segment, begin with the title in quotation marks. Then give the program title in italics. List important contributors (narrator, writer, director, actors), the network, and the date of broadcast.

> "Free Speech on College Campuses." *Washington Journal*, narrated by Peter
> Slen, C-SPAN, 27 Nov. 2015.
>
> "Obama's Failures Have Made Millennials Give Up Hope." *The Rush
> Limbaugh Show*, narrated by Rush Limbaugh, Premiere Radio
> Networks, 14 Apr. 2014, www.rushlimbaugh.com/daily/2014/04/14/
> obama_s_failures_have_made_millennials_give_up_hope.

47. Radio or television interview Begin with the name of the person who was interviewed, followed by *Interview by* and the interviewer's name, if relevant. End with information about the program as in item 46.

> Wang, Lulu. Interview by Terry Gross. *Fresh Air*, WNYC, 26 July 2019.

48. Podcast Cite a podcast as you would a short work from a website (see item 31).

> McDougall, Christopher. "How Did Endurance Help Early Humans
> Survive?" *TED Radio Hour*, National Public Radio, 20 Nov.
> 2015, www.npr.org/2015/11/20/455904655/how-did
> -endurance-help-early-humans-survive.

49. Short online audio segment or video Cite a short online audio segment or video as you would a short work from a website (see item 31).

Fletcher, Antoine. "The Ancient Art of the Atlatl." *Russell Cave National Monument*, narrated by Brenton Bellomy, National Park Service, 12 Feb. 2014, www.nps.gov/media/video/view.htm?id=C92C0D0A-1DD8-B71C-07CBC6E8970CD73F.

Nayar, Vineet. "Employees First, Customers Second." *YouTube*, 9 June 2015, www.youtube.com/watch?v=cCdu67s_C5E.

50. Live performance Begin with the title of the work performed and the author or composer of the work. Include relevant information such as the director, the choreographer, the conductor, or the major performers. End with the theater, ballet, or opera company, if any; the theater and location; and the date of the performance.

Concerto for Trumpet and Orchestra. By Detlev Glanert, conducted by Andris Nelsons, performances by Thomas Rolfs and Boston Symphony Orchestra, Tanglewood Music Center, Lennox, 8 July 2019.

51. Lecture or public address Cite the speaker's name, followed by the title of the lecture (if any) in quotation marks, the organization sponsoring the lecture, the location, and the date.

Ferrera, America. "My Identity Is a Superpower." *Ted.com*, Apr. 2019, www.ted.com/talks/america_ferrera_my_identity_is_a_superpower_not_an_obstacle.

Eugenides, Jeffrey. Portland Arts and Lectures. Arlene Schnitzer Concert Hall, Portland, OR, 30 Sept. 2003.

52. Personal interview Begin with the name of the person interviewed. Then write *Personal interview* followed by the date of the interview.

Freedman, Sasha. Personal interview, 10 Nov. 2018.

Other Sources

53. Government publication Treat the government agency as the author, giving the name of the government followed by the name of the department and agency.

United States, Department of Health and Human Services. *Keep the Beat Recipes: Deliciously Healthy Dinners*. National Institutes of Health, Oct. 2009, healthyeating.nhlbi.nih.gov/pdfs/Dinners_Cookbook_508-compliant.pdf.

54. Legal source For a legislative act (law), give the name of the act, neither italicized nor in quotation marks, followed by the Public Law number, the Statutes at Large information, and the date of enactment.

> Museum and Library Services Act of 2003. Pub. L. 108-81. Stat. 117.991.
>
> 25 Sept. 2003.

For a court case, name the first plaintiff and the first defendant. Then give the law report number, the court name, the year of the decision, and publication information. In a works cited entry, the name of the case is not italicized. (The name of the case is italicized in your in-text citation.)

> Citizens United vs. FEC. 558 US 310. Supreme Court of the US. 2010. *Legal Information Institute*, Cornell U Law School, www.law.cornell.edu/supct/pdf/08-205P.ZS.

55. Pamphlet

> Rainie, Lee, and Maeve Duggan. *Privacy and Information Sharing*. Pew Research Center, 14 Jan. 2016, www.pewinternet.org/files/2016/01/PI_2016.01.14_Privacy-and-Info-Sharing_FINAL.pdf.

56. Dissertation

> Thompson, Brian. "I'm Better Than You and I Can Prove It: Games, Expertise and the Culture of Competition." Dissertation, Stanford U, 2015.

57. Published proceedings of a conference

> Meisner, Marx S., et al., editors. *Communication for the Commons: Revisiting Participation and Environment*. Proceedings of Twelfth Biennial Conference on Communication and the Environment, 6-11 June 2015, Swedish U of Agricultural Sciences. International Environmental Communication Association, 2015.

58. Published interview

> Blume, Judy. "Judy Blume in Conversation with Lena Dunham." Interview by Lena Dunham. *The Believer*, vol. 12, no. 1, Jan. 2014, pp. 39+.

59. Personal letter

> Primak, Shoshana. Letter to the author, 6 May 2019.

23.4 Tutorial

MLA-Style Formatting

The following guidelines are consistent with advice given in the *MLA Handbook*, 8th edition (2016), and with typical requirements for student projects. If you are creating a nonprint project or have formatting questions, it's always a good idea to check with your instructor before preparing your final draft.

Formatting an MLA Project

First page and title page. The MLA does not require a title page. Type each of the following items on a separate line on the first page, beginning one inch from the top and flush with the left margin: your name, the instructor's name, the course name and number, and the date. Double-space between items; then doublespace again and center the title. Double-space between the title and the beginning of the text.

Margins and spacing. Leave one-inch margins at the top and bottom and on both sides of each page. Double-space the entire text, including set-off quotations, notes, and the list of works cited. Indent the first line of a paragraph one-half inch.

Page numbers. Include your last name and the page number on each page, one-half inch below the top and flush with the right margin.

Long quotations. Set off a long quotation (one with more than four typed lines) in block format by starting it on a new line and indenting each line one-half inch from the left margin. Do not enclose the passage in quotation marks.

Headings. MLA style allows, but does not require, headings. Many students and instructors find them helpful.

Visuals. Place tables, photographs, drawings, charts, graphs, and other figures as near as possible to the relevant text. Tables should have a label and number (e.g., Table 1) and a clear caption. For a table that you have borrowed or adapted, give the source below the table in a note like the following:

> Source: Boris Groysberg and Michael Slind, "Leadership Is a Conversation," *Harvard Business Review*, June 2012, p. 83.

All other visuals should be labeled *Figure* (abbreviated *Fig.*), numbered, and captioned. The label and caption should appear on the same line, followed by the source information. Remember to refer to each visual in your text, indicating how it contributes to the point you are making.

Formatting an MLA Works Cited List

Begin the works cited list on a new page at the end of the project. Center the title *Works Cited* one inch from the top of the page. Double-space throughout.

Alphabetizing the list.   Alphabetize the list by the last names of the authors (or editors); if a work has no author or editor, alphabetize by the first word of the title other than *A*, *An*, or *The*.

Indenting the entries.   Do not indent the first line of each works cited entry, but indent any additional lines one-half inch.

Breaking URLs.   If you need to include a URL in a works cited entry and it must be divided across lines, break it only after a slash or a double slash or before any other mark of punctuation. Do not add a hyphen. If you will post your project online or submit it electronically and you want your readers to click on your URLs, do not insert any line breaks.

Sample Pages from Student Writing in MLA Style

The following pages show samples from student writing using MLA style and following typical requirements for student projects.

- Basic MLA format   361
- Title page   362
- Long quotation   363
- Visual in text (created by student)   364
- Visual in text   365
- Works cited list   366
- Sample MLA research project   367

Basic MLA Format

Writer's name, instructor's name, course title, and date flush left on first page; title centered

Writer's last name and page number in upper right corner of each page

Double-spacing throughout

Page numbers in parentheses for quotation from source

1"

½" Larson 1

Dan Larson

Professor Duncan

English 102

19 April XXXX

The Transformation of Mrs. Peters:

An Analysis of "A Jury of Her Peers"

½" In Susan Glaspell's 1917 short story "A Jury of Her Peers," two women accompany their husbands and a county attorney to an isolated house where a farmer named John Wright has been choked to death in his bed with a rope. The chief suspect is Wright's wife, Minnie, who is in jail awaiting trial. The sheriff's wife, Mrs. Peters, has come along to gather some personal items for Minnie, and Mrs. Hale has joined her. Early in the story, Mrs. Hale sympathizes with Minnie and objects to the way the male investigators are "snoopin' round and criticizin' " her kitchen (249). In contrast, Mrs. Peters shows respect for the law, saying that the men are doing "no more than their duty" (249). By the end of the story, however, Mrs. Peters has joined Mrs. Hale in a conspiracy of silence, lied to the men, and committed a crime—hiding key evidence. What causes this dramatic change?

The first evidence that Mrs. Peters reaches understanding on her own surfaces in the following passage:

> The sheriff's wife had looked from the stove to the sink—to the pail of water which had been carried in from outside. . . . That look of seeing into things, of seeing through a thing to something else, was in the eyes of the sheriff's wife now. (251-52)

Something about the stove, the sink, and the pail of water connects with her own experiences, and she can imagine Minnie's life.

1"

Name, instructor, course, and date aligned at left

1"

Craig 1

½"

David Craig

Professor Turkman

English 219

18 December XXXX

Title centered

Messaging: The Language of Youth Literacy

The English language is under attack. At least, that is what many people seem to believe. From concerned parents to local librarians, everyone seems to have a negative comment on the state of youth literacy today. They fear that the current generation of grade school students will graduate with an extremely low level of literacy, and they point out that although language education hasn't changed, kids are having more trouble reading and writing than in the past. Many adults blame technologies such as texting and instant messaging. But although the arguments against messaging are passionate, evidence suggests that they may not hold up.

The disagreements about messaging shortcuts are profound, even among academics. John Briggs, an English professor at the University of California, Riverside, says, "Americans have always been informal, but now the informality of precollege culture is so ubiquitous that many students have no practice in using language in any formal setting at all" (qtd. in McCarroll). Such objections are not new; Sven Birkerts of Mount Holyoke College argued in 1999 that "[students] read more casually. They strip-mine what they read" online and consequently produce "quickly generated, casual prose" (qtd. in Leibowitz A67). However, academics are also among the defenders of texting and many recognize the power of informal language.

Indirect quotation uses *qtd. in* and author of Web source on list of works cited

Mercer-Golden 3

Two social enterprises, Nika Water and Belu, provide perfect examples. Both sell bottled water in the developed world with the mission of providing clean water to impoverished communities through their profits. Both have visionary leaders who define a critical lesson: financial pragmatism will add far more value to the world than idealistic dreams. Nika Water founder Jeff Church explained this in a speech at Stanford University:

> Social entrepreneurs look at their businesses as nine parts cause, one part business. In the beginning, it needs to be nine parts business, one part cause, because if the business doesn't stay around long enough because it can't make it, you can't do anything about the cause.

When U.K.-based Belu lost £600,000 ($940,000) in 2007, it could only give around £30,000 ($47,000) to charity. Karen Lynch took over as CEO, cutting costs, outsourcing significant parts of the company's operations, and redesigning the entire business model; the company now donates four times as much to charity (Hurley). The conventional portrayal of do-gooders is that they tend to be terrible businesspeople, an argument often grounded in reality. It is easy to criticize the Walmarts of the world for caring little about sustainability or social good, but the idealists with big visions who do not follow through on their promises because their businesses cannot survive are no more praiseworthy.

Walmart should learn from nonprofits and social enterprises how to advance a positive environmental and social agenda.

Long quotation indented ½" from left

Visual in Text (Created by Student)

Discussion of findings presented in Fig. 2

My research shows that the popular messaging culture contains at least some elements of its own language (Fig. 2). It also seems that much of this language is new: no formal dictionary yet identifies the most common messaging words and phrases. Only in the heyday of the telegraph or on the rolls of a stenographer would you find a similar situation, but these "languages" were never a popular medium of youth communication. Texting and instant messaging, however, are very popular among young people and continue to generate attention and debate in academic circles.

Writer's name and page number in upper right corner

     Messaging is certainly widespread, and it does seem to have its own particular vocabulary, yet these two factors alone do not mean it has a damaging influence on youth literacy. As noted earlier, however, some people claim that the new technology is a threat to the English language.

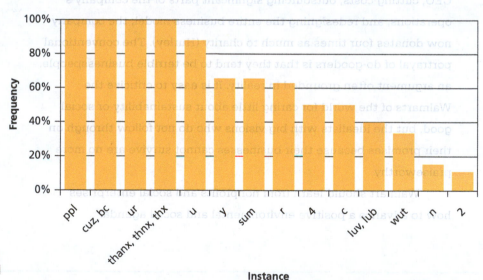

Figure labeled and captioned

Fig. 2. Usage of phonetic replacements and abbreviations in messaging

Song 3

The Bechdels' elaborately restored house is the gilded, but tense, context of young Alison's familial relationships and a metaphor for her father's deceptions. Alongside an image of her father taking a photo of their family, shown in Figure 2, Bechdel says, "He used his skillful artifice not to make things, but to make things appear to be what they were not" (*Fun* 16). The scene represents the nature of her father's artifice; her father is *posing* a photo, an image of their family.

Fig. 2. Alison's father posing a family photo (Bechdel, *Fun* 16)

In that same scene, Bechdel also shows her own sleight of hand; she manipulates the scene and reverses her father's role and her own to show young Alison taking the photograph of the family and her father posing in Alison's place (Fig. 3). In the image, young Alison symbolizes Bechdel in the present—looking back through the camera lens to create a portrait of her family. But unlike her father, she isn't using false images to deceive. Bechdel overcomes the treason of images by confessing herself as an "artificer" to her audience (*Fun* 16). Bechdel doesn't villainize the illusory nature of images; she repurposes their illusory power to . . . reinterpret her memories.

Reference to figure in text

Figure number, caption, and source citation

Works Cited List

Title *Works Cited* centered

List alphabetized by authors' last names (or by title when a work has no author)

Double-spacing used throughout; first line of each entry at left margin, additional lines indented ½"

Access date used for a Web source that has no update date

Works Cited

Gillmor, Dan. *We the Media: Grassroots Journalism by the People, for the People*. O'Reilly Media, 2006.

Glaser, Mark. "NOLA.com Blogs and Forums Help Save Lives after Katrina." *OJR: The Online Journalism Review*, Knight Digital Media Center, 13 Sept. 2005, www.ojr.org/050913glaser/.

Hazinski, David. "Unfettered 'Citizen Journalism' Too Risky." *Atlanta Journal-Constitution*, 13 Dec. 2007, p. 23A. *General OneFile*, go .galegroup.com/ps/.

Jones, Alex S. *Losing the News: The Future of the News That Feeds Democracy*. Oxford UP, 2009.

Sapin, Rachel. "Credit-Shy: Younger Generation Is More Likely to Stick to a Cash-Only Policy." *The Denver Post*, 26 Aug. 2013, www.denverpost.com/ci_23929523/credit-shy-younger -generation-stick-cash-only-policy.

"The 2006 Pulitzer Prize Winners: Public Service." *The Pulitzer Prizes*, Columbia U, www.pulitzer.org/prize-winners-by-year/2006. Accessed 21 Oct. 2013.

Weinberger, David. "Transparency Is the New Objectivity." *Joho the Blog*, 19 July 2009, www.hyperorg.com/blogger/2009/07/19/ transparency-is-the-new-objectivity/.

Benjy Mercer-Golden

Ms. Tavani

ENG 120

28 November XXXX

Lessons from Tree-Huggers and Corporate Mercenaries:

A New Model of Sustainable Capitalism

Televised images of environmental degradation—seagulls with oil coating their feathers, smokestacks belching gray fumes—often seem designed to shock, but these images also represent very real issues: climate change, dwindling energy resources like coal and oil, a scarcity of clean drinking water. In response, businesspeople around the world are thinking about how they can make their companies greener or more socially beneficial to ensure a brighter future for humanity. But progress in the private sector has been slow and inconsistent. To accelerate the move to sustainability, for-profit businesses need to learn from the hybrid model of social entrepreneurship to ensure that the company is efficient and profitable while still working for social change, and more investors need to support companies with long-term, revolutionary visions for improving the world.

In fact, both for-profit corporations and "social good" businesses could take steps to reshape their strategies. First, for-profit corporations need to operate sustainably and be evaluated for their performance with long-term measurements and incentives. The conventional argument against for-profit companies deeply embedding environmental and social goals into their corporate strategies is that caring about the world does not go hand in hand with lining pockets. This morally toxic case is also problematic from a business standpoint. A 2012 study of 180 high-profile companies by Harvard Business School professors

Writer's name and page number in upper right corner of each page

Title centered

Name, instructor, course, and date aligned at left

Robert G. Eccles and George Serafeim and London Business School professor Ioannis Ioannou shows that "high sustainability companies," as defined by environmental and social variables, "significantly outperform their counterparts over the long term, both in terms of stock market and accounting performance." The study argues that the better financial returns of these companies are especially evident in sectors where "companies' products significantly depend upon extracting large amounts of natural resources" (Eccles et al.).

Such empirical financial evidence to support a shift toward using energy from renewable sources to run manufacturing plants argues that executives should think more sustainably, but other underlying incentives need to evolve in order to bring about tangible change. David Blood and Al Gore of Generation Investment Management, an investment firm focused on "sustainable investing for the long term" ("About"), wrote a groundbreaking white paper that outlined the perverse incentives company managers face. For public companies, the default practice is to issue earnings guidances announcements of projected future earnings—every quarter. This practice encourages executives to manage for the short term instead of adding longterm value to their company and the earth (Gore and Blood). Only the most uncompromisingly green CEOs would still advocate for stricter carbon emissions standards at the company's factories if a few mediocre quarters left investors demanding that they be fired. Gore and Blood make a powerful case against subjecting companies to this "What have you done for me lately?" philosophy, arguing that quarterly earnings guidances should be abolished in favor of companies releasing information when they consider it appropriate. Companies also need to change the way the managers get paid. Currently, the CEO of ExxonMobil is rewarded for a highly profitable year but is not held accountable for depleting nonrenewable oil reserves. A new model

First author's name plus *et al.* for source with three or more authors

Shortened title for source with no author

Double-spaced throughout

should incentivize thinking for the long run. Multiyear milestones for performance evaluation, as Gore and Blood suggest, are essential to pushing executives to manage sustainably.

But it's not just for-profit companies that need to rethink strategies. Social good–oriented leaders also stand to learn from the people often vilified in environmental circles: corporate CEOs. To survive in today's economy, companies building sustainable products must operate under the same strict business standards as profit-driven companies. Two social enterprises, Nika Water and Belu, provide perfect examples. Both sell bottled water in the developed world with the mission of providing clean water to impoverished communities through their profits. Both have visionary leaders who define a critical lesson: financial pragmatism will add far more value to the world than idealistic dreams. Nika Water founder Jeff Church explained this in a speech at Stanford University:

> Social entrepreneurs look at their businesses as nine parts cause, one part business. In the beginning, it needs to be nine parts business, one part cause, because if the business doesn't stay around long enough because it can't make it, you can't do anything about the cause.

When UK-based Belu lost £600,000 ($940,000) in 2007, it could only give around £30,000 ($47,000) to charity. Karen Lynch took over as CEO, cutting costs, outsourcing significant parts of the company's operations, and redesigning the entire business model; the company now donates four times as much to charity (Hurley). The conventional portrayal of do-gooders is that they tend to be terrible businesspeople, an argument often grounded in reality. It is easy to criticize the Walmarts of the world for caring little about sustainability or social good, but the idealists with big visions who do not follow through on their promises because their businesses cannot survive are no more praiseworthy. Walmart should learn from nonprofits and social

Long quotation set off by ½" indent

enterprises on advancing a positive environmental and social agenda, but idealist entrepreneurs should also learn from corporations about building successful businesses.

The final piece of the sustainable business ecosystem is the investors who help get potentially world-changing companies off the ground. Industries that require a large amount of money to build complex products with expensive materials, such as solar power companies, rely heavily on investors—often venture capitalists based in California's Silicon Valley (Knight). The problem is that venture capitalists are not doing enough to fund truly groundbreaking companies. In an oft-cited blog post entitled "Why Facebook Is Killing Silicon Valley," entrepreneur Steve Blank argues that the financial returns on social media companies have been so quick and so outsized that the companies with the *really* big ideas—like providing efficient, cheap, scalable solar power—are not being backed: "In the past, if you were a great [venture capitalist], you could make $100 million on an investment in 5–7 years. Today, social media startups can return hundreds of millions or even billions in less than 3 years." The point Blank makes is that what is earning investors lots of money right now is not what is best for the United States or the world.

There are, however, signs of hope. Paypal founder Peter Thiel runs his venture capital firm, the Founders Fund, on the philosophy that investors should support "flying cars" instead of new social media ventures (Packer). While the next company with the next great social media idea might be both profitable and valuable, Thiel and a select few others fund technology that has the potential to solve the huge problems essential to human survival.

The world's need for sustainable companies that can build products from renewable energy or make nonpolluting cars will inevitably create opportunities for smart companies to make money.

No page number for unpaginated online source

In fact, significant opportunities already exist for venture capitalists willing to step away from what is easy today and shift their investment strategies toward what will help us continue to live on this planet tomorrow—even if seeing strong returns may take a few more years. Visionaries like Blank and Thiel need more allies (and dollars) in their fight to help produce more pioneering, sustainable companies. And global warming won't abate before investors wise up. It is vital that this shift happen now.

When we think about organizations today, we think about nonprofits, which have long-term social missions, and corporations, which we judge by their immediate financial returns like quarterly earnings. That is a treacherous dichotomy. Instead, we need to see the three major players in the business ecosystem—corporations, social enterprises, and investors—moving toward a *single* model of long-term, sustainable capitalism. We need visionary companies that not only set out to solve humankind's biggest problems but also have the business intelligence to accomplish these goals, and we need investors willing to fund these companies. Gore and Blood argue that "the imperative for change has never been greater." We will see this change when the world realizes that sustainable capitalism shares the same goals as creating a sustainable environment. Let us hope that this realization comes soon.

Works Cited List

Works cited list starts on new page; title centered

Works Cited

Sources arranged alphabetically by authors' last names or by title for sources with no author

"About Us." *Generation*, 2012, www.generationim.com/about/.

Blank, Steve. "Why Facebook Is Killing Silicon Valley."
Steveblank.com, 21 May 2012, steveblank.com/2012/05/21/
why-facebook-is-killing-silicon-valley/.

Church, Jeff. "The Wave of Social Entrepreneurship." Entrepreneurial
Thought Leaders Seminar, NVIDIA Auditorium, Stanford, 11 Apr.
2012. Lecture.

Source with three or more authors listed by first author's name followed by *et al.*

Eccles, Robert G., et al. "The Impact of a Corporate Culture of
Sustainability on Corporate Behavior and Performance." *Working
Knowledge*, Harvard Business School, 14 Nov. 2011, hbswk.hbs
.edu/item/the-impact-of-corporatesustainability-on-organizational
-process-and-performance.

Gore, Al, and David Blood. "Sustainable Capitalism." *Generation*,
15 Feb. 2012, www.generationim.com/media/pdf-generation
-sustainable-capitalism-v1.pdf.

Full name of publication given, including article *The*

Hurley, James. "Belu Boss Shows Bottle for a Turnaround." *The Daily
Telegraph*, www.telegraph.co.uk/finance/businessclub/9109449/
Belu-boss-shows-bottle-for-a-turnaround.html.

Knight, Eric R. W. "The Economic Geography of Clean Tech Venture
Capital." Oxford U Working Paper Series in Employment, Work,
and Finance, 13 Apr. 2010. *Social Science Research Network*,
doi:10.2139/ssrn.1588806.

DOI used if a source has one

Packer, George. "No Death, No Taxes: The Libertarian Futurism of a
Silicon Valley Billionaire." *The New Yorker*, 28 Nov. 2011,
www.newyorker.com/magazine/2011/11/28/no-death-no-taxes.

Double-spacing used throughout; first line of each entry at left margin, subsequent lines indented ½"

TOPIC 24

APA Documentation

The models used in the following tutorials follow the updated guidelines in the *Publication Manual of the American Psychological Association*, 7th ed. (APA, 2020).

Navigating Topic 24

The tutorials listed below provide information about APA in-text citations, References lists, and formatting for papers. You can work through the entire Topic on your own, learning about all the strategies and practicing them; work on items you've been assigned by your instructor; or choose those ones you would find helpful.

Introduction to APA Style   373

24.1	Tutorial	Documenting Sources in APA Style 373
24.2	Tutorial	APA In-Text Citations 374
24.3	Tutorial	APA Reference List 379
24.4	Tutorial	APA-Style Formatting 401

Introduction to APA Style

To cite and document sources in APA Style, you will need to use four main categories of information:

- **Author's (or authors') names.** The author's last name is used in in-text citations, and the last name with first and any middle initials is used in reference list entries.

- **Date of publication.** The year appears in in-text citations. The full date is used in reference list entries.

- **Title of the work.** The work you cite may be a stand-alone work such as a book, a report, or a film, or it might be part of a larger whole such as an article in a journal, a page on a website, or a chapter in an anthology.

- **Source of the work (retrieval information).** Retrieval information might include the publisher of a book; the volume, issue, and page numbers of a journal article; or a DOI (digital object identifier).

Like any documentation style, the APA guidelines present a system for citing many different kinds of sources, but they don't cover everything. At times you will have to think critically to adapt the guidelines to the source you are using.

24.1 Tutorial

Documenting Sources in APA Style

In most social science classes, you will be asked to use the APA system for documenting sources. APA recommends in-text citations that refer readers to a list of references.

An in-text citation gives the author of the source (often in a signal phrase), the year of publication, and at times a page number in parentheses. At the end of the paper, a list of references provides publication information for the source.

In-Text Citation

Yanovski and Yanovski (2002) reported that "the current state of the treatment for obesity is similar to the state of the treatment of hypertension several decades ago" (p. 600).

Entry in the List of References

Yanovski, S. Z., & Yanovski, J. A. (2002). Drug therapy: Obesity. *The New England Journal of Medicine, 346*(8), 591–602.

24.2 Tutorial

APA In-Text Citations

APA's in-text citations provide at least the author's last name and the year of publication. For direct quotations and some paraphrases, a page number is given as well.

NOTE: APA style requires the use of the past tense or the present perfect tense in signal phrases introducing cited material: Smith (2005) reported; Smith (2005) has argued.

Basic Format for a Quotation

Ordinarily, introduce the quotation with a signal phrase that includes the author's last name followed by the year of publication in parentheses. Put the page number (preceded by "p.") in parentheses after the quotation.

> Critser (2003) noted that despite growing numbers of overweight Americans, many health care providers still "remain either in ignorance or outright denial about the health danger to the poor and the young" (p. 5).

If the author is not named in the signal phrase, place the author's name, the year, and the page number in parentheses after the quotation: (Critser, 2003, p. 5).

NOTE: APA style requires the year of publication in an in-text citation. Do not include a month, even if the entry in the reference list includes the month.

Basic Format for a Summary or a Paraphrase

Include the author's last name and the year either in a signal phrase introducing the material or in parentheses following it. A page number is not required for a summary or a paraphrase, but include one if it would help readers find the passage in a long work.

> Yanovski and Yanovski (2002) explained that sibutramine suppresses appetite by blocking the reuptake of the neurotransmitters serotonin and norepinephrine in the brain.

> Sibutramine suppresses appetite by blocking the reuptake of the neurotransmitters serotonin and norepinephrine in the brain (Yanovski & Yanovski, 2002).

Directory to APA In-Text Citation Models

1. Work with two authors 376
2. Work with three or more authors 376
3. Work with unknown author 376
4. Organization as author 377
5. Authors with the same last name 377
6. Two or more works by the same author in the same year 377
7. Two or more works in the same parentheses 377
8. Personal communication 378
9. Indirect source 378
10. Sacred or classical text 378
11. Electronic source 378

Guidelines for In-Text Citations

1. Work with two authors Name both authors in the signal phrase or the parentheses each time you cite the work. In the parentheses, use "&" between the authors' names; in the signal phrase, use "and."

> According to Sothern and Gordon (2003), "Environmental factors may contribute as much as 80% to the causes of childhood obesity" (p. 104).

> Obese children often engage in limited physical activity (Sothern & Gordon, 2003, p. 104).

2. Work with three or more authors Use the first author's name followed by the abbreviation "et al." (Latin for "and others").

> In 2003, Berkowitzet et al. concluded, "Sibutramine . . . must be carefully monitored in adolescents, as in adults, to control increases in [blood pressure] and pulse rate" (p. 1811).

> Researchers have advised, "Until more extensive safety and efficacy data are available, . . . weight-loss medications should be used only on an experimental basis for adolescents" (Berkowitz et al., 2003, p. 1811).

> McDuffie et al. (2002) tested 20 adolescents, aged 12–16, over a three-month period and found that orlistat, combined with behavioral therapy, produced an average weight loss of 4.4 kg, or 9.7 pounds.

3. Work with unknown author If the author is unknown, mention the work's title in the signal phrase or give the first word or two of the title in the parenthetical citation. Titles of articles and chapters are put in quotation marks; titles of books and reports are italicized. (For online sources with no author, see item 11.)

> Children struggling to control their weight must also struggle with the pressures of television advertising that, on the one hand, encourages the consumption of junk food and, on the other, celebrates thin celebrities ("Television," 2002).

NOTE: In the rare case when "Anonymous" is specified as the author, treat it as if it were a real name: (Anonymous, 2001). In the list of references, also use the name Anonymous as author.

4. Organization as author If the author is a government agency or another organization, name the organization in the signal phrase or in the parenthetical citation the first time you cite the source.

> Obesity puts children at risk for a number of medical complications, including type 2 diabetes, hypertension, sleep apnea, and orthopedic problems (Kaiser Family Foundation, 2004).

If the organization has a familiar abbreviation, you may include it in brackets the first time you cite the source and use the abbreviation alone in later citations.

First Citation	(Centers for Disease Control and Prevention [CDC], 2009)
Later Citations	(CDC, 2009)

5. Authors with the same last name To avoid confusion, use initials with the last names if your reference list includes two or more authors with the same last name.

> Research by E. Smith (1989) revealed that . . .

6. Two or more works by the same author in the same year When your list of references includes more than one work by the same author in the same year, use lowercase letters ("a," "b," and so on) with the year to order the entries in the reference list. (See item 6 in the reference list section below.) Use those same letters with the year in the in-text citation.

> Research by Durgin (2003b) has yielded new findings about the role of counseling in treating childhood obesity.

7. Two or more works in the same parentheses When your parenthetical citation names two or more works, put them in alphabetical order, separated with semicolons.

> Researchers have indicated that studies of pharmacological treatments for childhood obesity are inconclusive (Berkowitz et al., 2003; McDuffie et al., 2002).

8. Personal communication Personal interviews, memos, letters, email, and similar unpublished communications should be cited in the text only, not in the reference list. (Use the first initial with the last name in parentheses.)

> One of Atkinson's colleagues, who has studied the effect of the media on children's eating habits, has contended that advertisers for snack foods will need to design ads responsibly for their younger viewers (F. Johnson, personal communication, October 20, 2009).

9. Indirect source If you use a source that was cited in another source (a secondary source), name the original source in your signal phrase. List the secondary source in your reference list and include it in your parenthetical citation, preceded by the words "as cited in." In the following example, Satcher is the original source, and Critser is the secondary source, given in the reference list.

> Former surgeon general Dr. David Satcher described "a nation of young people seriously at risk of starting out obese and dooming themselves to the difficult task of overcoming a tough illness" (as cited in Critser, 2003, p. 4).

10. Sacred or classical text Identify the title of the version or edition you used, the year of that version's publication, and the relevant part (chapter, verse, line).

> Peace activists have long cited the biblical prophet's vision of a world without war: "And they shall beat their swords into plowshares, and their spears into pruning hooks; nation shall not lift up sword against nation, neither shall they learn war any more" (*Revised Standard Version Bible*, 1952, Isaiah 2:4).

11. Electronic source When possible, cite electronic sources, including online sources, as you would any other source, giving the author and the year.

> Atkinson (2001) found that children who spent at least four hours a day watching TV were less likely to engage in adequate physical activity during the week.

Electronic sources sometimes lack authors' names, dates, or page numbers.

- **Unknown author.** If no author is named, mention the title of the source in the signal phrase or give the first word or two of the title in the parentheses (see also item 3). (If an organization serves as the author, see item 4.)

The body's basal metabolic rate, or BMR, is a measure of its at-rest energy requirement ("Exercise," 2003).

- **Unknown date.** When the date is unknown, use the abbreviation "n.d." (for "no date").

   Attempts to establish a definitive link between television programming and children's eating habits have been problematic (Magnus, n.d.).

- **No page numbers.** APA ordinarily requires page numbers for quotations, and it recommends them for summaries and paraphrases from long sources. When an electronic source lacks stable numbered pages, your citation should include information that will help readers locate the particular passage being cited. For example, you might include a paragraph number, a section heading (for a source that includes headings), a figure or table number (if you are citing a visual), a slide number (for presentation slides), or a timestamp (for a video).

   Hoppin and Taveras (2004) pointed out that several other medications were classified by the Drug Enforcement Administration as having the "potential for abuse" (Weight-Loss Drugs section, para. 6).

NOTE: Electronic files in portable document format (PDF) often have stable page numbers. For such sources, give the page number in the parenthetical citation.

24.3 Tutorial

APA Reference List

In APA style, the alphabetical list of works cited, which appears at the end of the paper, is titled "References." For advice on preparing the reference list, see Preparing the List of References on page 403. For a sample reference list, see the student essay on page 405.

Alphabetize entries in the list of references by authors' (or editors') last names; if a work has no author or editor, alphabetize it by its title. The first element of each entry is important because citations in the text of the paper refer to it and readers will be looking for it in the alphabetized list. The date of publication appears immediately after the first element of the citation.

In APA style, titles of books and periodicals are italicized; titles of articles and names of websites are neither italicized nor put in quotation marks. (For rules on capitalization of titles, see APA-Style Formatting on p. 401.)

General Guidelines for Listing Authors (Print and Online)

In APA style, all authors' names are inverted (the last name comes first), and initials only are used for all first and middle names.

Name and Date Cited in Text

Duncan (2008) has reported that . . .

Beginning of Entry in the List of References

Duncan, B. (2008).

Directory to APA References (bibliographic entries)

GENERAL GUIDELINES FOR LISTING AUTHORS (PRINT AND ONLINE)

1. Single author 381
2. Multiple authors 381
3. Organization as author 382
4. Unknown author 382
5. Two or more works by the same author 383
6. Two or more works by the same author in the same year 383

ARTICLES IN PERIODICALS (PRINT)

7. Article in a journal 385
8. Article in a magazine 385
9. Article in a newspaper 385
10. Article with up to twenty authors 385
11. Article with twenty-one or more authors 385
12. Abstract of a journal article 385
13. Letter to the editor 386
14. Editorial or other unsigned article 386
15. Newsletter article 386
16. Review 386

BOOKS (PRINT)

17. Basic format for a book 388
18. Book with an editor 388
19. Book with an author and an editor 388
20. Book with an author and a translator 388
21. Edition other than the first 388
22. Article or chapter in an edited book or an anthology 389
23. Multivolume work 389
24. Introduction, preface, foreword, or afterword 389
25. Dictionary or other reference work 389
26. Article in a reference work 389
27. Republished book 389
28. Book with a title in its title 390
29. Sacred or classical text 390

ONLINE SOURCES

30. Article in an online journal 392
31. Article in an online magazine 392
32. Article in an online newspaper 392
33. Article published only online 392

34. Article from a database 392

35. Abstract for an online article 393

36. Online book 393

37. Chapter in an online book 393

38. Online reference work 393

39. Document from a website 394

40. Section in a web document 394

41. Document from a government agency website 395

42. Article in an online newsletter 395

43. Podcast 395

44. Weblog (blog) post 397

45. Online audio or video file 397

46. Entry in a wiki 397

47. Data set or graphic representation 397

48. Post in an online forum 397

49. Email 398

50. Public post on social media 398

OTHER SOURCES (INCLUDING ONLINE VERSIONS)

51. Dissertation from a database 398

52. Unpublished dissertation 398

53. Government document 398

54. Report from a private organization 399

55. Legal source 399

56. Conference proceedings 399

57. Paper presented at a meeting or symposium (unpublished) 399

58. Poster session at a conference 399

59. Map or chart 399

60. Advertisement 399

61. Published interview 400

62. Lecture, speech, or address 400

63. Work of art or photograph 400

64. Brochure, pamphlet, or fact sheet 400

65. Presentation slides 400

66. Film or video (motion picture) 400

67. Television program 401

68. Sound recording 401

69. Computer software or video game 401

1. Single author

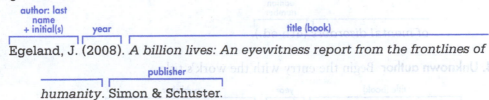

A billion lives: An eyewitness report from the frontlines of humanity. Simon & Schuster.

2. Multiple authors List up to twenty authors by last names followed by initials. Use an ampersand (&) before the name of the last author. If there are more than twenty authors, list the first nineteen followed by three ellipsis dots and the last author's name.

Up to Twenty Authors

all authors: last name + initial(s)   *year*   *title (book)*

Foer, J., Thuras, D., & Morton, E. (2016). *Atlas obscura: An explorer's guide*

publisher

to the world's hidden wonders. Workman Publishing.

Twenty-one or More Authors

first nineteen authors: last name + initial(s)

Sharon, G., Cruz, N. J., Kang, D.-W., Gandal, M. J., Wang, B., Kim, Y.-M., Zink, E. M.,

Casey, C. P., Taylor, B. C., Lane, C. J., Bramer, L. M., Isern, N. G.,

Hoyt, D. W., Noecker, C., Sweredoski, M. J., Moradian, A., Borenstein, E.,

ellipsis + last author   *year*   *title (article)*

Jansson, J. K., Knight, R., . . . Mazmanian, S. K. (2019). *Human gut*

microbiota from autism spectrum disorder promote behavioral

journal title   *volume, issue*   *page range*

symptoms in mice. Cell, *177*(6), 1600–1618.

3. Organization as author If the publisher is the same as the author, omit the publisher's name.

author: organization name   *year*   *title (book)*

American Psychiatric Association. (1994). *Diagnostic and statistical manual*

edition number

of mental disorders (4th ed.).

4. Unknown author Begin the entry with the work's title.

title (book)   *year*   *publisher*

New concise world atlas. (2007). Oxford University Press.

title (article)   *year + date (for weekly publication)*   *journal title*   *volume, issue*   *page range*

Order in the jungle. (2008, March 15). *The Economist, 386*(8571), 83–85.

5. Two or more works by the same author Use the author's name for all entries. List the entries by year, the earliest first.

> Barry, P. (2007, December 8). Putting tumors on pause. *Science News, 172*(23), 365.

> Barry, P. (2008, August 2). Finding the golden genes. *Science News, 174*(3), 16–21.

6. Two or more works by the same author in the same year List the works chronologically or, if they have the same date, alphabetize them by title. Following the year, add "a," "b," and so on. Use these same letters in the in-text citation.

> Conover, E. (2019a, June 8). Gold's origins tied to collapsars. *Science News, 195*(10), 10.

> Conover, E. (2019b, June 22). Space flames may hold secrets to soot-free fire. *Science News, 195*(11), 5.

Articles in Periodicals (Print)

Periodicals include scholarly journals, magazines, and newspapers. Most journals and some magazines are published with volume and issue numbers. If available, give the volume and issue numbers after the title of the periodical. Italicize the volume number and put the issue number, not italicized, in parentheses.

For all periodicals, when an article appears on consecutive pages, provide the range of pages. When an article does not appear on consecutive pages, give all page numbers: A1, A17. (See also Online Sources on p. 390 for online articles and articles accessed through a library's database.) For an illustrated citation of an article in a periodical, see Citation at a Glance: Article in a Periodical (APA) on page 384.

APA Citation at a Glance   Article in a Periodical

To cite an article in a print periodical in APA style, include the following elements:

1 Author

2 Year of publication

3 Title of article

4 Name of periodical

5 Volume number; issue number, if available

6 Page numbers of article

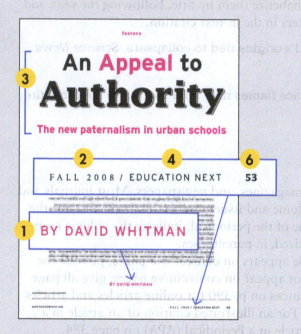

Reference List Entry for an Article in a Print Periodical

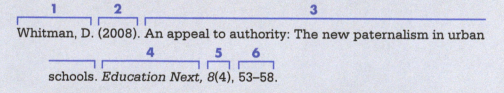

Whitman, D. (2008). An appeal to authority: The new paternalism in urban schools. *Education Next, 8*(4), 53–58.

Give the year, month, and day for daily and weekly periodicals. For variations on citing articles in print periodicals in APA style, see items 7–16 on the following pages.

Adapted from Hacker Handbooks (Bedford/St. Martin's).

7. Article in a journal

author: last name + initial(s) | year | article title

Zhang, L. F. (2008). Teachers' styles of thinking: An exploratory study.

journal title | volume, issue | page range

The Journal of Psychology, 142(1), 37–55.

8. Article in a magazine
Cite as a journal article, but give the year and the month for monthly magazines; add the day for weekly magazines.

McKibben, B. (2007, October). Carbon's new math. *National Geographic, 212*(4), 32–37.

9. Article in a newspaper

author: last name + initial(s) | year + month + day (for daily publication) | article title

Svoboda, E. (2008, October 21). Deep in the rain forest, stalking the next

newspaper title | page number

pandemic. *The New York Times*, D5.

10. Article with up to twenty authors

Ungar, M., Brown, M., Liebenberg, L., Othman, R., Kwong, W. M., Armstrong, M., & Gilgun, J. (2007). Unique pathways to resilience across cultures. *Adolescence, 42*(166), 287–310.

11. Article with twenty-one or more authors
List the first nineteen authors followed by three ellipsis dots and the last author.

Choi, H. M., Calvert, C. R., Husain, N., Barsi, J. C., Deverman, B. E., Hunter, R. C., Kato, M., Lee, S. M., Abelin, A. C., Rosenthal, A. Z., Akbari, O. S., Li, Y., Hay, B. A., Sternberg, P. W., Patterson, P. H., Davidson, E. H., Mazmanian, S. K., Prober, D. A., van de Rijn, M., . . . Pierce, N. A. (2016, October 1). Mapping a multiplexed zoo of mRNA expression. *Development, 143*(19), 3632–3637.

12. Abstract of a journal article [Abstract]

Lahm, K. (2008). Inmate-on-inmate assault: A multilevel examination of prison violence [Abstract]. *Criminal Justice and Behavior, 35*(1), 120–137.

13. Letter to the editor Letters to the editor appear in journals, magazines, and newspapers. Follow the appropriate model (see items 7–9), and insert the words "Letter to the editor" in brackets after the title of the letter. If the letter has no title, use the bracketed words as the title.

> Park, T. (2008, August). Defining the line [Letter to the editor]. *Scientific American, 299*(2), 10.

14. Editorial or other unsigned article [Editorial]

> The global justice movement [Editorial]. (2005). *Multinational Monitor, 26*(7/8), 6.

15. Newsletter article

> Setting the stage for remembering. (2006, September). *Mind, Mood, and Memory* [Newsletter], *2*(9), 4–5.

16. Review Give the author and title of the review (if any) and, in brackets, the type of work, the title, and the author for a book or the director for a film. If the review has no author or title, use the material in brackets as the title.

> Douthat, R. (2019, October 14). A hustle gone wrong [Review of the film *Hustlers*, by L. Scafaria, Dir.]. *National Review, 71*(18), 47.

> Agents of change. (2008, February 2). [Review of the book *The power of unreasonable people: How social entrepreneurs create markets that change the world*, by J. Elkington & P. Hartigan]. *The Economist, 386*(8565), 94.

Books (Print)

Items 17–29 apply to print books. For online books, see items 36 and 37. Take the information about a book from its title page and copyright page. Give the publisher's name as it appears on the book, but do not include terms such as "Inc" or "Co."

APA Citation at a Glance Book

To cite a print book in APA style, include the following elements:

1 Author

2 Year of publication

3 Title and subtitle

4 Publisher

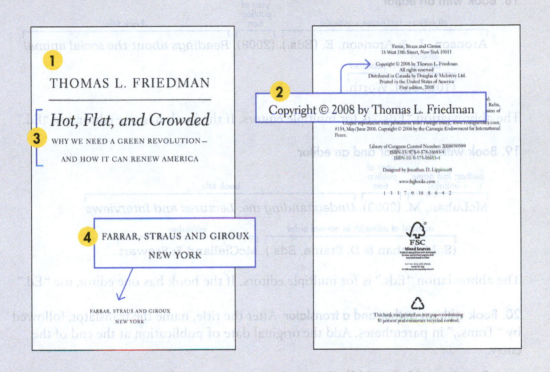

Reference List Entry for a Print Book

1   **2**   **3**

Friedman, T. L. (2008). *Hot, flat, and crowded: Why we need a green revolution—*

                                               4

and how it can renew America. Farrar, Straus and Giroux.

For more on citing print books in APA style, see items 17–29.

Adapted from Hacker Handbooks (Bedford/St. Martin's).

17. Basic format for a book

author: last name + initial(s)   year of publication   book title

McKenzie, F. R. (2008). *Theory and practice with adolescents: An applied*

publisher

approach. Lyceum Books.

18. Book with an editor

all editors: last name + initial(s)   year of publication   book title

Aronson, J., & Aronson, E. (Eds.). (2008). *Readings about the social animal*

edition number   publisher

(10th ed.). Worth.

The abbreviation "Eds." is for multiple editors. If the book has one editor, use "Ed."

19. Book with an author and an editor

author: last name + initial(s)   year of publication   book title

McLuhan, M. (2003). *Understanding me: Lectures and interviews*

name(s) of editor(s): in normal order   publisher

(S. McLuhan & D. Staine, Eds.). McClelland & Stewart.

The abbreviation "Eds." is for multiple editors. If the book has one editor, use "Ed."

20. Book with an author and a translator

After the title, name the translator, followed by "Trans.," in parentheses. Add the original date of publication at the end of the entry.

> Steinberg, M. D. (2003). *Voices of revolution, 1917* (M. Schwartz, Trans.). Yale University Press. (Original work published 2001)

21. Edition other than the first

> O'Brien, J. A. (Ed.). (2006). *The production of reality: Essays and readings on social interaction* (4th ed.). Pine Forge Press.

22. Article or chapter in an edited book or an anthology

author of chapter: last name + initial(s) — year of publication — title of chapter

Denton, N. A. (2006). Segregation and discrimination in housing.

book editor(s): in normal order — book title

In R. G. Bratt, M. E. Stone, & C. Hartman (Eds.), *A right to housing:*

page range for chapter — publisher

Foundation of a new social agenda (pp. 61–81). Temple University Press.

The abbreviation "Eds." is for multiple editors. If the book has one editor, use "Ed."

23. Multivolume work Give the number of volumes after the title.

Luo, J. (Ed.). (2005). *China today: An encyclopedia of life in the People's Republic* (Vols. 1–2). Greenwood Press.

24. Introduction, preface, foreword, or afterword

Gore, A. (2000). Foreword. In B. Katz (Ed.), *Reflections on regionalism* (pp. ix–x). Brookings Institution Press.

25. Dictionary or other reference work

Leong, F. T. L. (Ed.). (2008). *Encyclopedia of counseling* (Vols. 1–4). Sage.

26. Article in a reference work

Konijn, E. A. (2008). Affects and media exposure. In W. Donsbach (Ed.), *The international encyclopedia of communication* (Vol. 1, pp. 123–129). Blackwell.

27. Republished book

Mailer, N. (2008). *Miami and the siege of Chicago: An informal history of the Republican and Democratic conventions of 1968*. New York Review Books. (Original work published 1968)

28. Book with a title in its title If the book title contains another book title or an article title, neither italicize the internal title nor place it in quotation marks.

> Marcus, L. (Ed.). (1999). *Sigmund Freud's* The interpretation of dreams*: New interdisciplinary essays*. Manchester University Press.

29. Sacred or classical text Cite sacred and classical texts as you would a book.

> *New International Version Bible*. (2011). Biblica. (Original work published 1973)

> Dawood, N. J. (Ed., Trans.). (2006). *The Koran*. Penguin Books. (Original work published 1956)

Online Sources

When citing an online article, include publication information as for a print periodical (see items 7–16) and add information about the online version (see items 30–35).

Online articles and books sometimes include a DOI (digital object identifier). If a DOI is available for the work you are citing, include it using the format "https://doi.org/" followed by the specific identifier for the article. If no DOI is available, include a direct-link URL, if you can. If the URL is very lengthy, you may create a shortened form using a site like bitly.com. Do not include URLs to articles in databases if your readers will not be able to access them.

For most online sources, a publication date will be available. If the source has no date, use "n.d." Include a retrieval statement with your date of access only if the source is updated regularly and archived versions are not available.

Most of the examples in this section do not show a retrieval date because the content of the sources is stable; if you are unsure about whether to use a retrieval date, include the date or consult your instructor.

APA Citation at a Glance Article from a Database

To cite an article from a database in APA style, include the following elements:

1 Author(s)

2 Date of publication

3 Title of article

4 Name of periodical

5 Volume number; issue number

6 Page range

7 DOI (digital object identifier)

On-Screen View of Database Record

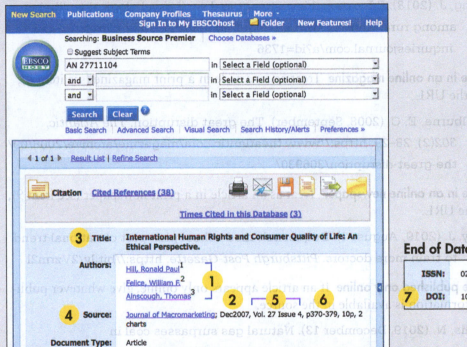

Reference List Entry for an Article from a Database

1
2
3
Hill, R. P., Felice, W. F., & Ainscough, T. (2007). International human rights and

4
consumer quality of life: An ethical perspective. *Journal of Macromarketing,*

5 **6** **7**
27(4), 370–379. https://doi.org/10.1177/027614670307128

For more on citing articles from a database in APA style, see item 34.

Adapted from Hacker Handbooks (Bedford/St. Martin's).

30. Article in an online journal

author: last name + initial(s) / year of publication / article title / journal title

Whitmeyer, J. M. (2000). Power through appointment. *Social Science*

volume, issue / page range / DOI

Research, 29(4), 535–555. https://doi.org/10.1006/ssre.2000.0680

If there is no DOI, include the URL.

Hung, J. (2018). Educational investment and sociopsychological wellbeing
among rural Chinese women. *Inquiries Journal, 10*(05). http://www
.inquiriesjournal.com/a?id=1736

31. Article in an online magazine Treat as an article in a print magazine (see item 8), and add the URL

Shelburne, E. C. (2008, September). The great disruption. *The Atlantic,
302*(2), 28–29. https://www.theatlantic.com/magazine/archive/2008/09/
the-great-disruption/306930/

32. Article in an online newspaper Treat as an article in a print newspaper (see item 9), adding the URL.

Daly, J. (2019, August 2). Duquesne's med school plan part of national trend
to train more doctors. *Pittsburgh Post-Gazette*. https://bit.ly/2Vzrm2l

33. Article published only online If an article appears only online, give whatever publication information is available in the source.

Karlis, N. (2019, December 13). Natural gas surpasses coal in
carbon emissions. *Salon*. https://www.salon.com/2019/12/13/
natural-gas-surpasses-coal-in-carbon-emissions/

34. Article from a database Start with the publication information for the source (see items 7–16). If the database entry gives a DOI for the article, use that number at the end and do not include the database name. For an illustrated citation of a work from a database, see Citation at a Glance: Article from a Database (APA) on page 391.

all authors: last name
+ initial(s)   year   article title

Eskritt, M., & McLeod, K. (2008). Children's note taking as a mnemonic tool.

journal title   volume,   page
issue   range   DOI

Journal of Experimental Child Psychology, 101(1), 52–74. https://doi.org

/10.1016/j.jecp.2008.05.007

If there is no DOI, do not include the name of the database or the URL because your readers might not have access to the database. Include that information only when the article cannot be found anywhere else.

35. Abstract for an online article

Brockerhoff, E. G., Jactel, H., Parrotta, J. A., Quine, C. P., & Sayer, J.

(2008). Plantation forests and biodiversity: Oxymoron or opportunity?

[Abstract]. *Biodiversity and Conservation, 17*(5), 925–951. https://doi

.org/10.1007/s10531-008-9380-x

36. Online book

Adams, B. (2004). *The theory of social revolutions*. Project Gutenberg. http://

www.gutenberg.org/catalog/world/readfile?fk_files=44092 (Original

work published 1913)

37. Chapter in an online book

Rubinstein, R. (2018). Telling the truth. In C. Helman (Ed.) *Doctors and

patients: An anthology* (pp. 49–52). CRC Press. https://doi

.org/10.1201/9781315375939 (Original work published 2003)

38. Online reference work Use a retrieval date only if the content of the work is likely to change.

Merriam-Webster. (n.d.). Adscititious. In *Merriam-Webster.com dictionary*.

Retrieved September 5, 2019, from https://www.merriam-webster.com/

dictionary/adscititious

39. Document or page from a website If the document fits another category such as article in an online magazine, follow that model. If the document is not part of a publication other than the website itself, list as many of the following elements as are available: author's name, publication date (or "n.d." if there is no date), title (in italics), name of the website (if different from author), and URL.

For an illustrated citation of a web document, see Citation at a Glance: Document on a Website (APA) on page 396.

Source with Date

author: last name + initial(s)   date: year + month + day   document title

Albright, A. (2019, July 25). *The global education challenge: Scaling up to*

site name   URL

tackle the learning crisis. The Brookings Institution. https://www

.brookings.edu/wp-content/uploads/2019/07/Brookings_Blum_2019_

education.pdf

Source with No Date

WebMD. (n.d.). *Types of Alzheimer's disease*. https://www.webmd.com/

alzheimers/guide/alzheimers-types

Source with No Author

If a source has no author, begin with the title and follow it with the date in parentheses.

40. Section in a web document If you use only a section of a web document or webpage, cite the specific section in your in-text citation(s) and cite the entire document or webpage in your references list.

In-Text Citation

(National Institute of Mental Health [NIMH], 2016, Risk Factors section)

Entry in the List of References

National Institute of Mental Health. (2016, March). *Seasonal affective disorder*. National Institutes of Health. https://www.nimh.nih.gov/health/topics/

seasonal-affective-disorder/index.shtml

41. Document from a government agency website If the work has no author, list the most specific agency involved in producing the document as the author.

> National Park Service. (2019, April 11). *Travel where women made history: Ordinary and extraordinary places of American women.* U.S. Department of the Interior. https://www.nps.gov/subjects/travelwomenshistory /index.htm

42. Article in an online newsletter Cite as an online article (see items 30–32), giving the title of the newsletter and whatever other information is available, including volume and issue numbers.

> National Science Foundation. (2008, May). In the face of extinction. *NSF Current.* http://www.nsf.gov/news/newsletter/may_08/index.jsp

43. Podcast

    host or producer   date of series   series title

National Academies (Producer). (2007–present). *The sounds of science*

    descriptive label   URL

    [Audio podcast]. http://media.nap.edu/podcasts/

    host or producer   date of posting   episode title   descriptive label

Boilen, B. (Host). (2019, September 11). Come from away [Video podcast

    series title   website   URL

episode]. In *Tiny desk concerts.* NPR. https://www.npr.org/2019/09/

11/758080813/come-from-away-tiny-desk-concert

APA Citation at a Glance Document on a Website

To cite a web document in APA style, include the following elements:

1 Author

2 Date of publication

3 Title of document

4 Name of website (if different from author)

5 URL

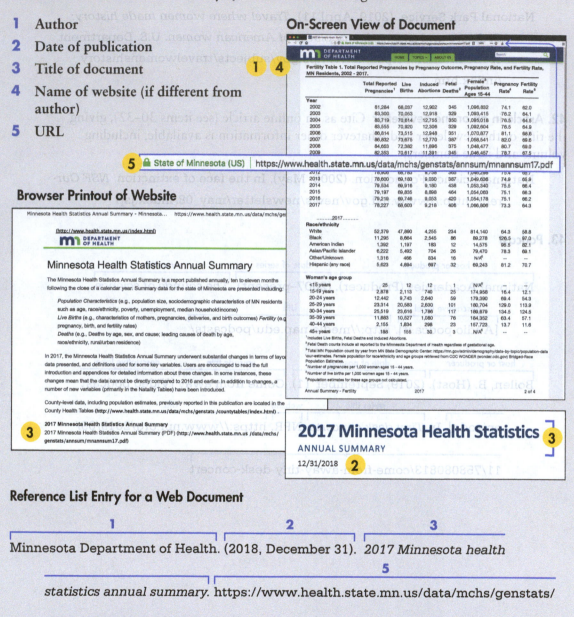

On-Screen View of Document

Browser Printout of Website

Reference List Entry for a Web Document

Minnesota Department of Health. (2018, December 31). *2017 Minnesota health statistics annual summary.* https://www.health.state.mn.us/data/mchs/genstats/annsum/mnannsum17.pdf

For more on citing documents from websites in APA style, see items 30–50.

Adapted from Hacker Handbooks (Bedford/St. Martin's).

44. Weblog (blog) post Cite a blog post as you would an article in a magazine or newspaper (see items 31 and 32).

Kellermann, M. (2007, May 23). Disclosing clinical trials. *Social Science Statistics*. http://www.iq.harvard.edu/blog/sss/archives/2007/05

45. Online audio or video file Give the medium or a description of the source file in brackets following the title.

BBC. (2018, November 19). Why do bad managers flourish? [Audio]. In *Business Matters*. https://www.bbc.co.uk/programmes/p06s8752

TED. (2019, September 20). *Britt Wray: How climate change affects your mental health* [Video]. YouTube. https://www.youtube.com/watch?v=-IlDkCEvsYw

46. Entry in a wiki Begin with the author (if identified), the title of the entry, and the date of posting, if there is one (use "n.d." for "no date" if there is not). Then add the name of the wiki and the URL for the entry. If versions of the entry are archived, give the URL for the version you used.

Behaviorism. (2019, October 11). In *Wikipedia*. https://en.wikipedia.org/w/index.php?title=Behaviorism&oldid=915544724

47. Data set or graphic representation Give information about the type of source in brackets following the title. If there is no title, give a brief description of the content of the source in brackets in place of the title.

U.S. Department of Agriculture, Economic Research Service. (2009). *Eating and health module (ATUS): 2007 data* [Data set]. http://www.ers.usda.gov/Data/ATUS/Data/2007/2007data.htm

Gallup. (2008, October 23). *No increase in proportion of first-time voters* [Graphs]. http://www.gallup.com/poll/111331/No-Increase-Proportion-First-Time-Voters.aspx

48. Post in an online forum

ScienceModerator. (2018, November 16). *Science discussion: We are researchers working with some of the largest and most innovative companies using DNA to help people* [Online forum post]. Reddit. https://www.reddit.com/r/science/comments/9xlnm2/science_discussion_we_are_researchers_working/

49. Email Email messages, letters, and other personal communications are not included in the list of references. (See Personal Communication in the in-text citations section [item 9, p. 378] for citing these sources in the text of your paper.)

50. Public post on social media If the post is not accessible to all readers, cite it in the text of your paper but do not include it in the list of references.

> Georgia Aquarium. (2019, October 10). *Meet the bigfin reef squid*
>
> > [Video]. Facebook. https://www.facebook.com/GeorgiaAquarium/
> > videos/2471961729567512/

Other Sources (including Online Versions)

51. Dissertation from a database

> Bacaksizlar, N. G. (2019). *Understanding social movements through*
> *simulations of anger contagion in social media* (Publication No.
> 13805848) [Doctoral dissertation, University of North Carolina at
> Charlotte]. ProQuest Dissertations & Theses.

52. Unpublished dissertation

> Degli-Esposti, M. (2019). *Child maltreatment and antisocial behaviour in*
> *the United Kingdom: Changing risks over time* [Doctoral dissertation,
> University of Oxford]. Oxford University Research Archive. https://ora
> .ox.ac.uk/objects/uuid:6d5a8e55-bd19-41a1-8ef5-ef485642af89

53. Government document

> U.S. Census Bureau. (2006). *Statistical abstract of the United States*.
> Government Printing Office.

> Berchick, E. R., Barnett, J. C., & Upton, R. D. (2019, September 10). *Health*
> *insurance coverage in the United States: 2018* (Report No. P60–267). U.S.
> Census Bureau. https://www.census.gov/library/publications/2019/
> demo/p60-267.html

54. Report from a private organization

Ford Foundation International Fellowships Program. (2019). *Leveraging higher education to promote social justice: Evidence from the IFP alumni tracking study.* https://p.widencdn.net/kei61u/ IFP-Alumni-Tracking-Study-Report-5

55. Legal source
Do not italicize the titles of court cases in the list of references. Italicize them in in-text citations.

Sweatt v. Painter, 339 U.S. 629 (1950). http://www.law.cornell.edu/supct/ html/historics/USSC_CR_0339_0629_ZS.html

56. Conference proceedings

Stahl, G. (Ed.). (2002). *Proceedings of CSCL '02: Computer support for collaborative learning.* Erlbaum.

57. Paper presented at a meeting or symposium (unpublished)

Vasylets, O. (2019, April 10–13). *Memory accuracy in bilinguals depends on the valence of the emotional event* [Paper presentation]. XIV International Symposium of Psycholinguistics, Tarragona, Spain. https://psico .fcep.urv.cat/projectes/gip/files/isp2019.pdf

58. Poster session at a conference

Wood, M. (2019, January 3–6). *The effects of an adult development course on students' perceptions of aging* [Poster session]. Forty-First Annual National Institute on the Teaching of Psychology, St. Pete Beach, FL, United States. https://nitop.org/resources/Documents/2019%20 Poster%20Session%20II.pdf

59. Map or chart

Desjardins, J. (2017, November 17). *Walmart nation: Mapping the largest employers in the U.S.* [Map]. Visual Capitalist. https://www .visualcapitalist.com/walmart-nation-mapping-largest-employers-u-s/

60. Advertisement

Xbox 360 [Advertisement]. (2007, February). *Wired, 15*(2), 71.

61. Published interview

Remnick, D. (2019, July 1). Robert Caro reflects on Robert Moses, L.B.J., and his own career in nonfiction. *The New Yorker*. https://bit.ly/2Lukm3X

62. Lecture, speech, or address

Grigas, A. (2019, October 8). *The new geopolitics of energy* [Address]. Freeman Spogli Institute for International Studies, Stanford University, Stanford, CA, United States.

63. Work of art or photograph

O'Keeffe, G. (1931). *Cow's skull: Red, white, and blue* [Painting]. Metropolitan Museum of Art, New York, NY, United States. https://www .metmuseum.org/art/collection/search/488694

64. Brochure, pamphlet, or fact sheet

National Council of State Boards of Nursing. (n.d.). *Professional boundaries* [Brochure]. https://www.ncsbn.org/Professional_Boundaries_2007 _Web.pdf

World Health Organization. (2007, October). *Health of indigenous peoples* (No. 326) [Fact sheet]. http://www.who.int/mediacentre/factsheets/ fs326/en/index.html

65. Presentation slides

Boeninger, C. F. (2008, August). *Web 2.0 tools for reference and instructional services* [Presentation slides]. http://libraryvoice.com/archives /2008/08/04/opal-20-conference-presentation-slides/

66. Film or video (motion picture) Give the director, producer, and other relevant contributors, followed by the year of the film's release, the title, the description "Film" in brackets, and the production company. You do not need to include the format in which you viewed the film unless you viewed a special version or edition.

Peele, J. (Director). (2017). *Get out* [Film]. Universal Pictures.

Hitchcock, A. (Director). (1959). *The essentials collection: North by northwest* [Film; five-disc special ed. on DVD]. Metro-Goldwyn-Mayer; Universal Pictures Home Entertainment.

67. Television program When citing an entire series, list the executive producers as the author. When citing a single episode, list the writer(s) and the director.

Waller-Bridge, P., Williams, H., & Williams, J. (Executive Producers). (2016–2019). *Fleabag* [TV series]. Two Brothers Pictures; BBC.

Waller-Bridge, P. (Writer), & Bradbeer, H. (Director). (2019, March 18). The provocative request (Season 2, Episode 3) [TV series episode]. In P. Waller-Bridge, H. Williams, & J. Williams (Executive Producers), *Fleabag*. Two Brothers Pictures; BBC.

68. Sound recording

Carlile, B. (2018). The mother [Song]. On *By the way, I forgive you*. Low Country Sound; Elektra.

69. Computer software or video game Include a description in brackets after the title. For software, also list the version in parentheses before the description.

ConcernedApe. (2016). *Stardew Valley* [Video game]. Chucklefish.

24.4 Tutorial

APA-Style Formatting

Many instructors in the social sciences require students to follow APA guidelines for formatting a paper.

APA Guidelines for Student Papers

The APA manual provides different guidelines for papers prepared for publication in a scholarly journal and for papers prepared for undergraduate classes. The formatting guidelines in this section and the sample paper are consistent with the requirements for undergraduate writing. The samples on the last page show APA formatting for a paper prepared for publication. If you are in doubt about which format is preferred or required in your course, ask your instructor.

Font. Use a 10- to 12-point font that is accessible to readers, such as Times New Roman, Calibri, or Arial.

Title page. On your title page, put the title of the paper in boldface type, centered, three or four double-spaced lines from the top of the page. Skip a line and then list the following information, centered: your name, your school and the department of the course, the course number and name, your instructor's name, and the assignment due date. See the Sample APA Research Paper on page 405.

Page numbers. Number all pages with Arabic numerals (1, 2, 3, and so on), including the title page, flush right.

Margins, line spacing, and paragraph indents. Use margins of one inch on all sides of the page. Left-align the text. Double-space throughout the paper, but single-space footnotes. Indent the first line of each paragraph one-half inch.

Capitalization, italics, and quotation marks. Capitalize all words of four letters or more in titles of works and in headings that appear in the text of the paper. Capitalize the first word after a colon if the word begins a complete sentence. Italicize the titles of books and periodicals. Use quotation marks around the titles of periodical articles, short stories, poems, and other short works.

NOTE: APA has different requirements for titles in the reference list. See Preparing the List of References on page 403.

Long quotations and footnotes. When a quotation is longer than forty words, set it off from the text by indenting it one-half inch from the left margin. Double-space the quotation. Do not use quotation marks around a quotation that has been set off from the text. See page 413.

Place each footnote, if any, at the bottom of the page on which the text reference occurs. Double-space between the last line of text on the page and the footnote.

Set the footnote in a 10-point font, single-spaced. Begin the note with the superscript Arabic numeral that corresponds to the number in the text. See page 407.

Abstract.   APA style does not require an abstract for student papers. If your instructor requires an abstract, include it immediately after the title page. Center the word *Abstract* in boldface one inch from the top of the page; double-space the abstract as you do the body of your paper.

An abstract is a paragraph of fewer than 250 words that provides readers with a quick overview of your essay. It should express your main idea and your key points; it might also briefly suggest any implications or applications of the research you discuss in the paper. See page 406.

Headings.   Although headings are not always necessary, their use is encouraged in long or complex papers. For most undergraduate papers, one level of heading is sufficient.

In APA style, major headings are centered and boldface. Capitalize the first and last word of the heading, along with any words of more than four letters. Secondary headings are bolded, capitalized, and aligned flush left. See page 407.

Visuals.   APA classifies visuals as tables and figures (figures include graphs, charts, drawings, and photographs). Keep visuals as simple as possible.

Label each table or figure in boldface with an Arabic numeral (Table 1, Table 2, Figure 1, and so on) and provide a clear title in italics. The label and title should appear on separate lines above the visual, flush left. Tables may be single-spaced, one-and-a-half-spaced, or double-spaced, depending on what is easiest to read.

Below the visual, give its source and any additional information in a note. If any data in a table require an explanatory footnote, use a superscript lowercase letter in the body of the table and in a footnote following the source note. See page 410.

In the text of your paper, discuss the most significant features of each visual. Place the visual as close as possible to the sentences that relate to it unless your instructor prefers it in an appendix.

Preparing the List of References

Begin your list of references on a new page at the end of the paper. Center the heading References in boldface one inch from the top of the page. Double-space throughout. For a sample reference list, see page 414.

Indenting entries.   Use a hanging indent in the reference list: Type the first line of each entry flush left and indent any additional lines one-half inch, as shown on page 414.

Alphabetizing the list. Alphabetize the reference list by the last names of the authors (or editors); when a work has no author or editor, alphabetize by the first word of the title other than *A*, *An*, or *The*.

If your list includes two or more works by the same author, arrange the entries by year, the earliest first. If your list includes two or more works by the same author in the same year, arrange the works alphabetically by title. Add the letters "a," "b," and so on within the parentheses after the year. Use only the year and the letter for articles in journals: (2002a). Use the full date and the letter for articles in magazines and newspapers in the reference list: (2005a, July 7). Use only the year and the letter in the in-text citation.

Authors' names. Invert all authors' names and use initials instead of first names. With two to twenty authors, use an ampersand (&) before the last author's name. Separate the names with commas. If there are twenty-one or more authors, give the first nineteen authors, three ellipsis dots, and the last author.

Titles of books and articles. Italicize the titles and subtitles of books. Do not use quotation marks around the titles of articles. Capitalize only the first word of the title and subtitle (and all proper nouns) of books and articles. Italicize names of periodicals and capitalize all major words.

Page numbers. Give the full page range of articles and parts of longer works.

DOIs and URLs. For DOIs, use the format "https://doi.org/" followed by the identifier for the specific work. For lengthy URLs, you can substitute a shortened form by using a site like bitly.com. Do not add a period at the end of a DOI or URL.

For information about the exact format of each entry in your list, consult the models in the section APA Reference List on page 379.

Sample Pages from Student Writing in APA Style

On the following pages is a research paper on the effectiveness of treatments for childhood obesity, written by Luisa Mirano, a student in a psychology class. Mirano's assignment was to write a literature review paper documented with APA-style citations and references. Marginal annotations indicate APA-style formatting and effective writing.

Sample APA Research Paper

Pages numbered in the upper right corner

Can Medication Cure Obesity in Children?
A Review of the Literature

Full title, centered

Luisa Mirano

Department of Psychology, Northwest-Shoals Community College

PSY 108: Introduction to Psychology

Dr. June Kang

October 31, 2017

Writer's name, department and school, course number and name, instructor's name, date, all centered

Abstract

In recent years, policymakers and medical experts have expressed alarm about the growing problem of childhood obesity in the United States. While most agree that the issue deserves attention, consensus dissolves around how to respond to the problem. This literature review examines one approach to treating childhood obesity: medication. The paper compares the effectiveness for adolescents of the only two drugs approved by the Food and Drug Administration (FDA) for long-term treatment of obesity, sibutramine and orlistat. This examination of pharmacological treatments for obesity points out the limitations of medication and suggests the need for a comprehensive solution that combines medical, social, behavioral, and political approaches to this complex problem.

Abstract (included at instructor's request) appears on a separate page.

Can Medication Cure Obesity in Children? A Review of the Literature

Full title, centered

In March 2004, U.S. Surgeon General Richard Carmona called attention to a health problem in the United States that, until recently, has been overlooked: childhood obesity. Carmona said that the "astounding" 15% child obesity rate constitutes an "epidemic." Since the early 1980s, that rate has "doubled in children and tripled in adolescents." Now more than nine million children are classified as obese.[1] While the traditional response to a medical epidemic is to hunt for a vaccine or a cure-all pill, childhood obesity has proven more elusive. The lack of success of recent initiatives suggests that medication might not be the answer for the escalating problem. This literature review considers whether the use of medication is a promising approach for solving the childhood obesity problem by responding to the following questions:

1. What are the implications of childhood obesity?
2. Is medication effective at treating childhood obesity?
3. Is medication safe for children?
4. Is medication the best solution?

Mirano sets up her organization by posing four questions.

Understanding the limitations of medical treatments for children highlights the complexity of the childhood obesity problem in the United States and underscores the need for physicians, advocacy groups, and policymakers to search for other solutions.

Mirano states her thesis.

What Are the Implications of Childhood Obesity?

Obesity can be a devastating problem from both an individual and a societal perspective. Obesity puts children at risk for a number of medical complications, including type 2 diabetes, hypertension, sleep

Headings, centered and bolded, help readers follow the organization.

[1]Obesity is measured in terms of body-mass index (BMI): weight in kilograms divided by square of height in meters. A child or an adolescent with a BMI in the 95th percentile for his or her age and gender is considered obese.

Mirano uses a footnote to define an essential term that would be cumbersome to define within the text.

In a signal phrase, the word *and* links the names of two authors; the date is given in parentheses.

apnea, and orthopedic problems (Kaiser Family Foundation, 2004, p. 1). Researchers Hoppin and Taveras (2004) have noted that obesity is often associated with psychological issues such as depression, anxiety, and binge eating (Table 4).

Because the author (Carmona) is not named in the signal phrase, his name and the date appear in parentheses.

Obesity also poses serious problems for a society struggling to cope with rising health care costs. The cost of treating obesity currently totals $117 billion per year—a price, according to the surgeon general, "second only to the cost of [treating] tobacco use" (Carmona, 2004). And as the number of children who suffer from obesity grows, long-term costs will only increase.

Is Medication Effective at Treating Childhood Obesity?

The widening scope of the obesity problem has prompted medical professionals to rethink old conceptions of the disorder and its causes. As researchers Yanovski and Yanovski (2002) have explained, obesity was once considered "either a moral failing or evidence of underlying psychopathology" (p. 592). But this view has shifted: Many medical professionals now consider obesity a biomedical rather than a moral condition, influenced by both genetic and environmental factors. Yanovski and Yanovski have further noted that the development of weight-loss medications in the early 1990s showed that "obesity should be treated in the same manner as any other chronic disease . . . through the long-term use of medication" (p. 592).

Ellipsis dots indicate omitted words.

The search for the right long-term medication has been complicated. Many of the drugs authorized by the Food and Drug Administration (FDA) in the early 1990s proved to be a disappointment. Two of the medications—fenfluramine and dexfenfluramine—were withdrawn from the market because of severe side effects (Yanovski & Yanovski, 2002, p. 592), and several others were classified by the Drug Enforcement Administration as having the "potential for abuse" (Hoppin & Taveras, 2004, Weight-Loss Drugs section, para. 6). Currently only two medications have been approved by the FDA for long-term treatment of obesity: sibutramine (marketed as Meridia) and orlistat (marketed as Xenical). This section compares studies on the effectiveness of each.

Sibutramine suppresses appetite by blocking the reuptake of the neurotransmitters serotonin and norepinephrine in the brain (Yanovski & Yanovski, 2002, p. 594). Though the drug won FDA approval in 1998, experiments to test its effectiveness for younger patients came considerably later. In 2003, University of Pennsylvania researchers Berkowitz et al. released the first double-blind placebo study testing the effect of sibutramine on adolescents, aged 13–17, over a 12-month period. Their findings are summarized in Table 1.

After 6 months, the group receiving medication had lost 4.6 kg (about 10 pounds) more than the control group. But during the second half of the study, when both groups received sibutramine, the results were more ambiguous. In months 6–12, the group that continued to take sibutramine gained an average of 0.8 kg, or roughly 2 pounds; the control group, which switched from placebo to sibutramine, lost 1.3 kg, or roughly 3 pounds (p. 1808). Both groups received behavioral therapy covering diet, exercise, and mental health.

These results paint a murky picture of the effectiveness of the medication: While initial data seemed promising, the results after one year raised questions about whether medication-induced weight loss could be sustained over time. As Berkowitz et al. (2003) advised, "Until more extensive safety and efficacy data are available, . . . weight-loss medications should be used only on an experimental basis for adolescents" (p. 1811).

In a parenthetical citation, an ampersand links the names of two authors.

Mirano draws attention to an important article.

Mirano uses a table to summarize the findings presented in the two sources.

Table 1

Effectiveness of Sibutramine and Orlistat in Adolescents

Medication	Subjects	Treatment[a]	Side effects	Average weight loss/gain
Sibutramine	Control	0–6 mos.: Placebo	Mos. 6–12: increased blood pressure; increased pulse rate	After 6 mos.: loss of 3.2 kg (7 lb)
		6–12 mos.: Sibutramine		After 12 mos.: loss of 4.5 kg (9.9 lb)
	Medicated	0–12 mos.: Sibutramine	Increased blood pressure; increased pulse rate	After 6 mos.: loss of 7.8 kg (17.2 lb) After 12 mos.: loss of 7.0 kg (15.4 lb)
Orlistat	Control	0–12 mos.: Placebo	None	Gain of 0.67 kg (1.5 lb)
	Medicated	0–12 mos.: orlistat	Oily spotting; flatulence; abdominal discomfort	Loss of 1.3 kg (2.9 lb)

A note gives the source of the data.

Note. The data on sibutramine are adapted from "Behavior Therapy and Sibutramine for the Treatment of Adolescent Obesity," by R. I. Berkowitz, T. A. Wadden, A. M. Tershakovec, & J. L. Cronquist, 2003, *Journal of the American Medical Association, 289*(14), pp. 1807–1809. The data on orlistat are adapted from *Xenical (Orlistat) Capsules: Complete Product Information*, by Roche Laboratories, December 2003, http://www.rocheusa.com/products/xenical/pi.pdf

A content note explains data common to all subjects.

[a]The medication and/or placebo were combined with behavioral therapy in all groups over all time periods.

A study testing the effectiveness of orlistat in adolescents showed similarly ambiguous results. The FDA approved orlistat in 1999 but did not authorize it for adolescents until December 2003.

Roche Laboratories (2003), maker of orlistat, released results of a one-year study testing the drug on 539 obese adolescents, aged 12–16. The drug, which promotes weight loss by blocking fat absorption in the large intestine, showed some effectiveness in adolescents: an average loss of 1.3 kg, or roughly 3 pounds, for subjects taking orlistat for one year, as opposed to an average gain of 0.67 kg, or 1.5 pounds, for the control group (pp. 8–9). See Table 1.

Short-term studies of orlistat have shown slightly more dramatic results. Researchers at the National Institute of Child Health and Human Development tested 20 adolescents, aged 12–16, over a three-month period and found that orlistat, combined with behavioral therapy, produced an average weight loss of 4.4 kg, or 9.7 pounds (McDuffie et al., 2002, p. 646). The study was not controlled against a placebo group; therefore, the relative effectiveness of orlistat in this case remains unclear.

Is Medication Safe for Children?

While modest weight loss has been documented for both medications, each carries risks of certain side effects. Sibutramine has been observed to increase blood pressure and pulse rate. In 2002, a consumer group claimed that the medication was related to the deaths of 19 people and filed a petition with the Department of Health and Human Services to ban the medication (Hilts, 2002). The sibutramine study by Berkowitz et al. (2003) noted elevated blood pressure as a side effect, and dosages had to be reduced or the medication discontinued in 19 of the 43 subjects in the first six months (p. 1809).

The main side effects associated with orlistat were abdominal discomfort, oily spotting, fecal incontinence, and nausea (Roche Laboratories, 2003, p. 13). More serious for long-term health is the concern that orlistat, being a fat-blocker, would affect absorption of fat-soluble vitamins, such as vitamin D. However, the study found that

For a source with three or more authors, the first author's surname followed by "et al." is used for the first and subsequent references.

this side effect can be minimized or eliminated if patients take vitamin supplements two hours before or after administration of orlistat (p. 10). With close monitoring of patients taking the medication, many of the risks can be reduced.

Is Medication the Best Solution?

The data on the safety and efficacy of pharmacological treatments of childhood obesity raise the question of whether medication is the best solution for the problem. The treatments have clear costs for individual patients, including unpleasant side effects, little information about long-term use, and uncertainty that they will yield significant weight loss.

In purely financial terms, the drugs cost more than $3 a day on average (Duenwald, 2004). In each of the clinical trials, use of medication was accompanied by an expensive regime of behavioral therapies, including counseling, nutritional education, fitness advising, and monitoring. As journalist Greg Critser (2003) noted in his book *Fat Land*, use of weight-loss drugs is unlikely to have an effect without the proper "support system"—one that includes doctors, facilities, time, and money (p. 3). For some, this level of care is prohibitively expensive. A third complication is that the studies focused on adolescents aged 12–16, but obesity can begin at a much younger age. Little data exist to establish the safety or efficacy of medication for treating very young children.

While the scientific data on the concrete effects of these medications in children remain somewhat unclear, medication is not the only avenue for addressing the crisis. Both medical experts and policymakers recognize that solutions might come not only from a laboratory but also from policy, education, and advocacy. A handbook designed to educate doctors on obesity called for "major changes in some aspects of western culture" (Hoppin & Taveras, 2004, Conclusion section, para. 1). Cultural change may not be the typical realm of medical professionals, but the handbook

Mirano develops the paper's thesis.

urged doctors to be proactive and "focus [their] energy on public policies and interventions" (Conclusion section, para. 1).

The solutions proposed by a number of advocacy groups underscore this interest in political and cultural change. A report by the Kaiser Family Foundation (2004) outlined trends that may have contributed to the childhood obesity crisis, including food advertising for children as well as

> a reduction in physical education classes and after-school athletic programs, an increase in the availability of sodas and snacks in public schools, the growth in the number of fast-food outlets . . . , and the increasing number of highly processed high-calorie and high-fat grocery products. (p. 1)

Addressing each of these areas requires more than a doctor armed with a prescription pad; it requires a broad mobilization not just of doctors and concerned parents but of educators, food industry executives, advertisers, and media representatives.

The barrage of possible approaches to combating childhood obesity—from scientific research to political lobbying—indicates both the severity and the complexity of the problem. While none of the medications currently available is a miracle drug for curing the nation's 9 million obese children, research has illuminated some of the underlying factors that affect obesity and has shown the need for a comprehensive approach to the problem that includes behavioral, medical, social, and political change.

Brackets indicate a word not in the original source.

A quotation longer than forty words is indented without quotation marks.

Mirano interprets the evidence; she doesn't just report it.

The tone of the conclusion is objective.

References

Berkowitz, R. I., Wadden, T. A., Tershakovec, A. M., & Cronquist, J. L. (2003). Behavior therapy and sibutramine for the treatment of adolescent obesity. *Journal of the American Medical Association, 289*(14), 1805–1812.

Carmona, R. H. (2004, March 2). *The growing epidemic of childhood obesity.* Testimony before the Subcommittee on Competition, Foreign Commerce, and Infrastructure of the U.S. Senate Committee on Commerce, Science, and Transportation. http://www.hhs.gov/asl/testify/t040302.html

Critser, G. (2003). *Fat land.* Houghton Mifflin.

Duenwald, M. (2004, January 6). Slim pickings: Looking beyond ephedra. *The New York Times,* F1.

Hilts, P. J. (2002, March 20). Petition asks for removal of diet drug from market. *The New York Times,* A27.

Hoppin, A. G., & Taveras, E. M. (2004, June 25). Assessment and management of childhood and adolescent obesity. *Clinical Update.* http://www.medscape.com/viewarticle/481633

Kaiser Family Foundation. (2004, February). *The role of media in childhood obesity.* http://www.kff.org/entmedia/7030.cfm

McDuffie, J. R., Calis, K. A., Uwaifo, G. I., Sebring, N. G., Fallon, E. M., Hubbard, V. S., & Yanovski, J. A. (2002). Three-month tolerability of orlistat in adolescents with obesity-related comorbid conditions. *Obesity Research, 10*(7), 642–650.

The list of references begins on a new page. Heading is centered.

The list is alphabetized by authors' last names. All authors' names are inverted.

The first line of an entry is at the left margin; subsequent lines indent ½".

Double-spacing is used throughout.

Roche Laboratories. (2003, December). *Xenical (orlistat) capsules: Complete product information.* http://www.rocheusa.com/products/xenical/pi.pdf

Yanovski, S. Z., & Yanovski, J. A. (2002). Drug therapy: Obesity. *The New England Journal of Medicine, 346*(8), 591–602.

Sample APA Title Page: Paper for Publication

A running head, which will be used in the printed journal article, consists of a shortened title in all capital letters. Page numbers appear in the upper right corner.

Can Medication Cure Obesity in Children?
A Review of the Literature

Luisa Mirano

Department of Psychology, Northwest-Shoals

Community College

The writer's name and affiliation are listed below the title.

An author's note lists other important information and contact information.

Luisa Mirano is an undergraduate student of Dr. June Kang in the Department of Psychology, Northwest-Shoals Community College.

We have no known conflict of interest to disclose.

All correspondence regarding this article may be directed to luisa.mirano@northwestshoals.edu

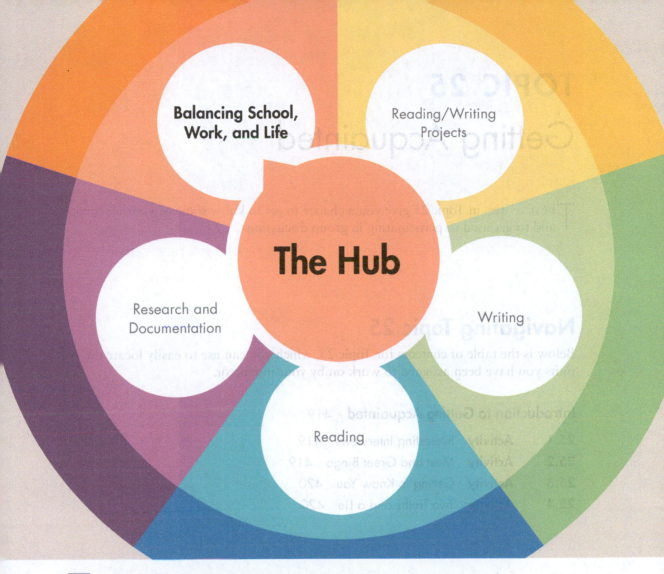

Balancing School, Work, and Life

Reading/Writing Projects

The Hub

Research and Documentation

Writing

Reading

5 Balancing School, Work, and Life

Topic 25 Getting Acquainted 418
Topic 26 Life Issues 421
Topic 27 Staying the Course 431
Topic 28 College Knowledge 435

TOPIC 25
Getting Acquainted

The activities in Topic 25 give you a chance to get to know some of your classmates and to get used to participating in group discussions.

Navigating Topic 25

Below is the table of contents for Topic 25, which you can use to easily locate the units you have been assigned to work on by your instructor.

Introduction to Getting Acquainted 419

25.1	Activity	Interesting Interviews	419
25.2	Activity	Meet and Greet Bingo	419
25.3	Activity	Getting to Know You	420
25.4	Activity	Two Truths and a Lie	420

Introduction to Getting Acquainted

The following activities are designed to help you and your classmates get to know each other and get used to working in groups.

25.1 Activity

Interesting Interviews

After the class is organized into pairs, you and your partner will interview each other with the goal of discovering something interesting—an unusual fact, an interesting experience, or a surprising attitude about each other. You might start by asking your partner to tell you three interesting things about him- or herself. You could then select one that you think is the most interesting and ask some follow-up questions about it. Then switch roles. You tell your partner three interesting things about yourself and then answer your partner's questions about one of them. After ten or fifteen minutes, each of you will report to the class on the one interesting thing you learned about your partner.

25.2 Activity

Meet and Greet Bingo

Walk around the room talking to people. For each of the boxes in the chart below (also available as a downloadable PDF in *Achieve for The Hub*), write the name of a person who fits the description in the box. When you've filled in five boxes in a row or in a column or diagonally, take your seat.

Hates to write	Speaks a language other than English	Is good at grammar	Owns a bicycle	Ate breakfast this morning
Plays Words with Friends	Has been out of high school at least ten years	Hated English in high school	Is a vegan	Keeps a diary
Is wearing something purple	Does crossword puzzles regularly	Loves to write	Reads science fiction	Writes poetry

Reads a daily newspaper	Knows where the next Summer Olympics will be held	Knows what haiku is	Has a full-time job	Knows what it means to "86" something
Tweets regularly	Has eaten dim sum	Works in a restaurant	Owns a dictionary	Knows who Matisse is

25.3 Activity

Getting to Know You

This activity is designed to help you get to know some of the other members of this class. Working with the members of your group, figure out the answer to each of the following questions.

1. In the group, who was born in the most interesting place? Where?
2. In the group, who has the most interesting nickname? What is it?
3. In the group, who has the worst boss? What's so terrible about his or her boss?
4. In the group, who is the best cook? What is his or her best dish?
5. In the group, who speaks the most languages? What are they?

Be prepared to share your group's answers with the rest of the class.

25.4 Activity

Two Truths and a Lie

To start, everyone in the group will take a few minutes to think of three statements about themselves, two that are true and one that is a lie. Next each person will tell the group their three statements, and the group will try to guess which statement is the lie. The process continues until everyone has told their three statements.

TOPIC 26

Life Issues

Attending college and trying to cope with the rest of life can sometimes be a challenge. The activities in this Topic are designed to help you develop strategies for balancing school, work, and the rest of your life.

Navigating Topic 26

Below is the table of contents for Topic 26, which you can use to easily locate the units you have been assigned to work on by your instructor or want to review for yourself.

Introduction to Life Issues 421

26.1	**Writing**	Money Matters 422
26.2	**Activity**	Renting 424
26.3	**Activity**	Health Care 424
26.4	**Activity**	Child Care 424
26.5	**Activity**	Time Management: Activity Log 424
26.6	**Activity**	Time Management: Analyzing Activity Logs 427
26.7	**Activity**	Time Management: Strategies 427
26.8	**Activity**	Time Management: Calendars 427
26.9	**Activity**	Plan B 430

Introduction to Life Issues

These activities are designed to help you think about and problem-solve on issues common to many students: money, renting, health care, child care, time management, and needing a Plan B.

Money Matters

At the same time that they are struggling to become more effective writers, many students in developmental writing classes are also struggling to figure out how to pay their bills and put food on the table. Financial pressures are one of the largest sources of stress in the lives of many students.

For this short writing assignment, you will do a little research, a little thinking, and a little writing about one of the financial topics listed below. The plan is that, as the class researches, discusses, and writes about these "financial" topics, many of you will learn things that will help with your financial pressures. At the same time, you should also begin to understand a little about doing research and incorporating the results into your writing.

Researching a Financial Topic

You will need to find some information about your topic. You can do this on the internet, using Google or a similar service, or you can find a book or journal that discusses your topic in the library. For more detailed information, see Research (Topic 22, p. 305).

You are not being asked to do a really thorough research project, just to find *one* piece of information that will be helpful as you write a short essay on one of the financial topics below. At this point in the course, you have probably not had any formal instruction in how to do research, so you're not being asked to give formal citations and lists of references. All you need to do is quote one brief passage—a sentence or more—that you found in your research and that helps to support the argument you are making in your essay. Of course, more than one quotation is fine, but only one is required.

Quoting Sources

Here's a little advice about how to include a brief quotation in your essay. Before the quotation itself, you want to include an introductory phrase that signals to the reader that a quotation is coming and provides a little information about the source of the quotation.

Here are some examples:

- Before being elected president, Senator Barrack Obama pointed out, "One of my favorite tasks of being a senator is hosting town hall meetings."

- One of the world's leading cosmologists, Brian Greene, reminds us that "[t]he ancient Greeks surmised that the stuff of the universe was made up of tiny 'uncuttable' ingredients that they called *atoms*."

- Noted art scholar John Berger suggests that "[i]mages were first made to conjure up the appearance of something that was absent."

Note that in each example, the writer identifies the source of the quotation, explains who the source is, and—using specific verbs like *pointed out, reminds us,* and *suggests*—helps us understand how the quotation was offered.

One more point about quoting: you must be careful to do it accurately. You must quote the words from your source exactly. If you need to change a word or two in the quotation, place brackets around the words or letters you have changed. Take a look at the following example.

Original

My grandparents left Jackson in the late 1940s and raised their family in Middletown, Ohio, where I later grew up.

Quotation

In his best-selling memoir, *Hillbilly Elegy*, J. D. Vance reports that his "grandparents left Jackson [Kentucky] in the late 1940s and raised their family in Middletown, Ohio, where [he] later grew up."

In the quotation, *Kentucky* was added in brackets to clarify where Jackson is, and *I* was changed to *he* (also in brackets) to make the quotation easier to understand.

Activity: Writing about Money

Select one of the questions below and search the internet for credible information to help you answer it. Then, write a short paper—about a page—in which you answer the question. In your paper, quote at least one sentence or phrase that you found in your research that supports your argument.

1. Is a "payday loan" ever a good idea?
2. What are the arguments for taking out a student loan?
3. What are the arguments against taking out a student loan?
4. What are the most important rules associated with a Pell Grant?

5. What rights do consumers have if they are behind in making payments on their credit card?

6. What should I know if I am threatened with eviction?

26.2 Activity

Renting

For this activity, working in your group, brainstorm a list of ideas for how you could lower the amount you are currently paying for rent. After twenty minutes, each group will report out on its list.

26.3 Activity

Health Care

If you or someone you care for became ill, what are your options for getting medical care? Working in your group, brainstorm a list of options for getting medical care. After twenty minutes, each group will report out.

26.4 Activity

Child Care

Working in your group, brainstorm a list of options for child care. List not only what you do but also options that other people you know have done. After twenty minutes, the groups will report out.

26.5 Activity

Time Management: Activity Log

Use the blank chart on page 426 (also available as a downloadable PDF in *Achieve for The Hub*) to keep track of how you use your time for one week. If you are also taking a course called something like "student success" or "first-year experience," a course designed to improve your ability to succeed in college, you may have been asked to complete an activity log in that course. If so, you don't need to do a second one; just use the one you compiled for that course.

Advice for the Specific Columns

1st Column	Enter a three-letter abbreviation for the day of the week.
2nd Column	Enter the time you spent on the activity. Example: 9:00–9:45
3rd Column	Enter a brief description of the activity.
4th Column	Enter a number indicating how important this activity is to you—4 is most important; 1 is least important.

Keep the log for one complete week.

Sample Activity Log

Name: _____

Day	Time	Activity	Priority
Mon.	11:10–12:00	English class	4
Mon.	12:00–1:15	bus home	4
Mon.	1:15–2:30	lunch and video games	1
Mon.	2:30–3:00	walk to Romano's	4
Mon.	3:00–9:00	wait tables	4
Mon.	9:00–10:00	have a beer with friends	1
Mon.	10:00–11:00	work on English paper	4

Activity Log

Name: _____

Day	Time	Activity	Priority

26.6 Activity

Time Management: Analyzing Activity Logs

Working in your group, look at the members' activity logs, one at a time, and then answer the following questions.

1. Are there any surprises in your activity log? Are you spending more time than you thought you were on some tasks? Less time on others?

2. Are there times of the day when you are most productive? Are you working on low-priority activities in these high-productivity times?

3. Are there little stretches of time that you could use to squeeze in small tasks?

4. Are you spending lots of time on low-priority tasks? Doing so can be a sign that you are procrastinating.

5. Are there things you are doing that don't need to be done? Things that can be delayed or cancelled or even done by someone else?

6. Is it possible to do everything you have committed to doing? If so, great. If not, what can you change to make it possible to accomplish everything you need to do?

26.7 Activity

Time Management: Strategies

Working together as a group, make a list of time-management strategies. To get you started, here's one strategy:

Do the hardest task first. Sometimes a difficult task gets pushed to later in the day or even later in the week. Then you spend time dreading it, which makes you less effective at completing other tasks. There's nothing more satisfying than taking on that hard task first, preferably earlier in the day when you are at your most alert, and getting it done.

26.8 Activity

Time Management: Calendars

Most busy people find that they cannot keep themselves organized, they cannot meet deadlines, and they cannot show up on time at events they need to attend without keeping a calendar.

Many versions of online calendars are available, although some people still prefer the old-fashioned calendar in a spiral notebook form. Both forms have their advantages, so you should choose whatever works best for you, but using a calendar is something that will definitely help with organizing your time.

Creating a Calendar

Print and online calendars can be arranged to display a day at a time, a week at a time, a month at a time, or even a year at a glance. Most students find a one-week-at-a-time format works best for them. Here are some suggestions for how to create an effective calendar:

- Set aside time to work on your calendar before the week begins—Sunday evenings work well.

- Start by filling in the times that are fixed: the times you are scheduled to be in class, the times you are scheduled to work, and the hours you will be sleeping.

- Then add any one-time events you know about that are coming up during the week. Your mother's 50th birthday party on Saturday night. The time you've volunteered to babysit your sister's daughter. A house concert you plan to attend.

- Be sure to build in time for studying. Don't just write "9:00–11:00 study." Make a specific plan: "9:00–11:00 Revise essay for English class."

- Don't forget to include travel time and time for household tasks like shopping for groceries or doing the laundry.

- Schedule breaks—time to relax, have a coffee, or talk to a friend on the phone.

Below, you will find a blank calendar for a week. Working with this form (also available as a downloadable PDF in *Achieve for The Hub*), plan out the next week for yourself. While you might normally do this planning on a Sunday, if you start working on some other day—say, Thursday—then just start with Thursday and plan for the next seven days. You should find the Activity Log you created (26.5, p. 424), the analysis of your Activity Log (26.6, p. 427), and the strategies you established (26.7, p. 427) to be helpful as you work on this calendar.

	Monday	Tuesday	Wednesday	Thursday	Friday	Saturday	Sunday
6:00–6:30							
6:30–7:00							
7:00–7:30							
7:30–8:00							
8:00–8:30							
8:30–9:00							
9:00–9:30							
9:30–10:00							
10:00–10:30							
10:30–11:00							
11:00–11:30							
11:30–12:00							
12:00–12:30							
12:30–1:00							
1:00–1:30							
1:30–2:00							
2:00–2:30							
2:30–3:00							
3:00–3:30							
3:30–4:00							
4:00–4:30							
4:30–5:00							
5:00–5:30							
5:30–6:00							
6:00–6:30							
6:30–7:00							
7:00–7:30							
7:30–8:00							
8:00–8:30							
8:30–9:00							
9:00–9:30							

	Monday	Tuesday	Wednesday	Thursday	Friday	Saturday	Sunday
9:30–10:00							
10:00–10:30							
10:30–11:00							
11:00–11:30							
11:30–12:00							
12:00–12:30							
12:30–1:00							

26.9 Activity

Plan B

Most students find going to college stressful. There's the pressure to do all the reading, to do all the homework, and to prepare for tests. But, for many students, there are also the stresses that come from life: financial pressures, family problems, health issues, legal problems.

Much of the time, the stress is manageable even though it's not pleasant. Most students deal with stress by digging down a little deeper, working a little harder, sleeping a little less, and remembering that the semester lasts just fifteen weeks or so. But sometimes the stress becomes unbearable, the student's efforts just grind to a halt, and he or she ends up dropping out of school.

If digging a little deeper and working a little harder is Plan A for dealing with stress, in this activity I want you to think about Plan B. If you felt that all the pressures of school, family, work, and life were approaching the point where you might have to give up on school, what could you do? What changes could you make *before* the stress overwhelmed you?

Activity: Listing Strategies for Coping with Stress

1. Working in groups, make a list of possible strategies that could help you avoid dropping out of school because of stress.

2. Share these strategies with the whole class.

TOPIC 27
Staying the Course

Going to college creates stress and anxiety for some students. The activities in this Topic provide suggestions for how to deal with these kinds of issues.

Navigating Topic 27

Below is the table of contents for Topic 27, which you can use to easily locate the units you have been assigned to work on by your instructor or want to review for yourself.

Introduction to Staying the Course 431

27.1	Writing	Why Are You in This Class?	432
27.2	Activity	Thinking about Why Are You in This Class?	432
27.3	Activity	What Worries You?	433
27.4	Writing	Who Is "College Material"?	433
27.5	Writing	Responding to Setbacks	434
27.6	Writing	Goal Setting and Planning	434

Introduction to Staying the Course

The activities in Topic 27 are designed to help you think, problem-solve, and develop strategies to address issues commonly experienced by students: questions about why you are in this class, things that worry you, concerns about whether you are "college material," ways to respond to setbacks, and goal setting and planning.

27.1 Writing

Why Are You in This Class?

For this short writing assignment, you don't need to write an essay or even a paragraph. Just write a list of the reasons why, at this point in your life, you find yourself in this writing class. This list doesn't have to be long; it could even be just one or two reasons. The point is to do a little thinking about why you are in this class.

27.2 Activity

Thinking about Why Are You in This Class?

1. Your instructor will share with the class a list of all the reasons you and your classmates gave in response to the request to "write a list of the reasons why, at this point in your life, you find yourself in this writing class."

2. After some discussion of that list, your instructor will ask you to study the following chart. Working in groups, what can you learn from this chart about why you might be in this writing class?

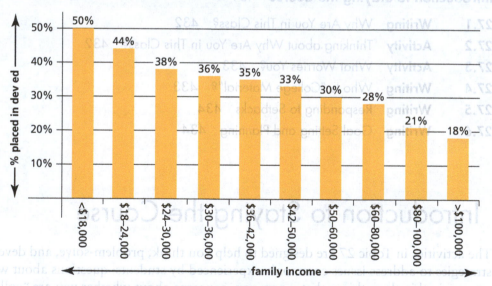

Republished with permission of Russell Sage Foundation from *Economic Inequality and Higher Education: Access, Persistence, and Success*, S. Dickert-Conlin & R. Rubenstein (Eds.) (pp. 69–100). New York, NY: Russell Sage Foundation; permission conveyed through Copyright Clearance Center, Inc.

3. Finally, again working in groups, come up with a list of observations from your life that would explain the conclusion you reached in question 2. In your life prior to enrolling in this class, what can you remember that would have contributed to the conclusions you reached in question 2?

27.3 Activity
What Worries You?

Write down one thing you are worried about on a piece of paper and hand it to your instructor. Don't put your name on it. Anything you are worried about is okay—something about school or work or your relationships or your family or the country or the world. Your instructor will read as many of these as possible to the entire class so the class can discuss them.

27.4 Writing
Who Is "College Material"?

Many students arrive in college with insecurities, doubts about whether they belong, doubts about whether they can succeed. In some cases, they express these doubts by saying something like this: "I'm just not sure I'm 'college material.'"

For this assignment, write a short essay—about a page—in which you discuss the term *college material*. You don't have to answer all of the following questions, or any of them, but they're here to help you think about the term.

1. What does *college material* mean?
2. Where do you suppose that students who wonder about whether they are *college material* learned the term? Who told them there was such a thing as students who are not "college material"?
3. Are you sure you are "college material"? If so, how did you avoid the doubt that comes from wondering whether you are?
4. Do you think anyone is not "college material"? What would put someone into that category? What keeps someone from being "college material"?
5. Do you know anyone who has these kinds of doubts about themselves? Are they "college material," in your opinion? Why do they have these doubts about whether they belong in college?
6. Do people get the idea they may not be "college material" in high school or does that doubt occur once they get to college?

27.5 Writing

Responding to Setbacks

Think about a setback you have experienced—a time you got a low grade in school, a time when you weren't hired for a job you wanted, a time your performance in a sport was publicly bad, or even a time when you learned that someone you loved did not return your affection. Write a short paper—about a page—in which you describe what you learned from that experience.

27.6 Writing

Goal Setting and Planning

Where do you want to be in five years? What do you want to be doing? Where do you want to be living? What kind of car do you want to be driving? How many children would you like to have (if any)? How much education do you want? Write a paragraph in which you answer at least some of these questions.

Activity: Twelve-Month Goals

Now think about what you need to do in the next twelve months to make those goals possible. Make a list of these "Twelve-Month Goals."

You will be discussing these "Twelve-Month Goals" with your group. During this discussion, you should feel free to add to your list, subtract from it, or revise it.

TOPIC 28
College Knowledge

The world of college can be quite different from the world outside. It has its own terminology, procedures, and expectations. The activities in this Topic are designed to help you understand and thrive in this specialized world.

Navigating Topic 28

Below is the table of contents for Topic 28, which you can use to easily locate the units you have been assigned to work on by your instructor or want to review for yourself.

Introduction to College Knowledge   435

28.1	Writing	College Terminology 436
28.2	Writing	Terms for Writing Assignments 436
28.3	Activity	Asking for Help 437
28.4	Activity	Locating Resources 437
28.5	Tutorial	What Is Group Work, and Why Are We Doing It? 439

Introduction to College Knowledge

The activities in Topic 28 are designed to help you become more familiar with the language, or terminology, used in college; understand the terms used in writing assignments to indicate the kind of essay an instructor wants you to write; recognize how important it is to ask for help when you need it; and learn what resources are available to you and how to access them.

28.1 Writing

College Terminology

Colleges and universities have a language of their own. Sometimes students new to college run into difficulty because of terms they don't know. The following is a list of such terms.

AA degree	department	plagiarism	transfer
appeal	essay	prerequisite	tutoring
books on reserve	FAFSA	probation	withdrawal
bursar	GPA	program	writing center
certificate	incomplete	registration	
composition	major	school	
dean	office hours	syllabus	

This list will be divided up among several groups of students. Each group will be responsible for writing a paragraph explaining each of the terms it is assigned. Groups should use the knowledge of the individuals in the group to define the terms. If necessary, it's okay for the group to Google a term, but then the definition should be translated into "student-friendly" language. The audience for this writing is next year's new college students. These paragraphs will be compiled into a document suitable to be given out to students.

28.2 Writing

Terms for Writing Assignments

Writing assignments in college frequently use terms like those listed below. In order to complete an assignment effectively, you will need to understand each of these terms and the differences in what they ask you to do.

Activity: Defining Terms

For this short writing assignment, you and your classmates will be compiling a document explaining these terms, which will be handed out to new students.

You will work in groups, each of which will be assigned some of the terms to work on. Each group will write a "student-friendly" paragraph explaining each of its assigned terms. Groups should use the knowledge of the individuals in the group to define the terms. If necessary, it's okay for the group to Google a term, but then the definition should be translated into "student-friendly" language.

agree or disagree	create	evaluate	state
analyze	defend	explain	summarize
argue	define	identify	support
classify	demonstrate	interpret	synthesize
compare	describe	list	
construct	develop	paraphrase	
contrast	discuss	solve	

28.3 Activity

Asking for Help

A website called Academic Tips (**search for "academic tips ask help" to locate the site**) contains great advice about asking for help when you're in college. Working in your group, discuss the tips on asking for help that you find on the Academic Tips website and list some additional tips you would add.

28.4 Activity

Locating Resources

Working in groups, your job for this activity will be to find out where to go on campus for each of the items listed in the chart on page 438 (also available as a downloadable PDF in *Achieve for The Hub*) and provide the following information about each place the group recommends. Of course, you may learn that your college doesn't have an office where you can go for several of these items. If that's the case, just write "Not available" next to those items.

- Location
- Phone number
- Email
- Hours
- Additional services available

		Location	Phone number	Email	Hours	Additional services available
1	Help with financial aid.					
2	Assistance with a disability.					
3	Help with doing research for a term paper.					
4	Advice about a career.					
5	Assistance with writing.					
6	Assistance with technology.					
7	The place to appeal a grade.					
8	A place to safely complain about harassment.					
9	Advice about transferring to a four-year school.					
10	Advice about getting into the Nursing Program.					
11	Help with child care.					
12	A copy of your transcript.					
13	To withdraw from a course.					
14	To look at a book that your instructor has placed on reserve.					
15	To pay your tuition bill.					

What Is Group Work, and Why Are We Doing It?

In this course, you will be doing a great deal of what is known as group work. Your instructor will often divide the class into small groups of three or four students and ask the groups to work on some task. These groups might be asked to answer questions about a reading, make sense out of a seeming contradiction, decide which of several arguments is most compelling, or make a list of ideas or experiences of the members of the group. Each group will regularly be asked to "report out" on what their group's conclusions were. At other times, groups will be asked to produce a written document, usually quite short, to be turned in, or to write their responses on large sheets of paper to be posted around the classroom.

If you're not sure why instructors include group work in the course, here are four important reasons why they do:

1. **Group work almost always involves a process known as *active learning* or *discovery learning*.** In more traditional classrooms, students learned by listening to instructors as they delivered information by means of lectures. In active learning students learn information by solving a problem or studying examples. They *actively* discover information for themselves, and there is considerable research to support the idea that what students learn through active learning stays with them longer that what they learn through lectures.

2. **Group work creates more of a community in the classroom.** Students get to know each other and develop a network of other students whom they can ask for advice or assistance. As a result, they feel more connected to the college and have a greater sense of belonging to a community of peers.

3. **Being able to work well in a group is a skill for which many employers are looking.** Many companies now have staff working together in groups on a wide variety of tasks, such as problem-solving design issues, creating new products, coming up with marketing campaigns, or trouble-shooting bad media coverage. Being able to work well with others, share and delegate responsibilities, brainstorm as a team member, and write joint responses to specific prompts or questions are all skills that prove very useful to students when they look for jobs.

4. **Group work can be fun.** Once students get over any initial anxiety, most find participating in group work much more enjoyable than listening to a lecture.

Tips for Successful Group Participation

Here are some tips to help you participate successfully in group work.

1. **Come to class prepared.**   If a reading was assigned, make sure you have read it. If you were supposed to bring a draft of an essay, make sure you bring it. If you were supposed to do anything else in preparation for the class, make sure you have done it.

2. **Don't be reluctant to participate.**   Everyone feels a little anxiety about expressing their ideas in a group at first, but once you join in, you will find it's easier than you expected. It's certainly more fun and more helpful if you are actively involved.

3. **It is also possible to participate too much, to take up more than your share of time for talking.** Dominating the conversation can be as harmful to the group as not participating. Take the time to listen to and understand the idea expressed by other members of your group in addition to sharing your own thoughts and opinions.

4. **If you have been assigned a specific role or responsibility in the group, be sure to perform that role diligently.**   Sometimes it's easy to get so caught up in the discussion that you forget your assigned role. For example, if you are the note-taker, be sure to come equipped with pen and paper, or your phone or laptop, to listen carefully, and to record what is being said as accurately as possible. This might mean talking less than you would if someone else was taking notes.

5. **Listen carefully to what your classmates are saying.**

6. **Be respectful of everyone's opinions.**   Avoid being judgmental.

7. **The most common problem groups have is when one or two members don't perform their share of the responsibilities.**   Make sure you come to class prepared to participate, that you make your share of contributions to the group's efforts, and that you follow through on any tasks assigned.

Tips for Group Success

Here are some tips to help *groups* be more successful.

1. The group's first task is to make sure every member understands and agrees on the task the group is asked to perform.

2. The group should take a little time to plan how they are going to use the allocated time.

3. The group needs to keep an eye on the clock. If they've used half of their time and are still discussing the first task of three, they need to move along faster.

4. If the instructor hasn't assigned roles to the group members, the group needs to think about taking on roles themselves. If there is to be a written project, who is going to do the actual writing? If the group will be asked to report out at the end of their work, who will do this reporting?

5. Perhaps the most important thing groups need to learn how to do is to settle disagreements. Sometimes a compromise can be reached. Sometimes, a group has to recognize that they cannot agree and, therefore, submit two reports or a primary report and a minority report in response to the assigned task.

6. The most common problem groups have happens when a member or two don't do their share of the work. Groups need to confront this problem directly. It is not an acceptable solution for the other members of the group to do most of the work. The group needs to confront the "slacker(s)" directly and discuss the problem. If it cannot be resolved within the group, then the instructor should be consulted. Learning how to handle the problem of a "slacker" is an important skill that will be beneficial in the workplace.

Acknowledgments

Jaison R. Abel and Richard Deitz. Reprinted by permission from Jaison R. Abel and Richard Deitz, "Do Big Cities Help College Graduates Find Better Jobs?" Federal Reserve Bank of New York, *Liberty Street Economics* (blog), May 20, 2013, http://libertystreeteconomics.newyorkfed.org/2013/05/do-big-cities-help-college-graduates-find-better-jobs.html. The views expressed in this article are those of the authors, and do not necessarily reflect the position of the Federal Reserve Bank of New York or the Federal Reserve System.

American Association of University Professors. "On Freedom of Expression and Campus Speech Codes." *Policy Documents and Reports*, Eleventh Edition, pp. 361–62. Copyright © 2015 American Association of University Professors. Reprinted with permission of Johns Hopkins University Press.

Julian Baggini. "The Nature of Truth." From *A Short History of Truth*. Copyright © Julian Baggini, 2017. Reproduced by permission of Quercus Editions Limited.

James Baldwin. "On Being White . . . and Other Lies." Copyright © 1984 by James Baldwin. Originally published in *Essence* magazine. Collected in *Cross of Redemption* by James Baldwin, published by Pantheon/Vintage. Used by arrangement with the James Baldwin Estate.

Bill Burnett and Dave Evans. Excerpts from *Designing Your Life: How to Build a Well-Lived, Joyful Life*. Copyright © 2016 by William Burnett and David J. Evans. Used by permission of Alfred A. Knopf, an imprint of the Knopf Doubleday Publishing Group, a division of Penguin Random House LLC. All rights reserved.

John Canaday. Excerpt from *What Is Art?* Copyright © 1980 by John Canaday. Used by permission of Alfred A. Knopf, an imprint of the Knopf Doubleday Publishing Group, a division of Penguin Random House LLC. All rights reserved.

Suresh Canagarajah. From "The Place of World Englishes in Composition: Pluralization Continued," *College Composition and Communication*, Vol. 57, No. 4 (June 2006), pp. 586–619.

Copyright © 2006 by the National Council of Teachers of English. Reprinted with permission.

Conference on College Composition and Communication. "Students' Right to Their Own Language." Adopted by the Conference on College Composition and Communication, 1974. http://www.ncte.org/library/NCTEFiles/Groups/CCCC/NewSRTOL.pdf. Reprinted by permission of the National Council of Teachers of English.

Arthur Danto. "Working Towards a Definition of Art." From *What Art Is,* pp. ix–xii. Copyright © 2013 By Arthur Danto. Reprinted by permission of Yale University Press.

Lisa Delpit. "The Silenced Dialogue." Originally published as text in Lisa D. Delpit, "The Silenced Dialogue: Power and Pedagogy in Educating Other People's Children," *Harvard Educational Review*, Vol. 58, No. 3, pp. 280–98. Copyright © 1988 by the President and Fellows of Harvard College. All rights reserved. Reprinted by permission.

Angela Lee Duckworth. Editorial review from the cover of *The Marshmallow Test: Mastering Self-Control* by Walter Mischel. Reprinted by permission.

Albert Elsen. "What Is Art?" From *Purposes of Art*, 4e. Copyright © 1981 South-Western, a part of Cengage, Inc. Reproduced by permission. www.cengage.com/permissions.

Daniel Goleman. Editorial review from the cover of *The Marshmallow Test: Mastering Self-Control* by Walter Mischel. Reprinted by permission.

"Gun Control. Now." https://petitions.moveon.org/sign/gun-control-now-1. Reprinted by permission of MoveOn.org.

Tim Harford. "The Problem with Facts," *FT Magazine*, FT.com, March 9, 2017. Used under license from the Financial Times. All rights reserved.

Anemona Hartocollis and Jacey Fortin. "Should Teachers Carry Guns? Are Metal Detectors Safe? What Experts Say," from *The New York Times*, February 24, 2018. Copyright © 2018 The New York Times. All rights reserved. Used under license.

Christopher Ingraham. "Want to Do What You Love and Get Paid for It? Choose One of These Majors," from *The Washington Post*, October 2, 2014. Copyright © 2014 The Washington Post. All rights reserved. Used under license.

Asao Inoue. Excerpt from *Antiracist Writing Assessment Ecologies: Teaching and Assessing Writing for a Socially Just Future.* Copyright © 2015 by Asao B. Inoue. Reprinted by permission of the author.

Daniel Kahneman. Editorial review from the cover of *The Marshmallow Test: Mastering Self-Control* by Walter Mischel. Reprinted by permission.

Eric R. Kandel. Editorial review from the cover of *The Marshmallow Test: Mastering Self-Control* by Walter Mischel. Reprinted by permission.

Celeste Kidd. "The Marshmallow Study Revisited." University of Rochester, http://rochester.edu/news/show.php?id=4622, posted October 11, 2012. Reprinted by permission.

Eugene Kiely and Lori Robertson. "How to Spot Fake News," FactCheck.org, November 18, 2016. Reprinted by permission of FactCheck.org, a project of the Annenberg Public Policy Center.

Daniel J. Levitin. "Dishonest Numbers: Evaluating the Accuracy of Statistics" and "Identifying Expertise." From *A Field Guide to Lies: Critical Thinking in the Information Age.* Copyright © 2016 by Daniel J. Levitin. Used by permission of Dutton, an imprint of Penguin Publishing Group, a division of Penguin Random House LLC. All rights reserved.

Walter Mischel. *The Marshmallow Test.* From *The Marshmallow Test: Why Self-Control Is the Engine of Success.* Copyright © 2014 by Walter Mischel. Reprinted with the permission of Little, Brown and Company. All rights reserved.

Walter Mischel, Yuichi Shoda, and Monica L. Rodriguez. "Delay of Gratification in Children." Republished with permission of the American Association for the Advancement of Science, from *Science*, Vol. 244, No. 4907, May 26, 1989; permission conveyed through Copyright Clearance Center, Inc.

Timothy Noah. From *The Great Divergence: American's Growing Inequality Crisis and What We Can Do About It.* Copyright © Timothy Noah, 2012. Reprinted by permission of Bloomsbury Publishing Inc.

Danielle Paquette. "What It's Like to Graduate from College with the Lowest-Paying Major," from *The Washington Post*, September 29, 2014. Copyright © 2014 The Washington Post. All rights reserved. Used under license.

"Periodic." From Merriam-Webster.com. Copyright © 2019 by Merriam-Webster, Inc. Reprinted by permission. https://www.merriam-webster.com/dictionary/periodic.

"Periodic." From *The American Heritage Dictionary*, Fifth Edition. Copyright © 2012 by Houghton Mifflin Harcourt Publishing Company. Reprinted by permission of Houghton Mifflin Harcourt Publishing Company. All rights reserved.

Steven Pinker. Editorial review from the cover of *The Marshmallow Test: Mastering Self-Control* by Walter Mischel. Reprinted by permission.

Steven Pinker. "Violence Vanquished." Adapted from *The Better Angels of Our Nature: Why Violence Has Declined*, published by Viking Press. The essay originally appeared in *The Wall Street Journal* on September 24, 2011. Reprinted by permission of the author.

Steven Pinker. "Words and Worlds." From *The Stuff of Thought: Language as a Window into Human Nature.* Copyright © 2007 by Steven Pinker. Used by permission of Viking Books, an imprint of Penguin Publishing Group, a division of Penguin Random House LLC. All rights reserved.

Mike Rose. "'Grit' Revisited: Reflections on Our Public Talk about Education" (blog), July 29, 2016. http://mikerosebooks.blogspot.com/2016/06/grit-revisited-reflections-on-our.html. Reprinted by permission of the author.

Bernie Sanders. "Medicare for All." Our Revolution. https://ourrevolution.com/issues/medicare-for-all/. Reprinted by permission.

Rebecca Skloot. "Prologue: The Woman in the Photograph." From *The Immortal Life of Henrietta Lacks.* Copyright © 2010, 2011 by Rebecca Skloot. Used by permission of Crown Books, an imprint of Random House, a division of Penguin Random House LLC. All rights reserved.

Emily Esfahani Smith. "There's More to Life Than Being Happy," *The Atlantic*, January 9, 2013. Copyright © 2013 The Atlantic Media Co., as first published in *The Atlantic Magazine*. All rights reserved. Distributed by Tribune Content Agency, LLC. Reprinted by permission.

Geneva Smitherman. From "Response to Hunt, Meyers, et al.," *College English Journal*, Vol. 35, No. 6, 1974, p. 731. Reprinted by permission of National Council of Teachers of English.

Rodney A. Smolla. "Speech Overview." Freedom Forum Institute: https://www .freedomforuminstitute.org/first-amendment-center/ topics/freedom-of-speech-2/speech-overview/. Reprinted by permission of the author.

Ashley Stahl. "Six Reasons Why Your College Major Doesn't Matter," from Forbes.com, August 12, 2015. Copyright © 2015 Forbes. All rights reserved. Used under license.

"Stop Animal Abuse." From the PETA website: https://www.peta.org/issues. Reprinted by permission of PETA.

Will Storr. "A Better Kind of Happiness," *The New Yorker*, July 7, 2016. Copyright © 2016 Condé Nast. Reprinted by permission.

Andrew Sullivan. "America Wasn't Built for Humans." Copyright © 2017 by Andrew Sullivan. Used by permission of The Wylie Agency LLC.

Margaret Sullivan. "When Reporters Get Personal." From *The New York Times*, January 1, 2013. Copyright © 2013 The New York Times. All rights reserved. Used under license.

United Nations Geneva Convention. From *International Convention on the Elimination of All Forms of Racial Discrimination*. Copyright © 2016 United Nations. Reprinted with the permission of the United Nations.

University of Chicago. "Report of the Committee on Freedom of Expression: College Policies on Controversial Speakers." Reprinted by permission of the University of Chicago.

University of Colorado Board of Regents. Policy 1.D: Freedom of Expression and Policy 7.C: Academic Freedom, from the University of Colorado Board of Regents Laws and Policies, Adopted September 14, 2018. Reprinted by permission of the University of Colorado Board of Regents.

Jeremy Waldron. From *The Harm in Hate Speech* by Jeremy Waldron, Cambridge, Mass.: Harvard University Press. Copyright © 2012 by the President and Fellows of Harvard College. Reprinted by permission.

Timothy Wilson. Editorial review from the cover of *The Marshmallow Test: Mastering Self-Control* by Walter Mischel. Reprinted by permission.

Excerpts from student papers adapted from Hacker Handbooks and Lunsford Handbooks (Bedford/St. Martin's).